FATHERLESS
IN GALILEE

FATHERLESS
IN GALILEE

Jesus as Child of God

ANDRIES VAN AARDE

TRINITY PRESS INTERNATIONAL
Harrisburg, Pennsylvania

Financial assistance from the National Research Foundation (ex: CSD programs until 2000) for research resulting in chapter 4 is hereby acknowledged. Opinions expressed in this research, or conclusions drawn, are those of the author and not necessarily of the NRF (South Africa).

Trinity Press International
P.O. Box 1321
Harrisburg, PA 17105
Trinity Press International is a division of the Morehouse Group.

Cover art: *Christ in the desert*, Ivan Kramskoi. Tretyakov Gallery, Moscow, Russia. Scala/Art Resource, NY.

Cover design: Corey Kent

Library of Congress Cataloging-in-Publication Data

Van Aarde, A. G. (Andries G.)
    Fatherless in Galilee : Jesus as child of God / Andries van Aarde.
       p. cm.
    Includes bibliographical references and index.
    ISBN 1-56338-345-4 (alk. paper)
    1 Jesus Christ—Person and offices. 2. Jesus Christ—Historicity.
  I. Title.

  BT202 . V23 2001
  232.9—dc21   00-052785

Printed in the United States of America

01 02 03 04 05 06   10 9 8 7 6 5 4 3 2 1

CONTENTS

~

DEDICATED TO

My father,
Johan Christian van Aarde
(22 March 1914–16 December 1974)

What?
Someone at school
Called you
A bastard...
Illegit...?

Is that all?
Tut-tut-tut-tut
Is that why you cry?
Come here, my boy,
Come and sit
On my lap.

Now tell me
Who was the greatest Man
That ever lived?
The Saviour
Redeemer
The Light...
King of Kings
The Prince of Peace...
My big boy,
Tell Mommy.

What was his father's name?
Was the carpenter
Really his father?
Stop crying
My love.

"Peals of Crying," from O. P'Bitek's *Song of Malaya* (1971)

CHAPTER 1

~

My Journey

What is at stake when one says that the study of the life of Jesus is important? Who is God and how is Jesus, in my mind, related to God? How much can we know about Jesus? Are our earliest Christian writings, including those in the New Testament and apocryphal and pseudepigraphical literature, in continuation or discontinuation with the Jesus of history? What is the status of the primary and secondary sources that first depicted Jesus? What is the status of the faith assertions expressed within the group of communities who produced these early writings? In other words, what is the role of the canon as a list of documents the church decided upon as sacred writings in contradistinction with extracanonical literature? Why do scholars distinguish between a pre-Easter Jesus and a post-Easter Jesus? What does it mean to refer to the first as the "historical Jesus" and to the latter as the "kerygmatic Christ?" Did Jesus regard himself to be Christ, or for that matter, Son of God? Why is it necessary to reflect once more on the continued importance of Jesus and on the interrelationship between the quest for the historical Jesus and the origins of the church?

Albert Schweitzer was right when he said at the beginning of the twentieth century that portrayals of Jesus by people in the nineteenth century mirrored in some way or another the lives and settings of those who had depicted it. In the last paragraph of his well-known book, *The Quest of the Historical Jesus*, Schweitzer spoke of Jesus as the "one unknown" to those, "wise or simple," who had obeyed his command to follow him but to whom he would "reveal himself in the toils, the conflicts, the sufferings which they shall pass through in his fellowship," and, then, as an unspeakable puzzle (in Schweitzer's words, "*unaussprechliches Geheimnis*"), "they shall learn in their own experience who he is."[1]

Well-founded research in the field of the psychology of religion demonstrates a clear relationship between images people have of God and images

---

1. Schweitzer, *Quest of the Historical Jesus*, 403.

of parental figures.[2] Building upon this research, a related study shows that the Christian believer, whether exegetically trained or not, tends to "shape a *self-concept* that corresponds . . . to some extent and in some sense to his or her image of Jesus."[3] From these studies the psychology of religion draws the plausible hypothesis that those "deep questions" about what human beings value, "underlie all 'readings of Jesus.'" The discord among scholars about the nature of either the historical Jesus or the risen Christ is "in part a function of disagreements about . . . values."[4] Nobody's portrayal of someone's life or of some event is an intact, objective reconstruction. This dictum also applies to the constructs of scholars with a well-trained historic consciousness, like Schweitzer.[5]

I can think of at least two New Testament writers who tell such "autobiographical" stories. They describe their own lives and worlds when they present their views of Jesus. Paul refers directly to Jesus, and Luke does so indirectly through parables he puts in the mouth of Jesus. Paul depicts his affliction using a "feminine" metaphor of a woman with birth pangs carrying her cross as "Christa" (cf. 2 Cor 4:10). Paul implies that when suffering causes death to a pregnant woman, others will give birth to the baby. The analogy is clear: participation in Jesus' cross brings about resurrection for his followers; the apostle's affliction as a result of his preaching constitutes such a participation and the believers of his words will enjoy the new life.

The other "autobiography" can be found in metaphorical stories in Luke's Gospel: a compassionate Samaritan becomes the neighbor of an unholy man in the ditch (Luke 10:25–37); a deviant second sibling becomes God's child (15:11–31); a half-dead Lazarus lying before the closed gates of the house of a man in royal drapery becomes Abraham's child (16:19–31).

---

2. E.g., Vergote and Tamayo, *The Parental Figure and the Representation of God*; Vergote and others, "Concept of God and Parental Images." (Francis and Astley, "Quest for the Psychological Jesus," summarize these authors' findings.) According to the latter study, the parental rather than the maternal image of God is for both males and females in North American samples more preeminent. This tendency is even stronger in males than in females. Also within Asian communities in North America, God is for boys and girls more like a father than a mother. According to another study, the correspondence between God and father, or between God and the masculine image, is basic in women, whereas in men the relation between God and mother, or between God and the feminine image predominates (cf. Francis and Astley, 249). They also show that among French-speaking Belgians, both males and females emphasize the parental image of God corresponding to their own gender. According to Francis and Astley, a more recent study among Canadian students draws attention to the "strong relation between the concept of God and the mother image for both male and female subjects."

3. Francis and Astley, "Quest for the Psychological Jesus," 248. Emphasis by Francis and Astley. By means of the "Revised Eysenck Personality Questionnaire," through which personalities are profiled, they quizzed 473 secondary school students between the ages of twelve and fifteen in the United Kingdom, 317 students studying religion at A level, and 398 adult churchgoers. The data exhibit significant correlations between the respondents' personality and their images of Jesus.

4. Ibid., 248.

5. See Schmidt, "Albert Schweitzer's Profile of Jesus."

In all of these biblical stories of suffering people who were resurrected as children of God, we encounter the truth of Schweitzer's words. Paul as "Christa," both the unholy man and the Samaritan, the sibling crossing boundaries but welcomed by the father at his homecoming, and the homeless Lazarus received as child of God in the bosom of father Abraham, are all, either explicitly or implicitly, Jesus-like figures. Both modern Jesus researchers and biblical writers find their own faces reflected in their descriptions of Jesus.

Schweitzer's truism, therefore, certainly applies to the portrayals by the first witnesses of Jesus' life that are found in the known and, for many, unknown Christian writings of the earliest centuries of the common era. This includes all of the precursors to Schweitzer, and both his concurrent and subsequent companions who have interpreted these narrated characters in the Bible and constructed their images of Jesus from reconstructed artifacts. However, there are certain constraints because not "anything goes." An image of Jesus can be either an alienation or an affirmation of the biblical model, even if the portrayal is only a shadowy etching.

The suppositions of this book reflect my own journey and the itineraries of scholars before me who have had an impact on my life and thinking. It would thus be wise to take Seán Freyne's advice to heart:

> I am convinced that the present "third wave" quest for the historical Jesus is no more free of presuppositions than any of the other quests that went before it. Nor could it be otherwise, no matter how refined our methodologies. If we are all prepared to say at the outset what is at stake for us in our search for Jesus—ideologically, academically, personally—then there is some possibility that we can reach an approximation to the truth of things, at least for now. Even that would be adequate. [6]

Leif E. Vaage, in a contribution entitled "The Scholar as *Engagé*," adheres to this position. According to him, the fact that there are as many faces of Jesus as there are Jesus researchers is not a matter of different modes of knowing or various angles of seeing different dimensions of one and the same object:

> What captivates, rather, is the social fact of situated discourses and their specific subjects. The oft-touted "subjectivity" of historical-Jesus research is simply a function of the fact that, unlike certain other forms of New Testament scholarship, the link here is still patent between who the particular scholar is, including the social

6. Freyne, "Galilean Questions to Crossan's Mediterranean Jesus," 91.

grouping(s) to which she or he belongs, and the preferred form(s) into which the Jesus data have been made to fit. Thus, the more honest and precise we can be about exactly what makes "the historical Jesus" worth discussing and what we hope to gain from our "Jesus," the better the chance there is that our conversation about the historical Jesus will produce not just scholarly smoke but intellectual fire and human warmth. [7]

MAPPING THE MILEPOSTS

The "situated discourse" of this book is not only a matter of ideological and academic concern, but one of personal engagement. In my own journey I long ago found great pleasure in knowing Jesus. My voyage began with a strenuous relationship with my father, but as a child and adult I experienced the warmth of the believing community. This chapter is a survey of my journey and those suppositions that illumine my image of Jesus.

My description of the itinerary of other Jesus researchers in chapter 2 consists of explaining two phases in a more academic fashion. One pertains to the growing realization among scholars that if one denies at the doorstep the quest for the historical Jesus, doubt concerning God comes in through the window. The second phase aims at showing that today, to some extent, scholars have established a new frame of reference within which to do historical Jesus research. In chapter 3, I argue that the starting point of the quest for the historical Jesus could be moved beyond Jesus' relationship to John the Baptist. Thus far, Jesus' baptism has been seen by historical-critical exegetes as the point of departure for the quest. However, one can move backward from the river Jordan to the cradle, in spite of all the legendary elements that cloud the nativity stories.

In chapter 4, entitled "The Joseph Trajectory," I demonstrate that Joseph, the father of Jesus, should probably be seen as a legendary figure. Such an argument will lead me to conclude that Jesus grew up fatherless. In antiquity, especially in first-century Galilee, fatherlessness meant trouble. Against the background of the marriage arrangements within the patriarchal mind-set of Israelites in the Second Temple period, a fatherless Jesus would have been without social identity. He would have been excluded from being called a child of Abraham, that is, a child of God. Access to the court of the Israelites in the temple, where mediators could facilitate forgiveness for sin, would have been denied to him. He would have been excluded from the privilege of being given a daughter in marriage.

With the help of cross-cultural anthropology and cultural psychology, I explain in chapter 5 in social-scientific terms an ideal-typical situation of

---

7. Vaage, "Recent Concerns," 181–82.

someone who bore the stigma of being fatherless but who trusted God as Father. In chapter 6, I demonstrate that the "myth of the absent father" was well known in antiquity, whether in Sepphoris, Galilee or in Pompeii, Italy, where it can be seen in mosaic or mural paintings. I argue that the motif of abandoned children who subsequently become adopted by God underlies the story of Jesus, son of Mary. The same motif is replicated in the story of Jesus' blessing of "street children."

In chapter 7, I retell Ovid's story of Perseus who was conceived virginally. My intention is to show why the second-century philosopher Celsus thought that the Christians unjustifiably mirrored this Greek hero, child of Zeus, in their depiction of Jesus. Other examples within Greek-Roman literature are the myths surrounding Hercules, a Greek hero who also had a divine conception. In explaining his adoption as child of Zeus (which means deification), the Greek writer Diodorus Siculus tells the story of an empty tomb and an ascension to heaven. (The same theme is to be found in the Lukan story of Jesus.) The Roman writer Seneca also tells the story of Hercules's divine conception and his adoption as child of Zeus. In the New Testament, Paul, Seneca's contemporary, is particularly known for using the concept of adoption to become God's child. This notion presumes that the followers of Jesus revered him as "child of God." Here the focus is no longer on the Jesus of history but rather on the Jesus of faith. In chapter 7, I explain the concept of adoption to become God's child against the background of Seneca's portrayal of Hercules and references by Diodorus Siculus and in the *Carmen Priapea* to miraculous conceptions of god-like human figures. Like Paul, John also attests to the idea that the believer, in some sense, shares Jesus' sonship. In John's Gospel, Jesus' "fatherlessness" is contextualized within a defamatory campaign that focuses on alleged illegitimacy. This offense is disputed by an argument that Jesus actually came from the heavenly region into the fullness of human condition and that Joseph is his biological father. Nonetheless, the Judean opponents of Johannine Christianity opposed this claim by showing that the children of the First Testament patriarch Joseph are believed to be the ancestors of the Samaritans and that "true" Israelites do not mix with the Samaritans.

Chapter 8 focuses on the origins of the church and the development of the dogma of the "two natures" of Jesus as human and divine. Here, toward the end of the book, the subversiveness of Jesus' cause is underlined. This is an important facet in answering the question concerning the continued importance of the historical Jesus. Therefore, in the last chapter I demonstrate why the quest for the historical Jesus could be called engaged hermeneutics. One of the most urgent social problems of our time is that millions of children are growing up fatherless; this is not only a concern in the Third World but also elsewhere, as can be seen in the title of David

Blankenhorn's book, *Fatherless America: Confronting Our Most Urgent Social Problem* (1995). On the dust cover of this book, Don Browning, professor of ethics and social sciences at the divinity school of the University of Chicago, writes: "*Fatherless America* is the strongest possible refutation to a thesis widely held in our society—that fathers are not really important. David Blankenhorn exposes the multiple ways our culture has convinced itself of this falsehood and shows how to reconstitute fatherhood for the future." My book is about the historical Jesus who filled the emptiness, caused by his fatherlessness, with his trust in God as his Father. Among the earliest faith assertions of Christians was their belief in Jesus as child of God. Searching for Jesus, child of God, could also restore authenticity in the lives of many people today.

My own sense of fatherlessness propelled me toward my present Jesus studies. A friend suggested that I tell my life story along with my interpretation of the Jesus story. Yet I did not begin my Jesus studies with the theme of fatherlessness in mind. Instead, it was my research that eventually convinced me that Jesus grew up as a fatherless son. This historic probability should be taken into consideration when trying to explain Jesus' behavior as reported in the documents of earliest Christianity. I did, however, become existentially impelled by Jesus' fatherlessness because it addressed my own situation. According to Albert Schweitzer's truism, I have come to learn through my own experience who Jesus was and still is, child of God. Yes, it is an "ineffable mystery" (*unaussprechliches Geheimnis*).

GOD-TALK

In biblical times, the name Jesus was fairly common. Influenced by Greek idiom, this name occurred frequently among Israelites around the beginning of the common era. Apart from Jesus "who is called the Christ" and Joshua the "son of Nun" mentioned in the Hebrew Scriptures, the first-century Galilean historian Josephus mentions at least twelve others called Jesus. They played a part in the history of Israel during the period of Greco-Roman geopolitical domination. The vast majority of these people belonged to priestly and governing families.[8]

However, when people today hear the word "Jesus," or use it themselves, they probably have in mind the Jesus to whom Christians pray as if to God. Many people today do not distinguish between the names "Jesus" and

---

8. See Whiston, *Josephus Complete Works*, 767. These Jesuses were Jesus son of Phabet, who was robbed of the high priesthood (*Antiquities* [*Ant.*] 6.5.3); Jesus son of Ananus (*Bellum Judaicum* [*B.J.*] 6.5.3); Jesus, also called Jason (*Ant.* 12.5.1); Jesus son of Sapphias, governor of Tiberias (*Vita* 12.27; *B.J.* 2.20.4); Jesus brother of Onias, who was robbed of the high priesthood by Antiochus Epiphanes (*Ant.* 15.3.1); Jesus son of Gamaliel, who was proclaimed high priest (*Ant.* 20.9.4); Jesus the oldest priest after Ananus (*B.J.* 4.4.3); Jesus son of Damneus, who was proclaimed high priest (*Ant.* 20.9.1); Jesus son of Gamala (*Vita* 38.41); Jesus son of Saphat, who was the leader of a band of robbers (*Vita* 22; *B.J.* 3.9.7); Jesus son of Thebuthus, a priest (*B.J.* 6.8.3); Jesus son of Josedek (*Ant.* 11.3.10).

"Christ." Christians use the name "Jesus" or "Christ" as synonymous with God. This equation already appears at the end of the second century of the common era, in Clement of Alexandria.[9] Similarly, the second-century Syrian Christian writer, Ignatius of Antioch refers to Christ as God, as though such a relationship were self-evident.[10] Ignatius often used the expression, "Jesus Christ our Lord." [11] In most instances the New Testament itself, however, has reservations about calling Christ "God."[12]

Expressing the otherworldliness of God amounts to "objectifying" in a paradoxical way an existence that is in essence no "object." However, there is no other means of God-talk. This process of "objectifying" the transcendent manifests itself in language that corresponds to the deep values of human existence. This kind of analogical language is foundational to studies in the field of psychology of religion, which establishes a relationship between God-imaging and self-conception. Theology as an intellectual enterprise is, therefore, in some sense a systematic reflection on a set of metaphorical expressions in which the transcendent is "objectified."

A theological metaphor is a means by which someone speaks about something he or she knows little or nothing about in terms of what is better known. Furthermore, the use of metaphors is always embedded within a particular context. One can say that a metaphor itself is always contextually bound. When believers in the first and second centuries referred to Jesus *as* God's Christ, *as* God's equal, *as* Child of Humanity, *as* God's image which manifests God, *as* Child of God who comes forth from God or who is legitimated by God or who was with God, or who emanated from God's "fullness," they used recognized cultural metaphors to speak about God.

TELLING AND SHOWING

To call Jesus "the Christ" on the basis of the New Testament is not altogether obvious. In the New Testament we do not have any statement by Jesus that he is the Christ, except in a very qualified and indirect sense in Mark 14:61.

---

9. Clement of Alexandria (*Protr.* 1:1): "We should think of Jesus Christ as we think of God."

10. See Ign. *Trall* 7:1; Ign. *Smy* 1:1; 10:1.

11. Ign. *Eph.* (prologue; 15:3; 18:2); Ign. *Rom.* (2x in prologue; 3:3); Ign. *Pol.* (8:3). Ignatius wanted to indicate that there is nothing self-evident in viewing God as being present in the shape of the human Jesus Christ. However, his concern was not with the idea that God appeared in the shape of a human. To people like the Greeks and the Romans, such an idea was far too general for this to have been the case. What concerned Ignatius is the mystery that God appeared in the specific shape of the *suffering* Jesus Christ. Therefore, there is to him a paradox expressed in the terms "incarnated God" (Ign. *Eph.* 7:2), "God's blood" (Ign. *Eph.* 1:1), the "suffering of my God" (Ign. *Rom.* 6:3), or the "bread of God, that is the flesh of Jesus Christ" (Ign. *Rom.* 7:3).

12. See, among others, Bultmann, "Christologische Bekenntnis," 248; Bultmann, *Theologie des Neuen Testaments*, 131 note 1; Richardson, *Was Jesus Divine?*; Harris, *Jesus as God*. Apart from John 1:1, where the preexistent *Logos* is called "God," and John 20:28, where Thomas glorifies the risen Jesus with the exclamation, "My Lord and my God," the assumption "Christ is God," at least on the basis of what may in all probability be said exegetically of these texts, is only made in 2 Thess 1:12; Titus 2:13, and 2 Pet 1:1. The doxology in Rom 9:5 can hardly be applied to Christ, and the readings in John 1:18 and 1 Tim 3:16 are, viewed text-critically, secondary.

However, to the believing community, Jesus is more than merely a historical figure. Since the second half of the first century and for two thousand years, Jesus has been proclaimed and confessed by Christians in the church *as* the Messiah of Israel, *as* Lord of the world, *as* the Child of God, *as* God—essentially equal to the Father, since the fourth century, and to the Spirit, since the eighth century, and formulated in a specific way in the Western church since the beginning of the eleventh century. This Jesus is the *Jesus of faith,* in contradistinction to, yet irrevocably bound with, the *Jesus of history.*

Different expressions are used to refer respectively to the one or the other. The Jesus of history has often been called the *historical Jesus* while, on the other hand, the Jesus of faith is known as the *kerygmatic Christ.* The word *kerygmatic* is derived from the Greek word that means "proclaimed." The distinction *pre-Easter Jesus* and *post-Easter Jesus,* respectively, is also used for this purpose. Considering the reasons for the use of these various terms may help us to get a grip on a very profound matter. It can help us to understand what the quest for the historical Jesus involves. It also illuminates why, even in secular society, the question about the continued importance of Jesus is still being asked. If Jesus was seen as merely a historical figure, the significance of his life would be no different from that of people like Aristotle, Plato, or Alexander the Great. Nobody would deny the value of the historical investigation of these figures. Jesus, like others from the ancient or more recent past, may be added to such a "who's who in world history" list. From a historical perspective, Jesus is important because he was influential in the course of world history.

For instance, in a note on the stoning of James, the brother of Jesus, the first-century historian Josephus found it worth mentioning that James is "the brother of Jesus, who was called Christ."[13] Here, in this report intended to be the product of historiography, we are not dealing with a honorific, as is the case with the same words ("Jesus, who is called 'Christ'") in the Gospel of Matthew (1:16; see also Matt 27:17, 22). This is also the case with the Roman historian Tacitus (ca. 110 C.E.), and with other "non-Christians" who subsequent to Josephus made pejorative remarks about "Christ" or "Christians."[14]

The reasons for the importance of Jesus to people outside the Christian believing community are different from the reasons of those who believe in him. In the concluding chapter, I indicate briefly why the quest for the historical Jesus, seen from the vantage point of both the church and the broader community, should be undertaken. For now, it is sufficient to emphasize that the question of the importance of Jesus is today irrevocably bound to

---

13. Josephus, *Ant.* 20.9.1—cf. Whiston, *Josephus Complete Works,* 423.
14. Tacitus, *An.* 15.44. Cf. Whiston, *Josephus Complete Works,* 639–47. Notable references to Jesus Christ in ancient sources by non-Christians are those by Tacitus, Suetonius, Pliny, Celsius, Lucianus of Samosata, Thallus, and Mara son of Serapion (see Evans, *Life of Jesus Research,* 291–98).

the fact that the historical Jesus is also taken to be dialectically linked to the kerygmatic Christ.

Sometimes the term *kerygma* is used to refer to the proclaiming Jesus and the proclaimed Christ. The terms *proclaiming* and *proclaimed* here constitute a dialectical conceptual pair. This means that they are two different grammatical constructs and therefore have semantically different connotations. However, they function as a unit. Their interrelatedness contributes to the establishment of meaning. *Proclaiming* refers to Jesus himself acting and speaking. *Proclaimed* refers to the interpreted Jesus whose words and deeds are retold by others. This constitutes the Jesus-kerygma—Jesus manifests as a becoming event through the retelling of his cause.

In *The Acts of Jesus: The Search for the Authentic Deeds of Jesus,* these terms are used somewhat differently by the Jesus Seminar.[15] In this book, the expression *telling* is used to refer to a probable act of the historical Jesus while *showing* refers to an act of faith by believers of later faith communities "retelling" Jesus. *Telling* refers to both authentic sayings and deeds, because sayings and deeds go hand in hand, even if one or the other is not reported. *Showing* refers to a saying or deed that could be based on either something authentic or unauthentic. Irrespective of the historicity of the case, the faith assertion expressed by the enactment or retelling is so overwhelming that authenticity is overshadowed and difficult to discern. Telling is thus not without showing and vice versa. Yet telling and showing must never be confused, even though they are dialectically intertwined.

The concepts *historic-kerygmatic* and *proclaimer-proclaimed* first appeared in the title of a book by Martin Kähler.[16] There he distinguished between the "historical Jesus" and the "real Christ" on the one hand, and the "*geschichtliche*," "biblical," and "proclaimed Christ" on the other. These concepts not only disclose a distinction in German between the *historisch-geschichtlich* and *wirklich-biblisch/gepredigt*, but also between the names *Jesus* and *Christ*. This distinction is related to the dialectic between pre-Easter Jesus and post-Easter Jesus.

Why do scholars draw these distinctions? The answer lies in the fact that historical-critical exegesis of the New Testament brought forth the insight that Jesus did not regard himself *as* the Christ, *as* the Child of Humanity, *as* the Child of God, *as* God. Nor was he recognized as, for instance, the Child of God by the people around him. Rather, the New Testament, the church fathers, and the drafters of the fourth-century creeds proclaimed and confessed him in these terms. It is, furthermore, not the case that all these names—Christ, Child of Humanity, Lord, Child of God, God—were used immediately by *all* followers of Jesus. An investigation into the development

---

15. Funk, and the Jesus Seminar, *Acts of Jesus*, 27–28.
16. Kähler, *Der sogenannte historische Jesus und der geschichtliche, biblische Christus.*

of the origins of Christianity and the handing down of traditions relating to Jesus, brings to light trajectories that indicate the succession of different historic phases in the development of the use of these terms.

Drawing an accurate picture of Jesus from these complicated particulars is certainly no easy task. The question regarding the historical Jesus is prodigiously complicated. Who is the "real Jesus?" We must remember that we do not have immediate access to what Jesus thought of himself and of God. However, for the Christian believer he is *the* manifestation of God. The different aspects of the influential nature of Jesus' life were handed down mainly after his death by those who met God on the basis of the traditions concerning Jesus. Jesus is therefore "God's becoming event"[17] for Christian believers.

At first, the handing down of traditions occurred orally. The first written record to be found today in the New Testament only appeared twenty-five years after Jesus' death, and was written by someone who had never met him personally: Paul (according to Acts 9:11, from the town Tarsus in the region of Cilicia in Asia Minor, today's Turkey). The Gospel according to Mark (ca. 70 C.E.) only came afterwards. Mark served as a source for the authors of the Gospel of Luke (ca. 85 C.E.) and of the Gospel of Matthew (ca. 85-95 C.E.). The Gospel of John originated independently of Mark, Luke, and Matthew, towards the end of the first century. During the second century, Gnostic writings with a "hidden" way of talking about Jesus, although very diverse in nature, content, and God-talk, became prolific. Though outnumbering the writings commonly used by the Roman-based church, these "hidden scriptures" were not regarded as being in accordance to the rule of faith by the dominating church. However, today a number of influential historians and exegetes argue that some of these documents contain authentic sayings of Jesus or, at least, present trajectories of Jesus traditions that lie beneath the New Testament Gospel material. A large number of these Gnostic writings are part of what is today called the Nag Hammadi library.

For some scholars, historical decisions are guided in particular by the criterion known as "multiple independent attestation." This means that multiple independent written evidence has greater historical probability than either singular evidence or a plurality of interdependent literary evidence. In other words, the same evidence in independent documents such as Paul and Mark should be more seriously considered historically than evidence in Matthew and Luke, much of which was taken from Mark. The same evidence independently reported in Matthew and John is also probably more historical than that of a single witness in Luke, for example. This does not mean that a single witness should be regarded as unauthentic. Yet an argu-

---

17. Cf. Ogden, *Doing Theology Today*, 248–52.

ment for authenticity in such a case lacks historical proof. Moreover, writers often amended material to suit their intentions and narrative structures. Material and statements that clearly exhibit the literary preference of a particular writer and the characteristics of a post-Easter ecclesiastical life situation (*Sitz im Leben*) often serve as directives toward those Jesus traditions that cannot historically be traced back to the oral period of 30–50 C.E. Such editorial material can hardly be deemed authentic.

However, the issue is much more complicated than meets the eye. Take as an example the well-known Jesus saying reported in Matthew 16:20 that the "church" is built upon "Peter." Seen from a historical-critical perspective, virtually no New Testament scholar would regard this as a saying of the historical Jesus. Yet telling and showing are so closely intertwined in this saying that it is almost impossible to differentiate between Jesus' telling and Matthew's showing. The reference to Peter's primacy among the core group of Jesus' followers is historically well attested in independent documents. This element in the particular saying could therefore, in all probability, be regarded as historical. However, historical-critical research indicates that the reference to an assembled faith community as "church" (ἐκκλησία) is not from the life situation of the historical Jesus or the pre-Easter disciples, but rather from the post-Easter faith community.

Concerning the search for Jesus (*Rückfrage nach Jesus*), the German New Testament scholar Ferdinand Hahn prefers to focus on "individual features" (*Einzelheiten*) rather than on complete sayings: "It is a matter of establishing a concise description of the interrelatedness between post-Easter and pre-Easter elements in the individual pieces of Jesus traditions."[18] This kind of historical research, applied to a search for Jesus, assumes that the followers of Jesus attributed or applied general wisdom derived from their experience of life and the world to him. It is similar to what writers did with regard to legendary sages such as Solomon, Socrates, and Krishna.

Thus, for example, Matthew represented Jesus in a way that conformed with the Greek translation of the Old Testament, the Septuagint. In doing so, he made use of apocalyptic-messianic themes derived from a late first-century Hellenistic-Israelite context. In these writings, Israel's messiah was depicted as, among other images, the coming Son of Man, a figure who would inaugurate God's perfect kingdom when the despondent believers (seeing that this human-like figure comes from above) will be justified and rescued.

In his representation of Jesus, Luke, in turn, used propaganda motifs that appeared in Greco-Roman stories about deities and in the emperor cult. It was presented in this way in spite of the fact that many of the traditions in

---

18. Hahn, "Methodologische Überlegungen," 28–29: "Es ist die Relation zwischen nachösterlichen und vorösterlichen Elemente in den einzelnen Überlieferungsstücken zu prüfen und Exakt zu bestimmen."

the sources of this Gospel originated in Israel and Roman Palestine. The Gnostic literature, on the other hand, located Jesus firmly within a heavenly realm, entering into the earthly context only apparently human.

All these examples are related to what may be called the "Christianizing" (German: *Christianisierung*) of Jesus. A more inclusive way of referring to this process would be to call it a technique of exalting Jesus by using honorific titles (German: *Würdeprädikationen*). Clear traces of such exaltation are already present in the New Testament and trajectories can be followed deep into the second century and even afterwards.

Suffice it to say that certain statements by Jesus clearly exhibit convictions characteristic of Christians after Easter. This is related to the phenomenon that the Christian community designed certain apologetic statements, which they attributed to Jesus, in order to oppose defamatory campaigns by opponents. Such information assists us in constructing a particular image of the historical Jesus that can be clearly distinguished from the images of Jesus found in the canonical and noncanonical Gospels. In this investigation, historical decisions are not made depending on what modern people, within the context of the Western tradition, deem rationally possible or acceptable.

At the time when the Bible was written, empiricism was not the prevalent theory of knowing or truth. Biblical thought does not distinguish between a "supernatural" occurrence and a "natural" happening. In the cultural context of first-century people in the area of the Mediterranean Sea, the primary distinction in this regard was between "creator" and "creation." From a modern perspective, the latter included not only "natural" things concerning humanity and its constituents, but also "spiritual" things concerning the world of God, angels, miracles, diviners, and magic, expressed by rituals and spells.[19] Those who encountered the spiritual experienced an altered state of consciousness.[20] Cultural psychology tells us that the particular nature of this condition is influenced by cultural associations and personality types. Without this insight, rationally oriented people in the Western world today would be inclined toward an anachronistic understanding of the context of Jesus and of its peculiar consciousness, which involved, among other things, faith healing and resurrection experiences.

At present, the quest for the historical Jesus is multidisciplinary in nature. Biblical archaeology, sociology, cultural anthropology, psychobiography, cultural psychology, medical anthropology, and sociolinguistics are some of the disciplines that provide a basis for the investigation of the his-

---

19. Pilch, "Altered States of Consciousness," 134.

20. See Pilch, "Insights and Models," and Davies, *Jesus the Healer*. However, Pilch (Review of *Jesus the Healer*, 71–72) blames Davies for not interpreting adequately the Mediterranean personality types and their contextual embeddedness cross-culturally. Davies' use of cultural psychology is also, according to Pilch, anachronistic and ethnocentric from a Western monocultural perspective.

torical Jesus. Even with all of these scholarly tools, however, no one will ever be able to determine exactly what Jesus would have said or done. Our attempts to fathom the core of his message can only be through the literary witness of believers who proclaimed him *as* Messiah, *as* Child of Humanity, *as* Lord, *as* Child of God, and *as* God.

Since Emperor Constantine (fourth century C.E.), an image of Jesus known as classical ontological Christology was developed with the help of complicated Greek philosophical metaphysics and Roman legal terminology. For example, terms such as *persona* and *substantia* were taken from the renowned Roman legal system. According to this system, the law provides for an individual to share some substance with someone else while retaining his or her own possessions. From this simple legal regulation the sophisticated and ingenious monotheistic dogma of the one triune God was developed. Sharing the same substance of being, three persons feature different aspects within the divine economics of salvation: begetting and providing (God the Father), conciliating (God the Son), managing (God the Holy Ghost).

Focusing on the second category, God the Son, the mode of the dogmatic discussion is to speculate about the two natures of the Son, divine and human. At this point Christianity becomes metaphysical and ontological. Since Plato (ca. 427–347 B.C.E.), metaphysics has focused on the distinction and relationship between the natural and the supernatural, human-like and God-like. As J. J. Pilch observes, "Christian thinkers up to the ninth century really did not develop theologically significant usages of the supernatural."[21] Christology emerged as an enterprise of theologians who reflected and systematized their thoughts about Jesus. They presumed that these thoughts were supported by witnesses in the New Testament, while most of their presuppositions actually originated in later Christian thinking.

Today, apart from the distinction between a Chistology from above and a Christology from below, a Christology *from the side* also has been introduced.[22] Most critical New Testament scholars are convinced that a Christology from above is not to be found in the New Testament, not even in Johannine literature. In John 1:1 we read that the *Logos* (Word/Jesus) was with God and was God. Here, however, we do not have a typical ontological metaphysical scheme, but rather a functional way of understanding Jesus' behavior. The term *Logos* originated in Greco-Semitic wisdom speculation and has clear traits of Gnosticism. In the Johannine literature, however, Gnosticism is "converted" into something less docetic. This is a form

---

21. Pilch, "Altered States of Consciousness," 134. Referring to Saler, "Supernatural as a Western Category," 46, Pilch notes that "theologically significant usages of the supernatural" were only then introduced into the theology of Western Christendom when the works of Pseudo-Dionysius were translated into Latin in the ninth century C.E.

22. Cf. Malina and Neyrey, *Calling Jesus Names*, x–xi.

of theology which says that God's becoming event in Jesus can be explained by using the honorific title *Logos*: from the heavenly realm God entered into the earthly context. The functional perspective emphasizes those words and deeds of the pre-Easter Jesus that, in the post-Easter period, gave rise to the "majesty titles" ascribed to Jesus by the earliest Christians. However, the perspective "from the side" does not endeavor to unravel the web of pre-Easter and post-Easter Jesus traditions. In this investigation, the issue is how Jesus would have been experienced by his contemporaries rather than how his later followers interpreted his words and deeds. The interpretation from a post-Easter faith perspective was filtered through experiences of resurrection appearances.

The historical investigation practiced in this book is multidisciplinary in nature. From a literary point of view, relevant documents are read against the background of their chronological periods and respective contexts. A multiplicity of congruent, independent evidence from a particular tradition carries relatively greater historical weight.[23] The influence of Easter on the handing down of Jesus traditions is taken into account. This is necessary to distinguish historically between the pre-Easter and the post-Easter Jesus. Pre-Easter traditions are interpreted within typical situations in terms of a first-century, eastern Mediterranean society. The contention of this book is that Jesus grew up as a fatherless son.

This point of departure is supported by a historical-critical deciphering of a post-Easter trajectory with regard to a legendary Joseph figure. Initially Joseph is found in the First Testament (Genesis 37–50). Here he is depicted as an abandoned sibling who becomes an Israelite sage in Egypt. Having been called from Egypt, he is the Moses prototype who rescues Israel in need. I will show that Joseph's offspring, believed to be the forefathers of the Samaritans, were marginalized by the Judeans as illegitimate children of Israel. Nevertheless, in the New Testament Joseph becomes, by God's intervention, the savior of Mary and her child. This tradition was conveyed in both intertestamental documents and the New Testament. It developed in a distinctive way in the literature of Roman Catholic and Protestant dogmatics. In the New Testament, we find this tradition behind and beyond Matthew, Luke, and John. In Matthew, there is the scene of a holy marriage and, as in Luke, the story of the adoption of Jesus by Joseph. According to John, Joseph is Jesus' biological father. Historically seen, the figure of Joseph as Jesus' father does not occur in the early sources behind Matthew and Luke. Joseph also does not play a role in the Pauline literature and the New Testament documents that build upon Paul.

After addressing more general issues related to the historical Jesus in chapters 2 and 3 , I come back to this Joseph trajectory in chapter 4. At this

---

23. Cf. especially Crossan, *Historical Jesus: The Life of a Mediterranean Jewish Peasant*, 427–50.

point, it is sufficient to postulate that the presence of such a trajectory satisfies the criterion of multiple independent attestation of the fact that Jesus probably grew up fatherless. Jesus' fatherlessness is probably a historical fact that should be taken into account when one considers his social identity, his nonpatriarchal ethos, his behavior towards women and children, and especially his trust in God as his Father.

HOW MUCH CAN WE KNOW ABOUT HIM?

Because we do not have Jesus' words as recorded by him, but only as transmitted by witnesses, two fallacies may develop. The first is that it would be impossible to determine the historical core of the mind-set of Jesus of Nazareth. The second is that it would be undesirable to undertake a historical Jesus investigation because the real Jesus is the Jesus to be found on the surface of the Bible and not behind the text. In orthodox theological circles, this is the Jesus of whom the ecclesiastical creeds bear witness. The title of Martin Kähler's book, *The So-Called Historical Jesus and the Historic, Biblical Christ* (1896), already indicates his opinion that only the Christ proclaimed ("gepredigt") in the New Testament really matters.

The work of Rudolf Bultmann has often been wrongfully used to validate the view that a quest for the historical Jesus is impossible. Bultmann was prompted by Albert Schweitzer's finding that exegetes who draft biographies of Jesus often project their own ideologies onto their images of Jesus. Such ideologies include the exegetes' own ideas regarding ethical-religious perfection, goodness, sinlessness, and holiness. These are projected onto the inner being of the person Jesus.[24] Bultmann called this the "psychological fallacy." One cannot describe another person's mind.

Earlier Kähler had pointed out that a biography of Jesus would be impossible since sources did not mention Jesus' psychological disposition.[25] This led Schweitzer to react against theories about supposed mental disorders in the mind of Jesus. In his doctoral thesis, *The Psychiatric Study of Jesus*, which served as the completion of his medical examinations, Schweitzer responds to the work of four "psychopathologists." These authors claimed to build upon Schweitzer's view that Jesus' activities were those of a "wild" apocalyptic prophet.[26] Using "the investigation of the mental aberrations of significant personalities in relation to their works"[27] these men depicted Jesus as suffering from hallucinations and

24. Cf. Joy, "Introduction: Schweitzer's Conception of Jesus," 23; Kähler, *Sogenannte historische Jesus*, 28, note 1a.

25. Kähler, *Sogenannte historische Jesus*, 14: "Der sogenannte historische Jesus ist für die Wissenschaft nach dem Maßstabe moderner Biographie ein unlösbares Problem; denn die vorhandenen Quellen reichen nicht aus."

26. See Schweitzer, *The Psychiatric Study of Jesus*, 46–53.

27. Schweitzer, *The Psychiatric Study of Jesus*, 33.

paranoia.[28] Schweitzer's reaction to these "psychopathologists" was similar to his reaction to the "liberal theologians" from the previous century. According to Schweitzer, they construct a "liberalized, modernized, unreal, never existing Jesus . . . to harmonize with [their] own ideals of life and conduct."[29] With regard to these "psychopathologists," Schweitzer states: "[They] busy themselves with the psychopathology of Jesus without becoming familiar with the study of the historical life of Jesus. They are completely uncritical not only in the choice but also in the use of sources . . . . We know nothing about the physical appearance of Jesus or about the state of his health."[30]

In his book *Jesus*, Bultmann agrees that, "psychologically speaking," we know virtually nothing of the life and personality of Jesus.[31] Bultmann's student, Ernst Käsemann, also agrees with this.[32] But according to Walter Schmithals (another Bultmann student) in the afterword to Bultmann's book, a gross misunderstanding could arise here.[33] It is misleading to believe that Bultmann, or Schweitzer, for that matter, considered it impossible to carry out a historical investigation of Jesus. Bultmann says that we know enough of Jesus' message to be able to draw a coherent picture of him.[34] The problem is not that we know too little of the historical Jesus. The question is whether this knowledge is at all relevant for faith.

One of the assumptions of this book is that historical Jesus research can be done. The question then would be whether it is necessary. Can one be a Christian without it? Marcus Borg points out that there have always been Christians who believed in Jesus as Christ, as Child of God, and as God without ever having engaged in the quest for the historical Jesus.[35] Kähler called it the "childlike faith" of millions throughout history.[36] According to Luke Timothy Johnson, the post-New Testament's "developed, dogmatic

---

28. See also Schweitzer, *Geschichte der Leben-Jesu-Forschung*, 362–67.

29. Joy, "Introduction: Schweitzer's Conception of Jesus," 19.

30. Schweitzer, *The Psychiatric Study of Jesus*, 44–45, 47.

31. Bultmann, *Jesus*, 8–10.

32. Käsemann, "Problem des historischen Jesus," 212–13: "Bei einem Leben Jesu kann man schlechterdings nicht auf äußere und innere Entwicklung verzichten. Von der letzten wissen wir jedoch gar nichts, von der ersten fast gar nichts außer dem Wege, der von Galiläa nach Jerusalem, von der Predigt des nahen Gottes in den Haß des offiziellen Judentums und die Hinrichtung durch die Römer führte."

33. Schmithals, "Nachwort," 149.

34. Bultmann, *Jesus*, 13. Cf. also Painter, *Theology as Hermeneutics*, 102. To my knowledge, the most concentrated summary of Bultmann's reconstruction of the historical Jesus is to be found in his *Das Verhältnis der urchristlichen Christusbotschaft zum historischen Jesus* (11): "Mit einiger Vorsicht also wird man über das Wirken Jesu Folgendes sagen können. Charakteristisch für ihn sind Exorzismen, der Bruch des Sabbatgebotes, die Verletzung von Reinheitsvorschriften, die Polemik gegen die jüdische Gesetzlichkeit, die Gemeinschaft mit deklassierten Personen wie Zöllnern und Dirnen, die Zuneigung zu Frauen und Kindern; auch ist zu erkennen, daß Jesus nicht wie Johannes der Täufer ein Asket war, sondern gerne aß und ein Glas Wein trank. Vielleicht darf man noch hinzufügen, daß er zur Nachfolge aufrief und eine kleine Schar von Anhängern—Männern und Frauen—um sich sammelte."

35. Borg, *Jesus in Contemporary Scholarship*, 184.

36. Kähler, *Sogenannte historische Jesus*, 44.

Christ of church doctrine (true God and true man)" is not the Jesus "limned in the pages of the New Testament."[37] The latter Jesus is "instantly graspable" by uncritical Christians, who let their lives be shaped by it and not by historiography. The problem, however, is that Johnson sees the writings of Paul and of 1 Peter and Hebrews "converging" with the canonical Gospels, but overlooks the New Testament's diversity. The "converging" picture, then, is the "instantly graspable" image of Jesus!

The issue here is: in whom or in what do we place our ultimate trust? The members of the Jesus Seminar are often accused of being positivists who place their trust in "historical" facts. The opposing opinion presents itself as trusting only in what the New Testament says. However, trusting in the New Testament as an "objective entity" also exhibits positivism. It is claimed that "truth" is to be found in the New Testament's "kerygma." How then is "truth" manifest in the witness regarding the "kerygmatic Christ?"

In a specific response to Johnson, John Dominic Crossan points out that the narrative form, as in the four canonical Gospels, is not the only gospel format.[38] There are also gospels in the form of collections of proverbs of Jesus, which undoubtedly came into being before the narrative type. The Sayings Gospel Q, hidden in the Gospels of Matthew and Luke, and the *Gospel of Thomas* (recovered in Greek fragments and in a Coptic translation found under the sand at, respectively, Oxyrhynchus and Nag Hammadi in Egypt) are examples of this format. Unlike the narrative Gospels and the letters of Paul, the "sayings" or "aphorisms" gospels do not attach any redemptive meaning to the death of Jesus.

What then is "true" with regard to the kerygmatic Christ found on the surface of the New Testament, in contradistinction with the historical Jesus who is rediscovered by means of historiography? After all, these two formats with their different messages of God's salvation cannot both lay claim to credibility. Even if one were to work only with the canonical Gospels, the problem would not be solved, since the interpretations of the death of Jesus by Mark and John differ radically, as Crossan notes:

> For Mark, the passion of Jesus starts and ends in agony and desolation. For John, the passion of Jesus starts and ends in control and command. But, I repeat, as gospel, both are equally but divergently true. Both speak, equally but divergently, to different times and places, situations and communities. Mark's Jesus speaks to a persecuted community and shows them how to die. John's Jesus speaks to a defeated community and shows them how to live.[39]

37. Johnson, "The Search for (the Wrong) Jesus," 20–44.
38. Crossan, "Why Christians Must Search," 42–43.
39. Ibid., 44.

Luke Timothy Johnson misses the important point. The issue is not that historical Jesus researchers want to ground their faith in historiography rather than in the normative nature of the scriptures. One cannot formulate it better than Crossan: "[O]ur faith is not in history, but in the meaning of history; not within a museum, but within a church."[40]

The contemporary dialectical systematic theologian Eberhard Jüngel says it in different words: "[F]aith in Jesus as the Christ cannot be *grounded* in the historical Jesus; it must nevertheless have a support in him."[41] Jüngel is correct when he states that God cannot be known historically, but only on the basis of God's revelatory acts in respect of which the faith of the one who receives the revelation corresponds.[42] God is revealed by God's own undertaking through the medium of historical events. By this I mean that, for Christian believers, God is manifested in the human Jesus of Nazareth. Another renowned systematic theologian, Edward Schillebeeckx, says, "Without Jesus' historical human career the whole of Christology becomes an ideological superstructure."[43] Without the historical Jesus, all of our reflections on Jesus' relevance for us as witnessed in documents written by biblical writers or afterwards would be ideas flying without identifiable roots in human existence. Such ideologies unjustifiably separate the supernatural from the natural without realizing that the authors of the Bible did not have such a dichotomy in mind.

Although God's becoming event in Jesus of Nazareth occurred historically and is therefore in principle open to historical investigation, the act of faith that confesses that Jesus is the Christ, the Lord, the Child of God, is not grounded in historiography as such: "No one can say that 'Jesus is the Lord' but by the Holy Spirit" (1 Cor 12:3). On the other hand, "if God has made *this* human being—and not just any human being—to be the Christ, as faith confesses, the faith must be interested to know what can be known about this person: but not in order to *ground* faith in Jesus Christ historically, but rather to guard it from docetic self-misunderstanding."[44]

The word *Docetism* is derived from a Greek word that denotes "apparentness." In other words, it presents the other side of empiricism. Yet Docetism provides a viewpoint that is not really less positivistic in nature than empiricism. Over against the viewpoint that someone's or something's credibility depends on its empirically observed or tested value in this earthly world, a docetic viewpoint would emphasize that someone's or something's value could manifest to the senses or mind as real or true on the basis of evidence that does not need to be empirically demonstrated.

---

40. Ibid., 45.
41. Jüngel, "Dogmatic Significance," 88.
42. Ibid., 83.
43. Schillebeeckx, *Jesus in Our Western Culture*, 13.
44. Jüngel, "Dogmatic Significance," 97.

Exegetes of the Johannine literature have therefore explained the references in the prologues of the Gospel (John 1:14) and the First Letter of John (1 John 1:1) to the seeing and touching of the Logos that became flesh as a polemic against Docetism.[45]

At the end of the first century, writings that advocated a world-escaping belief system originated. Among the documents of the Nag Hammadi library, discovered in 1945 in the desert close to Luxor in Upper Egypt, a fair number of such texts were found. In general, these documents view the material world negatively. The material world is seen as inherently evil, populated by evil powers, or as an imperfect creation because of its transitoriness.[46] When the Nag Hammadi writings refer to Jesus "who became flesh," their intention is, for the most part, that "Jesus who is a spiritual being hides his spiritual 'flesh' under shapes, likenesses or a human body."[47] This stands in contrast to the perspective of writers such as Paul and John, who emphasized that God's becoming event in Jesus Christ is trustworthy because it comes to believers by means of the apostolic kerygma. According to this kerygma, Jesus was equal to people in terms of human history and the human condition. In all probability, the apostolic kerygma originated in the Jerusalem church before the city was ruined by the Romans in 70 C.E. In chapter 4 (where the Joseph trajectory will be discussed) and in chapter 8 (where the "cradle of the church" will be discussed), I focus more critically on the role of the "pillars" of the Jerusalem church.

Bultmann's well-known observation that it is the *that* ("*daß*") of Jesus which is important for faith and not the *what* ("*was*") deals with precisely this type of dialectic between spirit and flesh.[48] According to this stance, stories in the Gospels about Jesus' work and life, his birth and death (the "whatness" of his life) are assertions of faith in which the Jesus kerygma is expressed. The Jesus kerygma is the "thatness" of God's becoming event in Jesus, the ground of Christian faith. However, it is on this point that students of Bultmann, such as Käsemann (and Jeremias), misunderstood their mentor. Bultmann[49] was not of the opinion that a "historical and material" antithesis[50] exists between Jesus and the kerygma of the early church. He spoke of a distinction between "historical continuity" and "material relation."[51] It seems that he meant that a continuity clearly exists between Jesus and Christ (the two names, after all, refer to the same historical person) but

---

45. See, e.g., Robinson, "Sethians and Johannine Thought," 663.
45. See, e.g., Robinson, "Sethians and Johannine Thought," 663.
46. Franzmann, *Jesus in the Nag Hammadi Writings*, 57.
47. Ibid., 72.
48. Bultmann, *Verhältnis der urchristlichen Christusbotschaft*, 9.
49. Bultmann, "Antwort an Ernst Käsemann," 191.
50. Käsemann, "Blind Alleys," 36.
51. Bultmann, *Verhältnis der urchristlichen Christusbotschaft*, 9; Bultmann, "Antwort an Ernst Käsemann," 191. Bultmann uses the phrase, "Unterschied zwischen *historische Kontinuität* und *sachliche Verhältnis*" (my emphasis).

that there is no historical continuity between the kerygma that takes the death of Christ Jesus as a redemptive event, and the historical Jesus himself who did not call on people to believe in him, but to depend, like him, on the presence of God. However, there is a material relation between the message of Jesus and the ecclesiastical kerygma: Both announce that life in the kingdom of God is qualitatively and radically different from the meaning that people find in cultural arrangements—life in the kingdom of God is life according to the Spirit and not life according to the flesh.[52] Paul, therefore, did not need to ground his kerygma in Jesus, the Jew, because then he would have grounded faith in the one who, as a human, came from the cultural context of the Israelites (Rom 9:5).[53]

Yet, as Robert T. Osborn rightly sees, it would be a misrepresentation of Paul to say "that Jesus in his flesh may well have been Jewish, but that as the resurrected Christ he certainly is not."[54] Indeed, to Paul, Jesus would be bound to particularism (that is, to a peculiar cultural arrangement) had the significance of Israel's messiah been solely of an ethnic nature. Such a messiah would be, according to Rom 9:5, "Christ according to flesh." But this is *not* the material essence of the traditions of Jesus that had been handed down to Paul. On the contrary, there is a material relation between Jesus of Nazareth and the Christ Jesus proclaimed by Paul. In other words, the Jesus of history is not irrelevant.

Faith assertions, according to Paul, do not need stories about miracles, pronouncements of controversies with Pharisees, or parables about God's patronage. These stories, however, are vehicles of the faith assertions found in the Gospel material. In other words, the authors of the Gospels regarded them as functional. Furthermore, Paul did not deem it necessary to use the Jesus kerygma as a source in order to reconstruct a historical Jesus *before* he could believe. However, Paul could only base the life "in Christ" (as he, from an existential perspective, formulated the Jesus kerygma compactly), because he in some way or another had knowledge of the Jesus tradition. According to this tradition, Jesus was subversive towards the culture of his time. For Jesus, living in God's kingdom meant that neither mediators nor specific cultural arrangements are needed to give someone direct and immediate access to God's love. God's becoming event in Jesus has universal relevance—no one is excluded, as Paul's notion of justification by faith puts it. The concept of "immediacy" is a functional, metaphorical way of explaining the cause of Jesus.

But, with regard to the Jesus kerygma, let me put it very concisely: The Jesus kerygma is merely another faith assertion that cannot claim to be the

---

52. Bultmann, "Significance of the Historical Jesus," 223–35.

53. NIV translates the Greek phrase in Rom 9:5 ("from whom the Christ, according to [the] flesh, comes") as "Theirs are the patriarchs, and from them is traced the human ancestry of Christ."

54. Osborn, "Christian Blasphemy," 221.

sole credible reflection of the cause of Jesus, that is, God's becoming event in Jesus of Nazareth. The observation by Joachim Jeremias that Bultmann runs the risk of replacing the message of Jesus with the preaching of Paul (and John) is therefore not entirely inappropriate.[55] Such an admittance, however, does not eliminate the fact that Bultmann indeed emphasizes the existence of a material link between the message of Jesus and the Pauline kerygma. In Robert Funk's version of Jesus' understanding of the kingdom of God, none other than Paul's statements are echoed in particular:

> God's domain was for Jesus something already present. It was also something to be celebrated because it embraces everyone— Jew, gentile, slave, free, male, female. In God's domain, circumcision, keeping kosher, and sabbath observance are extraneous. The kingdom represents an unbroken relationship to God: temple and priests are obsolete.[56]

The Gospels present this message in a version different from that of Paul, while John presents it in a version different from that of Mark, and the Gnostic writings in the Nag Hammadi library differently again. A harmonized composition of the Christ events, as recorded in the New Testament, is not "normative," as Johnson would have it, nor is a necessarily relativistic choice of one version above another. It is the mode of the dialectic between pre-Easter and post-Easter that is normative. Crossan says: "It is because of that normative process that each Christian generation is called both to consider the historical Jesus and simultaneously to reinterpret that figure as Christ or Lord. Each side of the dialectic must be done over and over again . . . .What is permanent is the dialectic."[57]

Seen in this way, the imposed injunction to repeat this same dialectic mode amounts to our always being oriented again by the evidence in the New Testament and extracanonical literature. Where else do we learn of God's revelation in and through Jesus of Nazareth? To the writers of the New Testament he was Christ, Child of Humanity, Child of God, Lord. To the authors of extracanonical literature such as the Nag Hammadi documents, Jesus was, among other things, the "Fullness of God." For me, Jesus *is* God, but not necessarily in the classical ontological sense.

In other words, when Funk deliberately chooses to turn his back on Paul, and, for that matter, decisively also on Bultmann as a dialectic theologian, one can have respect for his taking Jesus' subversiveness seriously.[58] However,

---

55. Cited in Käsemann, "Blind Alleys," 24. In an earlier work, I said that this remark by Jeremias "is . . . entirely inappropriate" (Van Aarde, "Continued Importance of Jesus," 784). However, by second thought, I have changed my mind.

56. Funk, *Honest to Jesus*, 41.

57. Crossan, "Why Christians Must Search," 45.

to go along in the new millennium with Jesus but without the New Testament or the church as the believing community of Christians would not be an act of faith that necessarily rests on or is implied by his cause. On the other hand, it does not mean that the New Testament should be put, as Willi Marxsen formulates it, "in the place of Jesus as *the* revelation."[59] William Thompson, building upon the insights of philosopher-theologians Paul Ricoeur and David Tracy, says,

> Christianity is not a religion of a book, but of a person, Jesus [as] the Risen One. But the Jesus event has left us "traces" of itself in the New Testament, and it is chiefly to this "text" that we must turn for "normative codification" of the Jesus event. That we go to Jesus *through the biblical text* is finally rooted in our tradition-bound character. Like all other things human, Christianity is an historically-mediated religion.[60]

FROM DOUBT TO INQUIRY

The aim here is to display the landscape where scholars have trod. This approach will help us to sketch a profile of the historical Jesus constructed from the contents of scholarly interaction. Within these boundaries I will explore the notion of fatherlessness in the Second Temple period and elucidate some aspects of Jesus' words and deeds in terms of the stigma of being fatherless in Herodian Galilee. The route passes two important mileposts. The first is Schweitzer's alarm against the unsophisticated and uncritical historical approach of scholars, not only in their choices but also in their use of the New Testament and its sources.[61]

The voyage by Rudolf Bultmann's students, despite all of the obstacles, represents the second milepost. Labeling contemporary historical Jesus research as the "New Quest" as distinct from the "Old Quest" was triggered by one of Bultmann's students, James Robinson, in 1959.[62] Robinson referred to the traverse into the newest phase of the itinerary as a "paradigm shift."[63] While Bultmann is often described as a proponent of the "No Quest," the fact that his students embarked on a journey they referred

---

58. Funk, *Honest to Jesus*, 304: "We can no longer rest our faith on the faith of Peter or the faith of Paul. I do not want my faith to be a secondhand faith. I am therefore fundamentally dissatisfied with versions of the faith that trace their origins only so far as the first believers; true faith, fundamental faith, must be related in some way directly to Jesus of Nazareth."

59. Marxsen, *Introduction to the New Testament*, 284.

60. Thompson, *Jesus Debate*, 115.

61. Schweitzer, *Quest of the Historical Jesus*, 44–45, 47.

62. Robinson, *New Quest of the Historical Jesus*.

63. Cited in Borg, "Portraits of Jesus," 2.

to as the "New Quest" demonstrates my opinion that a denial of the necessity of the search for Jesus can bring about doubt with regard to the quest for God. If inquiry is denied at the doorstep, doubt will come through the window.

Many articles that intend to give an overview of historical Jesus research have been published. It seems that many reviewers find their point of departure in the pattern of Albert Schweitzer's *The Quest of the Historical Jesus: A Critical Study of Its Progress from Reimarus to Wrede* (English translation published in 1910 from the German original, *Von Reimarus zu Wrede*, originally written in 1906). Reviewers classify three distinctive periods: the precritical phase (150–1778), the first period of the "critical quest" for Jesus (1778–1953), and finally, since 1954, the second phase of the "critical quest" for Jesus (the New Quest). The process of harmonization of the Jesus tradition found in the canonical gospels constitutes the first period. More than forty examples of such a harmonization appeared in the sixteenth century within both Roman Catholic and Protestant circles.[64] The second period is characterized by its radical historical skepticism and rationalism. The third period was introduced by the students of Rudolf Bultmann.[65]

In South Africa, the first consideration of the importance of the quest for the historical Jesus came in the late seventies from Andrie du Toit, emeritus professor of New Testament at the University of Pretoria.[66] Du Toit appraised the representatives of the New Quest positively. It appears to be the same within the academic circles in North America. Within the contour of Käsemann's (1954) reconsideration of Bultmann's stance, the quest for the "original" Jesus was regarded as not only desirable but also essential.[67] The need for the quest rests, according to these scholars, upon what one can call a theological accountability toward intraecclesiastical as well as extraecclesiastical truth claims.

---

64. See Du Toit, "Historiese Jesus en die Verkondigde Christus," 268. This was the very first article published in South Africa on the quest for the historical Jesus. It forms the seventh chapter of the series *Guide to the New Testament*, vol. 4, *The Synoptic Gospels and Acts: Introduction and Theology*, edited by Andrie Du Toit. This *Guide to the New Testament* series aims to provide textbooks for graduate theological students. Their main purpose is to provide background material on the New Testament documents, specifically in terms of introductory and theological issues. The very fact that the particular volume on the Synoptic Gospels and Acts ends with a treatise on the historical Jesus expresses the viewpoint of the editor of the series (who is also the writer of the specific treatise) that Jesus is indeed part and parcel of the "theologies" of the New Testament and not only its presupposition (267).

65. See Käsemann, "Problem des historischen Jesus"; Bornkamm, *Jesus of Nazareth*; Fuchs, *Zur Frage nach dem historischen Jesus*; Robinson, "New Quest of the Historical Jesus"; Conzelmann, *Jesus*; Schmithals, *Jesus von Nazareth in der Verkündigung der Kirche* (cf. Boshoff, "Proclaimer Became the Proclaimed").

66. Du Toit, "Historiese Jesus en die Verkondigde Christus."

67. Ibid., 272–74. Du Toit prefers to use Joachim Jeremias's notion of the "original Jesus" rather than the "historical Jesus" (cf. Jeremias, *Problem of the Historical Jesus*).

Concerning the intraecclesiastical truth claims, an authentic continuity between the life and proclamation of Jesus of Nazareth and the kerygmatic Christ proclaimed in the early church is essential, otherwise one can argue that the message of the gospel about the Jesus of history rests on myths and ideas.[68] More specifically, some have argued that the shocks Bultmann's influence caused for many believers in terms of the reliability of the gospel tradition of Jesus should be thwarted. The skeptical historians (influenced by Bultmann and Schweitzer) were challenged to overcome the "scandal of the New Testament" and to "accept God's singular revelation that was granted once and for all" in the Jesus of history. Concerning the "accountability toward extra-ecclesiastical truth claims," this has relevance for the interreligious dialogue and the demonstration of the rational basis of theology and the gospel embedded in the New Testament.[69]

But the quest for the "original" Jesus is also desirable because it helps the exegete to clarify in a responsible way the process by which the New Testament was handed down. We can therefore say that the historical quest for who Jesus was, what his vision was, what he said and did, has an expository power in guiding an analysis and an understanding of the varied traditions as vehicles of theological developments within the New Testament and the early church.[70] Scholarship has demonstrated that the Jesus tradition was "reduced," not only because of the editing process of the Gospel writers themselves, but also because of the shift from orality to literacy, the process of translation from Aramaic into Greek, and, especially, by means of the selecting, transforming, and remaking of the pre-Easter Jesus tradition in the light of post-Easter beliefs. This very process of reduction underlines the futility of a quest for an "objective" Jesus without and before any interpretation.

Therefore, according to some scholars, one can ultimately seek to establish the "original" Jesus' understanding of himself and the relation of this understanding to the understanding of Jesus by the early church.[71] One of the assumptions in this regard is that the Jesus tradition, as reflected in the canonical gospels, can be regarded as authentic until one

---

68. Apart from the "Radical Dutch Criticism," led by New Testament scholar Wim van Manen in the nineteenth century, Earl Doherty (*The Jesus Puzzle: Did Christianity Begin with a Mythical Christ?* [1999] recently has challenged again the existence of a historical Jesus. He builds his opinion on four arguments: (a) Why are the events of the gospel story, and its central character Jesus of Nazareth, not found in the New Testament epistles? (b) Why does Paul's divine Christ seem to have no connection to the Gospel Jesus, but closely resembles the many pagan savior gods of the time who only lived in myth? (c) Why, given the spread of Christianity across the Roman Empire in the first century, did only one Christian community compose a story of Jesus' life and death—the Gospel of Mark—while every other Gospel simply copied and reworked the first one? (d) Why is every detail in the Gospel story of Jesus' trial and crucifixion drawn from passages in the First Testament?

69. Du Toit, *Historiese Jesus en Verkondigde Christus*, 282.

70. Ibid., 275–79. Du Toit elaborates especially (but not exclusively) on Hahn's "Methôdologische Überlegungen zur Rückfrage nach Jesus".

71. Ibid., 279.

proves the opposite. The burden of proof lies with those scholars who argue for nonauthenticity.[72] Methodologically, however, it can be helpful to argue for absolute accuracy in a complementary fashion: authenticity is only accepted when it is really proved. Therefore, "criteria for authenticity" are needed, like the criterion of dissimilarity or the criterion of coherence.[73] New Testament professors such as Norman Perrin, Günther Bornkamm, Ernst Käsemann, and Joachim Jeremias were advocates of the criterion of dissimilarity.[74]

According to this yardstick, words of Jesus would be considered his own if they did not oppose, to a degree, the faith assertions found among the followers of Jesus in the period of earliest Christianity or among the Israelites after the destruction of the temple in Jerusalem by the Romans in 70 C.E. Criticism against this criterion is that it is difficult to imagine that the mind-sets of the historical Jesus and of formative Judaism and formative Christianity would be so very much unrelated to one another. In the end, this criterion may help to identify a *distinctive* Jesus, but not Jesus' own characteristics. Similarly, one cannot have outright peace with the criterion of coherence. According to this criterion, Jesus' sayings would be regarded as authentic if they make sense coherently within a framework of other sayings that have been established by historical-critical exegesis as probably part of Jesus' own thinking. The notion of coherency is today very much the constituent of the work of Jesus researchers, including myself. However, many scholars remain skeptical about the appropriateness of the different criteria because, among other reproaches, they cover only Jesus' words and not his deeds as well.[75]

Regardless of doubt and uneasiness about the perplexity of the search for the historical Jesus, the feeling among historically minded exegetes at this stage is that historical Jesus research does have a future.[76] However, some have pleaded for a reconsideration of some of the dispositions of the research, such as where the burden of proof should lie. Should a Jesus researcher accept the historical accuracy of a Jesus saying in the Gospels at face value until it is proved to be an interpreted faith assertion of a follower of Jesus from a post-Easter believing community? Or should one begin from a more skeptical vantage point by assuming that the burden of proof lies with the scholar who argues for authenticity? There are many scholars in the field of the study of the origins of Christianity who are not suspicious at all of the reliability of the New Testament writings, especially, so it seems

---

72. Ibid., 280.
73. Ibid., 282–86.
74. See Perrin, *Rediscovering the Teaching of Jesus*; Bornkamm, *Jesus of Nazareth*; Käsemann, "Problem des historischen Jesus"; Jeremias, *Problem of the Historical Jesus*.
75. See also Du Toit, 286–87.
76. Keck, *Future for the Historical Jesus*.

to me, those who are at present working in the United Kingdom.[77] Some of
these scholars are in constant debate with Jesus scholars who are inclined
not to accept so easily the historical trustworthiness of the documents
without critical scrutiny because of the faith biases of these writings.[78]

In the South African context (and seemingly in the North American context), these first attempts to explain the dynamics of historical Jesus research
serve as a breakthrough in many ways. For several years, the presence of
orthodoxy and the evangelical approach in church and theology inhibited
biblical scholars from operating freely within the historical-critical paradigm, sometimes to a greater and sometimes to a lesser extent. However, in
all fairness to many colleagues working within an evangelical framework, it
seems they at least explicitly rejected a fundamentalist and "precritical" presumption that all aspects of the Jesus tradition were to be simply identified
with the very own deeds and words (*ipssisima facta et verba*) of Jesus' life. In
the same vein, German New Testament scholar Peter Stuhlmacher tried to
break through the "antimetaphysical" historical research. In accordance with
what Ernst Troeltsch called "the principle of analogy in historiography," the
historian sees his or her own modern experience of reality as the norm by
which to judge what could be historically authentic in the past and what
could not. Stuhlmacher aimed at creating an atmosphere in which scholars,
as members of the Christian believing community, would regard aspects of
the Jesus tradition in the canonical gospels that do not have other analogies
in a historiographical sense as authentic. In particular, he had the resurrection narratives and the miracles of Jesus in mind.[79]

What is the status of present-day Jesus research concerning miracles and
resurrection appearances? With regard to the miracle stories, we are now
aware that they have become part of the quest for the historical Jesus.
However, they have not been studied exactly according to conservative
approaches. In, for example, the work of the Jesus Seminar and of Gerd
Theissen,[80] the miracles of Jesus have begun to be investigated along sociological and cultural-anthropological lines. At the same time, the New
Testament canon does not constitute the boundaries within which independent attestations are critically scrutinized for possible analogies. When
the Jesus Seminar started to compile a database of authentic deeds of the
historical Jesus after completing the study of the Jesus sayings, Robert Funk,
addressing the controversy with regard to the historicity of Jesus' miracles,
made use of Peter Berger's and Thomas Luckmann's treatise on the sociology of knowledge. In their study *The Social Construction of Reality*, Berger
and Luckmann note: "Theories about identity are always embedded in a

---

77. Cf. Wright, "Knowing Jesus," 15–27; Stanton, *Gospels and Jesus*; Stanton, "Jesus of Nazareth."
78. See, e.g., Borg and Wright, *Meaning of Jesus*.
79. Stuhlmacher, *Schriftauslegung auf dem Wege*, 14ff.
80. Theissen, *Urchristliche Wundergeschichte*, 38–41.

more general interpretation of reality; they are 'built into' the symbolic universe and its theoretical legitimations."[81] From this perspective of a "psychology of identity," Funk comments:

> The overarching issue for Fellows of the Seminar is thus whether to interpret stories of exorcism from late antiquity in terms of the then prevailing cosmology, or whether to put them to the test of the modern scientific world-view. The answer to the question whether such stories are historically plausible would depend on the universe [being] invoked as the test of plausibility. This issue goes together but is not identical with the question of whether biblical scholars belong to the community of faith or to the scientific community . . . . If the issue in this form is transposed back into the New Testament, it has to be asked: Did people really suffer from demon possession? Did Jesus then really heal them? This question can be stated in different terms: Were demons real because people believed in them? The Fellows of the Seminar will have to face this dilemma.[82]

However, it is a false dilemma to require an either/or case regarding the cosmology of people believing within the framework of a mythological symbolic world and modern scientific historiography based on the principle of analogy. To decide whether something is historically plausible demands, according to our insights today, independent multiple attestation. These witnesses should be attested to in documents that are chronologically stratified. It should also make sense coherently in terms of a social stratification of the period involved.[83] Attestation, however, does not apply only to the words of Jesus. We do not have direct access to the Jesus tradition. As in the case of his deeds, which are attested only by reference to them, we have access to Jesus' words, but solely by means of reference to them. Furthermore, these references came to us in many modes. Myths and metaphors are such modes.

Thus, metaphorical and mythological language is part of our assessment of the beliefs of Jesus' contemporaries about his identity, either as acclamation or defamation, like any other of their references to his sayings or deeds. From the perspective of the sociology of knowledge, these beliefs, expressed in language of analogy through myths and other metaphors, were built upon or arose from the social world in which Jesus and his contemporaries lived. In other words, myths and metaphors represent an interpreted reflection on the identity of Jesus, just as any other attestation to his words and deeds does. Therefore, myths and other metaphors in relevant documents,

---

81. See Berger and Luckmann, *Social Construction of Reality,* 174–80.
82. Funk, "Demons, Identity, and Worldview," 15.
83. Cf. Crossan, *Historical Jesus.*

relating to Jesus in one way or another, should also be submitted to a chronological stratification by which their historical reliability, in terms of their closeness to the historical Jesus, can be judged. Closeness, however, does not mean mere chronological nearness, but also accuracy in terms of nearness in cosmology and ideology. If an attestation in this regard does not have any analogy elsewhere, it should also be regarded with circumspection, like any similar attestation. Still, it does not mean that such a singular attestation is self-evidently untrue in the historical sense. A single attestation that is chronologically not far removed from the beginning of the common era can still be considered useful if it has explanatory power in an intelligible and internally coherent context. In short, such a context in which references to Jesus' identity make coherent sense should correspond with the social stratification of first-century Herodian Palestine.

This social stratification is a construct of the first-century social world dialectically built upon or arisen from a mythological symbolic universe. The chronological stratification of textual evidence is a construct on the basis of modern, painstaking historical and literary research. Where such attestation is lacking, as in the case of the empty tomb tradition, historical research is still possible, but then the relevant witnesses will be subjected to the question Why and with which results did the particular tradition develop or become enhanced at that particular point in time?[84] The older criterion of coherence has thus been adapted so that sociological and cultural anthropological models[85] are used in a heuristic and expository fashion to contextualize the historical Jesus within the Herodian Palestine of his day.

Other controversies which have brought about intense reconsiderations among Jesus scholars are the issues of the dissimilarity between Jesus and formative Judaism, and the Gospel of John as source for the historical Jesus. With regard to the former, Robert Funk puts it as follows:

> Scholars now by and large reject the older criterion of dissimilarity, by which Rudolf Bultmann meant: different from his Jewish context and different from the alleged hellenistic context of the early church. Scholars are now inclined to the view that Judea and Galilee were under powerful hellenistic influence, and that the early church retained more of its Jewish heritage than earlier interpreters allowed. Accordingly, the quest for the distinctive, or the peculiar, is understood as something different from the old criterion of dissimilarity.[86]

---

84. Cf. Van Aarde, "'He Has Risen," 20.
85. See Lenski, Lenski, and Nolan, *Human Societies*, 195–96.
86. Funk, "Criteria for Determining," 10.

The following five criteria were distilled by the fellows of the Jesus Seminar for determining those logia that possibly go back to Jesus: (1) Jesus said things that were short, pithy, and memorable; (2) Jesus spoke in aphorisms (short, pithy, memorable sayings) and in parables (short stories about some unspec-ified subject matter); (3) Jesus' language was distinct from that characteristi-cally used in the proclamation of the primitive church and from that charac-teristic of the common lore and cliches of the time; (4) Jesus' sayings and parables have an edge and were subversive in terms of the mainstream of social life; (5) Jesus' sayings and parables characteristically call for a reversal of roles or frustrate ordinary everyday expectations: they surprise and shock![87]

Significant developments have recently taken place also with relation to John's Gospel as a source for determining the historical Jesus. For example, in an appendix to his book *The Historical Jesus*, Crossan includes the Fourth Gospel in his "inventory of the historical Jesus tradition by chronological stratification and independent attestation."[88] The first stratum covers the ear-liest Christian texts, which originated in the period 30–60 C.E. Among these texts, Crossan considers a hypothetical document, a Miracles Collection, which is embedded within the Gospels of Mark and John. Among the documents that belong to the second stratum (originating in the period 60–80 C.E.) Crossan includes another hypothetical document that Johannine scholars Fortna and Von Wahlde, independently of each other, identified with a high degree of probability.[89] It contains a combination of miracles and dis-course, wherein the earlier Miracles Collection of the first stratum is inte-grated with an independent collection of the sayings of Jesus, and it is prob-ably independent of the Synoptic Gospels.[90] The relationship between the Gospel of Signs, the Sayings Gospel Q, and the *Gospel of Thomas* seems to require future investigation so that more clarity can be gained with regard to the use of the Fourth Gospel as a source for the historical Jesus.

The notion that has been bracketed so far is the concern for the rational base of historical Jesus research. As I have shown, what is at issue is the ques-tion of where the burden of proof should lie: with those who argue for nonauthenticity or with those who argue for authenticity? This kind inquiry has not, as far as I can discern, become a main issue in present-day histori-cal Jesus research. This does not, however, mean that reflection on theories of knowledge is not important for historical Jesus research. According to scholars such as N.T. Wright and the late Ben Meyer, the quest for the his-torical Jesus definitely needs more reflection in this regard.[91] By using the

---

87. Ibid., 8–10.
88. Crossan, *Historical Jesus: The Life of a Mediterranean Jewish Peasant*, 429–30.
89. Fortna, *Fourth Gospel*; Von Wahlde, *Earliest Version of John's Gospel*.
90. Cf. Crossan, *Historical Jesus: The Life of a Mediterranean Jewish Peasant*, 431.
91. Wright, *Christian Origins*, 1:10, 11, 18, 27, 32–46, 60, 61–64, 88–98, 101–2, 468; Wright, *Who Was Jesus?* 13; Meyer, *Aims of Jesus*; Meyer, "Jesus Christ."

"historiographical" theory of the German sociologist Max Weber[92] in the construction of typical situations in the past (rather than being too positivistic about the possibility of accurately reconstructing the past), I have deliberately tried in my own understanding of the historical Jesus to be realistic. This is a choice that requires putting on a different thinking cap.

PUTTING ON A DIFFERENT THINKING CAP

Since the 1980s, scholars have increasingly become occupied with a kind of historical Jesus research that, as we have seen, has been described as a "paradigm shift." Some systematic theologians refer to it as the *postmodern* quest of the historical Jesus.[93] Studies that are intentionally "post-historical" in nature have also proliferated (although these are not the products of historical Jesus research, which is by definition historically bound).[94] According to Marcus Borg, Jesus is now, from the perspective of the newest historical Jesus studies, regarded as a "teacher of a world-subverting wisdom"[95] and no longer as an "eschatological prophet" per se who "proclaimed the imminent end of the world."[96]

John Dominic Crossan, "the leading Historical Jesus scholar," according to Richard Horsley and Neil Silberman,[97] puts it more subtly. For Crossan, Jesus was not "noneschatological."[98] He sees in the Sayings Gospel Q and in the *Gospel of Thomas* two different "eschatologies" operating. Crossan endorses the findings of Stephen Patterson[99] that one-third of the sayings in these two gospels are common material. Editorial recension transformed this material in the Sayings Gospel Q into "apocalyptic eschatology," in contradistinction to what happened in the *Gospel of Thomas* where redactional activity changed it into "ascetic eschatology." Both eschatologies promote the belief that God's perfect world will be brought about by a termination of the created world, which has been domesticated by systemic evil. An apocalyptic perspective on the end of the world predicts a cosmic cataclysm, while an ascetic perspective envisions the world ending by means of celibacy.

The eschatology in these two "sayings gospels," which lies in the common material before them, underwent redactional changes that take us, according to Crossan, to the mind-set of the historical Jesus. Jesus tried to subvert

92. Weber, *Methodology of the Social Sciences*.
93. See, e.g., Breech, *Jesus and Postmodernism*; Breech, *Silence of Jesus*.
94. See, e.g., Hamilton, *Quest for the Post-Historical Jesus*.
95. Borg, "Portraits of Jesus," 15.
96. Borg, "Renaissance in Jesus Studies," 285.
97. Horsley and Silberman, *Message and the Kingdom*, 70.
98. During the Annual Meeting of the Society of Biblical Literature in San Francisco on November 22, 1997, Crossan explained at a panel discussion of the Historical Jesus Section his understanding of Jesus in relation to eschatology. This statement is based on notes I made of this discussion. See also Crossan, "Jesus and the Kingdom," 33–35.
99. Patterson, *Gospel of Thomas and Jesus*.

the systemic violence that was forced upon the marginalized peasants in Israel by the powers to be in Rome, Sepphoris and Tiberias, and Jerusalem—the centers of the empire, the Herodian family, and the priestly (Sadokite) elite respectively. One can call this an "ethical eschatology" or "social apocalypticism."

Marcus Borg construes more or less in the same vein a Jesus within the context of a cross-cultural conventional wisdom tradition and the subversive activity of "holy men" with revitalizing aims.[100] In 1984, Bernard Brandon Scott referred to this development as follows: "The historical quest for the historical Jesus has ended; the interdisciplinary quest for the historical Jesus has just begun."[101] The interdisciplinary aspect in this new development relates to archaeological, sociohistorical, and cultural-anthropological studies. But it does not mean that historical research as such is now dismissed. According to N.T. Wright, it only gives a "less artificial, historical flavour to the whole enterprise."[102] Wright has labeled this undertaking the "Third Quest."[103] In his 1992 book, *Who Was Jesus?* he refers again to this label:

> Schweitzer brought down the curtain on the "Old Quest." The "New Quest" has rumbled on for nearly thirty years without producing much in the way of solid results. Now, in the last twenty years or so, we have had a quite different movement, which has emerged without anyone co-ordinating it and without any particular theological agenda, but with a definite shape none the less. I have called this the "Third Quest."[104]

Wright also has his ideas about the appearance of this "shape." He describes its main features this way:

> One of the most obvious features of this "Third Quest" has been the bold attempt to set Jesus firmly into his Jewish context. Another feature has been that unlike the "New Quest," the [proponents] have largely ignored the artificial pseudo-historical "criteria" for different sayings in the gospels. Instead, they have offered complete hypotheses about Jesus' whole life and work, including not only sayings but also deeds. This has made for a more complete, and less artificial, historical flavour to the whole enterprise.[105]

---

100. Borg, *Conflict, Holiness, and Politics*; Borg, *Jesus: A New Vision*; Borg, *Meeting Jesus Again*; Borg, "From Galilean Jew," 11.
101. Cited in Borg, "Renaissance in Jesus Studies," 284.
102. Wright, *Who Was Jesus?* 13.
103. See Wright and Neill, *Interpretation of the New Testament*, 379–403.
104. Wright, *Who Was Jesus?* 12.
105. Ibid., 13.

These remarks were written in 1992, when Wright thought that the period of the "New Quest" was over. Four years later, in his magnum opus, *Jesus and the Victory of God*, he admitted that a "renewed New Quest" is still alive and well, and represents a survival of "the Bultmannian picture, with variations." According to Wright, the image of Jesus that has evolved out of this approach, is still preoccupied with the sayings of Jesus and not with his deeds—and this figure is a "deJudaized Jesus."

The method by which scholars representing the New Quest assess these sayings operates, according to Wright, with criteria by which the historical authenticity of the sayings is tested in terms of their date and multiple, independent attestations. The assumption behind this method is that "smaller-scale decisions" with regard to prejudiced sayings in the Gospels are selectively fitted into a "large hypothesis" of a particular "demytholo-gized" picture of Jesus. In other words, such a Jesus preaches a message in which "a vertical eschatology" is reinterpreted as "horizontal" subversive-ness to create a socially and politically minded Jesus. Within this frame of reference, the crucifixion of Jesus was not a theological event prior to the resurrection, and the resurrection itself represents a "coming to faith, some time later, of a particular group of Christians." Another early group of Christians was sapiental/Gnostic oriented. They were only interested in the retelling of aphorisms of Jesus but were "uninterested in his life story." The Gospels developed gradually as these sayings of Jesus solidified and "gath-ered the moss of narrative structure about themselves," while the "initial force of Jesus' challenge was muted or lost altogether within a fictitious pseudo-historical framework."[106]

For Wright, the Jesus Seminar and Burton Mack are examples par excel-lence of this "Renewed Quest."[107] People such as Marcus Borg and, to some extent, John Dominic Crossan, Geza Vermes, and Richard Horsley (who has "considerable affinity" to Crossan), are "straddling," in that they are walk-ing with legs wide apart, seemingly favoring two opposite sides. These two sides are respectively represented by the "Third Quest" and the "Renewed Quest." Wright describes the latter as the *Wredebahn* and the former as the *Schweitzer-straße*, referring to the two opposite roads that the two giants, Albert Schweitzer (1875–1965) and William Wrede (1859–1906), had taken with regard to the historical status of the Gospel of Mark.[108] Wrede consid-ered Mark's Gospel a theological treatise that already presents an apocalyp-tic interpretation of the historical Jesus, while Schweitzer's basic position was that the "Jewish eschatology" found in Mark's Gospel also represents the context for Jesus. The *Wredebahn* leads to the search for Jesus hidden in

---

106. Wright, *Jesus and the Victory of God*, 78–82.
107. See Mack, *Myth of Innocence*; Mack, *Lost Gospel*; Mack, *Who Wrote the New Testament?*
108. Wright, *Jesus and the Victory of God*, 80.

the sources behind Mark and in other early documents such as the Sayings Gospel Q and the *Gospel of Thomas*. Wright quotes Schweitzer from *The Quest of the Historical Jesus*, saying that there is no third option, "*tertium non datur*," and suggests that the time when the *Wredebahn* was a "helpful fiction" has now "come to an end."[109]

Yet for me there is a third option. It is not a middle-of-the-road stance but an uncommitted journey where both Jesus' nonapocalyptic response to Jewish eschatology and Mark's apocalyptic interpretation are not anachronistically understood. Moreover, the "cause of Jesus" challenges me to also reconsider the faith assertions that are found in the Gospel of Mark. Does this mean that I, by putting on a different thinking cap, belong neither to the Renewed Quest nor the Third Quest? Perhaps, but what is in a name? I shall learn from whatever is proffered from whatever direction, consider the insights scholars are proposing, make my choice, and proceed. For example, I am challenged by Robert Funk's description of what the Third Quest is about. According to Funk, "third questers" are only interested in the Jesus of history out of "historical curiosity."

> The Christian faith was born, for them, with Peter's confession, or at Easter, or at Pentecost, or at Nicea. . . . For third questers there can be no picking and choosing among sayings and acts as a way to determine who Jesus was. Instead, one must present a theory of the whole, set Jesus firmly within first-century Judaism, state what his real aims were, discover why he died, when the church began, and what kind of documents the canonical gospels are . . . . The third questers . . . take critical scholarship about as far as it can go without impinging on the fundamentals of the creed or challenging the hegemony of the ecclesiastical bureaucracy. In their hands, orthodoxy is safe, but critical scholarship is at risk. Faith seems to make them immune to the facts. Third questers are really conducting a search primarily for historical evidence to support claims made on behalf of creedal Christianity and the canonical gospels. In other words, the third quest is an apologetic ploy.[110]

However, my interest in historical Jesus research is neither born from neoorthodoxy nor from neoliberalism. For me, it is a matter of urgency to prioritize and contextualize the sources that could lead to Jesus. Furthermore, it is in the "subversive and dangerous memory of Jesus," as

---

109. Ibid.
110. Funk, *Honest to Jesus*, 65.

David Tracy[111] has called it, that this road should be simultaneously, though paradoxically, also named the *Wredebahn*. Without a critical attitude of challenging the tradition without treading along the *Wredebahn*— Schweitzer himself would never have been guided by the "cause of Jesus" to walk over from Strasbourg in Europe to Lambaréné in Africa. There is a third option, *tertium datur!*

The *Gospel of Mark: Red Letter Edition* by Robert Funk and Mahlon Smith includes a useful list of assumptions that have played a role in previous and in renewed historical Jesus studies. When one compares the presuppositions that underlie the New Quest with those currently present in the Renewed Quest, it becomes undoubtedly clear that scholars have put on a different thinking cap. The following assumptions describe the position of the New Quest.[112]

The historical Jesus is to be distinguished from the Gospel portraits of him.

Jesus taught his disciples orally.

Traditions about Jesus were circulated by word of mouth for many years after Jesus' death.

Oral tradition is fluid.

Jesus' mother tongue was Aramaic; the Gospels were written in Greek.

Oral tradition exhibits little interest in biographical data about Jesus.

Forty years elapsed after the death of Jesus before the first canonical Gospel was composed.

Mark was the first of the canonical Gospels to be written.

Mark was not an eyewitness to the events he reports.

Between them, Matthew and Luke incorporate nearly all of Mark into their Gospels, often almost word-for-word.

Matthew and Luke each make use of a Sayings Gospel, known as Q, often almost word for word.

---

111. For Tracy (*Analogical Imagination*, 233–47), the only adequate norm is the tradition as actualized anew in its role of "constituting" the Christian community (see also Thompson, *Jesus Debate*, 106-7; Hill, *Jesus the Christ*, 44–46.) According to Tracy, a reconstructed historical Jesus, on the tradition's own terms, cannot be our norm. However, Hill (*Jesus the Christ*, 45) rightly shows that "Tracy does recognize... that *the Jesus of history* is a secondary norm that preserves that which is 'subversive' and 'dangerous' in the memory of Jesus" (my emphasis). To me, seeking the cause of Jesus is the norm. Previously I used the expression *Jesus of history* interchangeably with the *cause of Jesus*. I realize now that a more subtle formulation is necessary. The *quest for this cause* keeps us in touch with the radical dimension of Jesus' message, a dimension that can easily be lost as the tradition develops inside the canon or outside the canon. "The development of the traditions needs always to be measured against the historical word and deeds of Jesus" (Hill, 45, reflecting on the insights of David Tracy).

112. The core of the lists that follow is taken from Funk and Smith, *Gospel of Mark*. Although Willem Vorster, "The Jewishness of Jesus," added to the lists, neither the compilation nor the completion of the lists was his intention. The purpose of the lists is to "compile a profile of presuppositions which determined the outcome of the historical study of Jesus" (see Van Aarde, "Tracking the Pathways"). In some instances I have changed the wording in order to comply with my own opinion.

Matthew and Luke each make use of additional material unknown to Mark, Q, and each other.

Mark has arranged the order of events in the story of Jesus arbitrarily.

Q is a collection of sayings without a narrative framework.

The portrait of Jesus in the Fourth Gospel differs markedly from that drawn by the synoptics.

John is a less reliable source than the other Gospels for the sayings of Jesus.

The Gospels are made up of layers or strata of tradition.

The original manuscripts of the Gospels have disappeared.

The earliest small surviving fragments of any Gospels date from about 125 C.E.

The earliest major surviving fragments of the Gospels date from about 200 C.E.

The earliest complete copy of the Gospels dates from about 300 C.E.

No two surviving copies of the same Gospel, prior to 1454 C.E., are exactly alike.

In the copying process, texts of the Gospels were both "improved" and "corrupted."

Scholars cannot assume that the Greek text they have in modern critical editions is exactly the text penned by the evangelists.

Jesus was not a Christian; he was a Jew.

The same methods of study that are used in the study of other ancient texts should be applied to the Bible.

The Bible should be studied without being bound to theological claims made by the Church.

Copies of the Bible suffered from textual corruption, loss of leaves, and devastation by insects and moisture.

Jesus should be studied like other historical persons.

Historians can approach but never achieve certainty in historical judgments on the probability principle.

Historians measure the unknown by the known on the principle of analogy.

Historians assume that biblical events occurred within a continuum of historical happenings but that each event or person is historically unique.

The canonical Gospels are more reliable than the extracanonical gospels with regard to Jesus.

Sources other than those found in the New Testament are not of any help in the historical study of Jesus.

Jesus was a unique person and differed considerably from his contemporaries.

The kingdom of God was a central theme in the teachings of Jesus.

The teachings of Jesus are embedded in eschatology.

There is a historical and material continuity between Jesus of Nazareth and the kerygmatic Christ.

The quest for the historical Jesus entails a historical as well as a theological problem.

The following assumptions describe the position of the Renewed Quest:

The canonical Gospels are not necessarily more reliable than the extra-canonical gospels with regard to the historical Jesus.

Sources other than those found in the New Testament are important for the historical study of Jesus.

The *Gospel of Thomas* has provided a new and important source for the Jesus tradition.

Thomas represents an earlier stage of tradition than that in the canonical Gospels.[113]

Thomas represents an independent witness to the Jesus tradition.

Jesus was not a totally unique person. He was a first-century Israelite from Galilee.

The kingdom of God was (according to some, but not to all) probably a central theme in the teachings of Jesus. If it was, it was not necessarily an eschatological concept.

The teachings of Jesus are (according to some, but not to all) embedded in eschatology.

There need not be a historical and material continuity between Jesus of Nazareth and the kerygmatic Christ.

The quest for the historical Jesus first entails a historical problem. The results have consequences for the theological interpretation of Jesus the Christ.

The difference between modern societies and first-century Judaisms in the eastern Mediterranean world should be studied by applying social-scientific methods to the sociohistorical phenomena of that period.

Historical research entails more than the application of the traditional historical-critical methods to the Jesus tradition. It also implies the study of the social world with the help of social-scientific methods and models.

---

113. My position with regard to the authenticity of the *Gospel of Thomas* is that it is a second-century document, extensively dependent on the synoptic tradition but with some logia independent and earlier than the Synoptic Gospels (see Riley, "Gospel of Thomas," 235–36). The logia should be scrutinized historical-critically one by one in order to decide in favor of independence or dependence (cf. Baarda "Concerning the Date").

The social world of Jesus is not studied for the sake of supplying background material, but in order to supply contexts of interpretation of texts of a different nature.

Judaism has to be studied from the perspective of a social system and not only from the perspective of ideas, persons, and events.

Palestine was fully hellenized in the first century and it is necessary to work out the implication of this for the study of Jesus of Nazareth.

The criterion of dissimilarity should be used with circumspection with regard to Jesus material.

Jesus, like many other Jews of his time, was probably bilingual and spoke Greek as a second language.

The stratification of the layers in the Jesus tradition is of great importance for the construction of the historical Jesus.

The hypothetical Sayings Gospel Q and independent logia in the *Gospel of Thomas* make it possible to conceive of Jesus as a wisdom teacher and social prophet and not as an apocalyptic impostor of a cataclysmic end of the world.

Most written sources about the first-century eastern Mediterranean world have been written from above, that is, from the perspective of the authorities and important people. In order to understand Jesus and his intentions, it is necessary to construct views from below and from the side.

In judging the historical value of Jesus material with regard to separate witnesses, it is necessary to take into account genetic relationships and attestation.

It is impossible to reconstruct past events, persons, contexts, and so on. These phenomena are constructed by scholars, using whatever material is available, and by applicable methods and models.

Only a few of the sayings of Jesus in the Gospels were actually spoken by Jesus himself.

A larger portion of the parables or the metaphoric gist in them goes back to Jesus because the parables were harder to imitate than other material.

The greater part of the sayings tradition was created or borrowed from common lore by the transmitters of the oral tradition and the authors of the Gospels.

Modern critical scholarship is based on cooperation among specialists.

The similarities and differences between the assumptions listed above indicate a clear shift between the New Quest and the Renewed Quest. It involves specifically the emphasis on sociohistorical aspects, the fact that prejudices and biases about the value of extracanonical material have been put aside, and the conviction that Jesus did not understand the notion

"kingdom of God" apocalyptically. Though Mark's apocalyptic interpretation of the kingdom of God and his apocalyptic framework of the teachings of Jesus were taken over from tradition, apocalypticism was therefore
not part of Jesus' mind-set. Subsequently, the "futuristic" Child of
Humanity sayings (with a titular connotation) are seen as later developments in the Jesus tradition.

This is not the road someone like Wright would take.[114] But to accept
Wright's invitation to busy oneself with a historical construct of Jesus'
"whole life" (in terms of the context of first-century Herodian
Palestine), would, in the words of Elisabeth Schüssler Fiorenza, hold
"out the offer of untold possibilities for (a) different christology and
theology."[115] What I have in mind, is a "christology from the side."[116] A
"Jesus from above" describes the conciliar debates about Jesus as a figure who descended from heaven and was incarnated on earth—a Jesus
who has been confessed as "true God" and "true man." A "Jesus from
below" refers to modern biblical scholarship where the focus is squarely
on the humanity of Jesus. Because both Christologies represent a dialectic of vertical classification, this perspective on the person of Jesus is
chiefly, if not exclusively, concerned with symbols of power or force.
"Jesus from above" reflects Christian tradition only after the time of
Constantine, when hierarchy became the expressive social structure,
with power or force the primary concern. "Jesus from below" expresses
twentieth-century concerns with the relationship between natural and
supernatural, and the possibility of transcendence in a secular world.
Both these views would be rather anachronistic for an adequate understanding of New Testament views on Jesus. Yet within Christian groups
before Constantine, the chief expressive social dimension for non-
Roman and Roman nonelite Christians was not vertical, but horizontal—"from the side." Jesus as a first-century Israelite from Galilee
should be studied like other historical persons and should not be
regarded as absolutely unique, using whatever material is available and
by applicable methods and models.

---

114. Wright, "Mission and Message of Jesus," 41–42, sees Jesus' crucifixion and resurrection
resemble the Son of Man saying borrowed from Daniel 7. So do I (see Van Aarde, "Matthew
27:45–53 and the Turning of the Tide"). However, contra Wright, I do not regard the use of the Son
of Man title as part of the authentic Jesus tradition.

115. Schüssler Fiorenza, Jesus—Miriam's Child, 187, has the reconstruction of the "historical"
Mary (in contradistinction with ecclesiastical traditions) in mind: "The 'dangerous memory' of the
young woman and teenage mother Miriam of Nazareth, probably not more than twelve or thirteen
years old, pregnant, frightened, and single. . . can subvert the tales of mariological fantasy and cultural femininity. In the center of the Christian story stands not the lovely 'white lady' of artistic and
popular imagination, kneeling in adoration before her son. Rather it is the young pregnant woman,
living in occupied territory and struggling against victimization and for survival and dignity. It is she
who holds out the offer of ontold possibilities for different christology and theology."

116. See Malina and Neyrey, Calling Jesus Names, xi.

A PROFILE OF THE HISTORICAL JESUS

I have already referred to N.T. Wright's evaluation of previous historical Jesus research as "artificial" with regard to historiography. In his book *Who Was Jesus?* Wright seems to simply be concerned about the monopoly of Jesus' sayings over his deeds in previous research. This issue, however, is epistemologically much more complicated and Wright has discussed it at length in *Christian Origins and the Questions of God*, vol. 1, *The New Testament and the People of God*.[117] The application of different criteria in the process of distinguishing authenticity is another issue that needs reflection with regard to real historiography, specifically, when such a historical-critical approach ignores the social contexts in which the analyzed literary units are embedded. Even the criterion of coherency needs to be adapted to our insights today concerning a responsible identification of a stratification of texts and the social world of the eastern Mediterranean. Content and context should fit together. Social history is therefore the "buzz word" with respect to the Renewed Quest for the historical Jesus.

Biblical scholarship today, like any other postmodern scientific reflection, is featured among other things by its multidisciplinary and interdisciplinary character. The use of narratological and sociological theories and models in exegesis is a demonstration of the issues that nowadays constitute the agenda of biblical scholarship. It is within this paradigm that social-scientific criticism is worth mentioning. This approach in biblical interpretation has brought several unexplored aspects of the cultural background of the New Testament to the fore. Former impasses in research are being studied anew. Earlier debates have been reopened in the hope that they can solve present-day societal issues or at least provide an intelligible, credible explanation of the problems of our day. A growing awareness of ethnocentrism is perhaps one of the many important advantages that has occurred as a result of social-scientific criticism.[118] Ethnocentrism occurs when the cultural distance between ancient and modern societies, and among particular cultures in a given period, is not reckoned with. Ethnocentrism yields to an adherence of irreconcilable cultural phenomena that cannot stand the test of a responsible cross-cultural enterprise.

---

117. Wright, *Who Was Jesus?*; Wright, *Christian Origins and the Questions of God*, 1:10, 11, 18, 27, 32–46, 60, 61–64, 88–98, 101–2.

118. This awareness has significant ethical implications for Christian practice inferred from biblical scholarship. With regard to ethics, the New Testament has often been interpreted without a sensibility of the historical distance between the first century and the twentieth century. Economic and political forces behind modern social dichotomies are often ascribed to the conditions that were presumably present in the world of Jesus or the early church. In other words, ancient preindustrial documents are being interpreted from the perspective of our present-day societal structures. The result is not only ethnocentrism but also reductionism.

Reductionism, on the other hand, occurs, for example, when someone tries to explain a broad spectrum of intertwined socioreligious phenomena from a perspective framed by the dynamics of either one or two social institutions. Proponents of such an approach are often found among historical-materialistic interpreters of the Bible. In this regard, references within the (preindustrial) Bible to alienation from resources and to social ostracism are ascribed to the kind of economic and political ideologies that Karl Marx identified in the modern industrial society. Social-scientific criticism, however, makes us aware not only of cross-cultural similarities, but also of differences in cosmology, ideology, and mythology.

CHAPTER 2

∽

An Itinerary of Scholars Through Shifting Sands

We are pretty sure about the historical Jesus' compassionate care for the social outcasts of his day. The thrust of my argument is that Jesus himself grew up as a fatherless figure and that his compassion toward ill-fated people came from his own experience of being ostracized. The social-scientific model that serves as the frame of reference within which I substantiate my understanding of Jesus as fatherless and of his defense of the fatherless (according to Isa 1:17) came at the beginning of my historical Jesus research and was largely triggered by the work of Bruce Malina and Paul Hollenbach.[1] According to this model, social interactions should be understood against the background of the hierarchical structures of a "total society." Ostracism corresponds to these hierarchical structures or the institutional order found in a particular society.

The expression "institutional order" implies that a balanced society consists of particular social institutions, one of which is the overarching one, while the others are integrated with it in subordinate fashion. At least four basic social institutions or structures can be discerned within any society: economy, politics, family life, and religion. In certain societies today, the economy forms the basis of social relations. One may also find that politicians exercise control over economic and religious institutions. There are, however, societies in which families and the heads of families exercise the control. The Mediterranean world of the first century is such an example. In such societies religion, politics, and economy are embedded in an institutional order of family life primarily determined through birth and nationality. Applying this insight to the world of the New Testament, Malina convincingly demonstrates that

> the Mediterranean world treats this institution [kinship] as primary and focal. . . . In fact in the whole Mediterranean world, the centrally located institution maintaining societal existence

---

1. See Malina, *Christian Origins and Cultural Anthropology*; Malina, "Interpreting the Bible with Anthropology."; Hollenbach, "Defining Rich and Poor."

is kinship and its sets of interlocking rules. The result is the central value of familism. The family or kinship group is central in social organization; it is the primary focus of personal loyalty and it holds supreme sway over individual life.[2]

This is tantamount to anachronism, misplaced concreteness, and reductionism, however, if the phenomenon of social injustice in the world of Jesus is to be understood only, or even primarily, in terms of modern economic and political concerns. Economic and political steps taken in the first century that led to ostracism, for example, should be interpreted in terms of the above social-scientific model and perspective in light of the primary familial structures of the period and the social, mythological, and religious symbols representing these structures. Several aspects of my portrayal of the historical Jesus have become to me more and more intelligible as my application of social-scientific criticism has increased over the years. What follows are the basic elements of my profile of the historical Jesus.

Jesus, the son of Mary, the peasant who came from the Galilean village of Nazareth, grew up fatherless; he was unmarried, probably a carpenter. He lived in a strained relationship with his kin, and sought and found company among the followers of John the Baptist, only subsequently to separate himself from them, along with his own core group of followers. He came to the Baptist to, in light of Isa 1:16-17, "wash himself" from (systemic) "evil" in order that he might give meaning to the life of people—among whom were women and children living on the fringe of society because they were the nobodies (the divorced and the fatherless, the widows and the orphans) and to whom patriarchy gave no place amidst the honorable. After he left the circle of the Baptist, his life began to be characterized by an absolute trust in God as his Father, while the insignificant, the nobodies of the Galilean society, formed his audience when he spoke about his "Father's rule." To them, he was a pneumatic sage and healer,[3] a "popular king" threatening the ambitions of Herod Antipas[4]—very much like those prophets who spoke out against the elite.[5] His sayings had an edge; they were short, pithy and memorable.[6] His stories were symbolic in nature, open-ended, and shocking.[7] His acts, particularly those of healing, were of the same nature and can be considered as metaphors in themselves pointing to the idea of resocializing.[8] Both his words and his deeds were unconventional

---

2. Malina, "Dealing with Biblical (Mediterranean) Characters," 131.
3. Cf. Borg, *Jesus: A New Vision*; Borg, *Meeting Jesus Again*.
4. Cf. Horsley, *Jesus and the Spiral of Violence*; Horsley and Silberman, *Message and the Kingdom*, 71–72; Sanders, *Historical Figure of Jesus*, 248.
5. Cf. Crossan, *Historical Jesus: A Revolutionary Biography*, 43.
6. Cf. Funk, "Criteria for Determining," 8–10; Crossan, *Essential Jesus*, 21.
7. Cf. Scott, *Hear Then the Parable*, 54–62.
8. Cf. Pilch, "Insights and Models"; Crossan and Watts, *Who Is Jesus?* 76–102.

in a radical sense, and always crossed the boundaries of his culture.[9] He envisaged the kingdom of God neither as primarily cataclysmic in nature, that is, as something at the end of time that would bring about the vindication of martyrs, nor as comparable to earthly kingdoms where humaneness vanishes behind various symbols of power and hierarchy. Instead, he saw it as comparable to a household in which distorted relationships are healed by means of the "ethos of compassion"[10] and God's unmediated presence.[11] His "alternative wisdom"[12] took offense at "conventional wisdom" embedded in the temple ideology of his day,[13] an attitude that was not fully understood by some of his prominent followers. He came into conflict with village leaders and Pharisees, was regarded as a threat by the Sadducees and priestly elite in Jerusalem, and was eventually crucified by Roman soldiers like a criminal. No family or fictive family took care of his body.[14] If he was buried,[15] it was "certainly not in a respectable family tomb."[16] Jesus of Nazareth died as he was born: a nobody among nobodies.

From this picture, Jesus' use of the metaphor of the Kingdom of God is remarkable. If social-scientific criticism were more widespread, the hot debate among scholars about whether Jesus was eschatological or noneschatological in outlook could really cool down. Jesus was a child of his day. Culturally, people of the first-century Mediterranean world did have a strong religious consciousness according to their social and symbolic worlds. The social world maintained a mind-set not separated from the symbolic universe where gods, angels, and demons came. God's "kingdom" was the perfect domain. The social world was elongated into this symbolic universe so that even the dead were "living dead" and the longing for being in the bosom of these "forefathers" was a utopia, something that would happen at the general resurrection of the dead. Crises within the social world were attributed to the influences of the demonic world. Often, when a crisis became almost unbearable, a group of people and the individuals therein experienced ostracism and tended to be aware of only two sides: the right and the wrong, the divine and the satanic, a world here and now and a world beyond.

This outlook became marked on the one hand by pessimism and determinism, and on the other by hope. The present was miserable, while the

---

9. Cf. Borg, *Jesus: A New Vision,*. 79–96; Borg, *Meeting Jesus Again,* 69–95.

10. Cf. Borg, *Meeting Jesus Again,* 46–68.

11. Cf. Crossan, "Divine Immediacy and Human Immediacy"; Crossan, *Historical Jesus: The Life of a Mediterranean Jewish Peasant,* 423.

12. Cf. Borg, *Meeting Jesus Again,* 69–95.

13. Cf. Crossan, *Historical Jesus: The Life of a Mediterranean Jewish Peasant,* 355.

14. Cf. Crossan, *Historical Jesus: The Life of a Mediterranean Jewish Peasant,* 354–94; Crossan, *Historical Jesus: A Revolutionary Biography,* 123–58; Horsley and Silberman, *Message and the Kingdom,* 84–87, 89–91.

15. Sanders, *Historical Figure of Jesus,* 275.

16. Horsley and Silberman, *Message and the Kingdom,* 89.

transcendent beyond was joyful. Such pessimism and determinism were eased by the conviction that the course of history might be changed, for the sake of the self and others, by means of the prayers and martyrdom of the righteous. Unbearable experiences caused the unfortunates—as a result of the embarrassment of being trapped in a cul de sac—to project their longing into an imaginary world where God exercises control. They expressed what they imagined in symbolic language by analogy with experience in everyday life. A corrupted temple was imagined as a heavenly temple, a brutal kingdom was imaginatively replaced by God's kingdom, a fatherless child became a child of the heavenly Father. By means of martyrdom, one could desperately try to break vehemently into the world of God. By whatever means, praying or dying, the purpose was to make a plea to God to intervene. Certain figures would focus on the future of God's re-creation and judgment in order to abide in the present. Scholarship has become accustomed to call these figures *apocalyptic prophets* because they were revealing God's future. Other figures would, almost paradoxically, live in the midst of stress as if God's imagined presence was already a reality. Such a prophet is no less eschatological in outlook.

Historical studies have demonstrated that Jesus did not escape his experiences by moving futuristically into "imaginary time" as some authors of apocalyptic writings often suggested. Jesus experienced God's presence in the midst of and despite depressing circumstances. His symbolic conception of God was often expressed, though not exclusively, in terms of a familial relationship between a father and a son. His temple critique led to his death as the result of a falsely assumed political program. He probably did not think of himself as a martyr. Jesus was a social outcast and not a kind of Robin Hood figure born within an imperial kingdom who only docetically fulfilled the role of being poor in his act of being the hero of the helpless in society. As to politics in the vision of Jesus, my position is very well stated by Marcus Borg:

> We are not accustomed to thinking of Jesus as a political figure. In a narrow sense, he was not. He neither held nor sought political office, was neither a military leader nor a political reformer with a detailed political-economic platform. But he was political in the more comprehensive and important sense of the word: politics as the shaping of a community living in history.[17]

To better understand Jesus' own vision, it is helpful to catch a glimpse of the worldview and mind-set of the people with whom the historical Jesus interacted. In this process I consider it important to gain clarity on the social stratification of the first-century Mediterranean world and, specifically, the advanced agrarian society of Herodian Palestine in which the his-

---

17. Borg, *Jesus: A New Vision*, 125.

torical Jesus lived. I make specific use of the insights of macrosociologist Gerhard Lenski and of the publications of David Fiensy and Dennis Duling, who structured their work upon Lenski's macrosociology.[18] The specific originality of my own contribution rests upon the assumption that the ideological function of kinship as a social institution shifted in an evolutionary fashion when horticultural societies changed into simple and then advanced agrarian societies.

Initially, kinship, and especially the extended family as social unit, was the primary and focal institution in society. According to cultural anthropologists such as Lenski, this was clearly observable at the surface level of horticultural and simple agrarian societies as well. However, the shift from a horticultural (7000–3000 B.C.E.) to an agrarian society (3000 B.C.E.–1800 C.E.) changed this dominant role of the extended family. Instead, political economy became the most dominant factor at the surface of society. This process reached its zenith during the advanced agrarian society that commenced around 500 B.C.E. A third phase began during the Industrial Revolution, which, in the latter part of the eighteenth century, was well under way. Political economy has since become an ideology in the sense of what Karl Marx referred to as "false consciousness."

Kinship had been put under tremendous stress during the time of the advanced agrarian society because of political and economical dichotomies. As a result, the extended family almost ceased to be visible on the surface level of Herodian Palestine, and family interests moved to the deep structure of society and developed into an ideology comparable with the notion of false consciousness. In other words, family interests in the world of the historical Jesus were as ideologically conditioned as materialism in industrial societies. Against this macrosociological background and especially in light of the advanced agrarian society of Herodian Palestine, Jesus' critique of the patriarchal family and, paradoxically, his experience of God's kingdom as a brokerless household, grew more intelligible to me.

As mentioned earlier, N.T. Wright rightly identifies present-day historical Jesus research as the attempt first to set the historical Jesus firmly into his first-century Israelite context and, second, to offer complete historical constructs about Jesus' whole life and work. My own historical method in this regard comprises a construct of an ideal-type of Jesus of Nazareth. I aim at focusing on Jesus' trust in God as Father and how his defense of the fatherless makes sense within such a construct. Proceeding from this construct, I shall demonstrate that some of the faith assertions of the earliest Christians who witnessed the value of believers as "children of God" form

---

18. Lenski, Lenski, and Nolan, *Human Societies*, 6th ed.; Fiensy, *Social History of Palestine*; Duling, "Matthew's Infancy in Social Scientific Perspective." Fiency and Duling structure their work upon Lenski's macrosociology.

a material link to the historical Jesus and that others do not. On this point, the *Schweitzerstraße* has become the *Wredebahn*.

In constructing an ideal-type of Jesus of Nazareth, I am not attempting to devise a record of concrete historical situations based on empirical data. According to Max Weber, an ideal-type is a theoretical construct in which possible occurrences are brought into a meaningful relationship with one another so that a coherent image may be formed of data from the past.[19] In other words, as a theoretical construct, an ideal-type is a conceptualization that will not necessarily correspond with empirical reality. As a construct displaying a coherent image, the ideal-type does influence the conditions of investigations into what could have happened historically, in that the purpose of establishing an ideal-type is to account for the interrelationships between discrete historical events in an intelligible manner. Such a coherent construct is not formed by or based upon a selection from what is regarded as universally valid—in other words, that which is common to all relevant cases of similar concrete situations of what could in reality have happened. It is therefore no logical-positivist choice based on either inductive or deductive reasoning.

The contribution to historical Jesus research I wish to make is the development of a construct of Jesus as a fatherless figure who called God his Father. In consciously using the social-scientific model of an ideal-type as the point of departure for my historical investigation, I am not, therefore, claiming that my historical Jesus construct is based on what is common to all fatherless people in first-century Galilee. That would amount to inductive historical reasoning. Neither is it based on what is common to most types of cases of fatherless people in Galilee. That would amount to deductive historical reasoning. The ideal-type model enables one to concentrate on the most favorable cases. What I mean by this is that, in my investigation into the Jesus of history, I am focusing on the data that can lead to a better understanding and explanation of the total picture and of particular aspects of the total picture. I am specifically interested in the question of why the historical Jesus linked up with John the Baptist and submitted to the "baptism for the remission of sins" and also why, once his road deviated from the Baptist's, Jesus, so unconventionally for his time, became involved with the fate of social outcasts, especially women and children. My construct of Jesus as the "fatherless son of God" can provide an elucidation of these questions. My aim is to provide an explanation of the historical figure of Jesus—who trusted God as his Father, challenged conventional patriarchal values, and, at the same time, cared for fatherless children and women without men in their lives—within the macrosociological framework of the "psychic data" of family distortion and divine alienation in the time of Herodian Palestine.

---

19. Weber, *Methodology of the Social Sciences*, 89–112.

This ideal-type should be historically intelligible and explanatory. It should rely on contemporary canonical and noncanonical texts (including artifacts) that have to be interpreted in terms of a chronological stratification of relevant documents. It should also make sense within a social stratification of first-century Herodian Palestine. In other words, my construct of the life of Jesus does not start with Jesus' relationship with John the Baptist, as usually portrayed. It begins with the traditions regarding Jesus' birth record and his relationship with his family.

My understanding of Jesus' baptism is that it was a ceremonial or ritual event through which "sinful sickness" was addressed and healed. Why would Jesus have wanted to be baptized? I argue that the unfortunate relationship with his family and his critique against the patriarchal family as such provide the probable clue. What does Jesus' birth record tell us about his relationship with his family and the townsfolk in Nazareth? What does his birth record reveal about his vision with regard to children and other "nobodies" in his society? To me, the answers to these questions rely on a construct of an ideal-type regarding a man in first-century Herodian Palestine who was healed from "sinful sickness" (for example, the stigma of being a fatherless son) and started a ministry of healing/forgiving "sinners" with the help of disciples who were also called upon to act as healed healers. Jesus died because of the subversiveness of this "ethos of compassion," to use an expression from Marcus Borg.[20] It all happened against the background of the ideology of the Second Temple and Roman imperialism (very well explained by Richard Horsley and Neil Silberman[21]). His followers were likewise threatened and some died in the same manner as their forerunner. It is my intention to demonstrate theologically, historically, and in a literary fashion how this construct is built upon available Jesus traditions in terms of chronological as well as social stratification.

But first, there is still an unsettled matter waiting for elaboration. This is the question of where one should begin the search for Jesus, child of God: at the river Jordan where Jesus was baptized and declared to be the child of God, or at the cradle where God let him be adopted as Joseph's son and, hence, Abraham's son and, hence, according to the covenantal ideology among Israelites, child of God?

In the second century C.E., Celsus, a Greek philosopher, attacked Christianity's belief that "a member of the lower classes, a Jewish peasant nobody like Jesus," is the child of God, and therefore divine:

> I must deal with the matter of Jesus, the so-called savior, who not
> long ago taught new doctrines and was thought to be a [child] of

---

20. Borg, *Jesus—A New Vision*, 131.
21. Horsley and Silberman, *Message and the Kingdom*, 65–87.

God....This savior, I shall attempt to show, deceived many and caused them to accept a form of belief harmful to the well-being of mankind. Taking its root in the lower classes, the religion continues to spread among the vulgar: Nay one can even says it spread because of its vulgarity and the illiteracy of its adherents. And while there are a few moderate, reasonable and intelligent people who are inclined to interpret its belief allegorically, yet it thrives in its purer form among the ignorant. . . . What absurdity! Clearly the Christians have used the myths of the Danae and the Melanippe, or of the Auge and the Antiope, in fabricating the story of Jesus' virgin birth. . . . After all, the old myths of the Greeks that attribute divinity to Perseus, Amphion, Aeneas and Minos are equally good evidence of their wondrous works on behalf of mankind and are certainly no less lacking in plausibility than the stories of your [Celsus's Jew refers to Jesus] followers. What have you done by word or deed that is quite so wonderful as those heroes of old?[22]

From this citation it is clear that Christianity was defamed from the earliest times. According to Celsus, Christians dared to compare the saving acts by an illegitimate peasant child Jesus, believed to be divinely generated, with the myths of the Greeks.

Theologians and exegetes know that historical-critical scholars do not hesitate to admit that the nativity traditions about Jesus should be considered as legendary and mythical in nature and, therefore, not subject to historical research.[23] However, contrary to both Celsus and Origen, the parallels between Jesus and the Greek heroes do not need to be regarded as something that discredits either Jesus or Christianity. Interpreting mythology in a cultural fashion, from the perspective of the sociology of knowledge, can be worthwhile.

MYTH AS EMPTIED REALITIES

Sociology of knowledge is a modern theory according to which the interrelatedness between the social world and the symbolic world can be elucidated. Seen from a modern Western perspective, this association is about the relationship between the "natural world" and "supernatural world." For the people living in a prescientific Mediterranean context, these worlds were, as indicated in chapter 1, not really separated. This context has often

---

22. Celsus, *On the True Doctrine*, trans. R. J. Hoffman, 1987. Quoted in Crossan, "The Infancy and Youth," 74–75.
23. See, among others, Meier, *Marginal Jew*, 1:229–30; Borg, "First Christmas," 4.

been described as "mythological," as distinct from "scientific." However, this does not mean that modern people do not live by myths as well. Yet with the peculiar first-century Mediterranean worldview in mind, we need to determine how myths work. Philosopher-anthropologist Roland Barthes describes the function of myth as "to empty reality" and to fill the "emptied history" with "nature."[24] What does this mean?

In a mythological context, everyday experiences are projected into an imaginary world; in other words, reality is emptied. The imaginary world consists of imageries analogous to everyday experiences; the "emptied history" is filled with "nature." Crises in life are often made bearable by living in such an altered state of consciousness. Bruce Malina says, "While [first-century Mediterranean] people are defined by others and because of others, they are in fact unable to change undesirable situations. Hence the need for divine intervention."[25] Or as another scholar, writing about a totally different context, notes: "[M]yth transforms history into nature by stealing language from one context then restoring it in another so that it appears like something 'wrested from the gods' when in fact it is simply recycled language."[26] Stephen of Byzantium, a sixth-century philosopher, said, "Mythology is what never was but always is." According to Philip Wheelwright, "Myth is to be defined as a complex of stories—some no doubt fact, and some fantasy."[27]

As "emptied realities," myths are not absolute taboos with regard to historiography. Historically, they should be treated in a different way than those discourses that refer directly to psychical data. Mircea Eliade begins his book *Myth and Reality* with these words:

> For the past fifty years at least, Western scholars have approached the study of myth from a viewpoint markedly different from, let us say, that of the nineteenth century. Understanding their predecessors, who treated myth in the usual meaning of the word, that is as "fable," "invention," "fiction," they have accepted it as it was understood in the archaic societies, where, on the contrary, "myth" means a "true story" and, beyond that, a story that is a most precious possession because it is sacred, exemplary, significant.[28]

For Carl Jung, the human mind tends to express symbolically that which is poorly understood intellectually. He argues that potential for formulating archetypal meanings is present in all humans before language is acquired.

---

24. Barthes, *Mythologies*, 142–43.
25. Malina, "Circum-Mediterranean Person?" 71.
26. Salyer, "Myth, Magic, and Dread," 267.
27. Quoted in Perrin, *Jesus and the Language*, 22.
28. Eliade, *Myth and Reality*, 1.

It seems that the archetypes are like templates for organizing the universal themes that recur in human experience, such as a fatherless child who becomes a heroic figure. In different cultures and at different times an archetypal content, according to Jung, will be symbolically expressed in somewhat different ways, but will still reflect the basic human experience underlying it.[29] Eliade's formulation is almost identical. For him, myths give sacredness, or religious meaning, to physical objects and human acts. As M. J. Meadows notes, "They are thus exemplary models, human acts through which one relives the myths that give meaning to religious life. Reliving the myth abolishes time and puts one in touch with the real."[30]

My goal is to bring into historical Jesus research the association of the historical-critically established "fact" of Jesus' baptismal initiation ritual and the social-historical notion of an ideal-type, introduced by the sociologist Max Weber.[31] I read the textual and social-historical evidence as if it says that Jesus came as someone who had been fatherless since infancy to be baptized by John the Baptist. It is my intention to revive the myth of the absent father within the conceptualized framework of the assumption that Jesus' fatherlessness was canceled by his trust in God as his Heavenly Father. Destroying conventional patriarchal values, he cared for women and children who were marginalized because of patriarchy at the same time. His life experiences should be seen as embedded within the macrosociological framework of family distortion and divine alienation in the time of Herodian Palestine.

---

29. Jung, "Symbols of Transformation," 181. Cf. Meadow, "Archetypes and Patriarchy," 188.
30. Meadow, "Archetypes and Patriarchy," 188–89.
31. Weber, *Methodology of the Social Sciences*, 89–112.

CHAPTER 3

~

Where To Begin–At the River Jordan or at the Cradle in Bethlehem?

JESUS' BAPTISM AS CONDENSED HISTORY

My quest for Jesus begins with the traditions regarding his birth and his relationship to his family. This starting point originated in my reading of Crossan's book, *The Historical Jesus: The Life of a Mediterranean Jewish Peasant*. As Crossan commences with the Pauline vision of the "crucified Jesus" as a death through which "sin was buried,"[1] I begin with Jesus' baptism as a ritual event through which "sinful sickness" was addressed and healed.

Crossan understands the Pauline vision as "condensed history," a plotted event that was preceded by a sequential series of other historical events prior to the crucifixion. He puts it as follows: "For Paul, the historical Jesus, particularly and precisely in the terrible and servile form of his execution, is part of Christian faith. It is to the historical Jesus so executed that he responds in faith."[2] Crossan refers to Paul's perspective on death through which sin is buried (1 Cor 15:3) as "historicization of prophecy."[3] He distinguishes this concept from "history remembered,"[4] which, in his article "The Historical Jesus in Earliest Christianity," is seemingly built upon Paul's reference to the "folly of the cross" in 1 Cor 1:18. In *Who Killed Jesus?* Crossan commences his argument with this concept of "prophecy historized" and focuses the "continuity" between the Jesus of history and the Jesus of faith again on Paul's words in 1 Cor 15:3ff. in particular (NIV):[5] "For what I received I passed on to you as of first importance: that Christ died for our sins according to the Scriptures, that he was buried, that he was raised on the third day according to the Scriptures, and that he appeared to . . ."

One can also focus on Paul's words in 2 Cor 5:14, 19 and specifically those in verse 21: "God made him for our sake sin, he who knew no sin"

---

1. From a conversation on his work presented at the Jesus and Faith Conference, DePaul University, Chicago, February 4–5, 1993.
2. Crossan, "Historical Jesus in Earliest Christianity," 10.
3. Crossan, *Historical Jesus: The Life of a Mediterranean Jewish Peasant*, 375.
4. Crossan, *Who Killed Jesus?* 1.
5. Ibid., 191, 203–4. Crossan crosses swords with mainly Brown, *Death of the Messiah*.

(author's trans.). According to Rudolf Bultmann, in these words of Paul, we have the resemblance of the "Jewish way of thinking." However, it was put in terms of a "new order," a "change or purification of human notions about God."[6] Death was viewed as a means of expiation, just as in most of the vicarious passages (ὑπέρ *passages*) such as 1 Cor 15:3. In these passages the death of Christ was understood as something performed for the benefit of the believers.[7] Bultmann points out that the typical Pauline formula "to be (one) in Christ" [ἐν χριστῷ] marks the "believers' new life," received by baptism (cf. Gal 3:26–28; 1 Cor 12:13), used as a "term for a new epoch" and "applied to the individual in the sense of external healing or rescue, especially of the forgiveness of sin."[8]

Whether Paul knew the tradition of Jesus' baptism by John the Baptist and the embarrassment it caused for Christians that Jesus needed to be purified from "sins" cannot be ascertained. Bultmann reckons the phrase "he who knew no sin" refers to the same phenomenon found in contemporary (Hermetic, Mandaic, and rabbinic) literature that "innocent babes" and "children" do not know "what wickedness is."[9] Children are simply ignorant with regard to systemic evil, and in Paul's thinking, Christ could be compared with an "innocent babe" caught within the web of sinful existence.

For Paul, Christ is "treated as sinner by the fact that God allows him to die like a sinner on the cross (Gal 3:13)."[10] This "Christ who knew no sin" refers, according to Bultmann, to "Christ according to the flesh"—that is, Christ in his plainness.[11] As with the authors of Hebrews (4:15) and the Johannine literature (John 7:18; 8:46; 1 John 3:5), who tried to get rid of the embarrassment of Jesus' baptism, Bultmann interprets Paul as agreeing that "[n]aturally, there is no reference to the earthly Jesus as having sinful qualities, at least to the extent he could be tempted."[12] Bultmann is correct in his understanding of the "resurrected Christ" (cf. Rom 1:4) as the Jesus of faith, that is, the "Christ according to the spirit and not to the flesh."[13] This does not, in my mind, alter the statement in 2 Cor 5:21 that Jesus, innocent as a

---

6. Bultmann, *Second Letter to the Corinthians*, 159–60. Bultmann concurs with E. Vischer in this regard.

7. Ibid., 160: The death of Christ is a demonstration of God's grace, and "this grace is available to the one who opens himself [or herself] to it . . . so that 'katallage' [redemption] . . . occurred apart from people, independent of their conversion; it is the surrender of Christ into death."

8. Ibid., 157.

9. Whatever it may be, the "sinlessness" of Christ is, according to Bultmann (*Second Letter to the Corinthians*, 165), maintained by Paul: "he had not sinned . . . whether at his incarnation or his death."

10. Bultmann, *Second Letter to the Corinthians*, 164–65.

11. Ibid., 155. Bultmann relates the expression "Christ according to the flesh" to the other Pauline expressions in Phil 3:21.

12. Ibid., 165.

13. Ibid., 155, note 154. Bultmann quite rightly sees the reference to the transformation of ὁ χριστὸς τὸ κατὰ σάρκα into υἱὸς θεοῦ ἐν δυνάμει κατὰ πνεῦμα ἁγιωσύνης ἐχ ἀναστάσεως νεκρῶν (Rom 1:4) as belonging to the same referential sphere than the expressions σῶμα τῆς δόξης αὐτοῦ in Phil 3:21 and ὅς ἐστιν ἐν δεξιᾶ τοῦ θεοῦ in Rom 8:34.

child—whether metaphorically intended or not—did not know what sin was and, nevertheless, died as a "sinner!" Here Paul helps one to track a pathway that goes beyond Jesus' remission of sin, that is, a road that leads to his sinful, though innocent, childhood. Therefore, in addition to Crossan's perception that Jesus' death can be seen as condensed history, Jesus' baptism can, in my mind, likewise be perceived as condensed history.

Why would Jesus want to be baptized? Is it because of "sinful sickness"? As I have mentioned, Jesus' unfortunate relationship with his family could provide a clue. Moreover, what does Jesus' birth record tell us about his relationship with his family and his kin in Nazareth? What does his birth record reveal about his ministry among, especially, children and other nobodies in his society? To me, the answers to these questions rely on a construct of an ideal-type of someone in first-century Herodian Palestine who was healed from "sinful sickness," for example, the stigma of being a "fatherless son." He subsequently started a ministry of healing/forgiving "sinners" with the help of followers who were called to act likewise as "healed healers," to use an expression from Crossan's insights. Jane Schaberg, author of *The Illegitimacy of Jesus*, considers this approach of mine "a promising direction for research."[14]

However, the immediate goal is to demonstrate in this chapter the reasons for my preference to start the quest for Jesus, child of God, at the nativity traditions. Within the parameters of both the New Quest and the Renewed Quest, the point of departure for the quest is Jesus at thirty. Yet I am convinced that we need to move backwards, from the river Jordan in Judea to the Galilee of the Gentiles, from Jesus' baptism to his birth. We have to go beyond the New Quest and the Renewed Quest.

There are two possible reasons why we have no references to Jesus' childhood, besides the apologetic-confessional and legendary material in the infancy narratives inside and outside the New Testament.[15] First, it could be that the preadult traditions about Jesus were simply unknown. Second, it could be that Mediterranean people attached legitimate authority only to men who went through an initiation rite that is regarded as transferring from childhood to adulthood.[16] The priority of the Markan text

---

14. Schaberg "Canceled Father," 32. See also Schaberg, *Illegitimacy of Jesus*.

15. Cf. Schaberg, "Infancy of Mary of Nazareth"; Schaberg, "Canceled Father."

16. From a cultural-anthropological perspective it is, therefore, worthwhile to take note of the interpretations of Jesus' baptism by African theologians. Maturity is very highly estimated in traditional African culture. Authority and legitimization depend greatly on adulthood. Jesus' baptism (as well as his resurrection, understood as an exaltation to become the authoritative elder brother among the living dead—see also LeMarquand, "Historical Jesus and African New Testament Scholarship," 11) is indeed seen as an initiation rite (cf. Nyamiti, "African Christologies Today," 8), just like the rituals of status transformation among the first-century Mediterranean people (cf. McVann, "Baptism, Miracles, and Boundary Jumping," 151–57). In traditional African culture this status transformation has to do with that phase in the life of a young man when he reaches maturity and, subsequently, is accepted as an "authoritative personality" (cf. Nyamiti, "Incarnation Viewed from the African Understanding," 45–47).

causes proponents of both the New Quest and the Renewed Quest to start their search for the historical Jesus with his baptism.[17] Jesus' "call story" starts with his relationship to John the Baptist. Joachim Jeremias links this call story with Jesus' announcement of the reign of God in Mark 1:15. However, he asks,

> But have we found the right starting-point if we begin with Jesus' announcement of the reign of God? Does that really take us to the beginning? Does this starting-point not forget something, the question of how Jesus came to make an appearance and to proclaim the good news? There can be no doubt that something preceded the proclamation of the gospel of Jesus. The only question is whether we can come to any historical understanding of this first and most profound stage. Are we not up against that which cannot be described? At least, we can put our questions here only with the utmost caution and the utmost restraint. Nevertheless, we can make some very definite and clear statements, which give us a clue to what comes before Jesus' appearance, to his mission.[18]

What comes *before*, to Jeremias, was Jesus' relationship to the Baptist![19] To depart from Jesus' relationship to John in the quest for the historical Jesus (irrespective of whether it is the New Quest or Renewed Quest), is such an overwhelming fact that mentioning only one or two prominent scholars representing these two paradigms, such as R. Bultmann and E. P. Sanders, will suffice.

BEYOND THE LACK OF TEXTUAL EVIDENCE

The New Quest, to oversimplify it, mainly adopts a historical-critical perspective, and the Renewed Quest, a social-historical one. Regarding the former, Bultmann (the scholar to whom the "No Quest" has been attributed) cautiously mentions a few characteristics of the deeds of the historical Jesus that could be deciphered:

> Characteristic for him are exorcisms, the breech of the Sabbath commandment, the abandonment of ritual purifications, polemic against Jewish legalism, fellowship with outcasts such as

---

17. Ernst, *Johannes der Täufer*, 337, expresses this consensus in research as follows: "An der Tatsächlichkeit der Taufe Jesu durch Johannes besteht . . . kein begründeter Zweifel. Möglicherweise kann man noch ein Stück weitergehen und sagen, *Jesus habe bei dieser Gelegenheit seines großes Berufungserlebnis gehabt*" (my emphasis).

18. Jeremias, *New Testament Theology*, 1:42.

19. Ibid., 42–56.

publicans and harlots, sympathy for women and children; it can also be seen that Jesus was not an ascetic like John the Baptist, but gladly ate and drank a glass of wine. Perhaps we may add that he called disciples and assembled about himself a small company of followers—men and women.[20]

In a footnote to this summary, Bultmann refers to his student Hans Conzelmann's classic article "Jesus" for a similar viewpoint. [21] Therefore, one could say that the students of Bultmann who moved beyond their mentor's alleged "No Quest" with their "New Quest," have not really come forward with new results.[22] To my knowledge, there is no other place in Bultmann's writings where we find such a concentrated glimpse of his historical reconstruction of Jesus. In this very short sketch we have the core of Jesus' life. As far as his deeds are concerned, these few nonchronological, organized pen strokes concur more or less with the "red choices" of the fellows of the Jesus Seminar. They also concur with the content of the red printed sayings in the Jesus Seminar's *Five Gospels*.[23] However, in his work on Bultmann's interpretation of the history of Jesus, John Painter says that Bultmann was convinced that much more could be said on the teaching of Jesus.[24] He refers to Bultmann's own words: "we know enough of his [Jesus'] message to paint a consistent picture for ourselves."[25] In his afterword to Bultmann's *Jesus*, Walter Schmithals emphasizes the same. [26]

With regard to Jesus' baptism, Bultmann says, "The account of Jesus' baptism (Mark 1:9-11) is legend, certain though it is that the legend started from the historical fact of Jesus' baptism by John."[27] According to Bultmann, it is "told in the interest not of biography but of faith."[28] In his

---

20. Quoted in Painter, *Theology as Hermeneutics*, 102. The original German is found in Bultmann, *Verhältnis der urchristlichen Christusbotschaft*. See chapter 1, note 34 for text.

21. Bultmann, *Verhältnis der urchristlichen Christusbotschaft*, 11, note 17.

22. See Keck, *Future for the Historical Jesus*, 41-42, note 12; Borg, *Jesus in Contemporary Scholarship*, 4; Scott, "From Reimarus to Crossan," 256.

23. See Funk and the Jesus Seminar, *Acts of Jesus*; Funk and Hoover, *Five Gospels*.

24. Painter, *Theology as Hermeneutics*,102.

25. My translation of Bultmann, *Jesus*, 13: "von seiner Verkündigung wissen wir so viel, daß wir uns ein zusammenhängendes Bild machen können."

26. Schmithals, "Nachwort," 149: "Als Bultmann nach dem ersten Weltkrieg sein Jesusbuch schrieb, stand darum für ihn fest, 'daß wir vom Leben und von der Persönlichkeit Jesu so gut wie nichts mehr wissen.' Es ist ein groteskes Mißverständnis, wenn man diesen Satz gelegentlich in dem Sinne zitiert findet, nach Bultmanns Meinung könne man von Jesus nichts mehr wissen. Bultmann hat nie daran gezweifelt, daß wir uns ein hinreichend deutliches Bild von der Lehre und also von den Absichten und dem Werk Jesu verschaffen können." Referring to Bultmann's writing in the period after the First World War, Schmithals probably has in mind the Old Quest. Over against N.T. Wright's opinion that the "new questers" did not take the first-century Jewish context seriously, it should however be acknowledged that the historical Jesus is treated by Bultmann "as a Jew in the context of the diversity of Judaism" (Painter, *Theology as Hermeneutics*, 101).

27. Bultmann, *Theology of the New Testament*, 26–27.

28. Ibid., 27.

reconstruction of the history of the Jesus traditions in Mark, Matthew, and Luke, Bultmann states in the same vein, "Without disputing the *historicity of Jesus' baptism by John*, the story as we have it must be classified as legend. The miraculous moment is essential to it and its edifying purpose is clear. And indeed one may be at first inclined to regard it as a biographical legend; it tells a story of Jesus" (my emphasis).[29] These words remind one of Norman Perrin's reference to Philip Wheelwright's dictum, to which I referred earlier when I related a myth to an "emptied reality": "Myth is to be defined as a complex of stories some no doubt fact, and some fantasy.[30]

Bultmann does not want to refer to the account of Jesus' baptism in Mark 1:9–11 as a "call story" (German: *Berufungsgeschichte*) in order to avoid a "psychological fallacy." He agrees that "Acts 10:37f., 13:24f. show that the historical fact of Jesus' baptism is not necessary for linking the ministry of Jesus to John's."[31] Bultmann does mention the embarrassment experienced by Christians with regard to the problem of how Jesus could undergo a baptism for the remission of sin. [32] He does not, as far as I can see (including in his *Jesus* book[33]), elaborate either on what Markan scholar R. Pesch refers to as a pre-Markan baptismal tradition[34] or the historical background of Jesus being a "sinner" who needed remission and, therefore, became linked to the Baptist's circle. In his reconstruction of the gospel tradition he is only interested in the reediting of this tradition by a (Hellenistic) Christian redactor.[35]

However, in his commentary on the Gospel of John, Bultmann appears to argue that the baptism of Jesus, though a historical fact, should be seen as irrelevant for John. This is because the account of Jesus' baptism is not mentioned in the Gospel of John, or, at most, John's Gospel (knowing the Q tradition in its final redactional phase only alludes to what is reported in Mark, Matthew, and Luke.[36] On the other hand, in the Gospel of John the ministries of the Baptist and Jesus are remarkably related to each other.

---

29. Bultmann, *Geschichte der synoptischen Tradition*, 263, note 1, uses the expression "Wirksamheit Jesu" for "ministry." Bultmann, *History of the Synoptic Tradition*, 247, note 2, adds: "yet not that this linking must be made by the story of a baptism, or that it could only be made if the baptism of Jesus were not an actual historical fact."

30. Quoted in Perrin, *Jesus and the Language of the Kingdom*, 22.

31. Bultmann, *History of the Synoptic Tradition*, 253.

32. This embarrassment is expressed in Matt 3:14–15 and by Jerome (*Against Pelagius*, 3.2) who derived it from the *Gospel of the Nazoreans*. Bultmann refers to this document as the "Gospel of the Hebrews," since Jerome "assigned all known quotations of Jewish-Christian gospels to this one document, the 'Gospel According to the Hebrews,' which, he held, was identical with the original Aramaic Matthew" (Quoted in Koester, *Introduction to the New Testament*, 201-2). The real *Gospel of the Hebrews* was used in Alexandria, while the *Gospel of the Nazoreans*, like the *Gospel of the Ebionites*, was used in the area of Syria and Palestine (see Koester 203, 223). The *Gospel of the Hebrews* is preserved in Jerome's commentary on Isaiah 4 and the relevant citation does not refer to this particular embarrassment (see Tatum, *John the Baptist and Jesus*, 89).

33. Bultmann, *Jesus*, 20–22.

34. Pesch, *Markusevangelium*, Vol. 1, 80.

35. See Reumann, "Quest for the Historical Baptist," 181–99.

36. See Tatum, *John the Baptist and Jesus*, 79–80.

Here we also have a sharp emphasis on "specific social and religious categories of people depicted interacting with John the Baptist. These include priests, Levites, and Pharisees (1:19, 24; also 4:1)."[37] Bultmann comments as follows on the inattentiveness of the Johannine evangelist with regard to Jesus' baptism by John the Baptist:

> Yet it would be wrong to conclude from this that Jesus' baptism was an embarrassment for the Evangelist, so that he [John] passes over it as quickly as possible. On the contrary he clearly refers to it without misgivings. Yet he does not give an account of it, firstly because he can assume that his readers are acquainted with the story, and secondly, because for him the mere historical fact is of no significance by comparison with the witness of the Baptist which is based on it.[38]

In a separate publication on the traditions in Mark, Matthew, and Luke, Bultmann admits that Jesus underwent a "baptism of penitence"[39] and says that Jesus did not need to do so. However, the historical grounds, if any, on which Bultmann bases this opinion are unclear. I could not find the answer in Bultmann's writings, other than the implicit reference in his interpretation of 2 Cor 5:21 which was discussed earlier. As we have seen, in this verse Paul says that Christ "who knew no sin" was nevertheless made a "sinner" by God. Could one infer that the historicity of Jesus' baptism is irrelevant in Bultmann's opinion as well? Is that then the reason why Bultmann does not bother with the question of why Jesus' sinfulness was experienced as an embarrassment by earliest Christians? Clearly, seen at least from the perspective in the *Gospel of the Nazoreans* and the *Gospel of the Ebionites*,[40] this embarrassment presumes the question, Why would Jesus want to be baptized?

Walter Schmithals's understanding of the baptismal account, like Bultmann's exegesis of 2 Cor 5:21, also does not take the social-historical dimension of the account and its apology into consideration. Schmithals describes the "preaching about penitence" and the "baptism of penitence" (*Bußpredigt* and *Bußtaufe*) of John the Baptist in light of the "apocalyptic expectation of the imminent shift of aeons." He then links the historical

---

37. See Tatum, *John the Baptist and Jesus*, 80.

38. Bultmann, *Gospel of John: A Commentary*, 94. In German, see Bultmann, *Evangelium des Johannes*, 65: "Man darf das freilich nicht so deuten, als sei die Tatsache der Taufe Jesu für den Evangelisten eine Verlegenheit gewesen, sodaß er sie möglichst verschweigt. Vielmehr nimmt er auf sie sichtlich unbefangen Bezug; aber er erzählt sie nicht, weil er sie als bekannt voraussetzen kann, und *weil ihm das bloße historische Faktum unwesentlich ist* gegenüber den in ihm begründeten Täufererzeugnis" (my emphasis).

39. Bultmann, "Erforschung der synoptischen Evangelien," 34.

40. The *Gospel of the Nazoreans* is referred to by Jerome in his *Against Pelagius* (3.2) and the *Gospel of the Ebionites* is referred to by Epiphanius in his *Heresies* (30.13.7–8); see Tatum, *John the Baptist and Jesus*, 89–90.

baptismal event with the already developed faith assertions in early Christianity about Christ's vicarious death that takes away the sin of the world.[41] This is precisely what Bultmann does with 2 Cor 5:21. Historically seen, however, Josef Ernst rightly emphasizes that we do have a reference to a decisive, discernible, historical notation that Jesus "in those days" came from Nazareth in Galilee to let himself be baptized in the river Jordan by John in Mark 1:9. Ernst continues by saying that no Christian theologian has given any thought to what lies beyond the clearly edited apologetics by the church. Christendom has disputed the possibility that Jesus, the child of God, could have experienced conversion and the forgiveness of sins.[42]

The problem, however, is that we do not have the "texts" to settle the vital question of why Jesus would want to undergo baptism for the remission of sin. Nevertheless, as social historians, we ought not to shrink back from the lack of evidence. We can proceed if the historical inquiry is understood as "a limited endeavour of probabilities and hypotheses linking its evidence together in intelligible patterns."[43]

BEYOND THE LACK OF SOCIAL-HISTORICAL EVIDENCE

According to E. P. Sanders, some statements about Jesus are "almost beyond dispute."

---

41. This interpretation can be regarded as one-sided because of its individualistic existentialism without social awareness. Clive Marsh, "Quests of the Historical Jesus," 415, puts it as follows: "Bultmann's individualism . . . is well known. The apparent lack of explicit social and political awareness, either in Bultmann's New Testament work or in that of the post-Bultmannians [including Schmithals] who sought Jesus by an existential route, has proved costly." With regard to Jesus' baptism, Schmithals, *Theologiegeschichte des Urchristentums*, 183, refers to an "apocalyptic expectation of the coming shift in dispensations." He links the historical baptismal event with the "belief in Jesus' vicarious death as it developed in early Christianity" and interprets it as an "eschatological redemption of sin" event (99); cf. Schmithals, *Evangelium nach Markus*, 83. Nevertheless, Schmithals (*Evangelium nach Markus*, 82), in spite of his "existential exegesis," still holds on to the historicity of Jesus' baptism. Jeremias does not "put on one side as lightly as usually happens" the explicit dispute of Josephus (*Ant.* 18.117) that the baptism of John had anything to do with the forgiveness of sin. He understands Jesus' baptism as follows: "Jesus experienced his call when he underwent John's baptism, in order to take his place among the eschatological people of God that the Baptist was assembling" (Jeremias, *New Testament Theology*, 44, 49).

42. Ernst, J. 1989, *Johannes der Täufer*, 337: "Kein christlicher Theologe wäre von sich aus auf den Gedanken gekommen, den Sohn Gottes mit Umkehr und Sündenvergebung in Verbindung zu bringen. Die biblische Überlieferung der Tauferzählung gibt in ihrer zunehmenden apologetischen Überarbeitung noch deutlich erkennen, wie schwer man sich mit der offenkundigen Subordination getan hat."

43. Perkins, "Historical Jesus and Christology," 23. However, it is important to realize that current historical Jesus research does not necessarily present less emphasis on serious historical-critical analysis of textual and social evidence. Besides its ideological-critical awareness and acknowledgement of "autobiographical" projection, postmodern historiography tries to avoid any positivism. Marsh, "Quests of the Historical Jesus," 406, illustrates this "new historicist" perspective by referring particularly to Crossan's *The Historical Jesus: The Life of a Mediterranean Jewish Peasant* (1991): "Crossan has responded recently to those who criticize him for such autobiographical elements, noting the inevitability of being influenced by one's life experience as a historical interpreter" (Marsh, 406, note 5).

Jesus was born circa 4 B.C.E., near the time of the death of Herod the Great.
He spent his childhood and early adult years in Nazareth, a Galilean village.
He was baptized by John the Baptist.
He called disciples.
He taught in the towns, villages, and countryside of Galilee (apparently not the cities).
He preached "the Kingdom of God."
About the year 30 he went to Jerusalem for Passover.
He created a disturbance in the Temple area.
He had a final meal with the disciples.
He was arrested and interrogated by Jewish authorities, specifically the high priest.
He was executed on the orders of the Roman prefect, Pontius Pilate.

Sanders continues by adding a short list of equally secure facts about the aftermath of Jesus' life:

His disciples at first fled.
They saw him (in what sense is not certain) after his death.
As a consequence, they believed that he would return to found the kingdom.
They formed a community to await his return and sought to win others to faith in him as God's Messiah.[44]

Sanders quite rightly says that a "list of everything that we know about Jesus would be appreciably longer" than these lists.[45] In the first list he refers to two episodes in Jesus' life prior to his baptism by John: Jesus' birth during the Herodian regime and Jesus' childhood in Nazareth. Sanders mentions only two "facts" with regard to these two episodes:

> "Jesus lived with his parents in Nazareth, a Galilean village. . . .
> When Jesus was a young man, probably in his late twenties, John the Baptist began preaching in or near Galilee. He proclaimed the urgent need to repent in view of the coming judgement. Jesus heard John and felt called to accept his baptism. All four gospels point to this event that transformed Jesus' life."[46]

With regard to Jesus' birth and the role of his parents in these accounts, Sanders correctly says that so many "novelistic interests" pervade the Gospel

---

44. Sanders, *Historical Figure of Jesus*, 10–11. Cf. Sanders, *Jesus and Judaism*.
45. Sanders, *Historical Figure of Jesus*, 10. In this book he abstracts many more details from the available sources and most of them are very convincing. There are a few exceptions, such as his constant, though more subtle now, peculiar idea of Jesus as an eschatological proclaimer of the kingdom.
46. Ibid., 12–13.

narratives. The consequence of this is that we "cannot write 'the life of Jesus' in the modern sense, describing his education, tracing his development, analyzing the influence of his parents, showing his response to specific events and so on."[47] Elsewhere in his book he points out that the Matthean and Lukan birth narratives "constitute an extreme case" because their uses were solely "to place Jesus in salvation history": "It seems that they had very little historical information about Jesus' birth.[48]

This insight concurs with that of Bultmann, Crossan, and Borg, to mention only three scholars. In the whole section of Bultmann's treatment of the infancy narratives, he never pays the slightest attention to the possibility that implicit individual apologetic features or conditions in these narratives could have a historical base in the life of Jesus. For him, this is simply legendary material.[49] He is also skeptical about the possibility that the defamations about Jesus' alleged illegitimate birth were already present in Matthew. According to Bultmann, these defamations are evidence of the second-century polemics by Origen against the Greek philosopher Celsus. A similar slur can be found in the Talmud.[50]

---

47. Ibid., 75.
48. Ibid., 88.
49. See Bultmann, *History of the Synoptic Tradition*, 292, 295, 298, 302, 304, 306.
50. Origen, *Against Celsus* 1.28; Talmud, e.g., *Sab* 104b. See Bultmann, *History of the Synoptic Tradition*, 293–94. Kee, *What Can We Know?* 12–13, refers as follows to the reference in the Talmud.

Allusions to [Jesus] in the rabbinic writings are of uncertain date, since the basic documents of rabbinic Judaism were not produced until the period from the second to the sixth centuries. It is impossible to date with certainty those traditions included in this material known in its final form as the Mishna and the Talmud which claim that they are quoting rabbis who were (allegedly) active in the first century. Jesus is referred to as "certain person," on the assumption that even to mention his name would be to give him undue honor. The specific details about this unnamed character and his followers point unmistakably to Jesus. In some passages of this Jewish material, he is called Ben Stadia or Ben Panthera, implying that he is the illegitimate son (Ben, in Hebrew) of a soldier or some other unworthy person. Similarly, his mother is pictured as disreputable. In a document known as Shabbath (104) the following incident is reported: *Rabbi Eliezer . . . was arrested for Minuth* [holding Christian beliefs] *and they brought him to the tribunal for judgment. The governor said to him, "Does an old man like you occupy himself with such things?" He said to him, "Faithful is the judge concerning me." The governor supposed that he was saying this of him, but he was not thinking of any but his Father who is in heaven.* [The governor] *said to him, "Since I am trusted by you, I shall be the same concerning you . . . Perhaps these societies* [the Christians] *err concerning these things. Dismissus, behold you are released." And when he had been released from the tribunal, he was troubled because he had been arrested for Minuth. His disciples came to him to console him, but he would not take comfort. Rabbi Aquiba* [early second century] *came in and said to him, "Perhaps one of the Minim* [Christians] *has said a word of Minuth and it pleased you." He said, "By heaven, once I was walking in Sepphoris, and I met Jacob of Chepat Sichnin, and he said to me a word of Minuth in the name of Jesus Ben Pantiri, and it pleased me. And I was arrested for words of Minuth because I overstepped the words of Torah* [the Jewish law]: *'Keep your way far from her, and do not come near the door of her house, because she has cast down many wounded'* [Prov 5:8]."

Schaberg, *Illegitimacy of Jesus*, 167, and Lüdemann, *Virgin Birth?* 59, do not consider the name Ben Panthera as legendary. Lüdemann interprets the reference to Mary's rape by the Roman soldier as authentic. Lüdemann regards Joseph as Mary's "later husband" (128). However, the reference to Mary as παρθένος does not need to denote an unmarried woman, because in Greek thought "virginity did not depend on the presence of a hymen" (Sissa, *Greek Virginity*, 170; 78–79).

Crossan interprets the tradition of the illegitimate Jesus as the "instant and obvious rebuttal" by the "opponents of Christianity" of the "claims of virginal conception and divine generation for Jesus."[51] In other words, according to Crossan, these claims were not invented for the purpose of rejecting the reproach from the "synagogue" (and later from Celsus and rabbinic Judaism) that Jesus' conception was premarital or illegitimate. Such an interpretation is found in the writings of, among others, Walter Schmithals and Jane Schaberg.[52] According to Crossan, the accounts in Matthew and Luke about the virginal birth and Jesus' place in David's lineage were invented as "historized prophecy." Such an opinion, seen from a historical point of view, presumes that these accounts originated within the Christian cult, to use Bultmann's term. This happened prior to the actual defamations by the opponents of Christians of Jesus' divine origins.[53]

In *A Marginal Jew: Rethinking the Historical Jesus*, J. P. Meier argues that the precise "origins of the virginal conception tradition remain obscure from a historical point of view."[54] Meier argues in the same vein as Bultmann by regarding the rebuttal of Jesus' divine origins as a reaction to the infancy narratives. He thinks that there is no clear attestation of a "polemic tradition of Jesus' illegitimacy until the middle of the second century."[55]

Jane Schaberg also reads the infancy narratives in Luke and particularly in Matthew "as a response to the truth of the illegitimacy charge."[56] With regard to these narratives she (while exposing Raymond Brown's unsubtle reading of her argument) asks, "But why could Jesus not be Son of God and son of an unknown or even son of a nobody?"[57] Schaberg argues that Joseph's paternity is denied in Matthew and Luke because it was known in some circles that he was not the biological father of Jesus. The Gospel of John (1:45; 6:42) refers apologetically to Jesus as Joseph's physical son[58] because, for

---

51. Crossan, *Historical Jesus: A Revolutionary Biography*, 18; Crossan, "Infancy and Youth," 68.

52. Schmithals, *Einleitung in die drei ersten Evangelien*, 337; Schaberg, *Illegitimacy of Jesus*; Schaberg, "The Infancy of Mary of Nazareth"; Schaberg, "Feminist Interpretation of the Infancy Narrative"; Schaberg, "Canceled Father."

53. Crossan, *Historical Jesus*, 18.

54. Meier, *Marginal Jew*, 1:229–30. According to Meier the "seedbed" for this idea should be sought in Jewish apocalyptic.

55. Ibid., 22.

56. Schaberg, "Infancy of Mary of Nazareth," 20.

57. Schaberg, "Canceled Father," 20.

58. The references in Rom 1:3–4 and 2 Tim 2:8 to Jesus being born of the "seed" of David should not be understood as allusions to the paternity of a historical Joseph (contra Schaberg, "Canceled Father," 19, note 35). Some have misunderstood Bultmann's (*Second Letter to the Corinthians*, 155, note 154) interpretation of Rom 1:3–4 by deducing from his insight into Paul's important distinction between the ὁ χριστὸς τὸ κατὰ σάρκα ("Christ in his plainness") and the ὁ χριστὸς τὸ κατὰ πνεῦμα ("the resurrected Christ") an absolute discontinuity between the historical Jesus and the kerygmatic Christ, so that the historical Jesus is not considered as part of Christian faith. In chapter 1, I demonstrated why I do not interpret Bultmann in this way (see also Bultmann, *Verhältnis der urchrislichen Christusbotschaft*).

John, "illegitimacy discredits Jesus."[59] However, Matthew knew Joseph was not Jesus' biological father. Luke (4:22) also referred to Jesus as Joseph's (adopted) son.

The infancy narratives in *Proto-James* and in *Pseudo-Matthew*[60] stretch this notion to such an extent that they radically transform the plainness of the historical Jesus into symbols of power and hierarchy. In these narratives Joseph is "exalted" to a wealthy benefactor and Jesus almost to a royal prince! Subsequently, this kind of faith assertion in *Proto-James* and *Pseudo-Matthew* skip the scandal of Jesus' plainness and tragically miss what God's love is about! Therefore, Schaberg disagrees that a disgraced Jesus should necessarily discredit Christian faith. Nevertheless, it is understandable that such a fact could be used "to smear Jesus and his movement, to weaken his credibility as a religious leader. The infancy narratives wanted to dispute this notion."[61] In other words, to me, historical information can be inferred from these narratives.

On the other hand, like Bultmann, Crossan is of the opinion that there is no biographical information about the historical Jesus in either the claim of Jesus' virginal conception or the claim that Jesus is of David's lineage.[62] Crossan calls these two claims a "historicization of prophecy," a process in which a "historical narrative" is written from prophetic allusions; that is, "hide the prophecy, tell the narrative, and invent the history."[63] However, he seems to take the names of Jesus, Mary, and Joseph (the "only common features" in the "long narrative accounts of Jesus' birth in Matthew 1–2 and Luke 1–2") historically for granted. This specifically pertains to the references to Jesus as a child of the carpenter Joseph and Mary in Matt 13:55–56, Luke 4:22, and John 6:42.[64]

This consideration seems to be similar to Marcus Borg's,[65] although he, in his article "The First Christmas," writes: "[A]ccording to Mark, the family of Jesus seems not to have known about the virginal conception and his being the 'Son of God' from birth."[66] In this same article Borg refers to J. P. Meier, who states, with regard to a reference to Jesus' family in Mark 3:21–35: "Jesus' brothers did not believe in him during the public ministry which hardly seems likely if they had known about his virginal conception."[67]

---

59. Schaberg, "Canceled Father," 19.
60. See Schaberg, "Infancy of Mary of Nazareth," 708–27.
61. Schaberg, "Canceled Father," 20.
62. Crossan, *Historical Jesus: The Life of a Mediterranean Jewish Peasant*, 371–72.
63. Crossan uses the expression "historicization of prophecy" also with regard to his understanding of Paul's perspective on "death through which sin is buried" (see Crossan, *Who Killed Jesus*, 195–97) and the "historical narrative" in the *Gospel of Peter* about the "resurrected, escorted cross that spoke" (see Crossan, *Cross That Spoke*).
64. Crossan, *Historical Jesus: A Revolutionary Biography*, 23–24.
65. Borg, *Meeting Jesus Again*, 25. Cf. Borg, "Meaning of the Birth Stories," 179–88.
66. Borg, "First Christmas," 10, note 3.
67. Meier, *Marginal Jew*, 1:221.

Borg adds, "It should be noted that the passage in Mark also includes his [Jesus'] mother."[68]

Crossan reads Matthew's citation of Isa 7:14 as though the evangelist had a woman in mind who "will conceive and remain a virgin." In other words, Matthew, according to Crossan, "takes it [the word *virgin*; Greek: παρθένος literally and applies it to the virginal conception of Jesus."[69] However, according to Crossan, Matthew is not the source of the idea of the virginal conception of Jesus. Crossan's opinion is that "the source is the competition with Rome: the desire of the evangelists to show that God is manifested in Jesus born of a virgin and not in Augustus who claimed to be descended from Venus." Consequently, the virginal conception is for Crossan "not a literal statement about the biology of Mary." It "should be taken metaphorically. . . . It is a credal statement about the status of Jesus."[70]

Robert Funk, in his book *Honest to Jesus*, claims that in the infancy narratives, just four items may be extracted that have a historical basis:

> [1] Jesus may have been born during the reign of Herod the Great, although that is not certain. Scholars can find no basis for the claim that Herod murdered babies wholesale in the hope of eliminating Jesus as a rival king. Jesus' home was almost certainly Nazareth, and he was quite possibly born there as well. [2] His mother's name may well have been Mary. [3] And we have no reason to doubt that the child was named Jesus. These constitute the meager traces of history in the birth stories. Everything else is fiction. [4] We can be certain that Mary did not conceive Jesus without the assistance of human male sperm. It is unclear whether Joseph or some unnamed male was the biological father of Jesus. It is possible that Jesus was illegitimate.[71]

What we have in common between the two infancy narratives in Matthew and Luke is, according to Funk, (1) that Jesus' "home was Nazareth," (2) that "Joseph was Jesus' alleged father," (3) that "Mary and Joseph [were] engaged but not married," (4) that "Joseph was not involved in the conception of Jesus," and (5) that "Jesus was born after Joseph and Mary began to live together."[72]

Matthew's story clearly presupposes that Joseph thought Mary was guilty of unchastity.[73] N. T. Wright rightly reproaches positivists who presume to

---

68. Borg, "First Christmas," 10, note 3.
69. Crossan, "Infancy and Youth ," 67.
70. Ibid., 72.
71. Funk, *Honest to Jesus*, 294.
72. Ibid., 293.
73. Cf. Beare, *Gospel according to Matthew*, 68; Brown, *Birth of the Messiah*, 125–28.

know, in contrast to the characters in the story, the "truth" behind the miraculous events in the life of Jesus:

> It is naive to suppose that first-century Galilean villagers were ready to believe in "miracles" because they did not understand the laws of nature, or did not realize that the space-time universe was a closed continuum. . . . As has often been pointed out, in Mt. 1.18f. Joseph was worried about Mary's unexpected pregnancy not because he did not know where babies came from but because he did.[74]

As I will demonstrate in more detail in the next chapter, the figure of Joseph does not occur in the early sources: not in Paul, the Gospel of Mark, the Sayings Gospel Q, or the *Gospel of Thomas*. We meet Joseph for the first time in those documents that dispute the defamatory claims of the opponents of the Jesus movement: Matthew, John, and Luke, and eventually the dependent *Proto-James* and *Pseudo-Matthew*. In the Christian tradition, the role of Joseph is part and parcel of either the polemics against Jesus' alleged scandalous birth or the underpinning of Mary's (perpetual) virginity and Jesus' two "natures."

It remains a dilemma that Jesus' father is altogether absent in the Gospel accounts of Jesus' public ministry while other members of his family are specified. This is even more remarkable when one takes the central role of a father in first-century Mediterranean culture into consideration. It is highly problematic from a scholarly perspective for Meier to judge that the "traditional solution" for Joseph's absence is still "the most likely" one because it is also found in the patristic period.[75] This "traditional" solution is that Joseph died before Jesus began his public activities. Historically seen, however, this explanation functions on the same level as other "Christian solutions" that originated because of embarrassment, such as the "sinless" Jesus being baptized by John.

Strangely enough, Crossan does not insist on a painstaking historical analysis with respect to the quite different Joseph traditions in Matthew, Luke, John, *Proto-James*, *Pseudo-Matthew*, and the *Life of Joseph the Carpenter*. As I will argue in the next chapter, an analysis of a unit of texts about Joseph reveals a clear picture of a trajectory. Could it not be possible that the references to Joseph in the Gospel tradition be considered what Crossan calls "confessional statements?"[76] According to Crossan, such statements served as a reply to the obvious rebuttal by the opponents of

---

74. Wright, *Christian Origins*, 2:186–87, note 160.
75. Meier, *Marginal Jew: Rethinking the Historical Jesus*, 317.
76. Crossan, *Historical Jesus: A Revolutionary Biography*, 23.

Christianity. Is not Crossan too indifferent about the difference between Mark 6:3 ("Is not this the carpenter, the son of Mary and brother of . . . ?") and Matt 13:55–56 ("Is not this the carpenter's son? Is not his mother called Mary? And are not his brothers . . . ?")[77] Why could not Mark 6:3 also be interpreted like Mark 1:9 "without any defensive commentary"?[78] I understand the Gospel stories about Jesus' genesis and birth record as confessional commentaries that, as I will argue in chapter 6, historically reveal much about Jesus' compassion towards women and children—perhaps the most distinctive aspect in the life of the historical Jesus.[79]

Being fatherless, as our earliest sources depict Jesus, he could fit into the Pauline description implicitly found in 2 Cor 5:21. With regard to Mediterranean culture, I have already indicated that institutionalization made a fatherless child unaware of systemic "sin" or "wickedness;" a fatherless child was someone who knew no sin, yet who was made in the eyes of God and the people to be a nobody in society. Such a person was doomed. He or she could never enter the congregation of the Lord. The reason for this, as I will argue, is that fatherless children within the Israelite society were not respected as "children of Abraham." Being ostracized, according to the ideology of the temple and its idea of systemic sin, Jesus would be refused the status of being God's child. How and where would he find "remission for his sin" if it could not occur, according to the priestly code, in the temple itself?

Departing from two remarks in Mark (1:9, 11), the one about the "Jesus of history" and the other about the "Jesus of faith," my understanding of the paternity of Jesus is neatly summarized by Jane Schaberg: "[T]he paternity is canceled or erased by the theological metaphor of the paternity of God."[80] According to the Scholars Version, this particular remark about the Jesus of history reads, "During that same period Jesus came from Nazareth in Galilee and was baptized in the river Jordan by John." The remark about the Jesus of faith reads, "There was also a voice from the skies: 'You are my favored son—I fully approve of you.'"

As we have seen with both Bultmann and Sanders, Crossan regards Jesus' baptism "as historically certain as anything about either of them ever can be." As a historian, Crossan, like Sanders, doubts "things that agree too much with the gospel's bias" and "credits things that are against their preference."[81] However, this "rule cannot be applied mechanically, since some things that actually happened suited the authors [the evangelists] very well."[82]

---

77. Ibid., 24.
78. Ibid., 44.
79. Cf. Bultmann, *Verhältnis der urchristlichen Christusbotschaft*, 11.
80. Schaberg, "Canceled Father," 14.
81. Crossan, *Historical Jesus: A Revolutionary Biography*, 44.
82. Sanders, *Historical Figure of Jesus*, 94.

In view of this, it is most unlikely that the Gospels or earlier Christians invented the fact that Jesus started out under John. Since they wanted Jesus to stand out as superior to the Baptist, they would not have come up with the story that Jesus had been his follower. Therefore, we conclude, John really did baptize Jesus. This, in turn, implies that Jesus agreed with John's message: *it was time to repent in view of the coming wrath and redemption.*

Sanders emphasizes this point because of his conviction (similar to that of Bultmann and the other Renewed Questers) that Jesus constantly held on to the Baptist's apocalyptic vision. I mentioned earlier that the Renewed Questers have a more subtle view on Jesus' eschatological viewpoint. Richard Horsley and Neil Silberman note that "Jesus did not believe that the Kingdom of God would arrive with fire and brimstone."[83] According to Robert Funk, Jesus "can hardly have shared the apocalyptic outlook of John the Baptist, Paul, and other members of the early Christian commmunity."[84] Conversely, and parallel to Sanders, Wright declares, "It should be clear that Jesus regarded his ministry as in continuity with, and bringing to a climax, the work of the great prophets of the Old Testament, culminating in John the Baptist, whose initiative he had used as his launching-pad."[85] Of course, much was shared between Jesus and John. Why else would Jesus come to him to be baptized? However, to handcuff these two, as if in a chained succession, does not fit historical reconstruction. Rather, it represents a description of the theology of Mark, elaborated upon by Matthew.

At this point we have an example par excellence concerning the difference in method between Wright and the Jesus Seminar with regard to the search for the historical Jesus in contradistinction to Gospel overlays. Wright does not assess adequately the peculiar theology of each Gospel writer or the traditions upon which the interpretations of the respective Gospel writers were built. To make the excuse that traveling on the *Schweitzerstraße* does not require such a historical differentiation is not a proper response. Schweitzer himself differentiated sharply between Mark, Matthew, and Luke, at least. Wright's method of not being guided by hypothetical source traditions tempts him to confuse a synchronic description of Gospel evidence with the traditions of the Jesus of history with which this evidence is interrelated. Certainly the fellows of the Jesus Seminar do not share the opinion that the program of Jesus is only to bring the Baptist's vision to a climax. They interpret the sources in such a way that "Jesus changed his view of John's mission and message."[86] But considering method is not my

---

83. Horsley and Silberman, *Message and the Kingdom*, 42. Cf. Crossan, *Historical Jesus: The Life of a Mediterranean Jewish Peasant*, 227–64; Crossan, *Historical Jesus: A Revolutionary Biography*, 29–53; Borg, *Jesus in Contemporary Scholarship*, 77; Hollenbach, "Conversion of Jesus."

84. Funk, *Honest to Jesus*, 167–68.

85. Wright, *Christian Origins*, 2:167.

86. Crossan, *Historical Jesus: A Revolutionary Biography*, 47.

concern now. My aim is to argue that one should move beyond Jesus' relationship with the Baptist in order to construct his "whole" life.

As often pointed out, first-century historian Josephus had a biased interest in the baptismal activity of John the Baptist.[87] According to Crossan, by deciphering Josephus' prejudiced account of the Baptist's conduct as "not a magical or ritual act that removed sin," one can establish as historical "fact" that John's baptism was about the remission of sin. It was an alternative to "the actions of the priests in Jerusalem's temple."[88] Crossan takes seriously Sanders's understanding of what the "reconstruction of history" is all about: "In the reconstruction of history, we must always consider *context* and *content*.[89] The better we can correlate the two, the more we shall understand."[90] But we have to be careful of "extravagant claims not undergirded by carefully screened evidence," alerts Funk. He emphasizes that any new historical construction" will not of course be the real Jesus, now set out for the final time," but "will be a reconstruction based on the best evidence currently available, submitted to the most rigorous collective and cumulative analyses, and shaped into a relatively consistent whole." He adds that it is "the best we or anyone can do." [91]

According to Richard Horsley and Neil Silberman, the picture we get of what happened at the river Jordan is that "John the Baptist was offering crowds of people who lived under the shadow of Rome and under the burden of Herodian control and taxation a new way to end the pain and uncertainty that plagued their daily lives."[92] They continue:

> Theology aside, we can say that the baptism of Jesus took place within the context of a popular revival movement that was spreading among a pre-dominantly rural population that was being taxed, exploited, and regimented in new—and to their eyes— extremely threatening ways. . . . A journey out to see John the Baptist in the wilderness would have taken Jesus—presumably in the company of other people from Nazareth—out across the fringe of the Jezreel Valley where they would have passed through other rural villages, meeting tenant farmers and migrant workers, and seeing, at least from the distance, the houses of the overseers and the great villas of the wealthy lords. . . . That is the most we can say of the immediate circumstances of Jesus' baptism. And of the

---

87. See, among others, Crossan, *Historical Jesus: A Revolutionary Biography*, 34.
88. Ibid.
89. In Crossan, *Essential Jesus*, 9–13, he explores this kind of combinational notion when he creatively and ingeniously links texts and pre-Constantine images in order to understand the "essential," the "historical," Jesus better.
90. Sanders, *Historical Figure of Jesus*, 76.
91. Funk, *Honest to Jesus*, 59–60.
92. Horsley and Silberman, *Message and the Kingdom*, 34, 40.

ceremony itself, little can be said except that he presumably joined the assembled throngs . . . making the public commitment—as Josephus described it—"to live righteous lives, to practice justice towards their fellows and piety towards God."[93]

But is this really all that can be said if we screen Josephus's words as scholars like Crossan and others have done? Firstly, the Gospel tradition shows that, besides the background of Roman and Herodian royalty maltreating and impoverishing the peasants, John's baptismal practice should also be understood in terms of the ideology of the Jerusalem temple authorities. According to this ideology, these authorities decided who could be redeemed from sin and find access to God, as well as where, when, and how this would take place. Secondly, the Gospel tradition illustrates that when Jesus returned to Galilee, he did not continue baptizing but started a ministry of healing sinners and teaching God's unmediated presence among them.

When and under what circumstances Jesus returned we do not know, except that the textual evidence directs us to John's imprisonment and eventual decapitation by Herod Antipas as the turning point. Crossan points out that "John's vision of awaiting the apocalyptic God, the Coming One, as a repentant sinner, which Jesus had originally accepted and even defended in the crisis of John's death, was no longer deemed adequate."[94] He reaches this conclusion because of his analysis of the relevant references in Josephus as well as in the "intracanonical" traditions in the *Gospel of Thomas* and the Sayings Gospel Q.

The consistent element in the life of the historical Jesus, prior to and after his baptism and breach with the Baptist, seems to be his being among and his continued friendship with sinners (see Luke 7:3–35 [Q]).[95] This is tantamount to identifying "himself with those he was addressing, to emphasize that he shared with them a common destiny as we poor or destitute human beings."[96] Sanders, in discussing the identity of the sinners, says, "The most reliable passages about the sinners are those in which Jesus discusses the Baptist and contrasts himself to him." The "sinners" were those people who were "outside the law in some fundamental way." They were the people who, unlike the chief priests and elders, "believed John the Baptist and repented" (cf. Matt 21:32 and Luke 3:3, 8), *people who "lived as if there were no God."*[97] Against this background Sanders asks, "What did he [Jesus] think he was up to?" According to Sanders, Jesus was not primarily a "repentance-minded reformer."

---

93. Ibid., 40–41.
94. Crossan, *Historical Jesus: A Revolutionary Biography*, 47–48.
95. Cf. Crossan, *Historical Jesus: The Life of a Mediterranean Jewish Peasant*, 260.
96. Crossan, *Historical Jesus: A Revolutionary Biography*, 51.
97. Sanders, *Historical Figure of Jesus*, 227, 229, 231–33 (Sanders's emphasis).

In the New Testament that title [a repentance-minded reformer] clearly belongs to the Baptist. . . . The prostitutes repented when John preached—not when Jesus preached. . . . And Jesus was a friend of tax collectors and sinners—not of former tax collectors and sinners [against Josephus's biased perception of John the Baptist]. . . . Jesus, I think, was a good deal more radical than John. Jesus thought that John's call to repent should have been effective, but in fact it was only partially successful. His own style was in any case different; he did not repeat the Baptist's tactics. On the contrary, he ate and drank with the wicked and told them that God especially loved them, and that the kingdom was at hand. Did he hope that they would change their ways? Probably he did. But "change now or be destroyed" was not his message, it was John's. *Jesus' was, "God loves you."*[98]

There is good reason to relate these insights of Sanders with those he mentions earlier in his book regarding repentance, punishment, and forgiveness, though he does not do so himself. Explaining the temple ideology to which both John the Baptist and Jesus took offense, Sanders says, "God will always forgive the repentant sinner. Those who did not repent were subject to divine punishment, which was manifested, for example, in sickness. If they accepted this as God's chastisement for their misdeeds, they were still worthy members of the covenant."[99]

Jesus shares John's vision that remission of sin could be granted by God outside of the structures of the temple, in other words, "not through the usual channels."[100] The consequence of his indifference about repentance is that both he and his company of "sinners" would be regarded by the chief priests and the other Jerusalem elite and their retainers as people who lived as if there were no God.[101] Likewise, a "sinner" belonging to this category, would not be respected as a "child of Abraham"—that is, according to this ideology, a "child of God." However, the historical Jesus' trust in God as his Father was just as certain as his baptism by John!

Yet Sanders, like both Bultmann and Crossan, never asks why Jesus was seen as or saw himself as a "sinner" who "heard John and felt called to accept his baptism."[102] Sanders, nevertheless, says that the context that "should immediately attract the attention of the modern historian" is "the

---

98. Ibid., 233 (Sanders's emphasis).
99. Ibid., 34.
100. Wright, *Christian Origins*, 2:274. Although Wright disagrees with Sanders to some extent with regard to who the "sinners" in the social world of Jesus could be and what it meant that Jesus offered people "forgiveness of sin," he concurs that "Jesus was replacing adherence or allegiance to Temple and Torah with allegiance to himself."
101. Sanders, *Historical Figure of Jesus*, 229.
102. Ibid., 12–13.

events that immediately preceded and followed Jesus' own ministry and that were closely connected to it . . . ,[in other words], the preaching of John the Baptist" and the fact that the authors of the "gospels and Acts" ("reveal[ing] that John had a sizeable following")[103] were a little embarrassed at having to admit that their hero, Jesus, had been at first a follower of the Baptist."

Likewise, the Jesus Seminar has not asked the question why Jesus would want to be baptized.[104] Even Robert Webb, a fellow of the Jesus Seminar, has not asked or even referred to this question, despite writing extensively in his dissertation on John the Baptist from a social-historical perspective. In a subsequent essay, published in a volume on current research of historical Jesus studies, he does not touch on the issue.[105]

To my knowledge, the only scholar in the field of historical Jesus studies who has come forward with an educated guess is Paul Hollenbach.[106] In two different contributions he investigates the social world of John the Baptist's preaching mission and the "conversion of Jesus." In the latter, he is particularly interested in "what Jesus was like before his conversion." Hollenbach assumes that Jesus "went to John in order to repent of his sin," but as to what Jesus repented of, he admits that "we are really in the dark because of lack of evidence."[107] The only allusions in the sources are those texts that express the embarrassment of Christians (among others, Heb 4:15).

Hollenbach finds his point of departure for inquiry in the Markan reference that Jesus was a carpenter (Mark 6:3).[108] As Jesus was a craftsman (τεκτών) "in the sense of 'contractor' or 'builder,'" Hollenbach sets Jesus in a social class that "enjoyed considerable standing in society." According to this view, carpenters "in particular offered a large number of varied services on which especially poorer members of society would depend as they attempted to eke out a living. . . . It is likely then that Jesus, as a substantial member of society, came to feel at least a general concern for the injustices that he could observe daily from this vantage point."[109]

Such a picture, however, is misleading. Only two arguments against it will be sufficient to prove this judgment. One is taken from Sanders's insights and the other from Crossan's. Why would Jesus seek repentance outside the structures of the temple? The temple ideology stipulated that people "who transgressed the law should make reparations if their misdeeds harmed other people, repent and bring a sacrifice. God will always

---

103. Ibid., 92, 93–94.
104. See Tatum, *John the Baptist and Jesus.*
105. Webb, *John the Baptizer*; Webb, "John the Baptist."
106. Hollenbach, "Social Aspects of John the Baptizer's Preaching"; Hollenbach, "Conversion of Jesus."
107. Hollenbach, "Conversion of Jesus," 198.
108. Ibid., 200.
109. Ibid., 200, note 9.

forgive the repentant sinner."[110] As far as Crossan's reception of Hollenbach's hypothesis is concerned, we have an explicit acknowledgment of the insight of Hollenbach that "Jesus developed very soon his own distinctive message and movement which was very different from John's."[111] However, with regard to Jesus' artisanship, he implicitly, and rightly so, repudiates Hollenbach: "If Jesus was a carpenter, he belonged to the Artisan class, that group pushed into the dangerous space between Peasants and Degradeds or Expendables."[112]

Although one could expect Crossan to be aware of the aim of Hollenbach's article, namely, to ask "why Jesus went to John for baptism,"[113] he nevertheless does not ask the same important question. Crossan also never says that a lack of evidence is the reason why this gap in the existing historical Jesus research is beyond investigation. Even in the Third Quest, if one would like to differentiate between the Renewed Quest and the Third Quest, the whole life and work of Jesus of Nazareth is clearly not really at stake yet, as N. T. Wright thinks it is.[114] What I have in mind is certainly not what Sanders calls so indelicately, "the current flurry of interest in Mary's hymen (and Jesus' corpse)."[115]

What I have in mind is to reconstruct history in the same sense that I am engaged in the process of correlating context and content (see chapter 1). My journey with Jesus leads me to travel first from where the river Jordan flows through the Judean Desert into the Dead Sea. The journey then goes to the north, through Samaria and the agricultural estates of the Jezreel Valley (farmed by peasants, some of them previously landowners but now landless tenant farmers), then to Nazareth in Galilee (a simple village of peasants that is only a few miles from the Greco-Roman city of Sepphoris, once the capital), and then eastward, to the lake where the river Jordan starts its southern flow, to Herod Antipas's building operations in Tiberias, the new capital of Galilee ("a heavily mixed-race area," a place where Israelites would "cling fiercely to their ancestral traditions, and to maintain as best they could the symbols of their distinctiveness"[116]), and to the plains and villages surrounding the Lake of Tiberias (Sea of Galilee).

I shall return to these symbols and traditions and their peculiar relevance for the Israelites in "Galilee of the Gentiles" (cf. Matt 4:14), especially to

---

110. Sanders, *Historical Figure of Jesus*, 34.

111. Crossan, *Historical Jesus: The Life of a Mediterranean Jewish Peasant*, 238.

112. Crossan, *Historical Jesus: A Revolutionary Biography*, 25. Cf. Fiensy, *Social History of Palestine*, 164; Lenski, Lenski, and Nolan, *Human Societies*, 7th ed., 216–18.

113. Hollenbach, "Conversion of Jesus," 199.

114. Wright, *Who Was Jesus?* 13. In his 1996 magisterial work, *Christian Origins*, vol. 2, 160–61, Wright refers affirmatively to Hollenbach's work on John the Baptist published in 1992 in the *Anchor Bible Dictionary*, but not to the above-mentioned articles by Hollenbach, published respectively in 1979 and 1982 in *Römischen Welt*.

115. Quoted in Wright, *Who Was Jesus?* 76.

116. Horsley and Silberman, *Message and the Kingdom*, 31, 76.

their marriage arrangements in light of the purity system of Jerusalem's temple ideology. For now, it should be clear enough that I am convinced that the story of Jesus of Nazareth begins prior to the "cleansing of his sins." He and others could hardly be blamed for this epistemic sin because people who were labeled as "sinners" were often only those miserables who were trapped in institutionalized evil. Therefore, for me, the point of departure is the tradition behind the polemical faith assertions made by Paul, Matthew, Luke, John, and others after them. These assertions were about the origins of the peasant boy who probably became a carpenter and then, definitely, a revolutionary teacher and compassionate healer.

We know that, in all probability, after his baptism in the river Jordan, Jesus went back to the region where he came from, to the "Galilee of the Gentiles," as Matthew described this region in light of Isa 8:23–9:1. The historical Jesus went back to his native land to live up to the Baptist's prophetic message. In other words, apart from a difference in their respective eschatological views that seemed to widen after John's imprisonment, no disagreeing notions on the fundamental distinction between God's kingdom and the kingdoms of this world emerged. Both John and Jesus repeated the message of the prophets in this regard. The prophetic message was about a light shining for people living in darkness. Isaiah spoke of God's people living among the Gentiles in the northern regions of Israel (cf. Josh 16:10; 17:12; 19:10–16; 19:32–39). Over the years, these people (the descendents of, among others, Joseph, Zebulun, and Naphtali) became despised by Jerusalemites. Living in the "shadow of death" (cf. Matt 4:15–16), they were victimized by Judean and foreign landlords who dispossessed their land and estranged them from their cultic practices. The Baptist's message exposed the monarchs of Galilee, Judea, and Rome as well as all people who cared nothing about what the prophet (Isa 1:16–17) said: "Wash yourselves; make yourselves clean; remove the evil of your doings from my eyes; cease to do evil, learn to do good; seek justice, correct oppression; *defend the fatherless*, plead for the widow" (RSV).

BEYOND THE AGE THIRTY TRANSITION

The Gospel stories of the birth of Jesus precede the accounts of his resurrection in both Scripture and the Christian creeds. Yet, according to Willi Marxsen, they should be understood "only on the basis of the faith of Easter, rather than the other way around."[117] These powerful narratives are classic in their own right. Over so many centuries, they have articulated a confession of faith so storylike, so aesthetically beautiful.

Despite the absence of clear historical proof, twenty-nine percent of the fellows of the Jesus Seminar judge it possible that Mary's pregnancy

---

117. Marxsen, *Exeget als Theologe*, 169–70; see Ogden, *Doing Theology Today*, 249.

might have been the result of either rape or seduction, while four percent are convinced of that.[118] Almost all of the members (ninety-nine percent) are convinced that the reports in Matthew and Luke that Jesus was conceived by the Holy Spirit constitute not a historical statement but a theological one. The majority of the fellows of the Jesus Seminar is also uncertain whether Mary was a virgin at the time of conception. They argue that she probably became pregnant when Herod the Great was the "king of the Jews." Luke's references to a worldwide Roman census, to Jesus being laid in a manger, and to shepherds being the first to acknowledge his birth, plus Matthew's reference to "wise men," must be declared unhistorical. This also applies to the reports in both Matthew and Luke that the birth took place in Bethlehem, the references in Matthew that children were murdered by Herod the Great as a result of Jesus' birth and that Jesus was taken to Egypt by his parents after his birth, and the references in Luke that John the Baptist was of priestly descent, that he was the cousin of Jesus, and that Jesus was taken to the temple as a child where Simeon and Anna saw him. Undoubtedly, according to the majority of the Jesus Seminar, all of these references are unhistorical.

In this case, the question of illegitimacy arises with regard to the birth of Jesus. What could the consequences of illegitimacy in the social world of Jesus have been? Sixty-two percent of the members of the Jesus Seminar are uncertain whether the birth of Jesus was the consequence of rape or seduction. This is related to the fact that there is no evidence to this effect in the documents. However, in the second century C.E., Justin responded to accusations of rape.[119] Yet the credibility of these accusations cannot be founded on the principle of multiple, independent evidence. It is only based on the "Yeshua ben Pantera" traditions in the Talmud and the medieval Toledot traditions, which are interdependent and extremely tendentious.

However, even if rape can be ruled out, illegitimacy is a historical probability in light of the Second Temple ideology, as I will demonstrate in chapter 5. Yet I will argue that illegitimacy need not necessarily mean that one's mother was a "bad woman." Within the familial structure of the Mediterranean world (against the background of the contemporaneous marriage arrangements), a pregnant woman who was abandoned by her husband (without the protection of a substitute) was often given the label "whore." The child of such a woman (usually the firstborn) was deemed "born as a result of adultery." This expression often pertained to marriages between Jews and non-Jews. Since the postexilic marriage reform measures (see Nehemiah 9–10; Ezra 9–10), and certainly also during the

---

118. Funk and the Jesus Seminar, *Acts of Jesus*, 497–526.

119. *Shabbath* (104). See discussions by Kee, *What Can We Know?* 12–13; Schaberg, *Illegitimacy of Jesus*, 167; Lüdemann, *Virgin Birth?* 59.

first century, there was an insistence on the basis of priestly purity codes that male Israelites divorce "foreign" women. The result was "fatherlessness," or, in other words, "illegitimacy." Fatherless men (boys older than twenty) were not allowed to enter the temple (see Deut 23:3), nor to marry a fellow "true" (full-blooded) Israelite (see [Bab] Yebamot 78b) because of their "sinfulness." Illegitimacy did, of course, also refer to a birth that resulted from immorality, rape, incest, or seduction. A proverb of Jesus found in the Gospel of Thomas (105) may indicate that if a person did not know who his or her father (or mother) was—that is, if someone had no identity because he or she was not a child of Abraham—then he or she would be called a "child of a whore" and would carry sin (see Gos. Thom. 104).

Three other references to this theme are found in independent documents, which confirm that the tradition of the illegitimacy of Jesus must be taken seriously. This tradition is independently attested to in the earliest stratum of intracanonical New Testament documents (sayings in the Gospel of Thomas that go back to probably 50 C.E.). This is also the case in the second (the Gospel of Mark, written around 70 C.E.), in the third (in Luke and Matthew, written around 80–90 C.E., in traditions independent of Mark) as well as in the latest stratum (the Gospel of John, written around the end of the first century).

Mark 6:3 (against the background of the rejection of Jesus by his family in Nazareth) refers to Jesus not as the "son of Joseph," but as the "son of Mary." This latter expression is an indication that Jesus is without identity, an illegitimate person without a father who could have given him credibility. The second reference is found in Matt 27:64. The phrase "the last deception will be worse than the first" may be interpreted as a reference to a defamatory campaign by the opponents of Matthew's community. According to this campaign, the legend of the resurrection of Jesus is the "last deception" that is "worse" than the "first." The latter may possibly refer to the legend of divine conception and the conviction that God legitimated Jesus, despite his fatherlessness. God's legitimization is expressed within the framework of the Joseph tradition. An angel orders Joseph in a dream to marry Mary, whose pregnant condition had been the doing of the Holy Spirit. The third reference occurs in John 19:9. In this passage (against the background of the accusation that Jesus was supposedly "king of the Jews"), Pilate asks Jesus, "Where are you from?" Jesus, however, remains silent. According to rabbinic literature (see Qiddušin 4:2), a person must remain silent when asked such a question if he or she does not know who his or her father is. The reference in Qiddušin 4:2 is related to "street children" whose parents are unknown.

This information calls attention to the social dynamics of marriage and family arrangements in the Mediterranean world during the time of Jesus.

Studying such arrangements enables one to form a good idea of how a society was organized. Marriage, in a sense, forms a microcosm of the macrocosm. Therefore, the world of the Bible can be understood better by focusing on marriage and family. The sketch of the historical Jesus given in the previous chapter leads to the insight that Jesus' life and work centered in his trust in God as his Father. He redefined the kingdom of God in terms of a fictive household in which everyone, including the "sinners," has direct and unmediated access to God. This does not mean, however, that all of our historical knowledge about Jesus must be reduced to the single aspect of kinship imagery.

Jesus escapes simplifying definitions. He was a child of Galilee. Galilee was known for its diversity with regard to both its topography and population. Galilee had a lake with simple farmers who fished for a daily catch on age-old boats and lords who ran fish-salting and pottery industries. There were cities along the lakeshore and a few miles away. In these cities there were temples devoted to deities and emperors, a royal palace, military fortifications, mansions with mosaics floors that depicted Greco-Roman deities around whom aristocrats reclined to enjoy festive meals served by servant-slaves who could be from nearby peasant farming communities that were transformed into estates.

Galilee was multilingual, inhabited by pagans and Israelites, many of mixed marriage heritages upon whom Judeans looked down. Though not necessarily living in Samaria, Israelite Galileans were sometimes labeled as Samaritans because of either their real or alleged mixed parentage or simply their living for centuries among the Gentiles in the northern part of the country. Visiting Judean Pharisees came to teach and enforce the purity laws of the sacred writings. Jerusalem temple authorities appeared in time to collect the temple taxes (said to be the will of God) from impoverished people who tried to live according to ancestral traditions. In the peasant villages, family courtyards served as places for communal gatherings or sometimes as synagogical space for reciting and listening to the Torah.

Farmers in Galilee survived on small pieces of agricultural land. Landless tenant farmers worked for absentee lords in the cities, incurring huge debts. Records of these debts were kept in mansions and in "sacred places" far away—even in the Jerusalem temple. Sons of broken, distorted families sometimes tried to survive elsewhere. Some peasants who were forced from their lands turned to carpentry as a profession. Bandits, outcasts, and rebels escaped to the mountains and found shelter in caves. This is "the Galilee of the Gentiles" where people lived in darkness. Somewhere there, Jesus is to be found. He was not with his family and he did not practice his career (if he was a woodworker at all). He was a revolutionary and healer, teacher and helper.

Many features identified by Jesus scholars are not at odds with this pro-file. Actually, I am indebted to their discernment. Of course, there are aspects of some scholarship that I will not endorse. For example, I am not convinced that the subversive sayings and deeds of a Galilean peasant would originate in a highly sophisticated Greek philosophical school. [120] Yes, the revolutionary biography of an itinerant philosopher belonging to such a school can be compared with the life of a homeless traveler. Jesus as such a traveler would sometimes find housing in the fishing village Capernaum, where the extended family of a fisher-friend lived (see Mark 1:29), but sometimes he did not have a "nest" or a "hole," like creatures of nature (see Luke 9:58 [Q]). Yet we cannot do more than compare. The philosophical sophistication and domestication of subversive itinerancy developed after Jesus' lifetime. Subversive itinerancy occurred when some "Christian" fac-tion or other tried to find its own identity among synagogical and philo-sophical activities. These factions probably accomplished this by passing on and writing down Jesus' prophetic wisdom and accounts of his healing per-formances. It can be called "revolution historized" or "subversion memo-rized" or even "historicization of myth."

Likewise, I am unconvinced that Jesus' initial prophetic association with the Baptist led to a self-consciousness of being a Joshua of old and an attempt to lead God's covenant people over the river Jordan into a new promised land. It does not seem that he perceived himself as the agent of God who forgave the sins of the people. The allusion by the historian Josephus (*Vita* 2) to the "baptizer" Banus (who lived and acted in the desert similarly to John the Baptist) may be interpreted as a reference to someone who acted like John with a political motive as the "revived" prophet Elijah (see Mark 6:15). It therefore does not come as a surprise that John was imprisoned and eliminated by the powers that be (Josephus, *Ant.* 17.5.2.; Mark 6:17). It is also possible that the Gospel tradition was correct in saying that these authorities and some others were ignited by Jesus and thought him to be the Baptist resurrected (see Mark 6:14). This same Gospel tradi-tion, however, tried to rectify this image of Jesus.

Discerning the respective prophecies memorized and prophecies histori-cized in the messages of Gospel writers like Mark and Matthew (although not fully in concordance with each other) from the historical facts, we see an altogether different portrait of Jesus emerging from that of a typical prophet. It is a picture of a "sinner," away from his home village, trapped in a strained relationship with relatives, but experiencing a fantasy homecom-ing in God's kingdom. It is probably within such circumstances that an imaginary reality (which the Spirit of God created) brought about Jesus' altered consciousness of encountering the care of a Heavenly Father. He

120. See Horsley and Silberman, *Message and the Kingdom*, 3, 25, 47.

both attested to and lived this reality. Through the stories and letters of associates who were likewise empowered, either by Jesus' personal healing or by the tradition of his "memorized" healing, Jesus became the icon of God's mercy and love.

In the next chapter, I will argue that the ethical example that the First Testament Joseph figure fulfilled in Hellenistic-Semitic literature served as a model for the transmitters of the early Christian tradition. The Joseph tradition was also known to the authors of the Gospels of Matthew, Luke, and John. They found themselves (like others during the period of 70 C.E. to 135 C.E.) in synagogical controversies about Jesus' illegitimacy. They counteracted by positioning Jesus as the "son of Joseph, the son of Jacob." I will show that in Hellenistic-Semitic literature (like the *Testaments of the Twelve Patriarchs*) the "righteous" son of Joseph, despite defamation, became the ancestor of children whose sins were forgiven, who were given their daily bread, who were instructed to forgive others their trespasses; this man gave them their share of God's daily bread and requested God that they not be tempted to disobey their Father's will. Against this background, Greek-speaking Israelites who became Christians retold the life of the Jesus of history. For some of them, Jesus, despite slander, became the image of God's forgiveness of sin and daily care, thanks to the God of his father (see Gen 49:25), Joseph, son of Israel.

However, no Christian writing that originated between the years 30 C.E. and 70 C.E. records any knowledge about Joseph's connection with the Jesus of history. From this assumption, I believe a historical construct of Jesus' life within first-century Herodian Palestine can be built according to an ideal-type of a fatherless figure living in Galilee. It is not an inflation of historical probabilities to say that the following features of Jesus' life go together:

Records show he was born out of wedlock.

A father figure was absent in his life.

He was unmarried.

He had a tense relationship with his mother and siblings.

He was probably forced from farming to carpentry.

He carried sinfulness that led to an association with a revolutionary baptizer.

He experienced an altered state of consciousness in which God was present and acted like a Father.

He abandoned craftsmanship, if he ever was a woodworker.

He was homeless, and led an itinerant lifestyle along the lakeshore.

His journey seemed never to take him inside the cities Sepphoris and Tiberias, but was restricted to the plains, valleys, and hills of Galilee.

He assembled a core of close friends.

He defended fatherless children, patriarchless women, and other outcasts.

He called these outcasts "family" by resocializing them into God's household by empowering healing as an agent of the Spirit of God.

He offended village elders by his subversive teaching and actions.

He outraged Pharisees, Herodians, chief priests, and elders in Jerusalem
by criticizing the manipulative ploys and misuse of hierarchical power
by the temple authorities.

He was crucified by the Romans after an outburst of emotion at the outer
temple square.

He died under uncertain circumstances, but his body was not laid down
in a family tomb.

He was believed to have been taken up to the bosom of Father Abraham
to be among the "living dead" as the scriptures foretold.

He was believed to be God's beloved child who was already with God
before creation and who is now preparing a place that is actually
already present for those who still live by his cause.

In other words, what comes before and after Jesus at thirty seems to be
his fatherlessness. This constructed portrait is my understanding of the
Jesus of history and the Jesus of faith. It cannot be proved that this image is
a representation of the "real" Jesus. However, this ideal-type should be historically intelligible and explanatory with regard to textual evidence and
archaeological findings. Vice versa, it should rely on contemporary canonical and noncanonical texts, including archaeological artifacts, which have
to be interpreted in terms of a chronological stratification of relevant documents. It also would have to be congruent with the social stratification of
first-century Herodian Palestine.

In light of all of these prerequisites, I am profoundly uneasy with John
W. Miller's recent book, *Jesus at Thirty: A Psychological and Historical
Portrait*. Miller believes that he can explain Jesus' unmarried status from the
traditional viewpoint that Joseph died early in Jesus' lifetime. Jesus' being
the firstborn, would "[become] the breadwinner and family head at an early
age."[121] Miller refers to New Testament scholar Robert H. Stein, who wrote,
"[O]nly one thing we really know is that with the death of Joseph the
responsibilities of caring for the mother and family fell on the oldest son
Jesus. . . . Thus for the period after Joseph's death to the time of his ministry,
Jesus was the active breadwinner and responsible head of the family."[122]
Jesus would not have had the opportunity to be given by Joseph in marriage
since Joseph was already dead. Therefore he did not marry. His relationship
with his mother was special, tender, and compassionate. But it was the
"father's memory" that was "more precious to him than his living mother,

---

121. Miller, *Jesus at Thirty*, 36. See also Connick, *Jesus, the Man, the Mission*, 131.
122. Stein, *Jesus the Messiah*, 85, in Miller, *Jesus at Thirty*, 130, note 20.

who did not understand him and whom he turned away when she and his brothers came to take possession of him."[123]

As a "psychohistorian," Miller works "backward to childhood from analogous experiences in the life of the adult."[124] This represents the developmental school of psychology, which "profess[es] to tell us in any detail how human personality in all its complexity develops from childhood onward." [125] According to Miller, the Freudian model "elaborated by neo-Freudians" is the only recognized developmental model in this regard that "thus far not only survived empirical testing but demonstrated a remarkable capacity for interacting with historical disciplines in fruitful ways." Specifically, the research of Erik Erikson on "life-stage developments during early adulthood" and that of Daniel Levinson on the "Age Thirty Transition" direct Miller to ask why Jesus' "vocational achievements" occurred at the age of thirty.[126]

The research of Erikson and Levinson demonstrates that "the desire for 'intimacy' and marriage, and then having children and caring for them" is typical for men at the age of thirty. On the presumption of Erikson's "in-depth interviews with a cross section of forty American men" and of Levinson's enhancement with the help of "typical experience resulting from cross-cultural factors inherent to the complex task of becoming an adult," Miller applies the "Age Thirty Transition" complex to his understanding of Jesus' mission of the "salvation of the sinners" and Jesus' concern about the "fate of his people and the world" in light of the "mounting tensions with Rome."[127] The portrait of Jesus that emerges is that of "a father now himself with a 'family' of his own, one 'born not of blood nor the will of the flesh nor the will of man, but of God,'" someone with "extraordinary faith and intuitively wise 'father-like' talent for relating helpfully to all types of people and situations."[128] According to Miller, this behavior is "the fruit in part, no doubt, of an emotionally secure childhood and his [Jesus'] years of leadership in his deceased father's family." Miller wishes to see "Jesus' baptism and temptations as a turning point during which he terminated an increasingly sterile role as surrogate 'father'. . . . By means of this awakening and struggle he came to experience himself as 'son' of a gracious heavenly father."[129]

My uneasiness with Miller's psychohistorical analysis of Jesus concerns not his use of psychology as such. In a similar way, the bottom line of Albert Schweitzer's protest against the psychopathological studies of Jesus was not

---

123. Miller, *Jesus at Thirty*, 47.
124. Ibid., 36.
125. Ibid., 10.
126. Ibid., 77–95. Cf., e.g., Erikson, "Galilee Sayings"; Erikson, *Young Man Luther*; Levinson, *Seasons of a Man's Life*.
127. Miller, *Jesus at Thirty*, 89.
128. Ibid., 99.
129. Ibid., 81.

whether their psychoanalytical theories were correct. Of course, these psychoanalytical theories should have been tested, as Schweitzer the medically trained psychiatrist did. As a biblical scholar, he was concerned about the unsophisticated historical analyses of the textual evidence in the New Testament found in these studies.

It is Miller's academic prerogative to differ from other psychoanalyses of Jesus. However, from the perspective of biblical scholarship, the question should arise as to whether both the psychohistorical and cross-cultural analyses are based on evidence that will pass the test of both historical-critical exegesis and social-scientific criticism. For instance, the Lukan episode of the child Jesus in the temple would not be found even in the historical Jesus database of conservative researchers, and would be explained by social-scientific critics in light of child-rearing practices in the first-century Mediterranean context.[130] The cross-cultural support from the talmudic *Sayings of the Fathers* (*Avoth* 5.24), which Daniel Levinson gives to Erik Erikson's study of twentieth-century North-American individualistic-minded men, that age thirty is the "time in life when 'full strength' is attained,"[131] would not really pass a cultural-anthropological test either. It does not mean that the "Age Thirty Transition" could by no means be a factor in the life of first-century Mediterranean men. For example, in Gen 41:46, we find a reference to Joseph the patriarch, who was betrayed by his brothers but, at the age of thirty, was exalted over all the Egyptians. The trustworthiness of such a theory should, however, be tested to a larger extent as it has been done thus far and, then, its characteristics should be explained against the background of first-century Mediterranean personality types.[132] The genuine problems with regard to Miller's image of Jesus are:

1. His uncritical acceptance of the historicity of the patristic tradition (like John P. Meier and Marvin Cain) that Joseph died early in Jesus' life. [133]
2. His presupposition that Jesus must be the firstborn among the siblings of Mary, built upon the legend of the birth story.
3. His deductionistic inference that Jesus performed duties as a "surrogate father."
4. His conclusion that Jesus had an "emotionally secured childhood" because of "Jesus' love of the word *Abba* as a term for addressing God," his positive sayings about children, and the father-son relationship imagery in his parables.

---

130. See Pilch, "'Beat His Ribs."
131. Miller, *Jesus at Thirty*, 80.
132. See Malina, "Dealing with Biblical (Mediterranean) Characters."
133. Meier, *Marginal Jew*, 1:317; Cain, *Jesus the Man*, 30.

Almost none of the examples that Miller presents with regard to the father-son imagery are exegetically convincing. [134] In the next three chapters I will argue respectively that a trajectory of traditions about Joseph historically illustrates the probable legendary nature of Joseph as a surrogate father figure, that fatherlessness socially explains Jesus' trust in God as Father, and that Jesus' blessing of children fits into the social context of defending the fatherless.

---

134. See, esp. Miller, *Jesus at Thirty*, 39–40. The *qorban* text in Mark 7:9–13 is, in my opinion, the only evidence that Jesus cared for parents. If this episode historically goes back to Jesus, the detail of almost haggadic elements that feature in the whole episode and that are typical Markan features underline the possibility that we could call this controversy story "true fiction" rather than history. Nevertheless, the moral of this story is about temple critique in light of an anti-hierarchical protest against economical exploitation. It presumes a defends of "childlesses" similar to "fatherlesses" and not a devotion to patriarchs. If this story is about devotion to parents, it does not compromise the overall picture of the historical Jesus' attitude toward "family values" (cf. Osiek, "Jesus and Cultural Values").

CHAPTER 4

~

The Joseph Trajectory

The Joseph-Jesus relationship is a matter of "like father like son." In Mediterranean culture, at least, this is a common ideal. In this regard, we have in the Gospel of John (5:17) a Jesus saying, undoubtedly not authentic, that he is at work as his father is at work. In the Johannine context, this saying refers to deeds of healing and compassion, and a relationship between Jesus and God as his Father. The context also involves the outrage of the Pharisees that Jesus could dare to see himself as a child of God. F. C. Grant valued this Johannine phrase as a probable indication that the son Jesus stood in the vocational shoes of his father Joseph.[1] Jesus was a carpenter like his father, but typical to Johannine style, the author of the Fourth Gospel draws an analogy between the physical son-father relationship and the spiritual relationship between Jesus and his heavenly Father. Other examples of similar analogies are John's comparisons of physical birth with spiritual birth (3:6), natural water and bread with water and bread that bring about eternal life (4:13; 6:27), worshipping God either in Jerusalem or on the Gerizim Mountain in Samaria with worshipping God "in spirit and in truth" (4:21), and resuscitation from sleep with the resurrection from death (11:12).

Thus, according to the interpretation in the Fourth Gospel, it is quite possible to understand the relationship between Jesus and Joseph in this manner. However, it is doubtful that the relationship between Jesus and his heavenly Father could be analogous to the "working" of father and son (5:17) in the sense of their mutual craftsmanship. Nowhere in the Gospel of John do we find an indication that the Johannine school knows or makes use of the Markan tradition (6:3) that Jesus himself was a carpenter. We know that this tradition was changed by Matthew (13:55) to read "the carpenter's son." Luke simply ignores Mark's notation of Jesus (or Joseph) being a carpenter in the particular passage. Luke proffers only the question: "Isn't this Joseph's son?" (Luke 4:22).

---

1. Grant, "Economic Background of the New Testament," 96–114.

Apocryphal gospels, such as the second-century *Proto-James*, and other documents and fragments, such as *The Life of Joseph the Carpenter* and *Pseudo-Matthew*,[2] took over the Matthean hunch that Joseph was a carpenter but without elaboration. The latter two documents were written (maybe translated into Coptic and Latin respectively) during the period from the end of the fourth century to the sixth century. They mention only: (a) Joseph's righteousness, (b) his old age, (c) the death of his wife while his youngest son James was still a child, (d) the names of other siblings (taken over from evidence in the New Testament itself), and (e) that Joseph was eighty-nine years old when he took Mary as a wife, though he never slept with her, and that he lived to the age of one hundred eleven.

The title of *The Life of Joseph the Carpenter* bears witness to the notation. In the first century, we find only in the Gospel of Matthew evidence that Joseph the carpenter adopted Jesus as his son. However, the alluded analogy between father and son in this text does not concern craftsmanship or even Jesus' relationship with Joseph. What we actually find is a similarity between two Josephs: Joseph the widower who took the pregnant Mary into his house and Joseph the First Testament patriarch. The equivalent to the parallel of the two Josephs is the parallels between the character of Mary and that of Eve (Gen 4:1) and Hannah (1 Sam 1:11).[3] The Mary-Hannah parallel is found in *Proto-James* and in the above-mentioned dependent apocryphal documents.

In the Coptic Arabic version of *The Life of Joseph the Carpenter* (chapter 7), the correspondence between father and son pertains to geographical issues.[4] Characteristic of Mediterranean mores, the residential site of a family or clan is located at the burial place of the founder of the group. The tomb, in turn, is the place where a future leader is expected to be born. This leader will continue the work of the forefather. In *The Life of Joseph the Carpenter*, the tradition is that Jesus was born in Bethlehem, as it is in the New Testament Gospels where this tradition is also taken up (Matt 2:6;

---

2. Among the many publications available I have had make use of Hennecke, *New Testament Apocrypha*, 404–17; Manns, *Essais sur le Judéo-Christianisme*, 80–114; Robinson, "Coptic Apocryphal Gospels"; Schaberg, "Infancy of Mary of Nazareth"; Sellew, Heroic Biography and the Literary Intent."

3. Concerning the parallel of the two Josephs, see Manns, *Essais sur le Judéo-Christianisme*, 82, 87; concerning the parallel of Mary and Eve, see Thompson, *Bible in History*, 328–29: "In the story's opening [Genesis 2 and 3], all our characters bear cue-names. There is Adam 'the human' of the garden story (Gen. 2:7) and Eve, his wife, whose name is interpreted: 'the mother of all living' (Gen. 3:20). Adam has sex with his wife, who bears a child whom she names 'Cain' (Gen. 4:1). Adam's involvement, as far as the story is concerned, is not terribly important. It provides only the occasion of Eve's pregnancy; human fertility is not his to give but God's. When she gives birth Eve tells the audience: 'I have made a man with Yahweh!' Eve creates her children with God! Eve, the great mother of all, makes men. Her child 'Cain,' whose name puns with Eve's word *qaniti* ('to make'), has the name of 'creature.' Human life is born of god and woman. The child who is born is the creature, divine and human: he is us."

4. Manns, *Essais sur le Judéo-Christianisme*, 87.

Luke 2:4; John 6:41; 7:27, 41). In all of these instances, the relationship between Jesus of Nazareth and Joseph, whose ancestors were claimed to be from Bethlehem, is in focus.

This particular geographical tradition, explicit in Matthew and implicit in Luke and John, originated in the prophetic witness (Micah 5:2) against the supposedly mighty Judean royalty and in favor of an allegedly inferior ruler whose roots were in Bethlehem.[5] The Bethlehem referred to in Micah lies six miles southwest of Jerusalem: "But you, Bethlehem, in the land of Judah, are by no means least among the rulers of Judah; for out of you will come a ruler who will be the shepherd of my people Israel" (Matt 2:6, quoting Mic 5:2, NIV). The prophetic voice in Micah (chapters 2–5) was raised against the lack of righteousness among the elite in Jerusalem.

Bethlehem (i.e., Ephrath—see Gen 48:7) was the burial place of Rachel, wife of Jacob and mother of Joseph and Benjamin.[6] According to the source behind Gen 50:1–12, Jacob was buried in a cave in the field of Machpelah near Mamre, while Joseph's burial place, according to Joshua 24:32, is to be found at Shechem.[7] Part of the fabric of Israel's political history is the connection between Rachel's tomb (which lies on the road to Bethlehem) and Joseph's tomb (at the foot of the Gerizim and the Ebal mountains in Samaria). Because of this link, Bethlehem was an ideal place to symbolize the unity of the northern tribes (with Samaria as capital since the time of King Omri) and the southern tribes. According to 1 Samuel 16, David was born there to an Ephrathite family (see also Ruth 1–4). After being chosen as leader of the united Israelite tribes, David, however, did not decide on either Shechem (at that time the main cultic center of the northern tribes) or Bethlehem as his capital. He probably learned from Saul's experience who "had greatly diminished his own effectiveness by locating the capital in

---

5. There were two villages in ancient Israel with the name "Bethlehem." Apart from the one in Judah, the other one was situated in Zebulon, seven miles northwest from Nazareth (see Judg 12:8, 10).

6. Bethlehem (Bit-Lahmi) in Judah is first mentioned in the Amarna letters (ca. fourteenth century B.C.E.); see Murphy-O'Connor, *Holy Land*, 198–99.

7. "And Joseph's bones, which the Israelites had brought up from Egypt, were buried at Shechem in the tract of land that *Jacob* bought for a hundred pieces of silver from the sons of Hamor, the father of Shechem. This became the inheritance of Joseph's descendants" (Josh 24:32, NIV). Joseph's tomb is described from a Palestinian's perspective in *Pace Tour Guide* (167) as follows: "Just north of Jacob's well, right at the foot of Tell Balata [Mount Ebal], is the traditional site of Joseph's tomb. This rather simple white-domed building is believed to be Joseph's grave. His remains, according to the Old Testament, were carried from Egypt and buried here [Josh 24:32]. Others believe that the remains were buried in Hebron [see the Judean tradition as reported in Gen 50:12–13; cf. Murphy-O'Connor, *Holy Land*, 273–77, esp. 276–77]. The place was occupied by Israeli settlers who started a religious school in it at the beginning of the 1980s. Although Nablus [present-day Shechem] was transferred to the Palestinian Authority late in 1995, the site remained in the hands of the settlers. It is heavily guarded by the Israeli army and closed to visitors."

In Stephen's speech (Acts 7:15–16), Luke, relying on the Samaritan Pentateuch and not the Greek translation (LXX) of the Masoretic text (see Coggins, *Samaritans and Jews*, 122) says both Jacob and Joseph were buried at Shechem in the land that *Abraham* bought from the sons of Hamor.

the territory of the tribe to which he belonged."[8] Jerusalem was chosen instead, because of its neutrality.

During the time of Micah, Bethlehem was an insignificant village, but still remembered as the town of David that once symbolized the unification of the tribes of Judah (Jerusalem) and Joseph (Samaria). According to prophets such as Micah (see also Ezek 37:15–25 and Zech 10:16), the messiah who came from the roots of David (i.e., Bethlehem), would restore this unity again.[9] In Matthew's and Luke's Gospels, the story of the birth of Jesus the messianic child is imbued with both the "Davidic" and "Josephic" spirits. When the prophet Jeremiah speaks of a unified Israel that the messiah would bring about from the ruins of both North and South, he refers to its devastated past by mentioning Rachel who is weeping about her lost descendants (Jer 31:15). Matthew 2:17–18 quotes this within the context of the good tidings that the child Jesus outlived the onslaught of Herod the Great so that he could inaugurate this "new" kingdom.

However, the story of Herod the Great's infanticide also emphasizes an opposition from the Jerusalem royalty against the descendants of Joseph that goes way back in the history of the people of the "holy land." In about the middle of the eighth century B.C.E., the dominant belief in Israel was that Israel was God's covenanted people and that the cultic shrine at Bethel was the visible guarantee that Israel would continue to exist as a kingdom (see, e.g., Amos 7:10–13).[10] Among the evidence in the Pentateuch, Deut 33:13–17; Gen 37:1–11; and Gen 49:26 witness to the belief that Joseph was the legitimate successor of his father Jacob and not Judah.[11] According to this tradition, the cultic site to which God's people were attached was Bethel, also called Luz (Gen 28:19; 35:6). At Bethel, heaven and earth met as God entered into a covenant with Jacob and Jacob's children. Here, on the road between Bethel and Bethlehem (Ephrath), Rachel died and was buried (Gen 35:19).

---

8. Murphy-O'Connor, *Holy Land*, 199.

9. Micah mentions the link between Rachel's tomb and the land to the north by alluding to Gen 35:19-20, where Rachel's tomb is noticed in juxtaposition to Migdal Edar, in the vicinity of Shechem. The Hebrew for this location is also found in Micah 4:8, translated in the NIV as "watchtower of the flock."

10. For the interrelatedness between the prophetic traditions in the First Testament and the Joseph trajectory, I am specifically indebted to the research of my colleague at the University of Pretoria, Andries Breytenbach (see Breytenbach, "Herfsfees en die Koningsrite"; Breytenbach, "Meesternarratiewe, Kontranarratiewe en Kanonisering"; Breytenbach, "'Seun van Josef'"). For a treatise on the Pentateuch traditions regarding the two settlements in the land of Canaan that explains both the occupations of the center of the land (by the tribes Ephraim, Manasseh, and Benjamin) and the plain of Esdraelon in the north (by the house of Makir, the adopted [grand]son of Joseph born in Egypt), see Michaud, *L'Histoire de Joseph*, 77–135. Manasseh and Ephraim were born to Joseph by Asenath, daughter of Potiphera, priest of Heliopolis (On) in Egypt (cf. Gen 46:19). As Jacob legitimated Manasseh and Ephraim (Gen 48:8–12), Joseph did the same to Makir, the son of Manasseh who also was born in Egypt (cf. Gen 50:23b).

11. Genesis 49:26 ("Let all these rest on the head of Joseph, on the brow of the prince among his brothers," NIV) stands in clear opposition to Gen 49:10 ("The scepter will not depart from Judah, nor the ruler's staff from between his feet," NIV).

At the time of the centralization of the cult in Jerusalem, earnest attempts were made to disfavor and even to destroy the Bethel tradition (see, e.g., Hos 4:15, where the expression Beth Aven serves as a caconym for Bethel; Hos 10:5; Amos 5:5; 8:14). The prophet Hosea (1:4–5), for example, announced that the vengeance of God would be wreaked against the Northern Kingdom because of the "massacre" of Judeans in the Valley of Jezreel by Jehu, the king of the Northern Kingdom (see 2 Kings 9:1–10:28). According to Hosea, the termination of the covenant entered into at Bethel would be the punishment of God.

Jehu's treachery, an act of familial betrayal, is symbolized in the book of Hosea (1:2–9) by the prophet's marriage to a prostitute and the conception of his children from this adulterous union. Lo-Ammi, the name of the third sibling, is specifically an indication of the annulment of the covenant. This name means "for you are not my people, and I am not with you" (1:8). The separation between God and the Northern Kingdom is sealed by the prophet's divorce. Yet his reconciliation with his adulterous wife (3:1–5) symbolizes that God would keep the covenanted promises, though in an unconventional way (see Hos 2:21–23).

During the Second Temple period, a final attack was made on the Bethel tradition. The destruction of Samaria (capital of the Northern Kingdom since the reign of Omri; see 1 Kings 16:23) by the Assyrians (2 Kings 17:7–23) gave birth to this onslaught. In the Judean kingdom, reestablished after the Babylonian exile, the conviction was nurtured that the Israelites of the Northern Kingdom were replaced by outsiders (2 Kings 17:24–26). The northerners came to be labeled "Kutim," that is "the Samaritans." According to this conviction, the revival of the northern Israelite cult was a failed endeavor by the king of Assyria, who let one of the priests (who had been exiled from Samaria) come to live in Bethel and teach the Samaritans how to worship (2 Kings 17:25–28).[12]

For the Judeans, Jerusalem became the uncontested "city of David." What both David and Solomon intended to be an act of peacemaking became an ideological instrument par excellence during both the First Temple period and the Second Temple period to marginalize and silence opposition. David's choice of Jerusalem, a "neutral location,"[13] as the site of the official cult was a conciliatory venture to bring the North and the South into one royal household (2 Sam 5:1–11).

After Solomon, unity failed and Jerusalem functioned as the cultic center for the Southern Kingdom only. Jeroboam, ruler of the Northern Kingdom, was immediately advised to choose "Shechem in the hill country of

---

12. "The following section, v. 29–33, is evidently drawn from another tradition, for it contains a different story concerning the origin of the priests among the new colonists" (Montgomery, *Samaritans*, 449).

13. Breytenbach, "Meesternarratiewe, Kontranarratiewe en Kanonisering," 1171.

Ephraim," then Peniel, and finally Bethel as cultic sites (1 Kings 12:25–33—a passage colored by a southern bias). These sites were chosen mainly for two reasons: (1) the ancient traditions concerning Abram (Gen 12:6–8) and Jacob (Gen 28:10–27; 32:30–31), and (2) the traditions concerning the settlement of the descendants of Joseph. According to the traditions of the northern tribes, Joseph was the legitimate successor to lead the house of Abraham and Jacob to the center of the land.

The bias of the editorial reinterpretation of the Bethel tradition by Judean priests, as if the northern tribes were inherently defiled by pagan syncretism, should not be overlooked by a naive reading of the above-mentioned references in the First Testament. The domination of the Jerusalem cult should also be judged in the light of prophetic protests. The prophets brought the Judeans' attempt to ensconce God's sovereignty within the boundaries of Jerusalem as "city of David" to light. They challenged the royal household in Jerusalem and its priestly retainers not to ostracize their opponents.[14] According to the prophet Jeremiah (23:1–6; 33:14–26), a newborn Davidic king would reign righteously over both Israel and Judea in the period after the Babylonian exile (see also Hos 3:5). This prophetic voice seems to be ambivalent.

Similar apparently conflicting announcements occur in the book of Micah (chapters 2–5), which simultaneously support the continuance of the Davidic dynasty and criticize the exploitation of the peasants by the elite. Ezekiel prophesies in the same vein, using the metaphor of two tribal wood sticks:

> The word of the LORD came to me: "[Child of Humanity], take a stick of wood and write on it, 'Belonging to Judah and the Israelites associated with him.' Then take another stick of wood, and write on it, 'Ephraims's stick, belonging to Joseph and all the house of Israel associated with him.' Join them together into one stick so that they will become one in your hand.
>
> "When your countrymen ask you, 'Won't you tell us what you mean by this?' say to them, 'This is what the Sovereign LORD says: I am going to take the stick of Joseph—which is in Ephraim's hand—and of the Israelite tribes associated with him, and join it to Judah's stick, making them a single stick of wood, and they will become one in my hand.' Hold before their eyes the sticks you have written on and say to them, 'This is what the Sovereign LORD says: I will take the Israelites out of the nations where they have

---

14. For evidence of ostracism, see 2 Kings 10:1–17, and for examples of the prophetic voice, see Jer 11:18–12:6; 18:18–23; 36:5, 19, 26; 37:11–38:13; cf. Breytenbach, "Meesternarratiewe, Kontranarratiewe en Kanonisering," 1172. However, the same bias against the Jerusalem royalty is to be found among the people from the north (see, e.g., the revenge of Athaliah who tried to destroy the whole royal family in Jerusalem, 2 Kings 11:1–21).

gone. I will gather them from all around and bring them back into their own land. I will make them one nation in the land, on the mountains of Israel. There will be one king over all of them and they will never again be two nations or be divided into two kingdoms. They will no longer defile themselves with their idols and vile images or with any of their offenses, for I will save them from their sinful backsliding, and I will cleanse them. They will be my people, and I will be their God.

"'My servant David will be king over them, and they will all have one shepherd. They will follow my laws and be careful to keep my decrees. They will live in the land I gave to my servant Jacob, the land where your fathers lived. They and their children and their children's children will live there forever, and David my servant will be their prince forever.'" (Ezek 37:15–25, NIV).

In the period subsequent to the exile, the priestly elite continued with the process of ostracizing. This can be seen, for example, in the command the priests authorized as the "law of God," that the "men of Judah and Benjamin" must divorce their foreign wives and abandon the children born of such allegedly illegitimate marriages (Ezra 10; Neh 13:23–28). In turn, the metaphorical story of the prophet Jonah undermines the tendency to marginalize outsiders. On the other hand, 1 and 2 Chronicles try to restore the role of the monarchy and its priestly retainers. According to Ezekiel (11:14–21; 33:23–26), however, the Israelites who were not exiled thought themselves to be the people to whom God's promise made to Abraham applies. However, one reads in 2 Chron 36:17–20) that nobody among God's people was spared by Nebuchadnezzar and, subsequently, no "true believer" could possibly be found in Jerusalem or Judea; "the land enjoyed its sabbath rests" until God made the king of Persia return God's people to reestablish the cult in Jerusalem (2 Chron 36:21–23). Supported by birth records in the books Ezra and Nehemiah, the returning exiles were designated as the "true" and "pure" inheritors of the land. Against this claim, one reads in 2 Kings 25:12 (deliberately changed by priestly writers in 2 Chron 36:17–20), that peasants ("some of the poorest people of the land") were left behind in Judea by the commander of Nebuchadnezzar's imperial guard "to work the vineyards and fields." Against this background, a postexilic prophet describes the truth and righteousness of God by specifying both Jerusalem's atrocities and God's sustenance for the needy:

Therefore this is what the Sovereign LORD says:
  "My servants will eat,
    but you will go hungry;

my servants will drink,
    but you will go thirsty;
my servants will rejoice,
    but you will be put to shame.
My servants will sing
out of the joy of their hearts,
    but you will cry out
    from anguish of heart
    and wail in brokenness of spirit.

         . . .

Whoever invokes a blessing in the land
    will do so by the God of truth;
he who takes an oath in the land
    will swear by the God of truth.
For the past troubles will be forgotten
    and hidden from my eyes.
Behold, I will create
    new heavens and a new earth
The former things will not be remembered.

         . . .

for I will create Jerusalem to be a delight
    and its people a joy.
I will rejoice over Jerusalem
    and take delight in my people;
the sound of weeping and of crying
    will be heard in it no more.
Never again will there be in it
    an infant who lives but a few days,
    or an old man who does not live out his years.
                        (Isa 65:13–20, NIV)

This positive attitude toward the poor is also to be found in literature that refers to the period prior to the Davidic dynasty and the establishment of the temple in Jerusalem. At the consummation of the period of the Judges, Hannah's hymnal prayer (1 Sam 2:1–10) also attested both to God's ubiquitous sovereignty and to God's act of humbling the strong and exalting the week. The background of Hannah's prayer is her unusual presence as a woman in the shrine at Shiloh (after she gave birth to the prophet Samuel who was miraculously conceived) and the references to the exploitative behavior of priests (Eli's sons) in 1 Sam 1:21–28 and 2:12–17.

The history of Eli, the chief priest of the shrine at Shiloh, ties in with our interest in the interrelatedness between Joseph the patriarch and the gospel traditions in the New Testament about Jesus, son of Joseph, son of Eli (Luke 3:23). According to John's Gospel, the Pharisees belittled Jesus because Joseph's family was known to them (6:42). Their accusation was that Jesus was not a "child of Abraham" as they were. He, and not they, was therefore "illegitimate" (8:42), a "sinner" (9:16), a "Samaritan" (8:48).

The traditional Pharisaic version sees the origin of the Samaritans "in the events related in 2 Kings 17." According to this view, the Samaritans were "a mixture of pagans and inhabitants of the Northern Kingdom that had not been deported."[15] The Samaritans themselves furiously denied this denunciation that had already become widespread during the first century C.E.,[16] as can specifically be seen in Josephus's *Antiquities*.[17] By this time, the opposition of the Judeans (and particularly of the Jerusalemites) to the Samaritans is "clear and unequivocal."[18] R. Pummer puts it as follows:

> . . . [the] modern critical view . . . recognizes that antagonism
> between north and south in Israel existed for many centuries, but
> it also realizes that there was no sudden break that brought the
> separation of Jews and Samaritans. . . . If one wants to name a
> definite date when the two communities began to exist as sep-
> arate entities, it would be the end of the 2nd cent. B.C.E. when
> John Hyrcanus[19] [captured Shechem[20] and] destroyed the Temple
> on Mt. Gerizim and the Samaritans in all probability, like other
> groups [e.g., the Pharisees and the Essenes], began to adapt cer-
> tain passages in the Pentateuch to their particular theology.[21]

15. Pummer, *Samaritans*, 3.

16. See the booklets of A. Ishak, Samaritan priest and president of the Higher Community of the Samaritan Religion, *History and Religion of the Samaritans*; and of H. W. Kahen, priest of the Samaritan Community, *Samaritan History*.

17. See especially Egger, *Josephus Flavius und die Samaritaner*.

18. Coggins, *Samaritans and Jews*, 53 (see Josephus, *Ant.* 11.96–97; John 4:9).

19. See Josephus (*A.J.* 13.9.1; *B.J.* 1.22.6). These expansionist activities should not be seen as driven by orthodox zeal. For further military operations by Hyrcanus's sons, Antigonus and Aristobulus, not long before 107 B.C.E. and by the Hasmonean Alexander Jannaeus in 88 B.C.E., see Josephus (*A.J.* 13.10.1–3; *B.J.* 1.2.7) and Josephus (*A.J.* 13.14.1–2; *B.J.* 1.4.4) respectively. Cf. Montgomery, *Samaritans*, 79–81.

20. See Montgomery, *Samaritans*, 79. According to Montgomery, this happened in the year 128 B.C.E. Josephus relates that John Hyrcanus crushed the "Kuthean sect." This expression was a pejorative label for the Samaritans. The label refers to the "Judean" report in 2 Kings 17:24 that the king of Assyria brought people from, among other pagan places, Babylon and Kuthah to dwell in Samaria to replace the people of Israel (cf. Pummer, *Samaritans*, 3). Kahen, *Samaritan History*, 9, does not mention the replacement of Israelites, though it refers to "Sinharib, King of Asure" who "destroyed its [the Samaria kingdom's] cities and scattered its people." However, "both Jewish and Samaritan testimony concerning the origin of their division must be rejected as unreliable" (Coggins, *Samaritans and Jews*, 56). Cf. Eybers, "Relations between Jews and Samaritans." Eybers unconvincingly argues that the schism originated at the occasion of the return of some of the exiled Judeans because of the degree by the Persian king Cyrus.

21. Pummer, *Samaritans*, 3.

This development could explain the striking similarities between Samaritan beliefs and those of the Sadducees, the party that came forth from Hyrcanus's Maccabean family. The "close relationship in theology and practice of the Samaritans with the later Sadducees, who were the party of the hierarchy, can best be explained by the supposition of the maintenance of intercourse between the priests of Jerusalem and of the Shechemites."[22] Correspondence in this regard (such as attesting to the five books of Moses as the only authoritative scriptures and denouncing the belief in resurrection) could be ascribed to the power of the stronger party to enforce conformation. However, conformation with "orthodoxy" does not necessarily make people sociologically acceptable, specifically by "puritans" trapped within an ideology that is based on a social and ethnic purity line! This can be seen in the fact that the only two references to Shechem that appear in First Testament pseudepigraphical writings reveal a hostile attitude. This antagonism of the Judeans toward the Samaritans is recorded in Josephus, the New Testament, and talmudic literature.

Today, research has established the scholarly opinion that the "Samaritans are associated not with Samaria but with Shechem."[23] A more appropriate geographical designation used by Josephus for the people who generally came to be known as Samaritans, is therefore "Shechemites."[24] In the Wisdom of Jesus Son of Sirach (50:25–26), the contempt for the Samaritans is clear: "With two races is my soul vexed; and the third is no nation: with the dwellers of Seir and Philistia, and with the foolish race that sojourns in Shechem." This is likewise true in the *Testament of Levi* (chapter 7): "From this day will Shechem be called the City of Fools."[25] In rabbinical literature, a separate treatise is taken up in the Mishnah tractate *Masseket Kutim* ("Tractate on the Samaritans").[26]

Not everything in the Talmud concerning the Samaritans is negative. A saying of the "very conservative" Rabbi Simon ben Gamaliel (ca. 165 C.E.) that is frequently quoted in the Mishnah is his remark that "every command the Samaritans keep, they are more scrupulous in observing than Israel." Therefore, "a Samaritan is like a full Jew."[27] But then, applied to sabbatical limits (*Gemara* 57a), among others, one picks up the antagonism in

---

22. Montgomery, *Samaritans*, 72.

23. Coggins, *Samaritans and Jews*, 9. Cf. Wright, "Samaritans at Shechem."

24. Montgomery, *Samaritans*, 70.

25. Citations in Montgomery, *Samaritans*, 154–55.

26. Montgomery, *Samaritans*, 165–66: "It is now generally recognized that its [the Talmud] basis, the Mishnah, was completed by the end of the IInd Century A.C., while the commentary thereon, the Gemara, was not finally redacted, at least in the case of the Babylonian Talmud, until the VIth Century."

27. In this regard, one has to be reminded that the Talmuds of Babylon and Jerusalem and their additional clusters of Toseftas originated over a long period of time. But it is also acknowledged that some traditions go back to the period of formative Judaism during the time of the New Testament. (R. Simon b. Gamaliel was the father of Juda ha-Nasi, who was responsible for editing the Mishnah.) Cf. Montgomery, *Samaritans*, 169–70; also note 8.

Masseket Kutim 16 (see also *Nidda* 7.4): "This is the rule: Whatever they are suspected in, they are not to be believed in."[28]

The designation "Kutim" for the Samaritans is intended to be negative. This label goes back to the first century and beyond. Josephus (*Bellum Judaicum* 1.63) reports that John Hyrcanus crushed the "Kuthean sect." He referrs to the "Judean colored" report in 2 Kings 17:24 that the king of Assyria brought people from, among other pagan places, Babylon and Kuthah to dwell in Samaria, displacing the people of Israel. In the First Testament, including 1 Maccabees, Kuthah refers to people somewhere in the western Mediterranean, probably either the Greeks or the Romans. In the Dead Sea Scrolls, Kuthah sometimes refers to the people of Assyria and sometimes either to the Egyptians or the Chaldeans, calling them the end-time enemies.[29] According to talmudic thought, the world was divided in line with these categorizations: Judeans, Samaritans, and Gentiles.[30]

This particular division is also evident in Acts 1:8. Samaritans were considered to be "Mamzerim," that is, people of uncertain parentage or illegitimate.[31] In the talmudic Tractate *Kiddushin* 75a (cf. *Mass Kut* 27) they were treated as "bastards."[32] A mishnah qualifies the status of the Samaritans with respect to marriage arrangements of the Jerusalem cult in like terms: "They are the people of uncertain condition (i.e., with whom one may not marry): those of unknown parentage, foundlings, and Samaritans."[33] The *Gemara* (*Nidda* 74b) also classes the "sect" among those peoples (Ammonites, Moabites, Egyptians, Edomites, and Nethinim [eunuchs, i.e., descendants of the ancient slaves]) whom priests are forbidden to marry. If the regulation of Deut 23:3–5 was followed, the Samaritans could not hope to marry Judeans until the tenth generation (which is practically indefinite). This application is actually made in *Kiddushin* 75a.

The Johannine report (4:1–26) of Jesus talking to the Samaritan woman at "Jacob's well" is all but an innocent tale. The well is situated on the plot of land "Jacob had given to his son Joseph." The land is near the Samaritan town of Sychar. The woman notes that Jacob and his sons drank from this well. Here again we have an indication of the dualistic Johannine mentality: the *physical* Joseph and his ancestors drank the physical water from the well, but the *spiritual* son of Joseph, Jesus, gives the water of eternal life.

The fact that this story pertains to a Samaritan woman is particularly striking. It is possible that the words "Judeans do not associate with Samaritans" (John 4:9) could be a euphemism for intermarriage. Of the

---

28. Montgomery, *Samaritans*, 170.
29. For textual references, see Egger, *Josephus Flavius und die Samaritaner*, 179–92.
30. Montgomery, *Samaritans*, 178.
31. Ibid., 181.
32. Ibid., 180–81.
33. Ibid., 181.

"principal points in which Judaism condemned the Samaritans, there is none more important and significant than its attitude toward women."[34] It capitalizes specifically on sexual matters. For example, *Nidda* (4.1) imbues a spirit that could throw light on Jesus' healing, probably authentic, of the suffering woman who had been bleeding for twelve years (Mark 5:25–29; Luke 8:43–48; Matt 9:20–24): "The Samaritan women are menstruous from the cradle."

The notation of Sychar in the above-mentioned Johannine story is understood by Eusebius and Jerome to be the site of ancient Shechem.[35] In the light of archaeological evidence, there can be no serious doubt that there were contacts with the Shechemites over several periods: in patriarchal times (see Genesis 34), the period of settlement (see Joshua 24), the first attempt to establish kingship in Israel (see Judg 8:30–9:57), and the circumstances surrounding the division of the kingdom after the death of Solomon (see 1 Kings 12).[36]

Ancient Shechem is today called Tell Balatah. The present-day Samaritan community in Nablus likes to identify its town near the Gerizim Mountain with old Shechem.[37] Nablus is the modern name of the city Neapolis ("New City"), which the emperor Vespasian founded but which the Roman writer Pliny (*Natural History* 14) assigned to a place originally called Mabartha. The ancient mosaic map of Madaba (in modern Jordan) also distinguishes between Neapolis and Shechem.

Sychar itself has now come to be identified with Ain Askar, which lies 1250 meters northeast of Jacob's Well. However, the ruins of Nablus extend a distance east of the modern town. It could be that (because of text corruption in the Gospel of John) Shechem (i.e., Nablus) accidentally became Sychar.[38] In John's Gospel, as in the case of Luke-Acts, we have the allusion to the Judean division of the world into Judea, Samaria, and Galilee/Gentiles. A clear distinction between Jerusalem and Sychar (Shechem) is made in the story line of the first five chapters of the Gospel. Over against both the Judeans in Jerusalem (2:12–25, esp. 23–25) and the Galileans in Cana (2:1–11) and Capernaum (4:43–45) who put their trust in Jesus because of their physical experiences of his heroic deeds to humankind that uphold finiteness, the Samaritans of Sychar believed in him as the savior of the world by virtue of the spiritual water he gave them to drink so that they could receive infinite life. The story line concludes with another scene in Jerusalem, at the pool of Bethesda, where the Judeans severely oppose Jesus, who proclaims that he is God's son (5:1–47).

---

34. Ibid., 179.
35. Ibid., 19–21.
36. Coggins, *Samaritans and Jews*, 104–5; Wright, "Samaritans at Shechem."
37. Kahen, *Samaritan History*, 8; Ishak, *History and Religion of the Samaritans*, 23.
38. Montgomery, *Samaritans*, 21.

Based on an interpretation of available textual evidence in the First Testament, Priest Hasanein Wasef Kahen of the Samaritan Community in Nablus explained in 1966 that the establishment of the Judean cult in Jerusalem was the result of a wrong political evaluation: "King Daoud who is the descendent of Yahuda tribe moved the capital to Jerusalem instead of Nablus."[39] According to this tradition, David thought that building the capital of a united kingdom in a neutral place (and not at "the political and religious capital of the kingdom Nablus") could contribute to "supervising successfully all parts of the kingdom." After that, Solomon constructed the temple in Jerusalem. This was built "by human hands" (see the tradition used in Stephen's speech in Acts 7:48–49), while God's tent, the tabernacle, was still "erected . . . on a big rock that can be seen in Gerizim Mountain until now."[40]

In agreement with the *Samaritan Book of Joshua* in Arabic (chapter 43),[41] retold slightly differently by representatives of the present-day Samaritan community in Nablus,[42] the Samaritans consider themselves as "original Israelites whom the Jews split off in a schism under Eli who moved the ark of the covenant from Shechem to Shiloh."[43] They claim to be descendants of Ephraim and Manasseh, sons of Joseph born in Egypt. The mother of Ephraim and Manasseh is Aseneth, the Gentile daughter of the Egyptian Potiphera (Gen 41:45, 50), priest at Heliopolis (On). Manasseh and Ephraim are the children God gave to Joseph and they were, according to Genesis 48:1–21, legitimized by the head of the covenanted family, Jacob (Israel), by a Near Eastern judicial practice of adoption (see esp. Gen 48:12).

Against the claim that Jerusalem is the "city of David," the Johannine school knew the ancient northern tradition that the nascence of the messiah, son of David, should rather be sought at Rachel's tomb at Ephrath (Bethlehem), where Rachel (Jacob's wife and mother of Joseph) died during Jacob's journey from Bethel.

Like Joseph the patriarch, victim of slander, rejected by his own people, sold for forty pieces of gold but exalted over all the Egyptians at the age of thirty (Gen 41:46), the son of Joseph from the Gospel tradition, Jesus of

---

39. Kahen, *Samaritan History*, 8.
40. Ibid., 5.
41. Coggins, *Samaritans and Jews*, 122.
42. Kahen, *Samaritan History*, 5–8; Ishak, *History and Religion of the Samaritans*, 8–16.
43. Pummer, *Samaritans*, 3. The intention of the beginning of Jesus' birth record in Luke (3:23), totally different from the ending of the genealogy found in Matt 1:16, requires more research in the light of the common tradition of the parallel between Joseph the First-Testament patriarch and Jesus. Luke's way of articulating this parallel is very striking: "And Jesus was about thirty years old [cf. Gen 41:46 with regard to Joseph] when he began [his ministry as Israel's messiah] against the background [the Greek participle ὢν is seen as circumstantial] of his sonship, so it was thought [ὣς ἐνομίζετο]: son of Joseph, son of Eli." Could it be that Luke thought of the messiah as someone who would "revive" an era before Israel's division began (in accordance with the Samaritan sources) in the time of Eli?

Nazareth, was hated by the Judeans and belittled as demon possessed, a sinner, a Samaritan, an illegitimate person. But like father like son, just as Joseph the patriarch became an example of compassion and forgiveness (Gen 50:17), Jesus, in Johannine terms, loved the cosmos (i.e., the Judeans) despite its hate.

Very few things that Joseph did are mentioned in the Gospel tradition. The only things we read about are the references to his righteousness, his Davidic ancestry, his dream and the angel's conversation with him, and his marriage to Mary (who stands in the line of the "impure" women Tamar, Rahab, Ruth, and Bathsheba). Matthew depicts Joseph in legendary fashion as taking his family—Mary and the child Jesus—to Egypt. With a fulfillment formula, Matthew (2:15) quotes the prophet Hosea (11:1) that God called back his child from Egypt to settle in Galilee. Galilee is referred to in Isa 9:1, 1 Macc 5:15, and Matt 4:15 as "Galilee where the heathens live." (Remember Hosea's connection with the Joseph tradition in terms of his marriage to an impure woman so that God's sovereignty to act outside the conventional cultic structures could be proclaimed.) Matthew also narrates an attempt by Herod the Great to kill the "newborn king" (Matt 2:18). Matthew reports this attempt in terms of another fulfillment quotation, taken from Jer 31:15: "Rachel weeping for her children . . . because they are no more." (Remember the context within which the prophet argues. While holding on to the importance of the Davidic household, he nevertheless expects a totally new beginning in order to make an end to the atrocities of the monarchs and their priestly retainers.)

The Gospel of Luke does not share this material from Matthew, but clearly has knowledge of the tradition that Bethlehem is the location of the Joseph family. He also knows that the origin of the savior of all people (Judeans, Samaritans, and Galileans alike), according to the prophets, is not in Jerusalem but in Bethlehem. When Luke, in the speech of the "Hellenist outsider" Stephen in Acts 7:55–56, draws an analogy between Stephen and Jesus by retelling the story of the patriarchs, research shows that Luke is dependent not on the Judean (Masoretic) but on the Samaritan Pentateuch.[44] In this speech (7:1–53), as well as the record about the "Samaritan mission" headed by Philip (8:1–4), the controversy between the two tribes of Judah and Joseph is to be read between the lines.

Whatever the origin of the Stephen-Philip group could be, they clearly did not share the majority view of the Judeans with regard to the Samaritans. According to this view, the Samaritans were descendants of foreigners who settled in the North after the fall of Samaria and that the "true" ten tribes were still in exile in some far distant land. The Samaritan mission implies an acceptance of the Samaritans as part of God's people (as the Samaritans themselves have always maintained). Perhaps the Stephen-Philip group

---

44. See esp. Scobie, "Origins and Development," 393–96.

had in mind the great prophetic hopes (Jeremiah, Ezekiel, Zechariah) for a reunion of North and South. Now that the new age had dawned, the time for such a reunion had come.[45]

Matthew's notation (also in other Gospel traditions) of forgiving one's brother is one of the central characteristics of the portrayal of Jesus. The motive of compassion and forgiveness of sin by Joseph the patriarch is also the most outstanding theme in the intertestamental pseudepigraph the *Testaments of the Twelve Patriarchs*.[46] The Gospel tradition shares and makes use of this tradition in striking ways in its depiction of Jesus, as noted by H. W. Hollander:

> [I]t is the patriarch Joseph above all who plays a pre-eminent role in the ethics of the Testaments. Not only in his farewell-discourse is Joseph put forward as a good example for his sons, but his brothers too refer to him on their deathbeds, exhorting their sons to be like Joseph. He was one who kept himself free from adultery, who never stopped loving his brothers, who was full of mercy, compassion and forgivingness, who humiliated himself. He was a righteous man tried by God and rewarded and exalted afterwards.[47]

In the *Testament of Benjamin* (4:2) one reads, "The good person has not a dark eye. For he shows mercy to all people, even though they are sinners" and, in 4:4d, "on the poor person he has mercy; with the weak he feels sympathy."[48] In the *Testament of Zebulon* (6:5; 7:3f.), the same attitude toward the poor and feeling of sympathy toward the weak are described as virtues of the patriarch Zebulun in imitation of the attitude and feeling of Joseph.[49] In the *Testament of Gad* (4:1–2), in a passage where Gad instructs his children, a remarkable phrase appears that the Gospel tradition attributes to Jesus: Gad reveals that "lawlessness" against the Lord amounts to disobedience to the words of God's "commandments concerning the love of one's neighbour, and its sins against God."[50] These instructions clearly go together with the confession of one's own sin and repentance and an ongoing forgiveness of the sin of others (see *T. Gad* 6:3–4, 7).

Here we have a clear resemblance of the Matthean Jesus' words in the Lord's Prayer (Matt 6:12) and in his identification of the essence of the Law and the Prophets (22:37–40). These words in the *Testament of Gad* refer to Gad's memory that Joseph wronged him several times. He also reminds

---

45. Ibid., 399–400.
46. Cf. Hollander, *Joseph as an Ethical Model*; Sklar, "Fighter of Horizons"; Zerbe, *Non-Retaliation in Early Jewish and New Testament Texts*; Argyle, "Influence of the Testaments," 256–58.
47. Hollander, *Joseph as an Ethical Model*, 65.
48. Ibid., 69–70. The Greek in the *Testament of Benjamin* 4:4d contains references to mercy shown to the poor (πὲνηϚ) and sympathy to the helpless (ἀσθενήϚ).
49. Hollander, *Joseph as an Ethical Model*, 73.
50. Sklar, "Fighter of Horizons," 51.

himself of his hatred toward Joseph, so bitter that he "very often ... wanted to kill him" (*T. Gad* 2:1), and of his (and Judah's) own covetousness by selling Joseph for "thirty pieces of gold" (cf. *T. Gad* 2:3–4).

In light of these quotations, powerful parallels exist between the Jesus of faith as recorded in the Gospel tradition and Joseph the patriarch as depicted in the *Testaments of the Twelve Patriarchs*. This deliberate resemblance should not surprise us. In the *Testaments of the Twelve Patriarchs*, next generations are instructed to imitate "our father Joseph." It is therefore noteworthy, also with regard to the first-century Josephus, that the "biblical Joseph's relationship with his brothers emerges as that part of the story which is most similar to Josephus' own life"[51] (compare *Ant.* 2.16 with *Vita* 314, 306, 333, 353, 389).

In her work, *The Figure of Joseph in Post-Biblical Literature*, Maren Niehoff finds that "for one reason or another, Joseph seems to represent for each narrator a certain Idealtype."[52] The same is true with regard to Matthew's Joseph and the Joseph depicted in the romance *Joseph and Asenath*. Whereas the *Testaments of the Twelve Patriarchs*, in its present form, is dated to the second or third century C.E. but actually goes back to probably the second century B.C.E., *Joseph and Aseneth* is dated to between 100 B.C.E. and 115 C.E.[53]

The latter is a Hellenistic-Semitic romance that focuses on God's intervention in the life of Joseph the patriarch (parallel to the Joseph in the Gospel tradition) to take Aseneth, an "impure" woman, though a virgin, into his house. It is a story of a "holy marriage." Most striking is the reference (in the shorter constructed version of Marc Philonenko)[55] where Sophia is replaced by the figure Metanoia (referring to Aseneth): "And Metanoia is a virgin, very beautiful and pure and chaste and gentle; and God Most High loves her, and all his angels do her reverence" (*Jos. As.* [Ph] 15:7–8).[54] A longer constructed version (that of Christoph Burchard) reads as follows: "(What a) foolish and bold (woman) I (am), because I have spoken with frankness and said that a man came into my chamber from heaven; and I did not know that (a) god came to me" (*Jos. As.* 17:9 [B]).[55]

One has to keep in mind that Aseneth's virginity is not mentioned in the Genesis account (Gen 41:45, 50).[56] However, both the nature of Joseph's marriage to Aseneth and her virginity were already widespread literary topics by

---

51. Niehoff, *Figure of Joseph*, 101.

52. Ibid., 52.

53. Cf. Chesnutt, "From Text to Context," 286.

54. Philonenko, *Joseph et Asenath*. Quoted in Standartinger, "From Fictional Text," 309.

55. Burchard, *Untersuchungen zu Joseph und Asenath*. Quoted in Standartinger, *Frauenbild im Judentum*, 311.

56. It is possible, as Knud Jeppesen ("Then Began Men," 158–63; esp. 162–63) suggests with regard to other issues (including sexual matters), that reports in Genesis and Exodus react against tendencies in extrabiblical pseudepigrapha that depict God humanlike. Jeppesen refers, among others, to *Jubilees* (and the Septuagint), a text contemporary to *Joseph and Aseneth*.

the first-century C.E. For example, Josephus refers to their "most distin-guished marriage" and Aseneth's virginity (*Jos. As.* 2.9).[57] This reference alone rules out the possibility that the author of *Joseph and Aseneth* took this topic over from the evidence in the New Testament. What is in all prob-ability the case, is that both the Gospel tradition and documents such as *Joseph and Aseneth* share a common idealization of Joseph's holy marriage. It is furthermore remarkable to notice that "rabbinic Midrash is . . . con-cerned with Aseneth's alien origin and [that] this disturbing fact is accounted for in numerous ways."[58]

There are New Testament scholars who regard both the *Testaments of the Twelve Patriarchs* and *Joseph and Aseneth* as totally or to a great extent dependent on the New Testament. This opinion is not convincing.[59] Arguments, however, will take us on a road that does not fit the purpose of the present study. My concern is to focus on the references to the corre-spondence between father and son, between Joseph and Jesus. Actually, in this regard, it is highly problematic to refer to Joseph as the father of Jesus at all. These references do not occur in writings prior to the beginning of the separation of the Pharasaic synagogue and the church after the destruc-tion of Jerusalem in 70 C.E. and the termination of the earliest Jesus move-ment in Jerusalem.

No known father played a role in the life of the historical Jesus. Such a conclusion has far-reaching consequences for historical Jesus research. It seems that Joseph did not die early in Jesus' life. Joseph actually entered the scene rather belatedly, after Jesus had been crucified. For Greek-speaking Israelites, Joseph was an ethical paradigm. For Pharisees, he was the sym-bolic adversary of Judah, the forefather of people who either came from the pagan world or mixed with them. In other words, the Joseph people were regarded by the Judeans as bastards because they were a mixture of the chil-dren of God and Gentiles.

Who claimed first that the fatherless Jesus was the son of Joseph? Was it the Pharisees who regarded such a charge as a denotation of illegitimacy? Or was it the Greek-speaking Christians among the Israelites who regarded such a claim as a denotation of the intervention of God who turns slander

---

57. Cf. Niehoff, *Figure of Joseph*, 106. Niehoff refers also to Philo's knowledge of the "marriage as a social distinction" (107).

58. See Aptovitzer, "Aseneth, the Wife of Joseph"; Niehoff, *Figure of Joseph*, 107.

59. With regard to the *Testaments of the Twelve Patriarchs*, see esp. De Jonge, *Testaments of the Twelve Patriarchs*, 96–110. With regard to *Joseph and Aseneth*, see Price, "Implied Reader Response." Over against De Jonge, Hollander ("Joseph as an Ethical Model," 10) would argue that the testaments "are certainly not a Christian composition." However, this does not mean that I deny any Christian interpolation at all. The reference in the *Testament of Joseph* to the "lamb of God" born from a vir-gin who takes away the "sin of the world" is in all probability such an interpolation. These arguments concern a set of complicated issues with regard to intracanonical relatedness, the order of passages caused by editorial activity, probable and less probable hypotheses regarding dates of documents, of the clustering of "canonical" groups of literature and locations of the audiences of these documents, corpora of documents in order to expect knowledge thereof, and so forth.

into exaltation? We do not know. What is important, though, is that these two different perspectives relate to the way one looks at Jesus! The eye is the lamp of the body (Matt 6:22). If you look with an evil eye as his *physical* brothers and sisters did, then he is insane (Mark 3:21), filled with an evil spirit (3:30); if you look with a good eye as his *spiritual* brothers and sisters did, he is the child of God, filled with the Spirit of God (1:9–11), the savior who casts away the evil spirit!

KEEP ON WALKING

This chapter started with a reference to the tomb of Rachel, which is on the road from Bethel to Bethlehem. In Mediterranean culture, as in Africa and elsewhere, tombs of special patriarchs, matriarchs, martyrs, or prophets are of crucial cultic and political importance.[60] The tombs of Rachel and Joseph have been special places of veneration up to this day. However, one of the Jesus sayings from the Sayings Gospel Q, which can probably be regarded as authentic, urges potential followers of his cause to "leave the dead to bury their own dead." The context of this saying in both the Gospels of Matthew (8:21) and Luke (9:59) is the veneration of the dead, which is used as an excuse not to follow Jesus on his journey of subverting conventional wisdom. More or less the same sort of saying can be found in the *Gospel of Thomas* 42: "Keep on walking."

Luke interprets this Jesus saying within an apocalyptic frame of reference and against the breach between Jerusalem and Samaria (cf. Luke 9:51–53). Luke 9:54 refers to the hostile attitude of the Jesus movement in Jerusalem (transparent in the reaction of the two disciple brothers James and John) toward the Samaritans. Samaria is compared with Sodom and Gomorrah (cf. Gen 19:24). The two brothers, as spokesmen for the Twelve, request fire down from heaven to destroy Samaria, provoking a reprimand from Jesus. Genesis reports that the family of Lot was advised not to look back but to keep on walking (Gen 19:17). Lot's wife did not, and she became petrified (Gen 19:26). According to Luke's apocalyptic message, nothing can warrant such behavior: "No one who puts his hand to the plow and looks back is qualified for God's kingdom" (Luke 9:62).

Therefore, those who would like to participate in Jesus' itinerary should take note of what the Samaritan woman in John's Gospel does. She responds positively to a similar Jesus saying by which Jesus shows his indifference to the cultic issue of whether "sinners" venerate their forefathers on

---

60. For the information on this particular topic, I am especially indebted to the unpublished article of Cathleen Corley, "Gender and Class." See also the independent but similar conclusions reached by Philip Sellew in 1996, "Death, Body, and the World," 530–34. I am responsible for drawing the parallel between the Sayings Gospel Q, the *Gospel of Thomas*, and the Gospel of John.

the Gerizim Mountain or in Jerusalem (John 4:19–24). Participating in Jesus' cause is to become a passerby, to keep on walking, to stay on track, to leave the "fathers" behind! Yet in order to join Jesus' journey, one has to know the direction of the trajectory.

All of these parallels and analogies between biblical characters, events, and even religions could easily create an impression of an environment where a monolithic unity seems to prevail. But that is certainly not the case. One should therefore act with caution to not be caught in the net of "parallelomania."[61] One needs to think along the lines of a particular development of the data. The result of not following a trajectory is to walk in circles.

The "background" or "environment" of the biblical world should not therefore "be mastered by reducing it to a mass of disorganized parallels to the New Testament; it must be reconceptualized in terms of movements, trajectories . . . ." These words are quoted from a book by James M. Robinson (emeritus professor at Claremont) and Helmut Koester (emeritus professor at Harvard) entitled *Trajectories through Early Christianity*. In the introduction of this work, Robinson writes:

> We now have, as a result of two centuries of critical historiography, its limitations notwithstanding, a history of early Christianity which makes indisputable the theological change from Jesus to Paul, from Paul to Mark or Ignatius, from Ignatius to Irenaeus or Origen, and then to Augustine or Athanasius. This is not simply a case of random variety, of pluralism. A more penetrating analysis reveals individual items to be exponents of intelligible movements. . . . Such sequences of development have come to the surface in the course of the critical historical research of the past generations. Yet the implications of their discovery have been obscured by the context in which they [the above-mentioned individual items] arose and continue to be used. These stages were generally found in the process of seeking a fixed date for a document, or at least enough chronological accuracy to rule out apostolic authorship; or as part of an argument to establish that one document attests to the existence and circulation of another.[62]

By applying these ideas, many aspects of the interrelatedness of the Jesus of history and the Jesus of faith could be described and explained in a more adequate way. Establishing a sequence of movement, attested by different documents, can do this. Although these writings originated in diverse con-

61. See Sandmel, "Parallelomania."
62. Robinson, "Introduction: The Dismantling and Reassembling," 10–11.

texts, many of them are interrelated in some way or another. However, it is a hermeneutical danger, as Robinson realizes, that the term *trajectory* "may suggest too much determinative control at the point of departure." But it does not need to be so. Robinson notes further: "At one stage of a movement a document may function in a specific way, have a certain meaning or influence on the movement; at a subsequent stage on the trajectory that document, unaltered, may function or cut in a different way, may mean in effect something different, may influence the movement differently."[63]

How does this work out in practice? Take the belief of Christians regarding the virginal conception of Jesus as an example. The *locus classicus* of this dogma is Matt 1:23 where the word "virgin" (παρθένος) occurs. Actually, Matthew is quoting here from the book of Isaiah (7:14). The prophet Isaiah lived in the eighth century B.C.E., and refers to a particular wartime situation where ancient Syrians were involved in the history of both the Northern and Southern Kingdoms. The Hebrew word that the prophet used did not intend to mean "virgin" at all; however, the authors of the Septuagint translated this word as "virgin." Matthew's quotation comes from this Greek translation. It is possible that Matthew did not have the virginity of Mary in mind at all when he quoted Isa 7:14. What he probably had in mind here (see also Matt 28:20) is the concept "Emmanuel" (i.e., "God-with-us"), a motive found in Isaiah 7:14 (which is an allusion to the motive of the "child of the king," mentioned in Isa 8:8 as "God with us").

Here, again, one has to beware of anachronistic exegesis. An illustration of this would be to interpret the term "Holy Spirit" not only in, for example, Ps 51:11(13), but also in Matt 1:18 (ἐκ πνεύματος ἁγίου) and in Matt 1:20 (ἐκ πνεύματος ἐστιν ἁγίου) from the perspective of the Christian dogma of the Trinity. Such an interpretation can be found in the edict of 1555 by Pope Paul IV against the anti-Trinitarians and the Socinians. These people taught that " . . . our Lord (is) not the true God . . . , not in all respects of the same being as the Father and the Holy Spirit, or that he was, according to the flesh, not received from the Holy Spirit in the lap of the most holy and always virginal Mary, but like the other people from the seed of Joseph."

It is worth pointing out that Pope Paul IV, by rejecting the anti-Trinitarians, in fact defended Roman Catholic Mariology. The interwoven dogmas of the Immaculate Conception and the perpetual virginity of Mary are part and parcel of this doctrine. It is built upon an early belief that Joseph withheld himself from sexual intercourse with Mary. This belief originated in apocryphal documents dating back to the second century. Protestants used this tenet in the Belgic Confession (Articles 18 and 19) as support of the belief in Jesus' "two natures." However, to point out that both

---

63. Ibid., 14.

of these tenets regarding Joseph's role (or lack of a role) and Mary's virginity are post-New Testament developments does not necessarily mean a rejection of the dogmas of Jesus' divinity or the Trinity.

The roots of Mariology come from the second-century church father Ignatius (*Ign. Eph.* 18:2; *Ign. Smyrn.* 1:1; *Ign. Trall.* 9:1) who was the first Christian to interpret Matt 1:23 explicitly as a reference to Mary's virginity in relation to Jesus' divinity. But it was specifically because of the elaboration on both themes regarding Joseph and Mary in the post-New Testament document *Proto-James* (and writings dependent on it, such as *The Life of Joseph the Carpenter* and *Pseudo-Matthew*) that Mariology firmly took root.

How can we keep anachronisms out of our understanding of Matthew's interpretation of Jesus' adoption as "son of Joseph" on the basis of the intervention of the Holy Spirit? We could take note of texts contemporary to Matthew that emphasize a particular tradition with regard to "Joseph, the son of Jacob." We have already seen that the pseudepigraphic document *Testaments of the Twelve Patriarchs* (containing material that probably goes back to the second century B.C.E.) witnesses to this tradition concerning the First Testament figure Joseph, the son of Jacob. According to this tradition, Joseph was not merely the innocent victim of the spiteful and jealous "evil eye" manifested in the envy of his brothers. He, in fact, successfully conquered the evil spirits.[64]

Against this background, rabbis of the Jamnia academy were of the opinion that the protection that Joseph enjoyed against the evil spirits also applied to his offspring.[65] These rabbis (belonging to the Pharisaic school) are generally viewed as opponents of the Jesus movement. Against this opposition, among others, Matthew defends the notion that Jesus is "child of God." In the Talmud (*b. Bava Mezia* 84a; cf. *Berakot* 20a), there is a tradition according to which a leader of the Jamnia academy sees himself as being of the "seed of Joseph." Therefore, the "evil eye" has no power over him.[66] Within the symbolic world of Israel, the Holy Spirit was the power that overcame evil. Similar evidence occurs a number of times in the Gospel of Matthew (e.g., 12:28). Wordplay emphasizes the opposites: "son(s) of God" versus "son(s) of evil." According to Matthew, the disciples, as "children of God," just like Jesus, (the adopted "son of Joseph" and "child of God"), were also supposed to have power over "evil" and the "children of evil" (e.g., 10:20, 24–26).[67]

In the context of J. Duncan M. Derrett's discussion on the "evil eye" in the Mediterranean social world, he remarks as follows with regard to the

---

64. *T. Simeon* 1–2; *T. Dan* 1:6; 2:5; *T. Gad* 1–3; *T. Joseph* 1:3, 7; *T. Benjamin* 3–6 (see Elliott, "Evil Eye and the Sermon."

65. See, e.g., Overman, *Matthew's Gospel and Formative Judaism*, 35–71; Stanton, *Gospel for a New People*, 113–281; Saldarini, *Matthew's Christian-Jewish Community*, 167–77; Van Aarde, *God-with-us*, xiii–xvii, 248–60.

66. See Elliott, "Evil Eye and the Sermon," 73, note 26.

67. See Van Aarde, *God-with-us*, 69–71.

view Israelites had of births in general: "The Hebrews viewed childbirth as symbolic of destiny in a most intimate way. No conception took place without the co-operation of the holy spirit."[68] If the use of the word "virgin" in Matthew's quotation of Isaiah 7:14 was indeed intentional, then Matthew probably had the divine conceptions such as those in the haggadic Moses paschal document (b. *Baba Batra* 120a) and in the *Midrash Rabbah* (*Ex Rab* 1:19) about Jochebed, the mother of Moses, in mind.[69] According to this tradition, God restored Jochebed's virginity. This happened before she, without the involvement of her husband Amram, gave birth to Moses.

But it is also a fact that the mythological idea of a son conceived by some deity or other was taken over by Hellenist Egyptians within the Israelite tradition and applied to the "holy people" of the First Testament.[70] This mythological idea was not only known to the Greek tradition (e.g., the birth story of Asclepios, son of a mortal mother Coronis, but conceived by the god Apollo, son of Zeus), it was also a general notion within the context of the Babylonian, and particularly, the Egyptian royal legend. Since this idea was well known in Hellenistic Egypt, it is not surprising that the legend of the virgin birth appeared early on in Hellenistic Christianity. Within the Greco-Israelite tradition, it is not unusual to be confronted by the mythological notion of divine beings impregnating mortal women.[71] In the Wisdom of Solomon 8:16–18, an erotic love affair between the preexistent Sophia ("Wisdom") and the "wise person" is mentioned: "(Always when) I come home I shall sleep with her,[72] for intercourse with her [LXX: συμβίωσις] has no bitterness and the marital communion with her no hurt, but joy and merriment."[73]

As far as the Lukan birth narrative is concerned, research has convinced me that placing it against the background of the divine son myths in contemporary Greco-Roman literature provides the clearest explanation. This research is particularly supported by the work of Rudolf Bultmann, Walter Schmithals, and John Dominic Crossan.[74] The fact that the legend relating to the virginal conception was unknown to Paul does not necessarily prove that this was not a common idea in non-Pauline Christian circles, even before Paul's time.[75] Virginal conception was a common notion in non-Christian circles.[76] Examples are the conceptions of Perseus and Romulus

68. Derrett, *Jesus's Audience*, 119.

69. Cf. Allison, *New Moses*, 147–55.

70. "Die Frommen"— Bultmann, *Theologie des Neuen Testaments*, 133.

71. See *1 Henoch* 6–7; *Genesis Apocryphon* 2; *Testament of Solomon* 5:3; *Proto-James* 4:1. Cf., Allison, *New Moses*, 147, note 14.

72. See Rahlfs, *Septuaginta*, 357.

73. Standartinger, "From Fictional Text," 309.

74. Bultmann, *Theologie des Neuen Testaments*, 133; Schmithals, *Evangelium nach Lukas*, 25–28; Crossan, "Infancy and Youth," 72–76.

75. Cf. Bultmann, *Theologie des Neuen Testaments*, 133.

76. See Brown, *Birth of the Messiah*, 522.

in Greco-Roman mythology, as well as of the pharaohs, Alexander, and Augustus in legendary material emanating from, on the one hand, Egyptian and Greco-Roman history and, on the other hand, from famous philosophers and religious thinkers such as Plato and Apollonius of Tyana.[77]

In this regard one cannot but agree with Raymond Brown. He points out that it is inconceivable that converts from heathendom to Christianity would have been unaware of these parallels from Egypt, Greece, Anatolia, and Latium. Sketches and portrayals of figures of divine birth and/or virginal conception—for instance Hercules, Perseus, Horus (the Isis cult), and Priapus—were found in houses in the cities Herculaneum and Pompeii and in surrounding villages.[78] These portrayals provide a clear indication that miraculous birth stories were common and well known.[79]

The notion of the divine birth of Jesus does not appear in the New Testament except in Matthew 1 and Luke 1. This is remarkable in the light of its common occurrence in the contemporary world. The words in Gal 4:4, "when the fullness of the time came, God sent forth his Son, *born of a woman* (γενόμενον ἐκ γυναικός)," offer absolutely no indication that Paul knows of the tradition relating to the virginal conception of Jesus.[80] Nonetheless, in my opinion, we cannot suppose that Paul is silent about how Jesus was conceived.[81] According to Paul, Jesus was at birth the preexisting child of God and therefore of a completely different order than that of people. At birth, however, he became equal to people in all respects. Paul does not think of the birth of Jesus in any other terms than those of a natural

---

77. Traditions about a ruler who was deemed a god also need to be mentioned in this regard (see Harris, *Jesus as God*, 26). On the Rosetta stone, 196 B.C.E., it is reported of Ptolemy V Epiphanes that he "is a god from a god and a goddess, as Horus is the son of Isis and Osiris" (*Orientis Graeci Inscriptiones Selectae* 90:10). An inscription from Ephesus dated 48 B.C.E. (see Dittenberger, *Sylloge Inscriptionum Graecarum*, 2:760.7) mentions that Julius Caesar "is the manifestation of a god, born from Ares and Aphrodite and (the) general redeemer of human life." As far as Augustus is concerned, a number of inscriptions refer to him as god. The *Oxyrhynchus Papyrus* (1453.11) from Egypt, dated 24 B.C.E., refers to Augustus as "Caesar, a god from god" (see Grenfell, Hunt, and Bell, *Oxyrhynchus Papyri*). Another inscription dated 24 B.C.E. has the same reference, namely, "god from god" (*Orientis Graeci Incritiones Selectae* 655.2). Sometime in the period before the writer Strabo's death in 21 C.E. (Berkowitz and Squitier, *Thesaurus Linguae Graecae*, xix), he also referred in his work *Geographica* (4.177) to Augustus as "the god Caesar" (cf. Taylor, *Divinity of the Roman Emperor*, 142–246, 270–83). The New Testament (Acts 12:22) knows a tradition according to which Herod Agrippa I was called a god, a tradition also known to Josephus (*Ant.* 19.345). Similar traditions exist with regard to the Roman emperors Nero and Domitian (Harris, *Jesus as God*, 28, notes 34 and 35). As far as Nero is concerned, Deissmann (*Light from the Ancient East*, 345, note 4) refers to the inscription of Gaius Stertinius Xenophon of Kos in which he addresses the emperor as " (to) the good god." Suetonius (*De Vita Caesarum: Domitianus* 13.2) refers to Domitian as "our ruler and god." Similar references to Domitian are found in the works of the Greek orator and popular philosopher Dio (Cocceianus) Chrysostom (*Orationes: Defensio* 45.1), ca. C.E. 40–ca. 112, and of Dio Cassius (67.4.7), ca. C.E. 2–3 (Harris, *Jesus as God*, 28, note 35).

78. Brown, *Birth of the Messiah*, 522–23.

79. See Maulucci, *National Archaeological Museum*, 86–87, 106–7, 115; Bonechi (Casa Editrice) *Art and History of Pompeii*, 48, 98–100.

80. Cf. Brown, *Birth of the Messiah*, 519.

81. Cf. Dibelius, *Jungfrauensohn und Krippenkind*, 29–34; contra Brown, *Virginal Conception*, 57.

birth.[82] Paul's expression, "born of a woman," appears elsewhere, for example in Job 14:14 and Matt 11:11. Here it pertains to natural birth. In other words, according to Paul, it is not Jesus' birth that determines his being the son of God; he was this already before being born of a woman. Paul (as in John's Gospel) emphasizes the anomaly, the paradox, that the "eternal child of God" experienced a brief life and remarkable suffering because he was born of a woman. This view of what being the child of God entails, cannot be reconciled with that offered by the concept of a divine birth.[83]

It is clear that Matthew's and Luke's narratives of the birth of Jesus represent an unusual position in the New Testament. Bultmann concludes therefore that the particular understanding of being the child of God that underlies the narrative of the virgin birth is overshadowed by the understanding of being the child of God to which Paul and John bear witness.[84] Both, each in a specific way, work with adoption as child of God. In chapter 7, I shall elaborate on the background against which writers like Paul reasoned.

A CHAIN OF SEVEN LINKS

It is clear that parallels exist between Matthew's understanding of Jesus as "son of Joseph," "son of Abraham," and "child of God," and conceptions in the Greco-Israelite and rabbinical world, as portrayed in texts such as *The Wisdom of Solomon* and *Joseph and Aseneth*. These parallels do not necessarily imply a direct source dependence, but they at least indicate common thinking.[85] However, the background material on the notion of Mary's virginity does not constitute a "mass of disorganized" parallels. A clear trajectory can be discerned.

In Matthew's Gospel, the Joseph trajectory begins with a quotation from the prophet Isaiah. The book of Isaiah appears within the Hebrew Scriptures, but the quotation comes from the Septuagint. Matthew's quotation focuses on the expectation of an ideal king as well as on the motive of a Moses-like deliverance. This focus should be understood in the light of

---

82. Dibelius, *Jungfrauensohn und Krippenkind*, 34: "Paulus spricht nirgends von der wunderbaren Geburt Jesu und zeigt deutlich die völlig entgegengesetzte Richtung seines Interesses: er legt entscheidenden Wert darauf, daß das Erdensein des Christus begonnen hat wie das eines anderen Menschen, durch eine näturliche Geburt."

83. Pannenberg, *Jesus—God and Man*, 143.

84. Bultmann, *Theologie des Neuen Testaments*, 133.

85. After having commented on the parallels in the tradition concerning the birth of Jesus and the remainder of the Gospel of Matthew, Anthony Saldarini (*Matthew's Christian-Jewish Community*) makes the following observation: "The author of Matthew drew upon this rich and varied tradition when he stressed God the Father of Jesus in the birth narrative (chap.1). At the same time, he brought a variety of titles, roles, and scriptural passages to bear on Jesus in order to establish him firmly within the biblical worlds and further mark him out as a special figure in Israel" (176).

the Bethlehem-Jerusalem controversy. We have seen the extent to which this controversy relates to the Joseph-Judah conflict.

Luke and John treat the notion of Mary's virginity in vastly different ways. The Lukan birth story is told within the context of Greek myths about deities and the emperor cult of the Romans. On the other hand, John does not mention the aspect of virginity. (However, the Joseph figure plays a remarkable role in John's Gospel. John's understanding of Joseph within the context of the Jerusalem-Bethlehem controversy is in some sense similar to Matthew's.) Both of these Gospels originated against the background of the antagonism of the Pharisaic academy in Jamnia toward the Jesus movement during the period after the destruction of the temple in Jerusalem in 70 C.E.

Paul and Mark wrote a few years earlier than Matthew, Luke, and, John. Neither Paul nor Mark seem to know anything about either Joseph or Mary's virginity. Even Mary, according to Mark, does not regard Jesus as someone of high esteem. Likewise, a complete silence falls, with regard to both Joseph and Mary, in the rest of the New Testament.

During the second century, a steady development in a totally new direction is discernable. It started with Ignatius's emphasis on Jesus' divinity over the Gnostic belief that God's becoming event in "flesh" was unthinkable. In *Proto-James*, the Joseph figure serves to support the new upcoming belief in the perpetual virginity of Mary. Other documents and theologians took up this line. During the Middle Ages, exactly the same Joseph motive that occurred in the previous stage was used to support the dogma of the Trinity. The Reformers obviously disliked Mariology. Nevertheless, from the sixteenth century onward, they implemented the role of Joseph to defend the tenets of Jesus' two natures and the dogma of the Triune God (see the Belgic Confession, Articles 18 and 19).

One can explain this development from beginning to end with the image of a chain consisting of seven links. However, the silence with regard to Joseph in the documents closest to the historical Jesus presents a missing link in the center. The thrust of each of the first three links is in some way or another transparent in the themes of the overlays in the Gospel tradition. These overlays fill the emptiness in the center.

The First Link: The Saga in the First Testament (The Wisdom Tradition)

The first link contains the Joseph saga in the First Testament. This story is well known. It is about acceptance despite rejection. It is a story of tension within Jacob's family. The twelve sons in the family do not have the same mother. Rachel, Jacob's beloved wife, is the mother of Joseph and Benjamin. All the sons, however, have the right to be called children of their ancestor Abraham. The records in the First Testament about the twelve sons are not fully in concordance with one another. One particular tradition would like to put Joseph on a pedestal. According to this bias, Joseph was not his brothers' equal because he did not work with them in the fields. His father had prevented him from doing manual labor with his brothers by giving him a special multicolored robe. Such a robe is not worn for labor. In the same vein, this tradition records that the birthright is taken away from both the oldest, Reuben, and the second in line, Judah, because both of them had shamed their father by their sexual misbehavior. Later in the story, Joseph reportedly stands steadfast against sexual temptation.

The father's favoritism is clearly seen when Joseph gossips to his father about his brothers and receives no reprimand. The direction of the story develops from slander into rejection as Joseph is betrayed by his brothers and abandoned. Outside of the Promised Land, he continues to play the role of the beloved son of his father. Pharaoh exalts him "because of his father's God" (Gen 41:38–39; 50:17–18). From the perspective of his brothers, he marries an impure woman. However, this becomes a "holy marriage" because the children born of this union, strictly speaking also impure, are legitimized by Jacob when he adopts them into the circle of God's covenant people.

Mediterraneans are accustomed to judicial retribution: an eye for an eye. However, Joseph, meeting his brothers again, responds with an act of forgiveness and compassion. This is the first link.

The Second Link: A Pair of Tribal Sticks (The Prophetic Tradition)

Joseph's children, born in Egypt, became the forefathers of the people living in the Holy Land in the region north of Jebus. They had their own places of political power and cultic worship. Since the Israelites entered Canaan, there was tension between the two tribal groups, the Makarites/Shechemites (Joseph's children) and the Judeans. After Joshua's return from Egypt the tension mounted. The restoration of Judah began when David, from the tribe of Judah, became the leader of all of Israel. David and Solomon were the peacemakers. To this end they chose Jebus/Salem, since then called Jerusalem, as a neutral location for political power and cultic worship. However, in the long run, it was of no avail.

Two empires came into being. Prophets tried to unify the two groups. Ezekiel, for example, would have liked to transform the "pair of sticks" (Ezek 37:15–28) into one. However, the northerners continued to pray to God on Mount Gerizim, close to Shechem, Joseph's burial place (see Josh 24:32). In Judea, Jerusalem was the symbolic center of the power of the Davidic family, the economy of the land, and the Yahwistic religion. The Judeans tried to silence their opponents by creating the myth of the lost ten tribes. The Judean priests legitimized this bias by canonizing their version of the books of Moses. The northerners, however, had their own version of the books of Moses, the Samaritan Pentateuch. For the puritan Judeans the name "Samaritan" was equivalent to being a bastard, a person with no right to enter the temple in Jerusalem because he or she was not a "true" child of Abraham. Here, the second link ends.

The Third Link: The Failure to Restore Defamation (The Judean Tradition)

One should probably not take the Judeans' restoration of the defamed house of David too seriously. Like the forefather, Judah, David had his own story of sexual misconduct despite efforts made by the priestly Judean writers of the Chronicles to erase this story from the royal annals in the books of the kings. Much less sensational than the sexual morality of kings were the atrocities of the elite exploiting the peasants. Small wonder the prophetic voice (of Micah) was looking to a new king in Jerusalem, who was expected to come from the grass roots of Bethlehem. In the same vein, another prophet (Hos 11:1) predicted that a divine son would come from Egypt. This failure to restore defamation is the third link. At this stage, the air was pregnant with the peasants' expectations of a popular king. For the northerners, the "son of Joseph" would be this king. For the prophets, the "son of David," the messiah of the united Israel, could encompass both expectations.

The Missing Link: Fatherless in Galilee (The Jesus Tradition)

But when this figure came, nobody recognized him. He did not see himself in the role of a king. No biological father played a role in his life. His family thought he was insane. His wisdom subverted conventional culture. His heart and deeds were filled with compassion and anger because of the pain against which the prophets had already protested. The powers that be killed him as a nobody. There was no family tomb in which his body could be laid. This link is about the story of the fatherless Jesus.

The Fifth Link: Overlays Filling the Empty Center (The Gospel Tradition)

The people who were attracted by Jesus' message about God's all-inclusive presence looked with new eyes at Jesus after his death. They began to adore him in terms of the expectations the prophets had of God's messiah who would inaugurate a dispensation of righteousness. They used names taken from Israel's scriptures and the surrounding world to express their adoration. Simultaneously, those who saw it as their task to maintain the conventional wisdom with regard to their images of God and culture opposed this movement by labeling its "founder" and its messengers. This can clearly be seen in the earliest Christian documents available, the authentic letters of Paul. The opposition was specifically directed against his notion that God's becoming event in Jesus meant that God's presence was available also to the people outside the boundaries of Israel.

Chronologically, the Gospel of Mark presents the second available Christian text. In this document, Jesus is called the "prince of the demons." As in Paul's letters, one can trace in Mark a tradition that went back to the earliest Christian movement in Jerusalem. Although both Paul and Mark used the traditions transmitted from the Jesus movement in Jerusalem, they changed some essential aspects. Thus, it is clear that from the very beginning, the community of Christian believers was diverse in their understanding of what the core of Jesus' message really was.

Common to this early phase is that no one knew about Jesus' miraculous conception or that Joseph was his father. The later documents (Matthew, Luke, and John) have "overlays" that fill up this empty center in the tradition that originated in Jerusalem and was adapted by Mark. One aspect in the tradition of the Jesus movement in Jerusalem that does not go back to the historical Jesus is the idea of "the Twelve." In Jerusalem, the first Jesus followers seemingly regarded the Jesus movement as the inauguration of the united Israel. The idea of "the Twelve" fulfilled the role of focusing on Israel as God's unified people. The death of Jesus, understood in terms of dying, being buried, and resurrected, is also part of this early tradition. This formula was taken over by both Paul and Mark. To them it accentuates the empty tomb tradition (which probably did not originate within the circle of the earliest Jesus movement in Jerusalem but rather in a Greco-Roman environment). The empty tomb tradition was seemingly understood as an indication of God's acceptance of Jesus as God's child.

A similar motive, also known in Roman Palestine of the time, is found in the stories of Hercules' "deification," as can be seen in the satires and tragedies of Seneca in the fifties of the Common Era. These correspondences are yet another indication of the extent to which Hellenization had taken place in the earliest Jerusalem faction. Jesus' death, however, was understood as if the Hebrew Scriptures foretold its vicarious intention. The same happened with regard to the resurrection tradition.

This earliest tradition knows neither about Joseph's link to Jesus nor the mission of the Christian movement among Samaritans. In this tradition, there is also no knowledge of the virginal conception of Jesus. Matthew and Luke, using Mark as a source, filled the gap against the background of a particular process and mind-set. The process was that of the separation between the synagogue and the church that started after the destruction of the temple in Jerusalem in 70 C.E. The mind-set was that of apocalypticism, which both Matthew and Luke took over from Mark and a later version of the Sayings Gospel Q. All three of the Synoptics present an understanding of the death and resurrection of Jesus in the light of an apocalyptic mind-set.

The apocalyptic expectation was that this world would be transformed into the final kingdom of God. The vicarious death of a martyr was an important dynamic in this expectation because the martyr died on behalf of others to procure a better future for them beyond death. According to a specific prophetic tradition, the new age would dawn when the messiah was revealed in Jerusalem as the Child of Humanity, and the nations would come to Jerusalem to join the unified Israel. In Mark and Matthew, this cosmic event happens when, in accordance with Amos 8:9, the sun goes down at noon (see Mark 15:33; Matt 27:45) and Jesus, in accordance with Dan 7:13–14, is revealed as the messianic Child of Humanity igniting the "discipling" of all the nations (see Matt 28:18–20; Mark 15:39; Matt 27:54).

In Mark and Luke, the focus moves from Jerusalem to the Gentiles. Luke, in particular, geographically divides the world into concentric circles: Judea, Samaria, and Rome, the latter symbolizing the greater world. The Joseph tradition, as we have seen, is very much intertwined with Samaria. Jesus, son of Joseph, is seen as the precursor coming from Bethlehem, entering Jerusalem as Israel's messiah after journeying from Galilee through Samaria to Jerusalem. For Matthew, the journey into the pagan world is not at issue anymore. The focus is on the "lost sheep of the house of Israel" so that the temple in Jerusalem can become the house of prayer for all nations, including the impure and the outcasts. Matthew is either a Syrian or Galilean Gospel in which there is a tendency both to conform to and separate from the (Pharisaic) synagogue. The Pharisees remained the advocates of the purity ideology related to the temple in Jerusalem even after the destruction of the temple. An aversion to the Samaritans formed part of this ideology. The defamation of Jesus on account of his illegitimate background seems to be part of this aversion. Matthew apologizes by explaining that Jesus' birth was the result of an intervention by God. However, he conforms to the synagogical view by explicitly denying that Jesus or his followers ever went to the region of the Samaritans (Matt 10:5). Matthew represents the Judean emphasis of only one Israel as if the "northern stick" did not exist at all.

For Matthew, the son of David is the messianic Child of Humanity who is expected to inaugurate the utopia for the lost sheep of Israel. Paradoxically, Matthew departs from synagogical policy by emphasizing the ingathering of the social outcasts into the symbolic temple (which did not concretely exist anymore) and, therefore, into God's kingdom. For Matthew, as for Mark, the Jesus kerygma is the message of an apocalyptic death, although he does not mention Jesus' death as being for the benefit of others. The only hint of such an idea in Matthew's Gospel is the eucharistic formula (cf. also Paul in 1 Cor 11:23–26), taken over from Mark's version (Mark 14:22–25) of the Jesus faction in Jerusalem.

Luke also knew of the illegitimacy charge. His audience was probably located in Ephesus in Asia Minor. The influence of the conflict between the synagogue in Jamnia and the Christian communities reached far beyond the boundaries of Roman Palestine. This was the case in Asia Minor where the emperor granted judicial rights over the synagogue to Israelites.

The defamation on account of Jesus' illegitimate background seemingly originated in the synagogue probably because of his fatherlessness. The Jamnia Academy did not see Jesus' illegitimacy as the outcome of rape, but, as we have seen, second-century rabbinic Judaism saw it this way on account of a satirical reading of the traditions of Jesus' birth found in Matthew and Luke. They created the Ben (son of) Panthera tradition as a satirical word-play on parthenos (παρθενός), the Greek word for virgin. Panthera was the name they gave the Roman soldier who allegedly raped Mary.

Luke represented the prophetic tradition of the reunification of the North and the South. This can be seen in his tripartite mission to the Judeans, Samaritans, and the Gentiles (Acts 1:8). The Samaritans were, according to Luke, a necessary link backward to the "mission" to the outcasts in Judea, and forward to the Gentile mission. In the parable of the Good Samaritan, Luke (10:30–35) depicts Jesus as both the Samaritan and the impure Israelite lying in the ditch. Jesus is also Lazarus who becomes one of the "dogs" (cf. Luke 16:21), a label conferred on Gentiles (cf. Mark 7:28). In the Israelite tradition, the name Lazarus was linked to Abraham's family, and it meant "God helps." In another story, Jesus is portrayed as a defiant sibling who moves from the land of his fathers into an impure country where he becomes one of the outcasts (Luke 15:11–32). Paradoxically, the outcasts (the Samaritans) rejected Jesus but he did not reject them, although Luke tells us that the disciples James and John (projecting the Jerusalem faction) expected him to do so (cf. 9:51–55).

Luke's apology for the slander concerning the scandalous birth memoir differs from that of Matthew's. Luke combines the Jerusalem faction's claim of Jesus' messianic origin with the tradition of the newborn baby. This combination is placed within the common context of Greco-Roman deification and emperor-cult motives. For the Jerusalem faction, Jesus was "messiah" in an adoptionistic sense: as "son of David" he was the messiah who became the "child of God." Analyzing this tradition historically, especially in light of how it was used in New Testament writings, one can infer that the post-Easter followers of Jesus in Jerusalem did not understand this adoptionistic motive as correlating with divine conception. The same is true for Paul and Mark.

For Luke, Jesus

1. was Israel's messiah (Luke 1:11; 2:26; 4:18; Acts 4:26–27), filled with the Spirit of God (Luke 4:1; Acts 2:33);

2. is savior and *kyrios* (Κύριῳ) of the world (Luke 1:11; Acts 2:34, 36; 4:12);
3. was virginally conceived (Luke 1:34–35a), like Perseus and Asclepios;
4. was the son, so people thought, of Joseph, who was the son of Eli, the son . . . of Perez, the son of Judah, the son of Jacob (Luke 3:33–34), the son . . . of Seth, the son of Adam, the child of God (Luke 3:23–37);
5. was adopted as God's child (Luke 3:21) because of his divine origins (Luke 1:35), similar to the emperor of the time, the deified Augustus; and
6. ascended to heaven (Luke 24:51; Acts 1:9) like Hercules, the godlike hero who had a human mother impregnated by Zeus and who was adopted as Zeus's son because of an empty tomb (pyre) tradition.

As with the virginal conception, I do not trace the empty tomb tradition back to the Jesus faction in Jerusalem, but to common Greek thinking that manifested in the stories of the deification of Hercules. In this respect, Luke shares the opinion of Paul, who apparently got his idea of the empty tomb (cf. 1 Cor 15:4) from the common thinking in the Greco-Roman world. This idea partly lies behind the Christ hymn in Phil 2:6–11.

Luke also knew of the resurrection appearances because of his acquaintance with the Pauline tradition. This can be seen, for example, in the correspondence between Paul's reference in 1 Cor 15:6 to the five hundred who experienced the risen Christ at the same time and in Luke's version in Acts 2:1–13 of the "pentecostal" experience of a multitude of believers. Paul, in turn, took over the core of the appearance tradition (it falls out in the traditional formula in 1 Cor 15:3–7) from the Jerusalem faction:[86]

Christ
died for our sins, according to the Scriptures;
was buried;
was raised on the third day, according to the Scriptures;
appeared to Cephas [i.e., Peter], then to the Twelve,
to James, then to all the apostles.

The Jerusalem faction seemingly understood the notion of "the Twelve" as exchangeable for "all of Israel," represented here by "all of the apostles." In Paul's version of the traditional formula, it is clear that he differed.[87] Apart from himself, he names Junia, Andronicus, Cephas, and probably James and Silvanus as apostles. For Paul, the concept "apostles" is an expansion of "the Twelve" in Jerusalem.[88]

---

86. Cf. Gaston, "Paul and Jerusalem," 69.
87. See Murphy-O'Connor, "Tradition and Redaction," 582–89; Gaston, "Paul and Jerusalem," 66–67.
88. "Apart from himself, Paul names Apostles Junia, Andronicus, Cephas and probably Barnabas, James, and Silvanus" (Gaston, "Paul and Jerusalem," 67, note 36).

Luke, like Matthew, knew that a man called Joseph was not Jesus' biological father (cf. Luke 3:23). We have seen that the earliest tradition does not reveal any knowledge of Jesus' parentage except the suggestion of his fatherlessness. I have proffered a solution to the question of where the perception that Jesus was the (adopted) grandson of either Jacob (Matt 1:16) or Eli (Luke 3:23), the father of Joseph, could have originated. Evidence directs us to the Pharisaic tradition from the Jamnia academy. In the next chapter I will demonstrate to what extent the Jerusalem ideology debarred someone from the privilege of being counted among the children of Abraham if he did not know who his father was.

For the puritans in the Judean tradition, it did not take much to label a "son of Joseph" for his alleged illegitimate background and his association with prostitutes and other outcasts. Seen from the Christian perspective, the Joseph legend was also used in the apology found in the Gospel tradition. This apology concerned both Jesus' subversion of the Judean ideology and the defamation it evoked. The post-Easter Jesus movement filled the gap caused by Jesus' fatherlessness in its own way. Christians exalted Jesus as the risen Christ and Lord. This exaltation was substantiated by placing him in succession to the forefather Joseph, the First Testament patriarch. According to the Joseph saga in the First Testament, God exalted Joseph despite slander.

Furthermore, early witnesses such as Paul and Mark knew the tradition that the historical Jesus called upon God as his Father. By calling God his Father, Jesus claimed to be a "child of Abraham" regardless of the defamation concerning his fatherlessness. In the same vein, the Q tradition (Luke 3:8//Matt 3:9) contains a statement by John the Baptist that critically rejects the self-confident assumption of the Israelites that they have Abraham as their father. This statement is made within the context of Jesus' baptism. According to John the Baptist, God can produce children of Abraham from desert stones. In Matt 3:7, this statement is directed at the Pharisees and Sadducees. In this respect, both Jesus and John the Baptist represented the critical voice of the prophets against the royal hierarchy, and both were also killed as a result. As we have seen, Jesus did not agree with John the Baptist's view that God would, only at the end of time, catastrophically intervene in an apocalyptic way in order to create the ideal condition of righteousness. According to Jesus, God was already fully present here and now, and would not be so only at the end of time.

With regard to this labeling of Jesus as a Samaritan and a sinner, Bultmann correctly recognizes traditional material in these passages.[89] For him, it attests to the compassion of the historical Jesus toward the outcasts. John, however, interpreted this tradition within a specific context and from

---

89. Bultmann, *Gospel of John*, 289.

a particular perspective. The Fourth Gospel shares the Semitic-Hellenistic wisdom speculation. God's wisdom (son) came from above. Salvation is grounded in the mission of the Savior from above to beneath, becoming human in all aspects from birth to death.

John's community, like those of Luke and Matthew, consisted of Israelites and Hellenists. Against the synagogical charge that Christians were deviant and impure, similar to their "founder" Jesus, John claims that his community of Christians is part of the one assembly of God (cf. John 10:16). Jesus, who came from above and went up again, is God's victorious deliverance of his people's incarceration.

The claim of unity in the Johannine community should be seen against the defamation of the Judean synagogue that the Christian community was of illegitimate offspring, that is, that they were descendants of the Joseph tribe. According to the synagogue, Jesus was therefore a Samaritan. John knew that there had been Judeans who followed Jesus, but to him they did not really continue the cause of Jesus. John created the Nicodemus legend to illustrate that some of the Judeans were not prepared to accept the scandalous message that Joseph's son came from the world of God. Others closer to Jesus, like Peter, had difficulty accepting the death of Jesus as God's victory over the flesh. John, therefore, created another legendary figure, the beloved disciple, to portray his understanding of the ideal way to follow Jesus. Against this background, we read that a disciple, Thomas, did not believe in Jesus' death and resurrection as the starting point for the mission of the Christian community. Against such skepticism, both Mary Magdalene and the beloved disciple show that Christians are sent just as Jesus was sent. The objective of this mission was to show compassion to the weak. The Samaritan passages in John's Gospel underline this message.

The Sixth Link: For the Sake of Dogma (The Orthodox Tradition)

Whereas the fifth link in the Joseph trajectory consists of the Gospel tradition that fills the absence of a Joseph figure in the life of Jesus, the material in the sixth link coincides mainly with the development of post-New Testament Mariology. This tenet concerns the figure of the Virgin Mary, Mother of God, "one of the most powerful imaginary constructs known in the history of civilizations."[90] During this phase we find Joseph "passively" active. Christians used the Joseph legend to support their later belief in Mary's immaculate conception and perpetual virginity.

According to the dogma of the virgin birth, Mary conceived without sexual intercourse. No male seed entered her womb. This dogma uses the Gospel of John to support its argument. John 1:13 refers to God's children as people who were not born of natural descent. They have the right to be

---

90. Kristeva, "Stabat Mater," in *Kristeva Reader*; cf. Schaberg, "The Infancy of Mary of Nazareth."

called "children of God," but this right is not comparable to being physically born as someone's child. To be "born from above" (John 3:5–7) eliminates human decision or a husband's desire. "Flesh gives birth to flesh, but the Spirit gives birth to spirit" (John 3:6). Neither the developing Mariology nor the sixteenth-century Belgic Confession (Articles 18 and 19), however, comprehended the thrust of this dualistic Johannine mentality. Instead, Roman Catholicism's Mariology and Protestantism's focus on Jesus' divinity have been supported by the use of the Joseph legend. Furthermore, the Joseph legend provides the material for later doctrinal development.

We have seen that the roots of this tenet came from the second-century church father Ignatius. He understood Matt 1:23 as a reference to Mary's virginity in relation to Jesus' divinity: "For our God Jesus the Messiah was conceived by Mary according to the plan of God: on the one hand of the seat of David [cf. Rom 1:3], on the other hand of the holy spirit [cf. Matt 1:18, 20]."[91] These two themes (Mariology and Jesus' divinity) specifically form the plot of the story about Mary in the second-century document *Proto-James*. In later centuries, writings such as *The Life of Joseph the Carpenter* and *Pseudo-Matthew* elaborate extensively on these themes.

The Seventh Link: The Carpenter Is Deadly Alive (The Patristic Tradition)

The seventh link is the last in the Joseph trajectory. The discussion of this trajectory makes it clear that there is an enormous distance between the empty center and the traditions in the Gospels and post-New Testament documents.[92]

J. P. Meier admits that "the total silence about Joseph is significant."[93] However, he does not think that this gap is an "unbridgeable gulf."[94] According to Meier, there is "converging evidence of the notable silences found in the Four Gospels and Acts, all of which have references to the mother and brothers (and sometimes the sisters)."[95] For him the traditional solution, already known in the patristic period, remains the most likely. According to some church fathers (e.g., Epiphanius), Joseph was already dead when Jesus began acting in public. The first hint of this idea can be found in *Proto-James*. Here Joseph is portrayed as a very old man when he takes Mary into his home. According to Epiphanius (*Panarion* 3.78.10, ca. 377 C.E.),

---

91. Ignatius, *Eph.* 18:2; see also *Smyrn.* 1:1 and *Trall.* 9:1. Notice also in Ignatius, "the typical blending of elements from the Johannine tradition (Jesus is God), Matthew (conceived by [the virgin] Mary by the power of the Holy Spirit), and the pre-Pauline tradition (of the seat of David)" (Meier, *Marginal Jew*, 1:237–38, note 43). The concept of Mary's descent from David becomes more explicit in Justin; see, e.g., *Dialogue with Trypho* 45: "the Son of God . . . submitted to becoming incarnate and being born of this virgin who was of the line of David." See also *Proto-James* 10:1 (cf. Meier, *Marginal Jew*, 1:238, note 43).

92. Cf. Oberlinner, *Historische Überlieferung*, 73–78.

93. Meier, *Marginal Jew*, 1:317.

94. Ibid., 353, note 7.

95. Ibid., 317.

Joseph died shortly after the family visited the temple in Jerusalem with the twelve-year-old Jesus (as recorded in Luke 2:41–52).[96]

I cannot see how Meier could seriously consider the patristic evidence as historically authentic. This evidence uncritically links Joseph's death with the episode of the twelve-year-old Jesus in the temple. It is almost impossible to argue for the authenticity of this scene. Meier quite correctly realizes that "there is a completely neutral stance [of Joseph as father] toward Jesus' ministry." However, it is less likely that this stance could be explained as being "of no symbolic use to the evangelists."[97] A male figure in the Mediterranean world, such as Jesus in light of Mark 6:3, without an explicit connection to his father was someone without identity. Even today when one crosses the border of Israel or an Arab country such as Jordan, one has to provide the name of one's father on the application form for a visa or entrance permit.

Meier is right when he argues that when Jesus mentions a sister belonging to the household of God, he has his earthly relatives in mind.[98] However, I find it difficult to see that the silence about his earthly father would imply that his father was already dead. One would rather expect that, if Jesus used his earthly family as an analogy for God's heavenly family, the role of the father would be important. Given the importance of the father in Mediterranean culture, the cancellation of the role of an earthly father is inexplicable.

In my view, the other possible explanation to which Meier also refers fits in better with the converging evidence in the relevant material closest to the historical Jesus. The father could have abandoned the family. It seems that the reason he would have done this has to do with the conception of Jesus. Historically seen, we know nothing at all of the circumstances of Jesus' conception. Furthermore, there is no historical reason (including New Testament evidence; cf. Luke 2:7) why Jesus should be seen as the first-born.[99] The suggested father's abandonment could have had certain consequences that would have conformed to the information that, in all probability, we can discern historically:

1. Jesus' tension with his family;
2. Jesus' defense of the fatherless;
3. Jesus' judgment of the abandonment of women (and children) by an act of divorce;
4. Jesus' calling upon God as his Father;

---

96. Cf. Bertrand and Ponton, "Textes patristique." See Meier, *Marginal Jew,* 353, note 6.

97. Meier, *Marginal Jew*, 1:317.

98. Ibid., 353, note 5.

99. Whiston (*Josephus Complete Works*, 415), the translator of Josephus's works, refers in a footnote to Izates, the "only-begotten" son of Helena, the queen of Adiabene, as the "one best-beloved": "Josephus here [*Ant.* 10.2.1] uses the word *monogene*, as only-begotten son, for no other than one best-beloved, as does both the Old and the New Testament; I mean where there were one or more sons besides (Gen. xxii.2; Heb. xi.7.)." In Luke 2:7 the expression τὸν πρωτότοκον is used.

5. Jesus' criticism of the Jerusalemites;
6. the absence of a family tomb as his last resting place.

Nonetheless, for other patristic fathers, Joseph the woodworker was still "deadly alive." The patristic fathers assumed that Joseph died during Jesus' childhood. They used Joseph as a symbol to model Christian life, so that in this way he was kept "alive." Using Joseph as a living symbol, they exaggerated too much in a moralistic sense; therefore, Joseph was "deadly alive." According to an expert among a previous generation of patristic scholars, A. W. Argyle, one does not find references to Joseph the First Testament patriarch in the prophets.[100] However, as I have shown, the prophetic voice with regard to the conflict between the Northern Kingdom and the Southern Kingdom is very much embedded in the Joseph tradition. For example, in Amos 6:1, 6 we read: "Woe to you who are complacent in Zion, and to you who feel secure on Mount Samaria . . . .You drink wine by the bowlfull but you do not grieve over the ruin of Joseph"(NIV, see also Ps 77:15; 78:67; 80:1–2; 81:5; 105:17; Ezek 37:15–19; 47:13; 48:38; Amos 5:6, 15; Obad 1:16; Zech 10:6). We have also seen that Joseph was more directly mentioned from the second century B.C.E. onward.[101]

A similar pattern with regard to Joseph being simultaneously "dead" and "alive," can be found in both Judaism and Christianity. In Judaism, Joseph became an ethical paradigm for repentance, a notion that also found its way into Christian thinking.[102] The First Testament saga of Joseph the patriarch provides an abundance of material for elaboration: he was "a righteous man afflicted and sold by his brethren, steadfast in resisting temptation, unjustly accused, arrested, the benefactor of others, tender hearted, forgiving his brethren who had wronged him."[103] The church fathers made use of this ethical paradigm in two ways: (1) as prefiguring the incarnation, passion, and exaltation of Jesus;[104] and (2) as providing a model for Christian character and conduct.[105]

100. Argyle, "Joseph the Patriarch in Patristic Teaching," 199–202.
101. See Wis 10:13f.; Sir 49:15; 1 Macc 2:53; *Jub.* 39–43; *1 Enoch* 89:13; *Jos. As.*; *Testaments of the Twelve Patriarchs.*
102. See Schimmel, "Joseph and his Brothers," 60–65.
103. Argyle, "Joseph the Patriarch," 199.
104. For Joseph as prototype of Jesus, see, e.g., Justin Martyr, *Dial. Trypho* 36; Tertullian, *Adv. Marcionem* 3.18, *Adv. Judeaos* 10, Origen, *Hom. Genesim*, 15, Cyprian, *Liber de bono patientiae* [Migne, P.L., 4.col. 652–53; Jerome, *Ep. Ad Riparium presbyterum*, n. 2 [P.L., 22. col. 908]; Chrysostom, in Gen. 37, Hom. 61[P.G., 54. col. 528]; Hom. 84, Matt 26:51–54]; Ambrose, *De Joseph Patriarcha*, 14 [P.L., 14. col. 646]; Augustine, *Ep. Cl.*, 3. c. 39 [P.L., 33. col. 919]; *Quaest. In Heptat.*, 148 [P.L., 34. col. 588]; Cyril of Alexandria (see P.G., 69. col. 376); Bede, in *Pentateuchum Commentarii* Gen 37–38 [P.L., 91. col. 265–266].
105. For Joseph as an allegory of Christian conduct, see, e.g., Athanasius, *Apologia ad Constantium Imp.*, 12 [P.G., 25. col. 609]; Gregory of Nyssa, *Contra Fornicarios* [P.G., 46. col. 493f.]; St Basil, *Sermo* 19 (*De Temperantia et Incontinentia* [P.G., 32. col. 1348]; *Epistles*, 2; 46 (*Epistolarum Classis*, 1); Cyprian, *Ad Fortunatum de Martyrio* [P.L., 4. col. 693]; *Liber de zelo et livore* [P.L., 4. col. 666]; Chrysostom, Hom., 44, Gen 41:46–49, n. 7; Bede, in *Marci Evangelium Exposito*, Lib. 4 [P.L., 92. col. 279].

The seventh link of the Joseph trajectory is therefore open-ended. Some think Joseph died early in Jesus' life. Others think he lives as an ethical symbol. To me, Joseph is a legend. Therefore, the search for Jesus as child of God cannot avoid the issue of his fatherlessness. Within Christendom, the Joseph tradition clearly developed as a trajectory. This line of thought was impelled by the anti-Christian calumny against Mary and the associated evolution of the idea of the "pure" (sinless) birth of Jesus. This idea led to the conviction that Mary remained a virgin after Jesus' birth, and even that she was herself the fruit of a divine birth. However, there is no trace of a father in Jesus' life in historical Jesus material. For Jesus, God filled this emptiness.

CHAPTER 5

What Was His Father's Name?

In peasant society of the first-century Mediterranean world, everyone had a social map that precisely defined one's position in terms of identity, kinship, and expected behavior.[1] Seeing Jesus in light of an ideal-type of a fatherless figure in the first century C.E. can help to explain in a coherent, systematic way the individual facets of his life we have thus far untangled, especially, when one keeps in mind that in the peasant society of Jesus' world, the family revolved around the father.

STATUS ENVY AND SOCIAL IDENTITY

The father and the mother were the source of the family in this society, not only in the biological sense, but because their interaction with their children created the structures of society. A peasant economy was geared toward subsistence, the mere maintenance of the family, rather than investment in the future. This was the peasant father's goal, and therefore the socialization process employed in such communities was one that fostered the child's dependence. In the 1960s, Harvard University conducted, from a social psychology perspective, a cross-cultural study on the father's position in the family as it relates to the process of identification of children.[2] This research, supported by cross-cultural material, was related to what is called the "status envy hypothesis." Specifically, the evidence focused on the effect of father absence in the household.

The outcome of the study differed from some other theories of identification in that, in terms of the hypothesis, a relationship that fully satisfies both parties is not conducive to identification. According to the status envy hypothesis, for a child to identify fully with adults, it is necessary that adults openly consume resources that are denied to the child. In other words, love alone will not produce identification unless the people a child

---

1. Scott, *Hear Then the Parable*, 79; depending on Jerome H. Neyrey.
2. At a symposium during which the evidence of this research was tabled, Roger V. Burton of the National Institute of Mental Health and John W. M. Whiting of Tulane University shared a paper. The following references are from a shortened revision of the paper published in 1961.

loves withhold from her something she wants. This is particularly true during the process of socialization. This process involves familiarizing the child with the privileges and disabilities fundamental to the structure of a particular society.

As part of the cultural rules in every society, there is a status system that gives the privileged access to resources in the system and, at the same time, debars others from controlling and consuming them. A resource is a material or nonmaterial commodity—such as food, water, optimum temperature, and freedom from pain, including punishment—that one person may desire, but over which some other person may have control. Symbolic resources include love, comfort, power, and success. Were these resources inexhaustible and equally and completely available to all, there would be no learning by identification because there would be no such thing as status envy. This, however, is never the case. Nobody in a household in any society has unlimited access to every resource. Societal taboos make it practically impossible. It is inevitable that some resources will be withheld and that someone will want them. It is particularly true in agrarian societies with limited goods that are patrilocal in nature. In societies with patrilocal residence, a man spends his whole life in or near his place of birth. This results in a core of blood-related male residents, supplemented by wives drawn from neighboring communities. The women are literally and figuratively outsiders. It is the men who are the locus of power and prestige: the "adult males are the ones to be envied."[3] This hypothesis about the process of identification and the development of identity may be summarized as follows: identification is achieved by the imitation of a status role that is envied. This happens not overtly but in fantasy, and the driving force is envy of the person who enjoys the privileged status.[4]

In every society, statuses have names or labels. In modern Western society, for example, there are the familiar kinship statuses of father, mother, uncle, aunt, brother, sister; the age-determined statuses of infant, child, adolescent, adult, and aged; occupational statuses such as doctor, lawyer, clerk, and workman; and the sex-determined statuses of male and female. As said, the family, and especially the father, was at the center of the first-century Mediterranean world. Beyond the family lay the village, beyond that the city, and further still the limits of the world. This understanding of society served as an analogy for the concept of the kingdom of God.[5] The father's role in the family was not only that of God's representative, but also the person who had to ensure that God was worshipped and obeyed. One had to belong to a family to enjoy God's blessing, and, within the family, the

---

3. Burton and Whiting, "Absent Father," 89.
4. Cf. Ibid., 85.
5. Scott, *Hear Then the Parable*, 79.

father's status was divinely ordained.[6] And so, the divine and the human met each other at the most intimate level, the familial.

The identity of a person is his or her position or positions in the status system of a particular society. Three kinds of identity can be distinguished. *Attributed identity* consists of the statuses assigned to a person by other members of the society. *Subjective identity* consists of the statuses one sees oneself as occupying. *Optative identity* consists of those statuses one wishes one could occupy but from which one is debarred.[7] The aim of socialization in any society is to produce an adult whose attributed, subjective, and optative identities are isomorphic: "I see myself as others see me, and I am what I want to be." However, such isomorphism necessitates a transition marked by status debarment, which produces status envy and a reaching out from attributed to optative identity. That is, when an adult fantasizes about having a father, according to the status envy hypothesis, he would to become an adult who was deprived of the privilege of having a father during infancy. When society then permits him to occupy this privileged status, there is agreement on what he wants to be, on what society says he is, and on what he sees himself to be.

One's optative identity derives from status envy and it should always be objective and realistic. In households where the father is absent, the wish to be a father is not as realistic as the wish to have a father. The wish to have a family seems realistic in a situation where the privilege of having a position in a family is debarred. According to this theory, a fatherless infant who has been given everything by his mother would not identify with her as he already occupies the privileged status. We can presume that if a man wishes to have a fictive family, he did not occupy a privileged status within his biological family during infancy. And one could continue on this line: If someone is said by members within the community of Israel to be the son of Abraham and the son of God, these labels could express status envy and optative identity. The former name is an expression of a position within the extended genealogical family of Israel; the latter is the symbolic/fantasied expression of the mentioned position of having or being a father. In normal conditions, both types of labels are expressions of attributed identity. Having a position in the family is an identification of secondary nature and having a father is a primary identification.

Applied to the eastern Mediterranean context, Crossan says that "to be a child was to be a nobody, with the possibility of becoming a somebody absolutely dependent on parental discretion and parental standing in the community."[8] In other words, arrangements in infancy lead to primary

---

6. See Hamerton-Kelly, *God the Father*, 27.
7. Burton and Whiting, "Absent Father," 85.
8. Crossan, *Historical Jesus: The Life of a Mediterranean Jewish Peasant*, 269.

identification, whereas those in childhood lead to secondary identification. But there could also be a discrepancy between these two identifications because of status debarment on the primary level that needs to be resolved by an initiation ritual.

Cross-cultural studies yield significant variables bearing upon the hypothesis as postulated. Specifically, the social structures of a sample of societies were judged for the degree to which the father and adult males in general occupy privileged statuses as perceived by the infant and later by the child.[9] One such measure of privileged status, and therefore of status envy in childhood, is provided by the sleeping arrangements that appertain to a society.[10] Because it is the place where resources of greatest value to a child are given or withheld, a child's bed is at the center of its world during infancy. Those who share sleeping arrangements with the child become the child's models for primary identification, and the key question in this regard is whether or not the father also sleeps with the mother. In thirty-six out of sixty-four societies examined, the parents sleep apart during the nursing period so that the infant can enjoy the mother's exclusive attention. In the remaining twenty-eight societies, the parents sleep together with the child either sleeping in the bed with them or placed in a crib or cradle within reach of the mother. It follows that, in terms of the hypothesis, the situation prevailing would have a profound effect on the child's primary identification. If the parents sleep together, they both bestow and withhold resources so that the envied status would be in either parent. The infant perceives the juxtaposition of privilege to be between himself or herself and an adult. On the other hand, where the parents sleep apart, the mother assumes a role of greater importance in the child's life. The juxtaposition of privilege is between the child and mother, and, because she sometimes withholds resources, she is the person who is envied. In societies where infants enjoy their mother's exclusive attention in terms of sleeping arrangements, the optative identity of boys may be expected to be cross-sexual in nature, while those reared in societies where, because of the sleeping arrangements both adults withhold resources and are therefore envied, the optative identity of boys is more likely directed to adulthood as such.

Residence patterns provide the conditions for secondary optative identity also in the case where sex-determined statuses are relatively unprivileged because of primary cross-sex optative identity. Patrilocal societies would produce a conflict between primary and secondary optative sex identity when there are exclusive mother-child sleeping arrangements. In societies with maximum conflict in sex identity—for example, where a boy initially sleeps exclusively with his mother but the domestic unit is patrilo-

---

9. See Burton and Whiting, "Absent Father," 88–89.
10. Cf. Whiting, Kluckhorn, and Anthony, "Function of Male Initiation Ceremonies," 359–70.

cal and hence controlled by men—initiation rites at puberty function to resolve this conflict in identity. In the above-mentioned sample of sixty-four societies, there are thirteen in which "elaborate initiation ceremonies with genital operations" takes place.[11] All thirteen have the exclusive mother-infant sleeping arrangements, which, according to the hypothesis, cause a primary feminine identification. Furthermore, twelve of these thirteen have patrilocal residence that produces the maximum conflict in identity and hence the need for an institution such as an initiation rite to help resolve this conflict. Initiation rites serve the psychological function of replacing the primary feminine identity with a firmly established male identity.[12] This is accomplished by means of hazing, deprivation of sleep, tests of manliness, and painful genital operations, which are rewarded with the high status of manhood if the initiate endures them unflinchingly. By means of the symbolic death and rebirth through these initiation rites performed at puberty, a male born in these societies leaves behind the woman-child status into which he was born and is reborn into his optative status and identity as a man.[13]

With regard to the first-century Mediterranean world, the nature of the roles performed in the family by men, women, and children correlated with the "division of honor into male and female."[14] The family from which someone came was called the "family of orientation." The "family of procreation" was involved in the roles of the women in the family whose "exclusiveness" was defended by the males. Male honor, symbolized by the testes, was associated with not accepting slights, standing up to other males, exercising authority over the family, and defending its honor. Female honor, symbolized by the hymen, related to sexual exclusiveness, reserve, caution, modesty, and timidity. Although a mother's sexual purity was the concern primarily of her husband, it impinged also on her male children. Furthermore, males were involved in the purity of their daughters and sisters. The father of a household was not merely a begetter, but also a provider and protector. So it was not a child's birth that made the child a part of a household, but the father's decision to adopt the child into the household.[15] This, rather than birth, was the beginning of life, and the father, who exercised the power of life and death over his offspring, was a "godlike being."

Although women fulfilled the primary, gender-specific role of childbearing, the mother of a household was empowered to ensure that the other female members of the household regularly bore children as well. Her role

---

11. Burton and Whiting, "Absent Father," 90.
12. Ibid.
13. Cf. Whiting, Kluckhorn, and Anthony, "Function of Male Initiation Ceremonies."
14. Malina, *New Testament World*, 48–55.
15. Cf. Matthews and Benjamin, *Social World of Ancient Israel,* 8, 10.

as manager of the household was not gender-specific. The responsibility for ensuring that everyone was fed and that the food would last entailed careful stewardship of the resources that the village allocated to her household. The responsibility necessitated absolute control over this aspect of household life.[16] The mother was not only the childbearer and the manager of the household, she was also the teacher of its women and children. For a boy, however, this role was transferred to the father once the boy became a young man and participated in the communal labor of the village. As storyteller, the mother communicated the traditions of the community to her children. Apart from practical skills, she taught them all kinds of wisdom as well.[17] Typical female behavior included taking the last place at the table, serving others, forgiving wrongs, having compassion, and attempting to heal wounds.[18] All these acts are to be found among the list of the authentic deeds of the historical Jesus.

Various studies that focus on the factor of father-absent households in the early life of boys support the postulated hypothesis of status envy.[19] Specifically, some of these studies indicate that "war-born" boys from father-absent households not only behave like girls in fantasy behavior but also show very little aggression.[20] This kind of performance derives from the boys' first or primary identification. Their secondary identification leads to behavior, overtly and in fantasy, that produces father-like performance.

In her book, *Beyond Patriarchy: The Images of Family in Jesus* Diane Jacobs-Malina poses an intriguing thesis that Jesus' role was most like that of the "wife of the absent husband."[21] Focusing on the "submerged and subordinated social world of women in patriarchal society," Jacobs-Malina considers the "nineteenth-century western debate over the Jesus of history versus the Christ of faith" as irrelevant to the discussion in her book.[22] However, exactly because of her focus, I regard the quest for the historical Jesus as central to her thesis, although I agree that in a particular sense, with regard to her hypothesis, it does not matter whether the perspective of theology or sociology provides one's point of departure. From the perspective of *theology*, fatherlessness would refer to an absent father in heaven; from

---

16. Cf. Ibid., 25.

17. Cf. Ibid., 28–29.

18. Cf. Malina, *New Testament World*, 54.

19. See Blankenhorn, *Fatherless America*; Bach, "Father-Fantasies and Father-Typing"; Grønseth, "Impact of Father Absence"; Lynn and Sawrey, "Effects of Father-Absence"; Tiller, "Father Absence and Personality Development"; Mitscherlich, *Society without the Father*; Tripp-Reimer and Wilson, "Cross-Cultural Perspectives"; Stearns, "Fatherhood in Historical Perspective"; Marciano, "Religion and Its Impact"; Adams, Milner, and Schrepf, *Fatherless Children*; Bowen and Orthner, "Effects of Organizational Culture"; Jurich, White, White, and Moody, "Internal Culture of the Family"; Herzog, "On Father Hunger"; Angel and Angel, *Painful Inheritance*; Mott, "When Is a Father Really Gone?"

20. Burton and Whiting, "Absent Father," 93.

21. Jacobs-Malina, *Beyond Patriarchy*, 2.

22. Ibid., 8.

the point of view of *sociology*, the same phenomenon would be studied in terms of analogies in everyday society—thus, in terms of the ideal-type of being fatherless in first-century Palestine.

From the perspective of the belief (attested to in Luke's Gospel and elaborated upon in some post-New Testament documents) that God, the absent Father who is in heaven, impregnated Mary, who gave birth to Jesus, Jacobs-Malina studies the behavior of the wife of an absent husband in patriarchal first-century eastern Mediterranean society. By investigating themes in Mark and in the Pauline tradition, Jacobs-Malina finds that Jesus, the "fatherless son," did not act according to the expected role of the eldest son in a patriarchal family, but rather like that of the wife of an absent husband. She suggests that the image of Jesus reflected in the Gospels is reminiscent of that of the idealized wife/mother in the social world of Jesus. Acting on behalf of an absent Father in heaven, his primary role was the maintenance of God's household on earth.[23]

In patriarchal societies, the belief is commonly held that a male presence is necessary lest a woman bring shame on the family. If her husband is absent, a woman has to serve his interest by strictly conforming to his wishes or instructions. This results in close social scrutiny. A husband's absence imposes on his unsupervised wife even more rigorous expectations of decorum than those that are normally applied. Although he is absent, he remains present to his children through his wife as his authorized agent, who has the responsibility to ward off any challenge to her husband's prerogatives. Jacobs-Malina claims that this role, with its attendant rights, obligations, values, and activities, furnishes a good analogy or conceptual frame of reference for the role we see Jesus fulfilling in the Gospels in his relationship to God, to his followers, and to outsiders.[24] Domestic settings, such as these in the concrete language of parables, serve as analogies for God's kingdom, revealing the absent Father, whose household Jesus was authorized to create and maintain.[25]

My hypothesis differs from that of Jacobs-Malina. I do not metaphorically regard Jesus' relationship to God as one of husband and wife but, according to textual evidence, as father and son. I see this relationship as the product of the historical Jesus' "fantasy" caused by being fatherless in life.

According to the Freudian Oedipal complex, a boy's identification with his father originates in his desire to be like his father, but this is later replaced by the drive to replace the father in the mother's affections.[26] Is my thesis just another modern version of the Oedipal complex? Or is my image of the first-century Jesus the very beginning of the process that Hubertus

---

23. Ibid., 2.
24. Ibid., 6.
25. Ibid., 7.
26. Cf. Hamerton-Kelly, *God the Father*, 38.

Tellenbach identifies?[27] Contrary to Freud's contention that the father is at the center of consciousness,[28] Tellenbach is of the opinion that the role of the father figure has vanished today from the Western psyche. In the seventies, Tellenbach was the chair of the Department of Clinical Psychopathology at the Psychiatric Clinic in Heidelberg, Germany. From years of observing young schizophrenics, he found that the father played no role whatsoever in their lives.[29] According to Tellenbach, the disappearance of the father today is the result of a long process. He traces this process back in art and literature. From a macrosociological perspective, it might be seen as having roots in the period in which simple agrarian societies in the Middle East developed into advanced agrarian societies.[30] Although kinship ties remained of great importance for individuals throughout the agrarian era, they were no longer the "chief integrating force" in advanced agrarian societies.[31]

Such profound economic changes, especially with regard to Herodian Palestine, had an inevitable effect on kinship patterns and social relationships. The extended family began slowly breaking up.[32] The Hellenistic period inaugurated far-reaching change for many Israelites who had previously lived in extended family units, subsisting through communal labor on isolated farms. They now found themselves most commonly in nuclear families living and working on large estates.[33] It seems that only two options were open to peasants when their families disintegrated because their "agroeconomic" base was removed.[34] They could either increase their production or reduce their consumption. The former strategy necessitated putting more labor into their pieces of land, but in terms of the returns, this was hardly worthwhile. So they were propelled to supplement their income. They could hire themselves out as day laborers for seasonal agricultural work or for temporary work in the fishing industry, or perhaps find work as craftsmen.[35]

Neighbors in the village, which became the only viable economic unit, started to function as a socially supportive unit. This was true of village life in the ancient Mediterranean world, and, as children seldom left the village

---

27. Tellenbach, *Vaterbild im Mythos*, 7–11. Against the backdrop of the revolutionary student protests of the late sixties, the University of Heidelberg organized a three-year seminar in the early seventies on the role of the father figure in Egypt, Greece, the Old Testament, and the New Testament. Tellenbach acted as the editor of the seminar proceedings, which were published as *Das Vaterbild in Mythos und Geschichte*. Jan Assmann made the contribution with regard to ancient Egypt; Lothar Perlitt with regard to the Old Testament; Hans-Georg Gadamer focused on Greek philosophy; Werner Lemke on Greek poetry; and Günther Bornkamm on in the New Testament.

28. Cf. Hamerton-Kelly, *God the Father*, 5.

29. According to Tellenbach, *Vaterbild im Mythos*, 7: "Die Phase des Vaterprotestes in der Vorgeschichte so gut wie immer fehlte."

30. Cf. Lenski, Lenski, and Nolan, *Human Societies*, 188–222.

31. Ibid., 213.

32. See Fiensy, *Social History of Palestine*, 132.

33. See Ibid., 121.

34. See Wolf, *Peasants*, 15.

35. See Fiensy, *Social History of Palestine*, 95.

on attaining adulthood, neighbors increasingly constituted the socioeconomic basis of relationships.[36] Villagers were generally related to each other
by ties of blood or marriage. Furthermore, marriage arrangements in
Judean society were very tightly linked to the way in which the temple cult
in Jerusalem was organized. The temple cult also determined both the classification of people and politics. This meant that "holiness was understood
in a highly specific way, namely as separation."[37]

> To be holy meant to be separate from everything that would
> defile holiness. The Jewish social world and its conventional wis-
> dom became increasingly structured around polarities of holi-
> ness as separation: clean and unclean, purity and defilement,
> sacred and profane, Jew and Gentile, righteous and sinner. . . .
> "Holiness" became the paradigm by which the Torah was inter-
> preted. The portions of the law which emphasized the separate-
> ness of the Jewish people from other peoples, and which stressed
> separation from everything impure within Israel, became domi-
> nant. Holiness became the *Zeitgeist*, the "spirit of the age," shap-
> ing the development of the Jewish social world in the centuries
> leading up to the time of Jesus, providing the particular content
> of the Jewish ethos or way of life. Increasingly, the ethos of holi-
> ness became the politics of holiness.[38]

When someone, according this politics of holiness, was considered as a
nobody, such a person would have no identity and would experience a tense
relationship with villagers and even with close relatives. Status envy would
therefore come as no surprise. Calling God father and negating the importance of patriarchy goes hand in hand. This disposition amounts to a redefinition of the whole system of holiness. It created not only tension between
Jesus and his relatives, but also between him and the proponents of the
Judean temple cult. Eventually it led to his killing by the Roman authorities.
At the center of Jesus' disposition lies a different understanding of who God
is and who humankind is. To apprehend this understanding we need to know
more about the Jerusalem cult and its ideology with regard to fatherlessness.

THE JERUSALEM CULT AND
MARRIAGE ARRANGEMENTS

The Israelites of the first century C.E., besides the Samaritans, were sub-
divided by Josephus into four factions: Sadducees, Pharisees, Essenes, and

---

36. Fiensy, *Social History of Palestine*, 135. Fiensy refers to the work of, among others, Harper,
"Village Administration," 106.

37. Borg, *Jesus—A New Vision*, 86.

38. Ibid., 86–87.

Zealots. The latter group was constituted as a group only in 68–70 C.E. during the Jewish War. Prior to this time, the term zealot had referred only to
those who were diligent about faithfully following the law. Whether the
Zealots were related to the militant group that since the late fifties of the
Common Era had become active and were known as the Sicarii ("sword-
fighters"), and whether both the Zealots and the Sicarii grew from the movement Josephus called the "Fourth Philosophy," are questions that are not relevant here.[39] What is important for the purpose of this study, however, is that
Israel was a temple state and that the "policies" of all these groups, as well as
the vision of Jesus, were determined by their respective perspectives on the
purity ideology of the Jerusalem temple cult—an ideology that marked the
conventions of the entire Israelite society as exclusivist and hierarchical. It
circumscribed familial, political, economic, and religious life.

The Sadducees, whose origin is found in the aristocratic Maccabean-
Hasmonean family, had ruled over the temple state in Jerusalem since the
Maccabean War in the second century B.C.E. Since then, high priests had
been appointed from the ranks of this family, which meant that the regulation of cultic acts by the priests (including the collection of offerings) was
being compromised by family interests. Offerings formed the basis of a taxation system that was supposed to be grounded in the economic values of
reciprocity and redistribution. By means of the products of their small-
scale farming, the "people of the land" supplied the aristocratic temple elite
with goods. Because of the system of patronage, the elite, as patrons, had to
reciprocate by looking after the needy. Religion, economy, family interests,
and politics were therefore interwoven in this society. The equilibrium
between "patrons" and "clients" in this hierarchically stratified society
teetered on a knife's edge.[40]

As the hierarchical ladder became longer as a result of additional taxes
that had to be supplied to the rulers on the higher rungs of the ladder, the
peasants towards the bottom had to supply more surpluses on smaller bits
of land. At the same time, less was passed down by the supposed "patrons"
to the needy. In this way, taxes more than doubled.[41] Galilean peasants, for
instance, not only had to pay temple tax and supply the Sadducean elite
with their offerings, but also had to pay the Herodian royal house. Herod
and the high priest, in turn, had to pay tributes to the emperor. The
extended families in the peasant community started breaking up and
poverty increased, and some unfortunate beggars even started finding it
difficult to survive on charity.

Thus, the following picture supplied the content for a story by Jesus in
Luke 16:19–31: A beggar lies before the closed gates of a wealthy master. Curs

39. Cf. Van Aarde, *Kultuurhistoriese Agtergrond*, 152–57.
40. Cf., among others, Stegemann and Stegemann, *Urchristliche Sozialgeschichte*, 43–44.
41. Fiensy, *Social History of Palestine*, 100–101.

overwhelm the weakened man by greedily grabbing from him the leftover food thrown outside the gates of the rich aristocrat and even mauling the man. He has only God to help him. This is what the name *Lazarus* means.[42]

Leftover food was not something that fit into the temple cult in Jerusalem. The purity regulations of this cult consisted of strict dietary prescriptions, among others. When Israelite men were older than twenty they could enter the outer court of the temple. They had to do this to entreat God by means of "gifts," which had really been given to them by God, to forgive them their infringements of the purity laws. The priests received these "gifts" and brought the offerings to God, although the emperor would also receive his share. However, Jesus questioned if God in fact received what was God's own![43]

Only the most important priest could enter the purest place in the temple, and only then on the purest Sabbath of the year, the Day of Atonement. In this way, the exclusive and hierarchical purity regulations were ordered by means of prescriptions governing the calendar, circumcision, and diet.[44] But the author of Luke-Acts tells us that Jesus lived as if the temple, by implication, did not have outer courts.[45] Matthew, in turn, emphasizes Jesus' indifference towards the rules relating to the Sabbath and the temple cult (12:1–8). Paul says that Jesus' death on the cross metaphorically refers to the hypocrisy that accompanied the practice of circumcision (Gal 6:12–13), while Mark hands down the tradition that Jesus ridiculed the customs relating to dietary prescriptions (7:14–23).

The Essenes and the Pharisees may be viewed as the parties in opposition to the Sadducees. The control by the Sadducees of "God's house," in the eyes of Jesus a "cavern where robbers live" (Mark 11:17), was to both the Essenes and the Pharisees a source of resentment. How could they neutralize this power? They were not of Hasmonean descent, and high priests were not born from them or appointed from their own elite families in power as a result of nepotism! What the Essenes did was simply to leave Jerusalem and replace the temple with their own community at Qumran.[46] The Essenes considered the Jerusalem temple cult to be completely corrupt (cf. 1 QpH 8:8–13; 12:9). To them, the Qumran community took the place of the temple (cf. 1 QS 5:6; 8:5, 9; 9:6).

The policy of the Pharisees was particularly ingenious.[47] Instead of replacing the house of God, they broadened it by extending the regulations that related to the temple cult in Jerusalem to the sphere where they could exercise control. Each house of each "son of Abraham" was seen by the

---

42. Cf. Scott, *Hear Then the Parable*, 141–59.
43. Mark 12:13–17 (parallel texts: Matt 22:15–22//Luke 20:19–26); *Gos. Thom.* 100:1–4; *Egerton Gospel* 3:1–6. See Funk and Hoover, *Five Gospels*, 102–3.
44. See Dunn, *Parting of the Ways*, 28–31.
45. See Conzelmann, *Interpreting the New Testament*, 123, 243; especially with regard to Acts 21:30.
46. See Gärtner, *Temple and the Community*, 18–21.
47. See Saldarini, *Pharisees, Scribes, and Sadducees*, 234.

Pharisees to be a replica of the temple.[48] Even the design of the house was modeled on that of the temple. Women and children were limited to their quarters, just as in the temple in Jerusalem. Above all, the regulations surrounding meals—in particular the Sabbath meal, which was a replica of the sacrificial temple meal,[49] together with the manifold dietary and purity prescriptions—transformed the country households into "holy places."

To a peasant community in which families were already poverty-stricken, these prescriptions by the Pharisees were a heavy yoke. Families had already started to disintegrate because of the heavy burden of temple taxes. In addition to cereal, animal, and sin offerings, tolls were demanded at strategic places on the roads to markets in the cities. A rebellious spirit, directed against their own royal elite as well as against their pagan oppressors, lay very close to the surface. The desire for a popular messianic king grew.[50] Gang leaders who sporadically opposed the authorities were sometimes seen as messiahs, and brigands who attacked patrols by the Romans or Herodians were offered hiding places. Tax collectors were hated as if they were thieves who had personally robbed the people.

An Israelite peasant, even in "Galilee where the Gentiles live" (1 Macc 5:15; Matt 4:15), could not ignore the cult of Jerusalem very easily. After all, as Jesus says in Matt 23:2, the Pharisees, as representatives of this cult, sit on the "chair of Moses." This means that they had the authority to interpret the Law of Moses. Moreover, convention insisted that "pious" peasants also make the journey to Jerusalem for big religious festivals and to pay the temple tax. The collectors of the temple tax even went from Jerusalem to the countryside to collect the taxes. This was done if the people had not deposited their share into the treasure chest in the outer temple court or had not exchanged their "incorrect" coins (at a considerable commission) for the correctly minted silver coins (as prescribed by the Torah) at the money tables.[51]

The marriage regulations determined by the temple are another aspect of life that would have continually reminded a Galilean of Jerusalem. Marriages took place in all households, including those in the Galilean countryside. The rules prescribing who could marry whom were determined by the Torah. The temple hierarchy's hand was clearly visible in the postexilic marriage regulations. The world of the Bible was patriarchal in nature, with the interest of the head of the family paramount. We have seen that this world can also be described as patrilocal. In communities with patrilocal residence, the man spent his entire life in or near the place of his birth. This led to a nuclear group of male persons that was determined

---

48. See Neusner, *From Politics to Piety*, 75; Elliott, "Temple versus Household"; Elliott, "Household and Meals."

49. See Neusner, *Way of Torah*, 47.

50. See Horsley and Hanson, *Bandits, Prophets, and Messiahs*.

51. See Richardson, "'Why Turn the Tables?'" 513.

through blood relations. The group was supplemented by spouses who came from neighboring towns. This society was characterized, for the sake of self-preservation and survival, by strong competition in politics and the economy. Identity functioned within the bounds of the group. Therefore, one must distinguish between the "family of procreation" and the "family of orientation." In the former case, one might refer to "Simon, son of Jonah," and, in the latter, to the "sons of Jonah."

Regulations for marriage during the Second Temple period were determined strongly by cultic purity regulations. Thus, for instance, marriages were only allowed when they took place within the ambit of one's own group of families, the "family of procreation"; that is, the house of Israel.[52] Marriages were geared toward the continuation of the "holy seed," that is, of the physical "children of Abraham."[53] The practice of circumcision and admission to the temple as the place of God's presence was closely related to this. The commandment on divorce, by means of the marriage reform regulations (Ezra 9–10; Neh 13:23–27), was meant to achieve the dissolution of undesirable "mixed marriages."[54]

These marriage arrangements were embedded in the stratification of people from holy to less holy to impure:[55]

1. priests
2. Levites
3. full-blooded Israelites
4. illegal children of priests
5. converts (proselytes) from heathendom
6. converts from the ranks of those who had previously been slaves, but had been set free
7. bastards (born from mixed marriages or through incest)
8. the fatherless (Aramaic: *štuqin*) (those who grew up without a father or a substitute father and therefore were not embedded within the honor structures)
9. foundlings (Aramaic: *'supin*)
10. castrated men (eunuchs)
11. men who had been eunuchs from birth
12. those with sexual deformities
13. hermaphrodites (bisexual people)
14. Gentiles (non-Israelites)

---

52. See Malina, *First-Century Mediterranean Persons*, 50.
53. See Malina, *New Testament World*, 137–38.
54. See Bossman, "Ezra's Marriage Reform."
55. See Jeremias, *Jerusalem in the Time of Jesus*, 271–73; Neyrey, "Symbolic Universe of Luke-Acts," 279; Funk, *Honest to Jesus*, 202. This hierarchical construct is inferred from *m. Kiddushin* 4:1; *m. Horayoth* 3:8; *t. Rosh hash-Shanah* 4:1 and *t. Megillah* 2:7.

The principle behind this system of classification was related to the marriage regulations of the Second Temple period. This classification also determined who could marry whom and who could enter the temple.

The above-mentioned groups may be organized into seven categories.[56] The priests, Levites, and full-blooded Israelites form the first three categories. Illegal (not illegitimate) children of priests were children born of marriages that were inadmissible to priests. A priest was forbidden to marry a woman who already "belonged to a man," such as a widow, divorcée, or a woman who had been raped. These illegal children of priests form, with both groups of proselytes, the fourth category. Bastards, the fatherless, foundlings, and the castrated form the fifth category. Jeremias said the following about the fatherless and the foundlings:

> We have no information worthy of note on the *fatherless* (men whose father was unknown) and the *foundlings*. They were [born of a] forbidden marriage with both Israelites of pure descent and with illegitimate children of priests (M. Kidd. iv.1), for their father, or their parents were unknown. In fact, they were suspected of bastardy (cf. M. Ket. i.8–9); and on the other hand the possibility could not be excluded that they might without being aware of it, contract a forbidden marriage with a relation (b. Kidd. 73a).[57]

Those born eunuchs, those with deformed genitals, and hermaphrodites—in other words, people who could not marry at all—make up the sixth category. People with another ethnic orientation, those, in other words, outside of the covenant, form the seventh category. Any involvement with these people was strongly discouraged in Israel.

Those in the sixth category could make no biological contribution to the continuation of the children of Abraham. "True Israel," actually, consisted only of the first three categories. They could, with certain limitations, freely marry. People from the fourth category (illegal children of priests and proselytes) did belong to Israel and were allowed to marry Levites and full-blooded Israelites, but daughters among these illegal children and daughters of proselytes were forbidden to marry priests. Those in the fifth category were simply deemed "impure." These were people outside of the covenant, doomed, as far as the temple in Jerusalem was concerned, not to approach any closer than the temple square (the "court of the Gentiles"). They were obliged to live as if God did not exist.[58] If a man like this wanted to get married, he could do so only with an "impure" woman, among whom the

---

56. See Malina, *New Testament World*, 159–61.
57. Jeremias, *Jerusalem in the Time of Jesus*, 343 (author's emphasis).
58. See Sanders, *Historical Figure of Jesus*, 229.

Gentiles too were categorized. Otherwise such a person remained unmarried. In a society in which the honor of a man, in fact his entire social identity, was determined by his status as a member of the family of Abraham and his contribution to the physical continuation of that family, his status as unmarried had serious implications.

The image of the historical Jesus as the fatherless carpenter, the unmarried son of Mary, who lived in a strained relationship with his village kin in Nazareth, probably because of the stigma of being fatherless and, therefore, a sinner, fits the ideal-type of the fifth category described above. Although innocent as a child who was not supposed to know the nature of sin, the historical Jesus was denied the status of being God's child, doomed not to transmit the status of proper covenant membership and, therefore, not allowed to enter the congregation of the Lord in the light of the ideology of the temple and its systemic sin.

Yet Jesus shared the vision of John the Baptist that remission of sin could be granted by God outside the structures of the temple. Both before and after his baptism and breach with John the Baptist, Jesus was noted for his association and friendship with "sinners," and his trust in God as his Father. This attitude is certainly subversive toward the patriarchal values that underlined the marriage strategy of the Second Temple period. The historical claim may therefore be made, in terms of the criteria of the Second Temple period, that Jesus was regarded as illegitimate due to his being fatherless. On account of this "permanent sin," fatherless men (boys over the age of twenty) were not allowed to enter the temple (cf. Deut 23:3) or to marry a full-blooded fellow Israelite.[59]

John Pilch has made a valuable contribution with regard to child rearing in the Mediterranean world and its application to the life of Jesus.[60] It is not Pilch's intention to distinguish between the historical Jesus and the Jesus of faith as recorded in the New Testament. Although I, therefore, disagree with his statement that Jesus' parents successfully socialized him into his cultural world, and Jesus' behavior bears witness to their success,[61] the results of Pilch's study remain of special importance for my own research. Pilch shows how ambivalent Mediterranean society was in respect of its value system, since both the feminine quality of nurture and the male quality of assertion were emphasized.

In early childhood, the boy learned nurturing values, but these became displaced by the "clarification of status" that marked his passage at puberty from the gentle world of women to the authoritarian world of men. It is a kind of transformation that developed out of a parenting style in the Near

---

59. Cf. [Babylonian] *Yebamot* 78b; see Fiensy, *Social History of Palestine*, 165.
60. Pilch, "Beat His Ribs."
61. Ibid.

East through which the boy learned from his father (or male next-of-kin) that "Abba isn't Daddy," to use the words of James Barr![62] In the aggresive and hierarchical world of men, Jesus learned, according to Pilch, to reject the comfort of childhood and the warmth of feminine values and to embrace instead the rigors of manhood, subjecting himself in unquestioning obedience to the severity of the treatment that his father and other males might inflict on him.

If a clarification of status is lacking because of fatherlessness, one can anticipate a diffused identity. It is likely that status envy could cause, as Donald Capps suggests with regard to Jesus, the "child . . . as an endangered self" to desire "to be another man's son."[63] In the words of Jane Schaberg, "the paternity is canceled or erased by the theological metaphor of the paternity of God."[64] The resources that were withheld in Jesus' case would be those that a father was expected to give his son. Since Jesus called God his Father, it seems that the followers of Jesus interpreted his suffering as a filial act of obedient submissiveness to God, his heavenly Father.

On the assumption that his primary identification was never "clarified" by a secondary identification, the fatherless Jesus seemingly behaved in womanlike manner as an adult. This can be seen in his sayings and deeds, in which he advocated taking the last place at the table, serving others, forgiving wrongs, having compassion, and healing wounds. Given this interpretation, status envy produced spontaneous, if not intentional, antipatriarchal behavior.

Jesus' attributed identity seems to consist of his fatherless status, or his being as the members of his society perceived him. This position, assigned to him because of the purity ideology during the Second Temple period, would lead to his debarment from being child of Abraham, that is, child of God. Jesus' subjective identity seems to consist of the status he saw himself occupying: the protector and defender of the honor of outcasts, like abandoned women and children, and giving the homeless a fictive home. And finally, Jesus' optative identity, which consists of that status he wished he could occupy but from which he was debarred, seems to be child of Abraham, that is, child of God. This could be the reason why the fatherless Jesus called upon God as his Father.

---

62. Barr, "Abba Isn't 'Daddy.'"
63. Capps, "Desire to Be Another Man's Son," 21.
64. Schaberg, "Canceled Father."

CHAPTER 6

~

Defending The Fatherless

In chapter 4, I argued that a biological father did not play a role in the life of the historical Jesus. I ended chapter 3 by stating that Jesus' baptism, according to Mark 1:9, fits into the social context of someone who went to John the Baptist to, in light of Isa 1:16–17, "wash himself" of (systemic) "evil," to "plead for the widow" and "defend the fatherless." According to this particular context in Mark, it is also clear that (the fatherless) Jesus, child of Mary (cf. Mark 3:31–35; 6:3), was believed to be child of God. By this remark, I anticipated my understanding of Jesus, child of God who, according to Mark 10:1–12 and 13–16, pleaded for the (patriarchless) widow and defended the (fatherless) street children. The latter passage, the one about Jesus blessing the children and seeing them as central to God's kingdom, is often referred to as the *Evangelium Infantium* ("Gospel for Children").

JESUS—KINGDOM OF GOD—CHILDREN

Without repeating the painstaking detail of historical-critical analysis, I accept John Dominic Crossan's finding on the "complex" of *Jesus—Kingdom of God—Children*.[1] Crossan is clear that, in terms of the sequence of strata, the first stratum contains data chronologically closest to Jesus. Literary units of Jesus tradition composed within the first stratum, however, are not necessarily historically the most accurate. Theoretically, a unit from the fourth stratum can be more original than one from the first stratum. Therefore, a hierarchy of attestation of units and, especially, complexes of units is necessary, beginning with the first stratum and working from there to the second, third, and fourth. The complex *Jesus—Kingdom of God—Children* comprises six units, namely the *Gos. Thom.* 22:1–2; Mark 10:13–16//Matt 19:13–15//Luke 18:15–17; Matt 18:3; and John 3:1–10. Thus, it is a complex that is attested by a textual unit belonging to the first stratum (Thomas) and that is supported by multiple independent attestations of the second stratum (Mark) and third stratum (Matthew and John).

1. See Crossan, *Historical Jesus: The Life of a Mediterranean Jewish Peasant*, xxxiii–xxxiv; Crossan, "Life of a Mediterranean Jewish Peasant," 120.

These multiple and independent attestations show how seriously Jesus' attitude toward children should be taken historically. I will argue that it is possible to consider these children, from a perspective of the social stratification of first-century Herodian Palestine, as part of the lowest class, namely, the "expendables." Neither Mark nor its parallel texts in the other Gospels refer to parents bringing these children to Jesus. It seems that the children were street urchins. I am interpreting, on the one hand, this episode of defending the cause of the fatherless from the perspective of Jesus' own fatherlessness and, on the other hand, in light of the notion of "child of God" in the context of Paul. In chapter 7, I will focus on Paul's implicit reference to Jesus' call upon God as *Abba* ("Father") and on Paul's explicit notion (and its Greco-Roman background) of believers' adoption by God as children of God.

Scholars have argued from a historical-critical perspective (especially from the exegetical point of view that is referred to in German as *formgeschichtlich*) that the original social setting of the *Evangelium Infantium* in Mark 10:13–16 should place it as a miracle story.[2] This passage in the *Scholars Version* reads as follows:

> And they would bring children to him so he could lay hands on them, but the disciples scolded them. Then Jesus grew indignant when he saw this and said to them: "Let the children come up to me, don't try to stop them. After all, God's domain is peopled with such as these. I swear to you, whoever doesn't accept God's imperial rule the way a child would, certainly won't ever set foot in (God's domain)!" And he would put his arms around them and bless them, and lay his hands on them.

This passage is one example where *telling* and *showing* have been dialectically interlinked. The result is that it is almost impossible to discern between authentic individual components that go back to the historical Jesus and individual components that were colored by early Christians during the process of oral transmission. However, in terms of individual features and not of sayings as units, there is no reason to see the thrust of the *Evangelium Infantium* as authentic, even if the thrust originally goes back to a healing episode (or episodes) in the life of Jesus. Mark 10:13–16 as literary unit is Mark's composition.

Since the time of the Reformation, Mark 10:13–16 has been associated with the practice of baptizing children.[3] Although such an association is still

---

2. Sauer, "Ursprüngliche 'Sitz im Leben'"; Robbins, "Pronouncement Stories and Jesus' Blessing"; Schmithals, *Evangelium nach Markus*, 447–48.

3. Cf. Ludolphy, "Zur Geschichte der Auslegung."

made by some,[4] today this direct link between the baptizing of children and the *Evangelium Infantium* is not generally accepted.[5] As far as form is concerned, Mark 10:13–16 demonstrates the characteristics of what Martin Dibelius calls a paradigm and Rudolf Bultmann an apothegm. What this amounts to is that the *Evangelium Infantium* is a short (almost aphoristic) narrative that should be formally distinguished from, for example, the parable and the miracle story. Bultmann points out that the children in this story should be seen as the "idea," that is, a symbol or parable of some concern.[6] The German exegete J. Sauer has, however, very convincingly shown that Mark 10:13–16 is a combined form of an apothegm and a healing story, although it shows more of the characteristics of the latter.[7] Influential studies have independently or consciously supported Sauer in this view.[8]

What is immediately noticeable is that the introduction to Mark 10:13–16 demonstrates strong similarities with other healing narratives where the disabled are brought to Jesus as a performer of miracles, with a call on him to heal them.[9] For our purposes the following terminological aspects of this research can be pointed out:

> *brought [προσφέρω] to Jesus*. In the Synoptic Gospels, this expression is often used to refer to the bringing of the disabled and the sick closer, so that they could be healed.[10]
>
> *that Jesus should touch them [ἅπτομαι]*. In the Synoptic Gospels, this expression is used only in relation to miracle stories and the raising of the dead.[11]
>
> *the disciples rebuked the people [ἐπιτιμάω]*. This expression is frequently used in the New Testament with regard to miracle stories.[12]

---

4. See, e.g., Cullmann, "Spuren einer alten Taufformel"; Jeremias, *Kindertaufe in den ersten vier Jahrhunderten*, 61–68; Lindemann, *Kinder und die Gottesherrschaft*, 77, 97–99.

5. See, e.g., Aland, *Säuglingstaufe im Neuen Testament*, 67–71; Klein, "Jesus und die Kinder," 68–69; Schweizer, *Evangelium nach Markus*, 112; Gnilka, *Evangelium nach Markus*, 81; Sauer, "Ursprüngliche 'Sitz im Leben,'" 27–29; Derrett, "Why Jesus Blessed the Children," 1–3; Ringshausen, "Kinder der Weisheit," 34–42; Schmithals, *Evangelium nach Markus*, 445–46.

6. Bultmann, *Geschichte der synoptischen Tradition*, 6th ed., 215: "das Bild wird zur Sache selbst."

7. Sauer, "Ursprüngliche 'Sitz im Leben,'" 41–45.

8. See Derrett, "Why Jesus Blessed the Children," 1–2; Ringshausen, "Kinder der Weisheit," 41.

9. Cf. Klein, "Jesus und die Kinder," 59; Sauer, "Ursprüngliche 'Sitz im Leben,'" 41; and particularly Schmithals, *Evangelium nach Markus*, 445.

10. See Mark 2:4; Matt 4:24 – 14:35; Matt 8:16; Mark 1:32 (ἔφερον); Matt 9:2; Mark 2:3 (φέροντες); Matt 9:32; 12:22; 17:16; Mark 9:17 (ἤνεγκα); cf. also φέρω: Mark 1:32; 2:3; 7:32; 8:22; 9:19–20; Luke 15:18; Matt 17:17; Acts 5:16; exceptions: Matt 18:24; Luke 23:14.

11. See Mark 1:41; Matt 8:3//Luke 5:13; Mark 3:10; Luke 6:19; Mark 6:56; Matt 14:36; Mark 5:27–28; Matt 9:20–21//Luke 8:44; Mark 5:30–31; Luke 8:45–46; Mark 7:33; 8:22 (ἵνα αὐτοῦ ἅψηται); Matt 8:15; 9:29; 17:7 (with reference to raising from the dead); Matt 20:34; Luke 7:14; 8:47; 22:51; exception: Luke 7:39).

12. See Mark 1:25; Luke 4:35; Mark 4:39; Matt 8:26//Luke 8:24; Mark 9:25; Matt 17:18//Luke 9:42; Mark 10:48; Matt 20:31//Luke 18:39; cf. also Luke 4:39 and the "Markan seal of confession" in Mark 3:12//Matt 12:16//Luke 4:41. Outside the framework of the miracle story, one finds the word

do not prevent them [κωλύω]. The Greek verb for "do not prevent," on its own, does not concern the baptism tradition.[13] Significantly, this verb appears in Matthew only in relation to the parallel context, namely, Matt 19:14, and in Mark 9:38–41 two times in the same pericope that has a miraculous exorcism as its theme.[14]

Jesus put his arms around [ἐναγκαλίζομαι] the children. This expression only appears in the New Testament here in Mark 10:13–16. On the strength of the Septuagint's tradition of Prov 6:10 and 24:33 (among other references), "put one's arm around" has an affective connotation of compassion. Diodorus Siculus (first century B.C.E.) used it in the context of the healing of children.[15]

Jesus placed his hands on the children and blessed them [τίθημι τὰς χεῖρας ἐπ' or ἐπιτίθημι τὰς χεῖρας]. According to Sauer, the phrase "to place his hands on them" expresses a typical ritual found in healing practices.[16]

Walter Schmithals understands Mark 10:13–16 against the background of the healing of ostracized children.[17] In line with this interpretation, my research demonstrates that the Greek word τίθημι, which is translated above as "to place," functions semantically as the antonym for the Greek word (ἐκτίθεμαι). In some contexts the latter is used to denote "being put out of the home," "left out of doors," "abandoned," while (τίθημι) denotes "accommodating someone." This accommodation especially concerns ostracized children. To bless your child or to give your child a name implies accepting the child into your house. When the father proclaims the name of the child, he recognizes it as his own. In the fifties, At van Selms, my teacher of Semitic languages at the

ἐπιτιμάω, as far as the Synoptic Gospels are concerned, only in the Petrine confession in Mark 8:30, 32, 33, and parallels, and in the Lukan redaction in, e.g., Luke 17:3, but also in the Lukan material in Luke 19:39 and 23:40.

13. I say this despite what Oscar Cullmann and Joachim Jeremias, among others, infer from Acts 8:36. A form of baptism could be expected to be formulated interrogatively, while, in the Synoptic Gospels, κωλύετε occurs only as an assertion in the indicative (cf. Klein, "Jesus und die Kinder," 69; Pesch, *Markusevangelium,*132; Sauer, "Ursprüngliche 'Sitz im Leben,'" 41.

14. "Es ist ganz evident, daß im Hintergrund dieser Perikope Probleme urchristlicher Wunderpraxis stehen. Μὴ κωλύετε erweist sich somit als ein Terminus, der Raum dieser Praxis zumindest nicht unüblich war" (Sauer, "Ursprüngliche 'Sitz im Leben,'" 42). First Corinthians 14:39 is the only place in the New Testament where the expression μὴ κωλύετε occurs outside the referential framework of the "Wunderpraxis."

15. "Kybele schließt die kleine Kinder in die Arme [ἐναγκ.] u. heilt sie [σώζω], wenn sie krank sind" (see Arndt and Gingrich, *A Greek-English Lexicon,* 261. According to Sauer, "Ursprüngliche 'Sitz im Leben,'" 42, it is therefore also possible that the Greek words ἐναγκαλίσαμενος in Mark 10:16 describe a healing scene.

16. Sauer, "Ursprüngliche 'Sitz im Leben,'" 42. Cf. Matt 9:18; Mark 5:23; 6:5; 7:32; 8:23, 25; 16:18; Luke 4:40; 13:13; Acts 3:7; 28:8.

17. Schmithals, *Evangelium nach Markus,* 447–48.

University of Pretoria, wrote about family life in Ugaritic literature and noted, "Through the proclamation of the name the child becomes legally existent."[18]

To bless your children is to accept them into your home; to not bless your children is to abandon them. Being put out of the home was often the lot of unwanted children, such as the handicapped. The same fate fell on children born of unlawful unions (cf. Wis 4:6). Physically and mentally disabled children, the blind, those with only one eye or one arm, the leprous, the deaf, and the mute were often ostracized in this way.[19] The Roman philosopher and statesman Seneca, who was a contemporary of Jesus and well known for his call for a charitable attitude, referred to incidents in this connection (*Controversiae* 10:4.16).[20]

In the second or third century C.E., the anonymous writer of the well-known *Letter to Diognetus* referred to the widespread phenomenon of children being put out of homes:

> For the distinction between Christians and other [human beings], is neither in country nor language nor customs. For they do not dwell in cities in some place of their own, nor do they use any strange variety of dialect, nor practise an extraordinary kind of life. . . . Yet while living in Greek and barbarian cities, according as each obtained his lot, and following the local customs, both in clothing and food, and in the rest of life, they show forth the wonderful and confessedly strange character of the constitution of their own citizenship. They dwell in their own fatherlands, but as if sojourners in them; they share all things as citizens, and suffer all things as strangers. Every country is their fatherland, and every fatherland is a foreign country. They marry as all [human beings], they bear children, but they do not expose [ἐκρίπτω] their offspring. They offer free hospitality, but guard their purity.[21]

The Greek word translated above as "expose" is used in several places to refer to the ostracizing action of "putting someone out of the house or country."[22] This casting away of children should probably be seen as a primitive means to control population growth and ensure survival.[23] "The society

---

18. Van Selms, *Marriage and Family Life*, 90.

19. Stockton, "Children, Church, and Kingdom," 90.

20. See Dibelius, s.v. "Seneca, Lucius Annaeus," 1694–95. See also Boswell, "*Exposito* and *Oblatio*," 21, note 26; cf. Rawson, "Children in the Roman 'familia.'"

21. *Lake,* "Epistle to Diognetus," 358–361; cf. Wilson, "Infanticide, Child Abandonment, and Female Honour," 763, note 4.

22. See Liddell and Scott, *Greek-English Lexicon*, 1572.

23. See Boswell, "*Exposito* and *Oblatio*"; Countryman, *Dirt, Greed, and Sex*, 22.

tends to mandate infanticide in areas affecting the entire society in either ecological (overpopulation) or social (illegitimate) domains."[24] In many societies, records witness that "adulterous conception was offered as grounds for infanticide."[25] In some tribes males were said to assist upon the death of any child whose features suggested a nontribal sire. Cases are recorded that "deformed children were described as ghosts or demons, with the rationale for infanticide expressed in terms of a struggle with hostile supernatural forces."[26] Susan Scrimshaw refers to stories told by the Yaudepu Enga of New Guinea about "supernatural beings who take abandoned children and rear them to live privileged lives."[27] The Greco-Roman legend of the rescue of the unborn Asclepios by the one who conceived him, the god Apollo, also is a remarkable example. Asclepios's mortal mother, Coronis, was accused of infidelity when she was found to be pregnant with Asclepios. She was exposed to die on a funeral pyre, but Apollo tore out his unborn child. After Asclepios learned the art of medicine, he became the healer god in the Greco-Roman world (which included first-century Palestine) and founder of a famous healing cult (of which traces are found at the Pool of Bethesda in Jerusalem).[28] In Somalia (in the days before Islam) "infanticide of healthy children was alleged to occur for purely magical reasons. . . . Somali parents used to dispose babies born under inauspicious astrological signs."[29]

Closer to the life and times of Jesus, several other references to the casting out of children are encountered in the writings of, among others, Lactantius (ca. 250–ca. 325 C.E.), Justin Martyr (died ca. 165 C.E.), Clement of Alexandria (ca. 160–215 C.E.), Seneca (ca. 4 B.C.E.–65 C.E.), and Tertullian (ca. 160–ca. 212 C.E.).[30] These writers use the Greek (ἐκτίθεμαι) and (ἐκθέσις) and the Latin *exposito* to refer to this ostracizing action, which often took place under the pretext that it was a sacrificial religious action. The practice in the Middle Ages of "donating" children to cloisters with ecclesiastical approval and regulation, should be seen in the same light.[31]

Just as the words *hot* and *cold* cannot be used in a semantically independent manner (the one finds its meaning in terms of the other) the meaning of the (ἐκτίθεμαι) is complemented by (τίθημι). The latter can indicate, among other meanings, an act of "assigning/appointing someone to a particular task, function, or role."[32] It is, in other words, an act of choosing.

24. Scrimshaw, "Infanticide in Human Populations," 448.
25. Daly and Wilson, "Sociobiological Analysis of Human Infanticide," 489.
26. Ibid., 492.
27. Scrimshaw, "Infanticide in Human Populations," 443.
28. Cimok, *Pergamum*, 84; White Fathers—Saint Anne, "Bethesda: St. Anne."
29. Daly and Wilson, "Sociobiological Analysis of Human Infanticide," 494.
30. Lactantius, *Institutiones Divinae* 5.9; Justin Martyr, *1 Apologia* 27; Clement of Alexandria, *Paedagogus* 3.3; Seneca, *Controversiae* 10.4.16; Tertullian, *Ad Nationes* 1.3.16.
31. Cf. Deroux, "Origines de l'oblature benedictine."
32. Cf. Louw and Nida, *Greek-English Lexicon*, 483.

Choosing need not always imply *selection*, but could also refer to the act of accepting into the home or even the vocation to fill a specific role. The name given to a child by the parents was sometimes related to a vocation to fulfill a particular role or perform a task.[33] In this connection, it is important to note that the parental custom of blessing a child and placing one's hands on that child (cf. the analogy in Mark 10:16) relates to the action of "accepting into the home" as opposed to "putting out of the home." To bless your child is to promise help and care.[34]

As a result of the (covenantal) relationship between a son and his father, one of the most important signs of honor that a son can show his father is to care reciprocally for him when he is old, and to bury him. The Greek word τίθημι is also used for this (see Acts 7:16), as well as προστίθημι (see Acts 13:36, where the word literally means "to entrust your father to his fathers").[35]

It seems that Old Israel took better care of its children than its neighbors took care of their children. For example, in Ps 106:37 Israel is called to abandon the heathen practice of child sacrifice.[36] This does not mean, however, that this custom was no longer practiced by the Israelites. In Ezekiel 16, God's covenant with Israel is compared to finding a little girl who had been rejected at birth, but who had been cared for by God as her parent in terms of a covenantal agreement. In Stephen's speech, the putting out of the child Moses is also described using the Greek verb (ἐκτίθεμαι) (Acts 7:21; cf. Exod 2:3 [LXX]).[37]

Children were abandoned for various reasons. Apart from survival motives or religious considerations, children were often "thrown away" because of an unwanted marriage and pregnancy.[38] In Wis 4:3–6, for example, these children were considered as "born of unlawful unions." Jane Schaberg understands first-century Mediterranean society's attitude toward the status of the child carried by the pregnant, betrothed woman (like Mary, as Matthew's story describes it) in light of the depiction that appears in the Wisdom of Solomon as well as in the Wisdom of Jesus, son of Sirach.[39] These texts contain references to the divorce of a "seductress" who became pregnant:

33. Cf. Patte, *The Gospel according to Matthew*, 23–28, with regard to Joseph's name of "son of David" in the Gospel of Matthew, as well as the designation of "God-with-us" given to Jesus.

34. Horst, "Segen und Fluch," 1650, refers in this connection to Ruth 4:13–16.

35. Louw and Nida, *Greek-English Lexicon*, 531. The Greek expression used in Acts 13:36 is: προσετέθη πρὸς τοὺς πατέρας αὐτοῦ.

36. See the comprehensive study by Stager and Wolff, "Child Sacrifice at Carthage," in this regard. Cf. Thompson, "Missing Hexateuchal Narrative;" Countryman, *Dirt, Greed, and Sex*, 27, note 11.

37. See Louw and Nida, *Greek-English Lexicon*, 728.

38. Boswell, "*Exposito* and *Oblatio*," 19.

39. Schaberg, *The Illegitimacy of Jesus*, 55–56.

So it is also with a woman who leaves her husband
And produced an heir by a stranger.
For first, she disobeyed the law of the Most High;
Second, she committed an offense against her husband;
And third, she committed adultery through fornication;
And produced children by a strange man.
She will be led away unto the assembly,
And punishment will fall on her children.
Her children will not spread out roots,
And her branches will not bear fruit.
She will leave her memory for a curse,
And her disgrace will not be blotted out. (Sir 23:22–26)[40]

A similar attitude toward the "children of adultery" appears in the
Wisdom of Solomon:

But the children of adultery will not come to maturity,
and the offspring of an unlawful union will perish.
Even if they live long they will be held of no account,
and finally their old age will be without honor.
If they die young, they will have no hope and no consolation in the day
    of decision.

                               . . .

For children born of unlawful unions
are witnesses of evil against their parents when God examines them.
    (Wis 4:3–6)[41]

The abandonment of a child referred to in Ezek 16:3 was precisely the
result of an undesirable mixed marriage. Incisive studies have been done on
the prohibition of mixed marriages during the reign of the last Judean kings
in particular.[42] This prohibition was mainly the effect of Ezra's postexilic
marriage reforms.[43] At the time of first-century Judean purification, these
reforms led to divorce being justifiable on the basis of Mosaic law (see Mark
10:1–10 and parallel texts). This state of affairs allowed for the ostracism of
the "impure" wife and her oldest child.[44] The debate between Jesus and the

---

40. Translation by Trenchard, *Ben Sira's View,* 95; cf. Schaberg, *Illegitimacy of Jesus,* 217, note 154.
41. Wisdom of Solomon 4:3–6 (RSV); cf. Schaberg, *Illegitimacy of Jesus,* 56.
42. See, e.g., Epstein, *Marriage Laws in the Bible.*
43. See, e.g., Bossman, "Ezra's Marriage Reform."
44. Cf. Bakon, "Jacob, Man of Destiny," 119; Meijer and Meijer, "Matriarchal Influence in the
Bible," 81–87; Goodnick, "Saga of the First Born"; Weaver, "Status of Children," with regard to the
period of the Roman Empire.

Pharisees (reported in at least three independent sources: Mark 10:1–12; Luke 16:18; Matt 5:32; and 1 Cor 7:10–11[45]) on whether or not divorce was justified should probably be understood against this background. The story of Jesus' empathy for an impure woman who was called a "sinner" and who had been put out of her house seems to reflect similar circumstances.[46]

This is still a modern-day phenomenon, as attested by the following newspaper report:

> In an unusual demonstration in Nazareth, Israel, yesterday [24 June 1991], about fifteen young Arab women protested against the killing of women by their male relations as a result of shame they had brought on their families. These women say that about forty young women are killed every year after extramarital pregnancies, unsanctioned love affairs, and wanting to marry men not considered suitable by their families.[47]

On 20 September 1994, Sapa-Reuter reports about a "girl killed in 'crime of honour'" in Amman, Jordan:

> A Jordanian teenager killed his 18-year-old physically handicapped sister after she gave birth to an illegitimate child. The 17-year-old stabbed his sister several times before shooting her while their parents ululated. The Jordan Times newspaper, quoting relatives and officials, said the girl, identified only as Jizia, was attacked a day after her family freed her from jail and signed a paper saying they would not harm her. The pregnant girl had been kept in custody until the baby was born to protect her from what is known in the Middle East as a "crime of honour." The brother surrendered to police.[48]

A woman, remains, in some sense, "a member of the father's house in which [she] was born . . . . and would return to [her family] if she was divorced or left widowed and childless."[49] When a woman with an

---

45. See Funk and Hoover, *Five Gospels*, 88.

46. "There are three quite different versions of this story, which appear to derive from three independent sources: Mark [14:3–9], Luke [7:36–50], John [12:1–8]. Matthew has simply copied Mark, so his version provides no additional information. The affinity of these stories with one another is unmistakable. Yet the differences suggest that the story (or stories) had a long and complicated history . . . . The Fellows of the Jesus Seminar were of the opinion that the original form of the story is beyond recovery. As a consequence, they also doubted that any of the words preserved by the evangelists could be attributed to Jesus" (Funk and Hoover, *Five Gospels*, 115–16).

47. "Vroue maak beswaar," *Transvaler*, 25 June 1991, 7 (my translation from the original Afrikaans).

48. "Girl killed in 'crime of honour,'" *The Pretoria News*, 20 September 1994, 4.

49. Countryman, *Dirt, Greed, and Sex*, 160.

unwanted pregnancy (whether married or betrothed or not) escapes death, yet is abandoned, the child could be cast away at birth. It seems that in New Testament times, people of other fringe groups who tried to exist outside the circle of normal family care were often the only refuge of the outcast woman and/or child. It is possible that among these people was the socioeconomic group that Josephus frequently refers to as "bandits."[50] Also among them seemed to be people such as we encounter in Matt 15:29–32

> Then Jesus left there and went to the sea of Galilee. And he climbed up the mountain and sat there. And huge crowds came to him and brought with them the lame, the blind, the maimed, the mute, and many others, and they crowded around his feet and he healed them. As a result, the crowd was astonished when they saw the mute now speaking, the maimed made strong, and the lame walking and the blind seeing. And they gave all credit to the God of Israel. Then Jesus called his disciples aside and said: "I feel sorry for the crowd because they have already spent three days with me and haven't had anything to eat. And I do not want to send these people away hungry, otherwise they'll collapse on the road." (Scholars Version)[51]

"Unclean" and "imperfect" people were seen as estranged from God. From the perspective of the politics of holiness, they were the "sinners" who were under the influence of demons. It is with this in mind that Matthew refers to some of the Galileans as living in the "land of the shadow of death" (Matt 4:16).

According to Matthew (who developed his understanding of Jesus' healing activities from themes in the Hebrew Scriptures, such as in Isa 8:23–9:2; 58:10), Jesus' message that God's kingdom was near at hand was for the peripheral people (the outcasts, the "people who lived in darkness") and was like the dawning of a light. According to purification customs, these people were the socially despised who were put out of homes and were refused admittance to the temple and synagogues. Jesus' miracles were aimed at the outcasts in Galilee.[52] Matthew 4:23–5:4ff. is also an example of such a report:

> And he toured all over Galilee, teaching in their synagogues, proclaiming the good news of (Heaven's) imperial rule, and healing

---

50. See Horsley, "Josephus and the Bandits."
51. Miller, *Complete Gospels*, 86.
52. Cf. Theissen, *Miracle Stories*, 249.

every disease and every ailment the people had. And his reputa-
tion spread through the whole of Syria. They brought him everyone who was ill, who suffered from any kind of disease or was in
intense pain, who was possessed, who was epileptic, or paralytic,
and he cured them. And huge crowds followed him from Galilee
and the Decapolis and Jerusalem and Judea and from across the
Jordan. Taking note of the crowds, he climbed up the mountain,
and when he had sat down, his disciples came to him. He then
began to speak, and this is what he would teach them:

> Congratulations to the poor in spirit!
> Heaven's domain belongs to them.
> Congratulations to those who grieve!
> They will be consoled.... (Scholars Version) [53]

I do not think that this report is historical in its entirety, but it signals
in all probability a clear picture of the fact that Jesus did not act only as a
healer of disease but also as a critic of society.[54] As Gerd Theissen notes,
"The healings must be seen against the background of the community
that recounted them, as collective symbolic actions by which distress was
remedied and in which the members found strength to combat it in their
ordinary lives by actions that were not merely 'symbolic.'"[55] The people
who were ill were the people who were poor, who grieved. These people
are mentioned in the first two beatitudes (Matt 5:3–4) that preface
Matthew's Sermon on the Mount. The Jesus Seminar regards these two
and the one about hunger and thirst (Matt 5:6) as already having been
interpreted by Matthew as "religious virtues rather than .... social and
economic conditions."[56] However, the "Fellows of the Seminar were virtually unanimous in their view that [the historical] Jesus is the author of
the[se] three congratulations."[57] The Lukan versions of those congratulations that are addressed to the poor, the weeping, and the hungry (Luke
6:22–23) are probably more original. They are not like the Matthean spir-
itualizations because they do not have the stipulations "poor *in spirit*" and
"hunger and thirst *for justice.*"

Yet what Matthew does should not go unnoticed or be seen as irrelevant.
Matthew has a "typifying style of composition."[58] He often summarizes his
understanding of Jesus' miracles. When Matthew adds religious virtues to

---

53. Miller, *Complete Gospels*, 65.
54. See Crossan and Watts, *Who Is Jesus?* 84.
55. Theissen, *Miracle Stories*, 251.
56. Funk and Hoover, *Five Gospels*, 139.
57. Ibid., 289–91.
58. Theissen, *Miracle Stories*, 207.

Jesus' talk on political and economic conditions, he certainly does not distance himself from the concrete social consequences of Jesus' healing activities. Theissen describes Matthew's method: "The programmatic miracle summary in [Matt] 4:23–25 precedes the Sermon on the Mount. In it teaching and healing are linked. What Matthew has joined, let not the exegete put asunder. Distinguishing between the two is a different matter."[59]

Theissen notes that belief in miracles among the humble people was "concentrated . . . . on specific situations of distress, on possession, disease, hunger, lack of success and danger."[60] And it is true, the Matthean miracle summaries "leave no doubt about the sort of people who flocked to [Jesus]; it was the *ochlos*, the 'crowd,' the humble people." They were part of the expendable class, "about 5-10%, for whom society had no place or need. They had been forced off the land because of population pressures or they did not fit into society. They tended to be landless and itinerant with no normal family life and a high death rate."[61]

Street children were to be found among them. It is striking that, in many places in Matthew, the "crowd" is called the "least" (25:40, 45), the "children" (15:26; 18:3), the "little ones" (18:14), and "sheep" (18:12; cf. 10:36 and 15:26). The metaphorical use of "sheep" in Matt 9:36 and 18:12 correlates with the expressions "the lost sheep of Israel" in Matt 10:6 and "the little children" in Matt 18:3–5, as well as "the little ones" in Matt 18:6, 10, 14 (cf. 10:42).

In the first century C.E., the casting out of children generally meant abandoning them to all types of social evils. The Christian apologist Lactantius pointed out that children abandoned thus often fell prey to wild animals or sexual abuse (*Institutiones Divinae* 5.9). Also Justin Martyr argued that Christians should be taught not to put their newly born children out of their homes, since almost all such children, both daughters and sons, would be abused as prostitutes (1 *Apologia* 27). Clement of Alexandria also called attention to this wretchedness and noted that men would later unwittingly have sexual intercourse with their own children, who had become prostitutes (*Paedagogus* 3.3). Tertullian objected to the custom of putting children out of the house, since the children would suffer (*Ad Nationes* 1.3.16). He acknowledged that it was not usually the parents' intention to harm their children, that strangers would sympathetically adopt the children and care for them better than their biological parents could because of the parents' limited resources.

Throughout the Middle Ages, the church received children who had been ejected from their homes. Thomas Aquinas studied in detail the teaching of children in the cloisters and questioned whether children who

59. Ibid., 207.
60. Ibid., 249.
61. Saldarini, *Pharisees, Scribes, and Sadducees*, 44.

did not yet understand what it was all about could be bound by a life-long oath, and whether such children had any place in the cloister.[62] It would appear that this did not, in fact, reflect true concern for the children, but that the large number of children put out of their homes and given to the church by their parents disrupted church life.[63] This practice of "sacrificing children" was called *oblatio*, and by the first century C.E. it had already been identified as distinct from *expositum* by Seneca (*Controversiae* 10.4.16).[64]

By the Middle Ages it had become important for the church to regulate the baptism and the reclaiming back of *expositi*. Ecclesiastical practices of the sixth century that even organized the sale of children are known to us. Within the Benedictine Order, in particular, we find that *oblatio* was sanctioned. Parents were forbidden to have any further say in the instruction and formal education of these children. The instruction of these children was also distinct from the normal instruction given to children in the cloisters.[65] At first, only the children of aristocrats were received, but later children from parents in the peasant society were also taken in. In the thirteenth century, the papal Decretum Gratiani began to forbid the practice of *oblatio*, and attempts were made to avoid receiving children under the age of eighteen in the monasteries.[66]

We have seen that Schmithals describes the original social location of the *Evangelium Infantium* (as far as it can be discerned historically) as the healing of ostracized children. He also notes that Jesus' acceptance of the children, which is apparent from his actions, should be seen as a condemnation of the practice of turning the children out of the home.[67] Persons such as widows and orphans, who had no connection with a patriarch, were necessarily marginal to the society.[68] From the sociohistorical information given above, one can argue that the social world mirrored in the *Evangelium Infantium* (and in the contexts of both Jesus' birth record in Matt 1:1–17 and the birth narrative itself in Matt 1:18–25) correlates with what is found in the contextual world in which Matthew's story as a whole makes sense.

I already mentioned that the infancy narratives are so filled with legendary content that almost no history can be inferred from them. James Veitch puts it as follows in a published lecture:

---

62. See *Summa Theologiae* 2a.2ae.88.9; 2a.2ae.189.5; 2a.2ae.189.5.2; *Quodlibetales* 3.5.11.12; 4.12.23; 4.12.23.7.
63. See Boswell, "*Exposito* and *Oblatio*," 29.
64. See Ibid., 14, note 4.
65. See Ibid., 16–17.
66. See Ibid., 25.
67. Schmithals, *Evangelium nach Markus*, 447–48.
68. Cf. Countryman, *Dirt, Greed, and Sex*, 167–68.

Matthew's birth stories were created out of stories in the Hebrew Bible. They are not accounts of what actually happened. . . . The third gospel, known to us as "Luke," probably circulated in the wake of the persecution of Domitian around the mid-90s of the 1st century. Its communities were Greek Christians. . . . In the light of persecution, they wished to present a story of Jesus using language and thought-forms of their contemporaries living in cities throughout the empire. Since the Roman Senate deified its emperors from Julius Caesar onwards, it is not surprising to find Christian writers doing the same for Jesus. . . . So what can be gleaned from "Matthew" and "Luke" about the actual historical circumstances of Jesus' birth? Very little. . . . There is the admission that the circumstances of the birth were not straightforward but quite special, prompting a suggestion of illegitimacy or premarital activity. Perhaps in a small village like Nazareth, set in a mixed-Jewish and non-Jewish area, a conception like this would give rise to speculation and gossip. But religious concerns prompted by creative human imagination have already taken over by the time we reach "Matthew," and the human Jesus is already lost from sight. . . . So forget the history and enjoy the myth.[69]

Yet, when one sees myths as emptied realities and one fills the emptied history with nature (as I suggested in chapter 3), one catches a glimpse of how the stories about Jesus' birth gave meaning to the life of oppressed people, among whom were women and children living at the fringe of society because they were the nobodies (the divorced and the fatherless, the widows, and the orphans) to whom patriarchy gave no place amidst the honorable.

Connecting the infancy narratives with Jesus' defense of patriarchless women and fatherless children is one way to demonstrate how Matthew's showing and Jesus' telling (and acting) interlink. To realize this dialectic is to take into consideration that the Jesus of history is retold as the Jesus of faith—that the *proclaimer* became the *proclaimed*.

A TALE OF TWO KINGS

I have argued that the accommodation of the abandoned child forms the original social setting of both Mark 10:1–12 (Jesus' critique of divorce) and Mark 10:13–16 (Jesus' blessing of street children). It seems also to be the fundamental social setting of the Matthean parallel in Matthew 19:13–15.

---

69. Veitch, *Birth of Jesus*, 11–13, 17.

Here the *Evangelium Infantium* in Mark serves as the source for Matthew's version of the complex "Jesus-Kingdom of God-Children." In my view, the same social setting can be assumed to be part of the background of the narrative about the birth of Jesus, at least as told in Matthew's story.

Matthew's story about the genesis and infancy of Jesus forms an appropriate parallel to what many find to be perhaps the most distinctive aspect of Jesus' ministry: his association with the "least," the "children," the "little ones," the "sheep." The use of these names portrays the care and love of Jesus as shepherd of God's people (cf. Matt 2:6). Against this background, it is so much more comprehensible that the *Evangelium Infantium* (in both Mark 10:13–16 and Matthew 19:13–15) should have been placed between the debate on divorce (Mark 10:1–12//Matt 19:1–12) and the rich young man's question about the implications of obeying the law in terms of compassion and the constitution of a "new" fictive family (Mark 10:17–31//Matt 19:16–30).

A genealogical record is a kind of certificate of status in terms of someone's attributed identity: "it certified the bearer as an official member of his culture in good standing, and conferred upon him the cultural credentials of role and status apposite to his ancestral heritage."[70] According to Matthew's narrative strategy, the birth record of Jesus (1:1–17) paves the way for the birth narrative as such (1:18–25). And the birth narrative in its turn paves the way for the story of King Herod versus the newborn king of the Jews (2:1–23). Instead of leading God's people, Herod (appointed by Caesar as "king of the Jews") killed children (see Josephus, *B.J.* 1.431–440) and in response was feared (see *Assumptio Mosis* 6:2–9).[71] Susan Scrimshaw, therefore, postulates dynastic politics as the proximate reason for Herod's infanticide.[72] Jesus, on the contrary, being an adopted child (Matt 1:19–20), touched (19:13–15) and healed children (21:14) and, in response, was honored in the temple by children as Son of David (21:15). The Matthean infancy narrative can thus be interpreted from the perspective of the social pattern of *challenge* and *response* in terms of the ascribed and acquired honor of two kings.

This challenge and response pattern can be studied from the social-scientific perspective of honor and shame as pivotal social values.[73] In the first-century Mediterranean world, some social interactions that took place outside one's family or group of friends was perceived as an affront to one's honor. Bruce Malina helps exegetes of Jesus' birth record to understand that "being born into an honorable family makes one honorable, since the family is the

---

70. Yaghijan, "How Shall We Read?" 3.
71. See Tromp, *Assumption of Moses*, 17, 211–13.
72. Scrimshaw, "Infanticide in Human Populations," 445.
73. Cf. Malina, *New Testament World*, 28–55.

repository of the honor of past illustrious ancestors and their accumulated acquired honor."[74] Malina notes that one of the purposes of genealogies as birth records is to legitimize a person's ascribed honor.

The "game" of challenge and response can only be played among equals. This is a problem where Jesus is concerned. Jesus was not the equal of Herod the Great. We know that Antipater, the father of Herod the Great, was ascribed honor by Caesar when he was declared king of the Judeans in 47 B.C.E.[75] Herod the Great himself was made king by the Roman Senate.[76] However, although he was a Judean by religion, his racial descent was Idumean.[77] Herod acted as patron among the people through agriculture and commercial enterprise, but the response to his program was fear and hostility.[78]

Matthew's version of Jesus' genealogy places him among the disreputable. Matthew's reference to Tamar (as the mother of Perez, Matt 1:3) alludes to the tortuous way in which Judah begot Perez and Zerah (Gen 38:6–30); Rahab, the mother of Boaz (Matt 1:5), was the foreign prostitute who helped the Israelite spies at Jericho (see Joshua 20); Ruth, the mother of Obed (Matt 1:5), was also a foreigner (see Ruth 4); finally, the very designation of the mother of Solomon as "the wife of Uriah" (Matt 1:6) reminds the readers of David's dubious behavior (see 2 Samuel 11).[79]

These foremothers of Jesus were dishonorable people. A prostitute had no honor because of her unconventional lifestyle. She was not sexually exclusive to a patriarch. She symbolized chaos.[80] According to the Mediterranean culture, such people had no honor at all. In other words, there was no honor to defend. They were comparable to other defenseless people: orphans, widows, destitute poor, resident aliens. This meant that a patron with honor was needed in order to defend a person without honor.

According to Matthew, God was the one who intervened on behalf of Jesus. "While [first-century Mediterranean] people are defined by others and because of others, they are in fact unable to change undesirable situations. Hence the need for divine intervention."[81] In the Matthean infancy narrative, the life of the child Jesus is threatened by Herod the Great. Though Jesus is portrayed as born from and among despised outcasts, he is God's "adopted son" (see Matt 3:17).

74. Ibid., 33.
75. Josephus, *B.J.* 1.201–3.
76. Ibid., 2.14.4.
77. See Botha, "Herodes die Grote," 1015–16. See also the reference to "the hated Idumaean" in Brandon, *Jesus and the Zealots*, 27.
78. Josephus, *Ant.* 15.8.1b; *B.J.* 100.21.1; Cf. Botha, "Herodes die Grote," 1012.
79. Cf. Patte, *Gospel according to Matthew*, 19.
80. Malina, *New Testament World*, 53.
81. Malina, "Circum-Mediterranean Person?" 71.

It is clear that the thrust of the Matthean genealogy is that Jesus was an adopted child. Because of God's intervention, he became Joseph's adopted son (see Matt 1:25). Combining the messianic interpretation of Jesus and the tradition that Jesus was from the tribe of Joseph (see chapter 4), Matthew says that Joseph's line goes back to both David and Abraham. Yet children of Abraham were God's children. From the Matthean point of view, a son of David and of Abraham was not characterized primarily by biological offspring, but by what he would do, his vocation.[82] In Matt 3:7–9, the "true children of Abraham" are described as people who do certain things: they bear fruit that befit repentance.

Matthew's story presupposes that Joseph knows something about Mary's pregnancy. It seems that he thinks that she has committed adultery.[83] However, the narrative does not describe how Jesus was conceived but rather the reason why Mary's pregnancy should not be perceived as shameful; that which is conceived in her is not impure but is of the Holy Spirit, and thus holy. The Greek syntax of this sentence puts the emphasis on the word holy. The text opposes diverging evaluations of Mary's pregnancy, either as something that is shameful and a cause of disgrace and rejection (Matt 1:19) or as something that one should not fear because it is of God (1:20).[84] The divine is defined in terms of holiness. Joseph, when wanting to divorce Mary, is described as her husband, just (or righteous) and unwilling to put her to shame (1:19). Joseph, when assured by the angel that he need not be afraid to take Mary into his home, is described as son of David, obeying (1:24), without fear (1:20), adopting Jesus by giving him his name (1:25), and transmitting the vocation to be son of David and son of Abraham (see 1:1).

From Matthew's perspective, "true righteousness" (δικαιοσύνη), which "exceeds the righteousness of the scribes and Pharisees" (5:20), is expressed in love, given without discrimination to deserving and undeserving alike (5:44–48). Four of the five instances of the verb "to have compassion" (σπλαγχυίξομαι) and five of the eight instances of the verb "to have mercy"(ελεέω) occur in Matthew in connection with healing, and in almost every case the names "Lord" (Κύριο5) and/or "Son of David" appear in the same context.[85] Except for the narrator, it is only the crowd (9:27; 12:23; 20:30; and 21:15) and the Gentiles (15:22) who address Jesus as "Son of David" and not the disciples or the Judean leaders. All of these passages

---

82. Cf. Patte, *Gospel according to Matthew*, 23–28.
83. Cf. Brown, *Birth of the Messiah*, 125–28. Beare, *Gospel according to Matthew*, 68, puts it as follows: "Since he [Joseph] plans to divorce her [Mary] at all events, he must be taking it for granted that she is guilty of unchastity."
84. Patte, *Gospel according to Matthew*, 27.
85. Duling, "Matthew's Son of David," 10.

deal with healing and all, except Matt 15:21–28, deal with the healing of the blind in one way or another. Matthew 21:9, the entry into Jerusalem, is an exception because it does not deal directly with healing. However, the entry bears a close relation to the subsequent incident of healing that takes place inside the temple and leads to a climax when "children in the temple" honor Jesus as the "Son of David" (21:15). From a medical-anthropological perspective, we know that the healing incidents (for example, the healing of lepers) in the Gospels provide evidence that human illnesses "were thought to be a source of pollution, not contagion, and that Jesus' cure invariably involved establishing new self-understandings so that these formerly unclean and excluded from the holy community now found themselves clean and within the holy community."[86]

In the Mediterranean world, children were considered nobodies. Herod the Great, the challenger of Jesus, was also the murderer of children. Research on infanticide from a cultural-anthropological perspective mentions resource competition among individuals and families in preindustrial societies competing for other valuables besides land and geopolitical power. "Human history is full of cases of competition for access to office (read: economic and reproductive dominance) most especially among royalty. We should expect that the greater the value of the office, the greater the benefit of assassination of potential competitors."[87] These studies have found that the practice of infanticide was used in hunter-gatherer, horticulturist, and stratified agrarian societies for purposes ranging from population control to maintenance of the social structure.[88]

In order to maintain his power, Herod the Great murdered those sons who would be more readily acceptable to the Judeans as king. The legend about Herod's infanticide in Matthew should be understood against this background. Matthew narrates that Jesus escaped being murdered by Herod. This was a result of God's intervention. In Matthew's story Jesus, in turn, becomes the protector of defenseless children. Matthew encompasses the beginning and end of Jesus' public ministry within the context of Jesus' relationship to children. Jesus' baptism by John (so that they both can fulfill "all righteousness," Matt 3:15) and Jesus' entry into Jerusalem (Matt 21:1–17) form the two poles of his ministry. Both episodes can be described as cleansing of the temple—the last episode is told explicitly and the first implicitly. Both incidents were (in midrashic fashion) understood by Matthew as fulfillment of scripture. The baptism scene is a Matthean allusion to Isa 1:13–17, and the record of the entry into Jerusalem is an explicit interpretation of Jer 7:1–8:

---

86. Pilch, "Understanding Biblical Healing," 60; cf. Pilch, "Sickness and Healing," 181– 210.
87. Dickemann, "Concepts and Classification," 429–30.
88. Dickemann, "Demographic Consequences of Infanticide"; cf. Scrimshaw, "Infanticide in Human Populations," 440.

"Stop bringing meaningless offerings!
   Your incense is detestable to me.
New Moons, Sabbaths and convocations—
   I cannot bear your evil assemblies

   . . .

   I am weary bearing them.
When you spread out your hands in prayer,
   I will hide my eyes from you;
even if you offer many prayers,
   I will not listen.
Your hands are full of blood;
   wash and make yourselves clean.
Take your evil deeds
   out of my sight!
Stop doing wrong,
   learn to do right!
Seek justice,
   encouraged the oppressed.
Defend the cause of the fatherless,
   plead the case of the widow."

                         (Isa 1:13–17, NIV)

This is the word that came to Jeremiah from the LORD: "Stand at the gate of the LORD's house and there proclaim this message:

"Hear the word of the LORD, all you people of Judah who come through these gates to worship the LORD. This is what the LORD Almighty, the God of Israel, says: Reform your ways and your actions, and I will let you live in this place. Do not trust in deceptive words and say, "This is the temple of the LORD, the temple of the LORD, the temple of the LORD!" If you really change your ways and your actions *and deal with each other justly, if you do not oppress the alien, the fatherless or the widow and do not shed innocent blood in this place,* and if you do not follow other gods to your own harm, then I will let you live in this place, in the land I gave your forefathers for ever and ever. But look, you are trusting in deceptive words that are worthless."

                         (Jer 7:1–8, NIV)

In the beginning of Matthew's story, the "authorities" in Jerusalem almost murder the infant Jesus with other "expendable" children. In the middle part of the story, Jesus acts as the protector of the honor of the miserable. At the end, quite unconventionally, Jesus is honored by infants. Here, near the end of Jesus' life, Matthew unexpectedly places the children in the temple. Children were not permitted to enter the temple, yet, according to Matthew, they were the ones to honor Jesus. Jesus, seemingly a fatherless person, born from among the despised, was also not expected to be found in the temple. We have seen that honor could only be ascribed by notable persons.[89] The implication of this is that Matthew treated both Jesus and the children as notable people.

It becomes clear that in Matthew's story, God is shown "to be one who sides with the outcast and endangered woman and child."[90] Matthew retells the tradition of the divine intervention that brings about Joseph's acceptance of the messianic child and his mother. Therefore, Jane Schaberg is on the right track when she understands Matthew's emphasis of God as Father as an indication that the Jesus movement is the commencement of a new (fictive) family (cf. Matt 19:29), a family of God (cf. Matt 23:9). By making the child and not the father the model for entry into the reign of God, the fatherless Jesus "reversed the hierarchical assumptions that governed all of life."[91] The Matthean Jesus' attitude toward the status of women and children represents the deliberate breaking down of boundaries. The new way was for all to assume the position of children (cf. 23:11–12).[92] Jane Schaberg says about her work on Jesus' illegitimacy, "If my reading of Matthew's infancy narrative is regarded as a possible reading, other ears may recognize its echoes in the rest of this Gospel."[93] This is what my reading scenario does: the fatherless Jesus defended the fatherless street urchins. Jesus erased and replaced the godlike status of the biological father with God as "our Father in heaven." He opened the door for the fatherless to call upon God as their Father.

At this point, it is as if we have crossed a bridge. We have moved from seeing Jesus as child of God to seeing his followers as children of God. It represents a movement between what can be historically discerned with regard to the words and deeds of Jesus on the one hand, and the faith assertions of his followers on the other hand. What is at issue is engaged hermeneutics. While bridging the transition between pre-Easter and post-Easter, the scholar is critically testing whether the cause of Jesus has been adequately conveyed in the process of transition.

---

89. See Malina, *New Testament World*, 34.

90. Schaberg, *Illegitimacy of Jesus*, 74.

91. Countryman, *Dirt, Greed, and Sex*, 188. Likewise, Riches, *Jesus and the Transformation*, 132–33, connects the antipatriarchal tendency with Jesus' disregard for the politics of holiness.

92. Cf. Countryman, *Dirt, Greed, and Sex*, 189.

93. Schaberg, *Illegitimacy of Jesus*, 77.

CHAPTER 7

~

From Child of God
to Children of God

In light of the central aspect of the book, the focus of this chapter is the transition between Jesus' foundational experience of being child of God to the confession of Christians in a metaphor that Jesus is God's son. This movement simultaneously represents the elements of distance and engagement.[1] It is part and parcel of the telling and showing process in which Jesus is seen, on the one hand, as the defender of the fatherless and the notion, on the other hand, found in the Christian tradition, that God adopted people as God's children.

THE METAPHOR "SON OF GOD"

The dogma of the two natures of Jesus can be traced back to Paul's thinking and to Johannine literature. Its foundation, however, is to some extent Jesus' invocation of God as "Father" (*Abba*). The expression "Abba, Father" is uttered by Jesus in Mark 14:36. Matthew (26:39) contains only the expression "my Father," while Luke (22:42) has "Father." This invocation does not have exactly the same connotation as when Paul had Christians address God in this way. However, what Jesus and Paul do have in common is that "children of God" are not necessarily biological children of Abraham, as thought conventionally by the Israelites. By means of the expression "adoption as child," Paul gives expression to the conviction that believers are not by nature children of God, but on the basis of their being bound to Jesus, the Son of God.

In Phil 2:9–11, Paul uses the designation "Lord" (Κύριος) to describe the crown of Jesus' redemptive work: "God gave him . . . the name which is above each name, so that in the name of Jesus . . . each tongue would confess: 'Jesus Christ is Lord.'" Similarly, the designation "Son" is a metaphorical label with which the resurrected Jesus is addressed. Thus we read, for instance, in Heb 1:3–4 that the "most excellent name" that God gave the exalted Jesus and that lifted him above the angels, was the designation

---

1. See Ricoeur, "Philosophische und theologische Hermeneutik," 38, 42–43.

"Son." In the *Shepherd of Hermas* (*Sim.* 9.14. 5) we learn that the "name Son of God is firm and supports the whole world."[2]

The names *Kyrios* and "Son of God" belong together.[3] Son of God refers to the divine nature of the *Kyrios* who is honored as a cultic figure. Inversely, *Kyrios* refers to the status and function of the figure called *Son of God*. It was in Hellenistic Christianity that the label *Kyrios* was first given to Jesus to express his divine nature. Previously, Jesus was already called *Kyrios* by Aramaic-speaking Christians, but for another reason. In the synagogue, teachers of the law were called *Rabbi*. The Aramaic-speaking Christians, influenced by Greek idiom, translated the word *Rabbi* with *Kyrios* and referred to Jesus as such, as can be seen, for example, in Matthew.[4] Hellenistic Christians used the label *Son of God* as part of their missionary message. In the First Testament, this name referred to a messianic king. Now it attained a new meaning. For Christians today it seems that *Son of God* applies uniquely to Jesus in an ontological way. However, in the Hellenistic environment, it was commonly used for people who were considered divine. At this stage, the metaphor *Son of God* started referring to the divine being of Jesus. Jesus was distinguished from the human sphere on the basis of his divine nature. The metaphor thus had a confessional function. With the confessional metaphor *Son of God,* the claim was made that Jesus had a divine origin and was filled with divine power.

To Christians from the Israelite tradition, the idea that a messianic figure could be represented as subject to suffering was offensive. However, to Hellenistic Christianity, such a representation regarding a Son of God figure was not an obstacle, but a "mystery."[5] This paradoxical mystery consisted of the fact that a figure, divine in being, appeared in human form and accepted the fate of suffering as a human. This can be seen in the Christ hymn quoted by Paul in Phil 2:6–11. For Hellenistic Christians, the divine origin and power of the Son of God were not belied by his humanness.

One way in which divinity and humanness came together in the ancient world was in a child conceived through the sexual intercourse of a deity with a human. The lives of people who were born as a result of such a union were characterized by heroic acts and spiritual contributions to humanity—benefactions far beyond ordinary human measure.[6] Many such figures were known in the Hellenistic period. Such a figure claimed to be "son of god." Some of them were honored in cults. In these cults, the

---

2. Cf. Bultmann, *Theologie des Neuen Testaments,* 130.
3. See ibid., 125.
4. See Sand, *Gezetz und die Propheten,* 164; Van Aarde, *God-with-us,* 62.
5. See Bultmann, *Theologie des Neuen Testaments,* 131.
6. See ibid., 132.

combination of divinity and humanness was not an issue. The prevalent view in Greek thought was that the soul of each person was a "divine entity."[7] From the perspective of Greek mythology, interest was not as much in the ontological interrelationship of someone's divine nature and human nature, as in later Greek metaphysical philosophy, but more in the content of the divine figure's life (βιoς) that was characterized by charismatic phenomena and miracles.[8]

Another way in which divinity and humanness came together during the time when the New Testament was written was in the idea of sons of gods. This was a legacy from eastern Hellenism and, initially, from ancient Eastern mythology. The sons of gods were honored in the cults of the mystery religions. They were taken to be savior figures. The myths about them recounted how they suffered the human fate of death but rose again from death (cf., e.g., the dying and rising Osiris myth in Egypt). Worshippers could partake in the redemption if they experienced the god's death and resurrection in the form of rites. The origin of these divine figures lies in ancient fertility religions.

The figure of the redeemer in Gnostic myth is related to these "mysteries." Some of the Christians who came from the heathen world made the birth and death of Jesus comprehensible by making use of the concepts "sonship of God" and the Gnostic "redemptive figure" who comes from above. Thus we read that the writer of the Gospel of John says the following about Jesus: "Such is God's love for the cosmos: He gave his 'only begotten' Son" (John 3:16). Likewise, the writer has Jesus say on the eve of his death: "I was born for this and entered the cosmos for this" (John 18:37). In 1 John 3:16 we read: "In this way we know what love is: that man [Jesus Christ, the Son of God; cf. 1 John 3:23] gave his life for our sake." In this kind of statement we see that the paradoxical concept of a divine being (a son of god) who became human and suffered a human fate may be related to the Gnostic idea of a redeemer who entered from above into the cosmos here below. The conceptualization of Jesus as Son of God varied in Hellenistic Christian circles, depending on which tradition more greatly influenced it—that of the Greek mythological or that of the Eastern mythological-Gnostic "son of god."

The Synoptic Gospels in essence represent the first type (the Greek tradition) insofar as they represent Jesus as the Son of God who reveals his divine authority.[9] This mode of representation fit into that part of Christian

---

7. In works by Epictetus, Marcus Aurelius, and Plotinus, we learn that those who were deemed to be people with "good sense" were taken to be people with a "god in them." See Harris, *Jesus as God*, 28, note 38.

8. See Bultmann, *Theologie des Neuen Testaments*, 132.

9. Ibid., 133; Betz, "Jesus as Divine Man"; Koester, "One Jesus and Four Primitive Gospels."

thought that was determined by Israelite views. Within this structure, the power manifested in the life of the divine figure is attributed to the Divine Spirit. This phenomenon, according to Hellenistic interpretations, also appeared in the lives of First Testament "holy men of God," such as David and the prophets. To those Christians influenced by Israelite thinking, this served as an analogy for their confession that the Christ was the Son of God. The faith assertion found in the Markan report about Jesus' baptism can be seen as an illustration of this conviction.[10]

In the first type of the combination of the divine and human, the divine figure was a miracle worker filled with the Divine Spirit. According to the second type (Eastern mythology), Jesus was seen as the preexisting Son of God who became human. Paul (like John) takes this notion as his point of departure. The pre-Pauline Christ hymn (Phil 2:6–11) also indicates that Paul was not the first person to have imported this idea into Christian thought. It is a pre-Christian concept that is found in the writings of Greek-speaking Israelites.[11] Paul, therefore, did not see Jesus as a miracle worker.[12] In a certain sense, these two types were mutually exclusive.

Both types are represented in the various New Testament texts. The Synoptic Gospels portray Jesus the Son of God as a miracle worker; Paul and John portray him as a divine figure who became human. Church fathers combined these two (incompatible) types in their homilies and writings. Ignatius seemingly had a sense of this incompatibility. Therefore, he referred to the virginity of Mary, her becoming pregnant, and the death of Jesus as "three enigmas." [13] He was probably also aware of the paradox found in the second type (the preexistent Christology).

---

10. Cf. Bultmann, *Theologie des Neuen Testaments*, 133. According to Mark 1:9–11, Jesus manifested himself as Son of God when, on the occasion of his baptism, he was filled with the Spirit of God. Bultmann points out that this same view appears quite clearly in the "Western" manuscript tradition of Luke 3:22 up to Augustine (see, e.g., the Latin version of the fifth-century Codex Bezae Cantabrigiensis [D^{it}], Justin, Clement, and Latin documents by a number of Western church fathers—see Aland and others, *Greek New Testament*, 207). According to this tradition, a voice came from heaven that said, in the words of Ps 2:7: "You are my Son; today I have begotten you." In line with this way of thinking, Acts 2:22 recounts that "God made Jesus of Nazareth known to you through powerful deeds, through the miracles and signs that God let him do in your midst."

11. See, e.g., the *Similitudes of Enoch* (*1 Enoch* 39:4ff.; 70:4—cf. Casey, *From Jewish Prophet*, 79–85) and the "love romance" *Joseph and Asenath*, in which Joseph is not only called the "son-of-god" (*Jos. As.* 6:3, 5; 18:11; 21:4—see Chesnutt, "From Text to Context," 296), but also the "firstborn" (*Jos. As.* 18:11; 21:4; 23:10—see Standhartinger, *Frauenbild im Judentum*," 203; Standhartinger, "From Fictional Text," 314. The view in Paul that the preexistent Son of God became human should be seen in connection with the above-mentioned paradox of the redemptive events. The total emphasis in this regard is on the fact of the humanity and the human fate of Jesus the Son of God who became human. This fact, as clearly witnessed in Phil 2:6–11, is, however, contradicted by the idea that Jesus, in the last days of his (earthly) life, showed himself to be God's son through miracles.

12. Cf. Bultmann, *Theologie des Neuen Testaments*, 134.

13. Ign. *Eph.* 19:1; cf. Ign. *Smyrn.* 1:1.

On the periphery of the New Testament, a third type can be found. In this type a preexistent divine figure was cocreator of the *cosmos*.[14] For Gnostics, however, the cosmos, because of its transience and corruption, could not possibly be the realm of the loving God (the Father of Jesus). The genesis of the cosmos is found in the creating work of the God witnessed to in the First Testament, who is to be distinguished from the Father of Jesus. Therefore, in relation to their witness of Jesus, Gnostic Christians tried to get rid of First-Testament elements. They denied that God's Son could take on human form.

In Ignatius's letter to the Ephesians (19:1), he combines all three types. He refutes the Gnostic heresies that a "Creator-God" (revealed in the First Testament) could not possibly be the Father of Jesus and that God could not associate with perishable humanness.

Polemics employing the metaphor of the Son of God, such as those of Ignatius, originated from various cultural backgrounds and formed the

---

14. Bultmann, *Theologie des Neuen Testaments*, 134. The Gnostic notion of the divine son has not only a soteriological but also a cosmological meaning. In fact, the cosmological meaning was probably the primary one and developed independently in mythologies and religio-philosophical speculations like those of Philo. In Philo, the cosmic Logos is the Son of God. A similar development is also found in Hermetic writings. A parallel phenomenon is the personification of Wisdom as a cosmic figure, which is found in the wisdom literature in the Israelite tradition (e.g. Prov 8:22–30) and which became an object of speculation in Judaism, especially among Greek-speaking Israelites. Very early, this speculation about the Logos and Wisdom opened a way into Hellenistic Christianity. Early in the fifties, Paul already refers to Jesus as "he through whom everything exists and through whom we live" (1 Cor 8:6), a formula in which the cosmological and soteriological roles of Jesus have been combined. Whether it was Paul who first attributed a cosmic role to Christ as "creation mediator" cannot be determined with certainty. The way in which he refers to it does create an impression of generality and indicates, again, that Paul was not the only one to have attributed such a role to Jesus. The self-evident way in which he calls Jesus the "image of God" in 2 Cor 4:4 strengthens this impression. The term "image of God" also forms part of the speculative context relating to a cosmological Son of God. This speculation occurs in Philo and in Hermetic and Gnostic literature. After Paul, this cosmological meaning of Christ is found, in particular, in Col 1:15–17. Here Jesus is represented as the "image of the invisible God," the "firstborn of the entire creation," "because in him everything was created which is in heaven and on earth [that is, everything which is visible and invisible]"; "everything was created through him and for him"; "and he is before everything and in him everything keeps existing together." Bultmann, *Theologie des Neuen Testaments*, 135, points out that the writer of the epistle to the Ephesians also knew about this speculation. The author of Ephesians, after all, found it in Colossians when he used that letter as a source. In Eph 1:20–22, the cosmology has been changed into an ecclesiology, a change that had already been initiated by Colossians (1:18a). Apart from the prologue to the Gospel of John, the epistle to the Hebrews may be taken as evidence that, apart from Paul and his school, there were others who also saw Jesus as the Son of God in the appearance of a cosmic figure. Hebrews 1:3 describes Jesus as the one who "through his word of power maintains all things." Jesus is called, in the first part of this verse, the "brightness of the glory [of God]" and "the image of his [God's] being." The latter expression is nothing but a paraphrase of the concept "image." Similarly, we read in the *Shepherd of Hermas* (*Sim.* 9.12.2): "The Son of God is older than all of creation, as a consequence of which he was God's advisor for all of creation." Proverbs 8:27ff. is clearly the basis for these words. It is particularly in the *Shepherd of Hermas* (*Sim.* 9.14.5) that the cosmological role of the Son of God finds expression: "the name of the Son of God is firm and incomprehensible and supports the whole world. If then all of creation is maintained by the Son of God . . . ?" The answer that was given to the question posed for the first time here draws an ecclesiological conclusion from the particular cosmological premises.

basis for confessional creeds that were used as the building blocks for the formation of the fourth-century ontological-metaphysical dogma of the two natures (divine and human) of Jesus. It is clear that this is a long way from Jesus' foundational experience of being child of God, the defender of the fatherless, and subverter of conventional wisdom. He who proclaimed unmediated access to God now became the mediator—the iconoclast became a cultic icon as a result of the combination of two traditions (the Israelite and the Greek). The following statement by Robert Funk is a good summary of this irony:

> The paradox of the dead god represents the marriage of the imageless tradition of Israel with the iconic mentality of the Graeco-Roman world. For descendents of Abraham, no one has ever seen God, and God cannot be pictured. For the Greeks, to consort with the gods was an everyday matter, and it was commonplace to make images of every imaginable deity. For hellenized Christians, Jesus the iconoclast became Christ the icon. Because Christianity has a twin heritage, its ancestors are both Jews and Greeks, it has never quite made up its mind whether it is iconic or iconoclast.[15]

The intention of the metaphor Son of God, applied to Jesus in the New Testament according to his experience of being child of God, was to convey unmediated access to God. This metaphor functioned in two spheres, that of divine origin and of divine power. In the first type (the miracle worker filled with the Divine Spirit), the divine origin pertains to the miraculous birth of the Son of God; in the second, the Son of God was preexistent and became human. In the first type, divine power was the result of the miraculous birth. Some myths represented the mother of the son of god as a virgin. For instance, Perseus was born from the union of the virgin Danae and Zeus. Other traditions placed no emphasis on the virginity or nonvirginity of the woman. Examples are Coronis and Alkmena. Coronis was impregnated by Apollo, and her unborn child, Asclepios, was torn out of his mothers' womb by Apollo to be reared as a deified diviner and "medicine man." Hercules was born from the union of the married woman Alkmena and Jupiter. Both traditions, however, placed the emphasis on the benefactions and heroic deeds of the son of god. In the second type the divine power of the son of god manifested in his victory over death.

In the first type, intermediary figures like angels and the Divine Spirit played a role in the life of a divine figure. Against this background, the "holy men of God" in the Israelite tradition were represented as having been filled

---

15. Funk, *Honest to Jesus*, 44.

with the Spirit of God, something that would have occurred either at birth or at their "adoption as sons of God," which was not necessarily represented as having occurred at birth. We have seen that Paul did not take up the tradition of Jesus as the miracle-working Son of God. We can assume, in light of what Paul says in Philippians 2:7–8 and 2 Cor 8:9 about the self-humiliation of the preexistent Christ, that Paul did not view the miracle stories about Jesus as being reconcilable with his (Paul's) gospel. The miracle narratives represented Jesus as having divine power, while, according to Paul, Jesus' deeds were characterized not by power but by weakness and vulnerability even upon his death on the cross. In Romans 1:3–4, Paul relates that Jesus' preexistent sonship was manifested in the resurrection event. A few years later, Mark would attest to Jesus' "adoption" as Son of God on the basis of the work of the Spirit of God in the life of Jesus.[16]

Mark, like Paul, does not relate this status as Son of God to a divine birth. For Mark, Jesus was declared Son of God at his baptism, at the beginning of his activity as miracle worker when he was filled with the Divine Spirit. Some years later, Luke, who used Mark as a source, took over the tradition of fulfillment with the Spirit that occurred with the baptism of Jesus. Luke, however, sees Jesus' adoption as Son of God as already anticipated in the story of Jesus' virginal conception on the basis of the work of the Spirit of God.

In chapter 4, I mentioned that the divine births in the mythological narratives of the gods and the emperor cult form the background against which Luke (as a sophisticated Greek) represents the birth of Jesus (and the ascension) in light of the hellenistically interpreted First Testament traditions concerning the "holy men of God." Matthew, chronologically the third literary witness within the Synoptic tradition, relates Jesus' being filled with the Spirit (as does Luke) to Jesus' role as the Messiah and as the apocalyptic Child of Humanity. The adoption as Son of God theme is related by Matthew to the motif of the holy marriage into which Joseph, on the basis of a divine intervention, enters with an impure, pregnant Mary. We have seen that a similar motif is found in the First Testament pseudepigraphic document *Joseph and Asenath*.

John stands outside of the Synoptic tradition and, like Paul, represents the second type. This second type, of which traces are to be found in the New Testament, emphasizes an anomaly, a paradox. Here the point of departure is the assumption that a preexistent figure, equal in status to God (John 1:1–2), took upon himself the fate of being completely human. A normal,

---

16. Paul describes in Rom 1:3–4 Jesus' adoption as Son of God in terms of the antinomy spirit-flesh. The expression "spirit of holiness" used here is not a reference to the Holy Spirit within the sphere of the (later) ontological dogma regarding the triune God. The expression "according to the spirit of holiness" in Rom 1:4 must be seen as the dialectical (tacit) antipode of the expression "the Christ according to the flesh," that occurs in Rom 9:5.

natural birth was one way in which this complete participation in human-ness was represented (cf. Gal 4:4 and John 1:14). In the Gospel of John (3:5–6; 7–8), the brothers of Jesus and bystanders see him as completely Galilean. Both Paul and John proclaimed something at which, paradoxically, Judeans took offense: namely, that the preexistent Son of God was born in the shape of an insignificant human, and also died as one. However, in this apparent anomaly the divine redemptive events lie hidden. John portrays this redemption as the suspense resulting from the fact that people born nat-urally could, on the basis of sharing in Jesus as the only begotten Son of God, also be born out of the Spirit of God and could therefore be designated chil-dren of God. More or less, the same idea also occurs in Paul. As far as Paul is concerned, people were, on the basis of sharing in the fate and suffering of the preexistent Son of God, adopted as children of God.

As said, parallel stories of both types (miraculous birth and victory over death) were well known in the first century and it comes as no surprise that both traditions were applied to Jesus. An example of the first type (virginal conception) is the story of Perseus. The story of the birth, death, resurrec-tion, and ascension of Hercules is a combination of both types.

OVID'S PERSEUS

The mythological legend of Perseus is a model of a fatherless son becoming a hero. This story is told in Ovid's *Metamorphoses*.[17] According to the myth, Perseus was the abandoned son of Danae by Zeus. Danae was the daughter of King Acrisius of Argos. The king was warned by prophecy that a son born to his daughter would kill him, so he shut her away in a brazen tower. (According to another version, it was in an underground chamber.) There through a narrow window Zeus went to her in the form of a shower of gold and she became pregnant. Danae called her son Perseus. In an act of dynas-tic politics, Acrisius enclosed the son and his mother in a chest and set it afloat on the sea. Acrisius's name means "ill judgment" and Perseus means "the destroyer."

Earlier in this study I mentioned that cultural-anthropological studies show that resource competition among individuals and families in prein-dustrial societies, that is, competition for other valuables besides land and geopolitical power, was one of the reasons for infanticide.[18] Acrisius was threatened by the oracle, he denied his vocation of fatherhood, and he

---

17. *Metamorphoses* (4 and 5), translated by Innes; see esp. 110–22. Cf. Kirkwood, *Short Guide to Classical Mythology*, 76–77. A version of the myth is also found as *The Doom of King Acrisius* in William Morris's *The Earthly Paradise* (1868) and as *Andromeda* by Charles Kingsley (1858); see Pirani, *Absent Father*, 3. My discussion of the story of Perseus is heavily dependent on Pirani's work.

18. See Dickemann, "Concepts and Classification."

absented himself from the child Zeus provided. It is ironic that the very attempt to make sure an oracle's prediction would not come true caused it to happen as foretold. By getting rid of a male heir, Acrisius weakened his line and thereby harmed himself.[19]

Zeus was the "god of illegitimacy," and appeared whenever what was "legitimate" needed to be called into question. (See, for example, the story of the infidelity of Coronis after she was impregnated by Apollo, son of Zeus, and Zeus who interfered to safeguard Coronis who was destined to die on a funeral pyre as punishment.) The implication is that the divine and the human cannot be separated. Though humans do not always realize it, there is a higher meaning to their bodily existence in the world. Against human heartlessness, Zeus combines divinity and humanity. The child that results from this union will carry forth this spirit. According to the myth, Acrisius did not believe that it was the work of Zeus. The myth gives an indication of what awaits a person who is burdened with restoring meaning and value to human life. "Every single mother and fatherless son is playing our drama of a society in need of a new father, as surely as Mary and Jesus did."[20]

The chest (compare to this the "death basket" in which the endangered child Moses was set afloat) floated to the island of Seriphus. A fisherman named Dictys, the brother of Polydectes, the king of Seriphus, found the chest. He rescued the endangered mother and son, and gave them shelter. Polydectes tried to force Danae into marrying him. However, the protection of Perseus, who was growing into manhood, hindered him in his pursuit of Danae. To get rid of the son, Polydectes sent Perseus off on a quest to bring back the head of Medusa, one of three winged sisters, the Gorgons, whose heads were wreathed with serpents instead of hair. The Gorgons had the power to turn whoever looked upon them into stone.

The goddess Athena, who hated Medusa and who was responsible for the serpented heads of the Gorgons, aided Perseus in various ways. She gave him a brightly polished shield so that he could see Medusa's head reflected in it and not face her directly. Hermes, the son of Zeus and Maia, daughter of Atlas, was the messenger of the gods and the guide of travelers. He guided Perseus to the cave where the three Graeae ("Gray Ones"), sisters of the Gorgons, dwelt. These women were gray from birth and had among them just one tooth and one eye. Perseus seized the communal tooth and eye and would not give it back until the Graeae told him how to find certain nymphs who could act as helpers. They had the equipment he needed to perform his commission. Thus Perseus was able to behead Medusa.

---

19. See Pirani, *Absent Father*, 9.
20. Ibid., 13–14, 18.

During an eventful return trip, Perseus rescued Andromeda, the daughter of Cepheus and Cassiope, the king and queen of Joppa in Philistia. (Andromeda had been turned over to a sea dragon to appease the furious Poseidon.) After Perseus slayed the monster he was rewarded with Andromeda's hand in marriage. Ovid recounted that Cassiope and Cepheus "were filled with joy: they greeted Perseus as their son-in-law, calling him the saviour and preserver of their house." Perseus and Andromeda returned to Seriphus, where Polydectes was still harassing Danae. She, fearing Polydectes's violence, took shelter in a temple with the fisherman Dictys. There Perseus found them. Polydectes was petrified when Perseus showed him Medusa's head. Dictys succeeded his deceased brother and became the king of Seriphus. Perseus, Danae, and Andromeda set out for Argos. On hearing of their approach, Acrisius fled to Thessaly. (According to another version, it was Larissa.) Later Perseus went to Thessaly (or Larissa) to participate in athletic contests. These were the funeral games that the king (of Larissa) held in honor of his dead father.[21] At the games, Perseus threw a discus that was diverted by the wind and killed Acrisius, who was there as a spectator.

Perseus refused to succeed Acrisius as king of Argos. He established himself elsewhere as king and father of a new dynasty, the Tiryns. Thus he became the model of the destroyer of patriarchy and, at the same time, as the "father of outsiders," the savior of the endangered woman.

> Perseus does not look back—but he does go back, to the beginning—by way of Seriphos to Argos. . . . His first concern is with his mother and Polydectes: he goes back to the place in which he grew up but could not come to manhood: something must be resolved there. His second concern is with his origins, the place, the mystery of his birth. The myth doesn't clarify the extent of Perseus's knowledge of his relationship to Acrisius. It is unlikely that he knows of the oracle's prediction. There is a feeling, created by the silence of the myth, of some unknown guilty secret being tracked down. Was it maintained in silence by Danae? Perhaps Perseus has doubts about his patrimony, cannot believe his mother's story about Zeus—or whatever she has told him—suspects incest, rape, illegitimacy?[22]

Perseus's return to the fatherland can be seen as his search for kinship and ancestry. The loyalty shown to a blood-bond can be very strong, but is often betrayed. As adults, adopted and illegitimate children often attempt exces-

---

21. Cf. ibid., 101–7.
22. Ibid., 95.

sively to reconnect with their missing fathers or original parents. As is often the case with such children, Perseus was proffered a kinship relationship in an imperfect way. He was thus separated from his origins, a common occurrence in times of social upheaval and restructuring.[23] Nevertheless, the image of Danae and Dictys in the temple is a powerful symbol. Perseus needed affirmation, which he received from the man who played a positive role in his life. Dictys, "the father in the temple,"[24] who had saved Perseus at birth, now became a father figure. The temple added a spiritual dimension to the qualities he brought to Perseus's life.

PAUL'S SON OF GOD AND SENECA'S HERCULES

Contemporary sketches and portrayals of divine birth and/or virginal conception and adoption (for instance of Hercules, Perseus, Horus, and Priapus) were well known in the time when the New Testament was written. Among these, the figure of Herakles ("Hercules" to the Romans) stands out not only because of his divine conception but also his adoption as child of Zeus when he conquered death.[25] The concept of being adopted as a child of God is also eminent in Paul's writings. One can therefore imagine that Paul's use of this idea was a common feature with the surrounding world.

The word "adopted as child" ($\upsilon\iota o\theta\varepsilon\sigma\iota\alpha$) occurs four times in the epistles of Paul, namely, in Rom 8:15; 8:23; 9:4; and Gal 4:5. Apart from these four instances, the word turns up only once in the remainder of the entire New Testament, in the deutero-Pauline epistle to the Ephesians (1:5). In the epistle to the Romans, Paul uses the expression against the background of his argument that the "house of Israel" was expecting God to fulfill his promises.[26] Paul was concerned with a "new" Israel, with people who did not necessarily physically belong to the "children of Abraham" but who nonetheless were adopted as such by God. (In Galatians, too, Paul uses the metaphor "inheritance" in order to refer to the reception of God's promises.) It would no longer be the physical "sons of Abraham" who would inherit (Rom 9:8). Children of God are the people who *in Christ* have, in a fictional way, become part of Abraham's family.

Paul calls Christ the "first of many brothers" in Rom 8:29. These brothers (and sisters) are family, not because they are blood relatives, but because they share in the preexistent Son of God, "who made everything and gives us life" (1 Cor 8:6). They became part of God's family by God's having adopted them as God's children. God predestined that they would conform to Christ, the preexistent Son of God. The precise phrase employed by Paul

---

23. See ibid., 97.
24. Ibid., 98–99.
25. See Kirkwood, *Short Guide to Classical Mythology*, 48–54.
26. See Atkins, *Egalitarian Community*, 172.

in Romans 8:29 is "conforming to the image of [God's] Son." Paul apparently uses the term "first" (πρωτότοκον) to indicate that the aspect of being the preexistent child of God does not apply to other believers and that Christ Jesus, in this respect, was the unique child of God.

Some are of the opinion "that there are analogies in the ancient world that might serve as parallels or even sources for such an evaluation of Jesus."[27] The notion of adoption occurs once in Greek mythology.[28] This incident concerned Hercules. In the works of Diodorus of Sicily and in the tragedies of Lucius Annaeus Seneca (*Hercules Furens* and *Hercules Oetaeus*), it is clear that this Greek hero is the biological son of Zeus. According to the myth, Zeus, who was notorious for his escapades, disguised himself as Alkmena's husband and begot a child. Directly after this incident, Amphitryon slept with his wife. (Amphitryon was the son of Alcaeus, who in his turn was the son of Perseus, the fruit of a virginal conception and also the doing of Zeus.[29] Amphitryon had taken Alkmena, the widow of his deceased brother Electryon, as his wife.) When he found out that Alkmena was pregnant with Zeus's child, he was so angry that he built a pyre and would have burned her (and Hercules) alive had Zeus not sent two clouds that poured water on the flames and so saved the life of the woman and her unborn child.[30] Amphitryon then fulfilled his role as Hercules' adoptive father with honor.

Diodorus Siculus reinterpreted this Greek myth during the first century B.C.E.[31] His entire Book Four deals with Greek mythology and with the myths relating to Hercules, among others. It is assumed that it was in Alexandria where Diodorus derived the information pertaining to these myths from a certain Dionysius of Mytilene, and that he assembled his narratives with supplementary material from the library in Alexandria.[32] Diodorus himself said that the reason he retold the Greek myths was that the narratives concerning the "honored heroes and demi-gods" had such an important effect on the everyday lives of people (*Bib. Tet.* 1.5).

Diodorus begins by telling the divine birth of Dionysus because this deity brought about great bounty for humankind. Earlier in his work, he referred to certain "barbarians" who did not speak Greek, who claimed the significance of the "birth of this god" for themselves (*Bib. Tet.* 6.2–3). By "barbarians," he meant the Egyptians, whose god Osiris was called Dionysus by the Greeks. According to Diodorus, the Greeks related that

27. Tabor, "Firstborn of Many Brothers," 295.
28. In Greek: υἱοθεσία/υἱοποιήσασθαι/θετὸν υἱὸν ποιεῖσθαι. Cf. Schweizer, "huiothesia."
29. Cf. Kirkwood, *Classical Mythology*, 76–77.
30. See Burn, *Greek Myths*, 16–17.
31. See Oldfather, "Introduction"; Wülfing von Martitz, υἱος, υἱοθεσία, 401.
32. See Oldfather, "Introduction," ix.

Cadmus took Harmonia, the daughter of Aphrodite, as his wife and that they had a daughter called Semele. Zeus was attracted to Semele because of her beauty and had sexual intercourse with her secretly. Because he did not talk to her during their sexual intercourse, Semele believed that Zeus held her in contempt. She therefore asked him to embrace her in the same way that he embraced his wife, the goddess Hera. He then appeared to her as befitting a god: with thunder and lighting. He embraced her, but the pregnant Semele could not endure the majesty of such a divine presence and gave birth prematurely, while she herself was destroyed by the lightning. Zeus picked up the baby and ordered Hermes to lay it down in a cave in Nusa, somewhere between Phoenicia and the Nile River, while nymphs were ordered to bring it up with the greatest possible care. Diodorus writes that Dionysus was therefore given a name made up of Zeus (in Greek: *Dios*) and Nusa (in Greek: *Nuses*). However, this Dionysus, according to Diodorus, must not be confused with the much earlier Dionysus, son of Zeus and Persephone (*Bib. Tet.* 4.1–2).[33]

According to Diodorus, the birth of the earlier Dionysus, as well as the sacrifices and honor related to it, was celebrated secretly at night because of the shame of the orgiastic beastliness it involved. This religious practice is usually referred to as the Dionysian mysteries.[34] The later Dionysus gave people the "gift of the vine." The above-mentioned orgiastic feast was a result of confusion between the two Dionysuses. Fasting was followed by an ecstatic orgy, the slaughtering of cattle, and the eating of bloody flesh. The later Dionysus (or Bacchus), as Diodorus related the myths told by the "ancient people," was under the influence of wine when he had an erotic urge and begat a son with Aphrodite (*Bib. Tet.* 4.6.2–4). The son was named Priapus.[35]

Diodorus mentions that the Egyptians equated the birth of Priapus with the miraculous birth of Horus (*Bib. Tet.* 6.3). Horus was the son of Isis and he was born after Isis's husband, Osiris, was murdered by the Titans.[36] The Isis-Osiris myth in Egypt gave rise to the practice of a phallic religion. On the island Philae (covered today by the waters of Lake Nasser), high in Upper Egypt, the temple of Isis, standing alongside the statues of emperors like Augustus and Claudius, indicated clearly the influence of the Ptolomeans and later the Romans in the Greco-Roman period. To the western side of the temple court lay the birth room, which contained reliefs of a papyrus marsh where, according to legend, Horus was born.[37] The northern wall contained a relief of Isis with the newborn Horus in her arms. This

---

33. Cf. Van Aarde, *Kultuurhistoriese Agtergrond*, 23.
34. See ibid., 23.
35. See Parker, *Priapea*, 1.
36. According to Diodorus, by Typhon (*Bib. Tet.* 1.21–22).
37. Farid and Busath, *Temple of Philae*, 16.

picture was an early influence on the Christian image of the Madonna and Child. This can be seen in wall paintings from the Coptic period in Nubia and Egypt, which are being preserved in the Coptic Museum in Cairo.[38]

The Priapus cult was popular particularly in Alexandria.[39] The practices of a phallic religion entailed worshipping the creative power of nature as symbolized by the male sexual organ. Even though Diodorus does not mention the particulars of the Egyptian version of the birth of Priapus/Horus, he does refer to phallic religious practices in Egypt as well as to the beliefs regarding the "eye of Horus," the "evil eye," that related to these practices (*Bib. Tet.* 6.4).

Paul undoubtedly knew the beliefs relating to the evil eye well.[40] The apostle writes in Gal 3:1, "O, foolish Celts, who cast the evil eye on you? You before whose eyes Jesus Christ was exhibited as the crucified one!"(my translation). The practice of crucifixion in ancient times served as a deterrent to evildoers.[41] According to the Israelites, a wrongdoer who was hanged on such a "pole of shame" was cursed by God (Deut 21:23). In Gal 3:13, Paul quotes from the Greek translation of Deuteronomy in order to argue that the crucified Jesus became a curse on behalf of his followers and in this way liberated them from the curse. Seneca (1 B.C.E.–65 C.E.), in his work *Dialogi* (6.20.3), refers to the Roman practice of crucifixion and says that some victims were nailed to the cross through their genitals. This type of deed evoked a greater degree of ridicule among the passersby and onlookers.

The following case to which Josephus refers,[42] and which was also mentioned in 1 Macc 1:60–61, is another example of the cross as a particular object of ridicule.[43] The Syrian monarch Antiochus Epiphanes IV ordered parents whose children were circumcised, to be seriously maltreated physically, then crucified alive. The children were to be strangled and hung over the necks of their crucified parents. The reference in 1 Macc 1:60–61 also mentions that the families of the victims and those who had carried out the circumcision were put to death as well. Massyingbaerde Ford comments that "The motif of shame is important here; not only do the parents suffer the public shame of crucifixion, but a mockery is made of the very mark of the covenant, namely, circumcision (cf. Gen 17)."[44]

Paul declares in Rom 1:16 that he is not ashamed of the gospel. As far as he is concerned, he proclaims the "crucified Christ" who offends Israel and is considered to be foolish by Gentiles (1 Cor 1:18, 23). In Gal 6:11–14, Paul

---

38. See Gabra, *Cairo*, 44, 92.
39. See Parker, *Priapea*, 1.
40. See Elliott, "Paul, Galatians, and the Evil Eye."
41. Cf. Van der Watt and Joubert, "Hoe is Jesus Gekruisig?" 635.
42. See Josephus, *De Bello Judaeorum* 5.551; cf. Van der Watt and Joubert, "Hoe is Jesus Gekruisig?" 636.
43. See Ford, "Crucifixion of Women in Antiquity," 294.
44. Ibid., 295.

writes that the "cross of Christ" has resulted in the persecution of Christians, but as a "new creature" he exults in the cross of his *Kyrios*, Jesus Christ, and describes the cross as "marks" that he too must bear.[45] By this he means that the cross, seen against the background of magical beliefs, is like an amulet that wards off the harmful influence of evil.[46] The historiographer Herodotus used the word "marks" as well in the context of Egyptian slaves who fled into the temple of Hercules and burned "marks" (that is, tattoos) onto their bodies as signs that they had become the property of the god Hercules and would be protected by that god (*Historiae* 2.113).[47]

When, in the second century, the Greek philosopher Celsus attempted to make Christian belief about Jesus' deification seem ridiculous, he used the nature of Jesus' death as the deciding evidence.[48] According to Celsus, Jesus is a "magus" (μάγος) rather than a "god" (θεός). Celsus first ridicules the illegitimate birth of Jesus and his humble peasant origins.[49] Mockingly, he wants to know how someone with such a background could be assumed to have had a divine birth like that of Perseus, Amphion, Aecus, or Minos.[50] Then Celsus, arguing, from an Israelite perspective, asks, How could the shameful death of Jesus lead to him being called a god?[51] If God was his "Father," as Jesus himself and the Christians afterwards claimed, how can one begin to imagine, in contrast to Dionysus and Hercules whose father was Zeus, that a father could let his divine son undergo such a death?[52]

An interesting graffito from the third century C.E. was found on the Palatine hill in the Roman Forum.[53] In this cartoon, to the right of a crucified man is a figure with the head of a donkey, and a young man is pointing his arm to the "crucified donkey." A badly written inscription reads, "Alexamenos worships God." In a similar vein, Polybius relates how, in 214 B.C.E., Achaios was killed in Sardis by the Seleudic monarch Antiochus III after Achaios had attempted to usurp the throne. He was beheaded and his body woven into the skinned hide of a donkey, after which it was crucified in public on a pole in order to serve as a deterrent.[54] Tertullian, in turn, describes a painting in which Jesus is portrayed as a teacher in a gown and with a book in the hand, but with the ears of a donkey and one-hoofed leg.[55]

Such satires ridiculing gods occurred regularly in Roman literature. In Seneca's tragedies about Hercules, it is particularly evident how the

---

45. Galatians 6:17: τὰ στίγματα τοῦ Ἰησοῦ ἐν τῷ σώματί μου.
46. See Oepke, *Brief des Paulus an die Galater*, 206–7.
47. See Schlier, *Brief an die Galater*, 196–97; Oepke, *Brief des Paulus an die Galater*, 206–7.
48. Callagher, *Divine Man or Magician?* 127.
49. Ibid., 49.
50. Celsus, *Alethes Logos* 1.28; cf. Callagher, *Divine Man or Magician?* 53.
51. Celsus, *Alethes Logos* 1.67; cf. Callagher, *Divine Man or Magician?* 61.
52. Celsus, *Alethes Logos* 8.41; cf. Callagher, *Divine Man or Magician?* 127.
53. See Hanfmann, "Crucified Donkey Man," 206.
54. Polybius in Hanfmann, "Crucified Donkey Man," 206.
55. Tertullian, *Adversus Nationes* 1.14. 1; *Apologia* 16.12.

triumphant descent into Hades of the hero correlates with his divine birth, and how his deification is confirmed by his ascension. Carolyn Osiek refers to this mythical constituent as follows:

> Most texts [about the relationship between resurrection beliefs and resuscitated bodies in the first-century Mediterranean world] are ambiguous, but some. . . . seem to suggest a close connection, as does one Greco-Roman apotheosis story, that of Hercules by the first-century B.C.E. historian, Diodorus Siculus (*Bibliotheca Historica* 38.3–5). Hercules mounts the funeral pyre, which is consumed by a bolt of lightning. Those who came afterwards to gather the remains find no bones, and conclude that Hercules has been translated to the realm of the gods. Paul's analogies to seed sown and astral bodies in 1 Cor 15:35–44 are open to a variety of interpretations, but it does seem as if some continuity with the physical is supposed in the pneumatic transformation.[56]

Yet in Seneca's satire on the "deification" of the emperor Claudius (which should rather be called a "pumpkinification"), Seneca reaches the apogee of his satiric discourse *Apocolocyntosis* when he mockingly describes the descent to Hades of Claudius. This Latin writer-philosopher uses a Greek expression derived from the Isis-Osiris myth relating to the incarnation of the god Osiris in the form of a bull, the annual rebirth of this Egyptian god: "We have discovered him; let us be glad."[57] Seneca's ridicule is sharp: it is not the discovery of the incarnated god but the descent to Hades, from which one never returns, that is the source of joy (*Apoc.* 11.28). Seneca clearly has his knife into Claudius. In his satire, he implies that the emperor was a "pumpkin" and that it was ridiculous to call him a god. Instead of having "immortality" (ἀπαθανατίοις), the pumpkin was "yanked by the neck"[58] from heaven, from Olympus: a motif that suggests condemnation (*Apoc.* 11.27).

The strong suspicion that we are dealing here with satiric wordplay on "pumpkinification" and "immortality" is derived from Seneca's brother, Lucius Junius Gallio, proconsul of Achaia in 51/52 C.E., resident of Corinth (cf. Acts 18:12–17). It is the writer Dio Cassius who tells us that Gallio was aware of his brother's intentional wordplay. Claudius was poisoned with mushrooms, "heavenly food," by his wife Agrippina and his son Nero (ironically the very people who requested the senate to "deify" him). According

---

56. Osiek, "Women at the Tomb," 102.
57. Seneca, *Apocolocyntosis* 13.12. See Ball, *Satire of Seneca*, 231–32; Eden, *Seneca "Apocolocyntosis,"* 139; Schönberger, *Lucius Annaeus Seneca*, 54.
58. Eden, *Seneca "Apocolocyntosis,"* 3.

to the satirist, his death was characteristic of Claudius (blood relative of the first emperor Augustus but murderer of members of his own family).[59] At the emperor's death, Seneca mockingly says that the truth comes from the mouths of the "magi" (Latin: *mathematicos*).[60] His premature birth and the probable cause of his physical disablement resulted in no one announcing his birth; for this reason, his existence may be ignored and he may be delivered to death (*Apoc.* 3.2)!

Seneca lets the heroic divine figure Hercules ridicule Claudius by having Hercules say that it was only the "barbarians" in Britannia who erected a temple for the fool and who honored him as if he was a god.[61] Hercules asks the fool, "Who are you and from where? From what town are you and who are your parents?" (*Apoc.* 8.3). Seneca continues with the "divine Augustus," himself a blood relative of Claudius, asking how it was possible that such a person could have been made a god! "Look at his body, born when the gods were angry!" (*Apoc.* 10.1).

In chapter 3, I mentioned that, according to John 19:9, a similar question was addressed to Jesus of Nazareth by the governor in Jerusalem, Pontius Pilate. In John's report on the trial of Jesus by the governor, Pilate reacts to the accusation of the head priests that Jesus claimed to be a "king" and the "Son of God" by asking, "From where are you?" According to chapters 7 and 8, everyone, the brothers of Jesus as well as the bystanders, knows that Jesus is from Galilee. But what good can come from Nazareth (John 1:46)? An aspiring disciple of Jesus first has to overcome the offense created by this paradoxical question before he can become a follower of the man of Nazareth. At the beginning of his narrative (1:41, 45), the narrator identifies Jesus, through his followers, as the "Messiah of Israel" and the son of Joseph. The offense in question is thus overcome by acknowledging that Jesus is "Rabbi," the "Son of God," and "King of Israel" (1:49).

However, it is significant that Jesus does not respond to Pilate's question with regard to his social identity (John 19:9). According to rabbinical literature (*Kiddushin* 4:2), a person had to remain silent when confronted with a question about his origins if he did not know who his father was. John's reason for Jesus' silence cannot be accepted as being historical. However, we are told that Jesus was more than the son of Joseph. In John 1:18, Jesus is the preexistent Son of God, unique in kind, the one best beloved.[62] Jesus' sonship is, according to the Johannine vision, related to the conviction that

---

59. Dio Cassius, *Historiae Romanae* 60.35.3ff.; cf. Eden, *Seneca "Apocolocyntosis,"* 1.

60. See Ball, *Satire of Seneca,* 203.

61. See Eden, *Seneca "Apocolocyntosis,"* 73.

62. The phrase "only begotten [unique in kind] Son of God" appears only in a certain manuscript, translation and patristic tradition; see Aland and others, *Greek New Testament,* 314, note 18. Another tradition reads the word "God" (θεός) in the place of the word "son" (υἱός). In any case, that Jesus is "the only begotten Son of God" is further professed in John 3:16 and 18, as well as in 1 John 4:9; see Metzger, *Textual Commentary,* 198.

Jesus is the "one sent by God."[63] Jesus also has the authority to grant the right to all "those who believe in his name" (an expression that is "typically and exclusively Johannine"[64]) to be called "children of God" (1:12). They are children "not born from sexual union, not from physical desire, and not from male willfulness: they were born of God."[65] Therefore, Jesus says to Pilate, "My kingdom is not of this world" (18:36). This is the way in which John deals with the ridicule that the man of Nazareth was confessed to be God after his shameful death.

However, in terms of the ridicule that followed the poisoning of Claudius, there were no devotees who could react apologetically to Seneca's satire following the deification of the emperor. The fact that the appellation "pumpkin" (Greek: κολοκύντη; Latin; *cucurbita*) rather than "god" was used to name Claudius is most probably related to the fact that the *cucurbita* has a phallic form.[66] This comparison places the climatic denouement of Seneca's *Apocolocyntosis* in a particular context. We have seen that Seneca's ridicule resulted in the ironic comparison of the godlike human Claudius with the godlike human Osiris, the symbol of phallic religious practice. This reminds us of the Priapus cult and the satires in the contemporary Greek-Roman literature that ridicule this god and his characteristic phallic representation.

It is understandable that Amy Richlin has related Seneca's *Apocolocyntosis* to the *Priapea,* the collection of poems that were either written about, addressed to, spoken by, or meant to ridicule Priapus.[67] Because the male sexual organ was seen as an amulet to ward off the evil eye, the representation of Priapus with an erection made him the "god of the garden"—the symbol of fertility and the protector of the fruits of the garden. The first references to Priapus in Greek appeared from the third century B.C.E. and were found in literature until the sixth century C.E. The reference to the function

63. Whiston, *Josephus Complete Works*, 415, refers in a footnote to Izates, the "only-begotten" son of Helena, the queen of Adiabene, as the "one best-beloved": "Josephus here [*Ant.* xx.ii.1] uses the word *monogene*, as only-begotten son, for no other than one best-beloved, as does both the Old and the New Testament; I mean where there were one or more sons besides (Gen. xxii.2; Heb. xi.7.)"

64. Schnackenburg, *Gospel according to St John*, 262–63. For references about the link between fatherlessness and silence when one was asked about his heritage, see Fiensy, *Social History of Palestine*, 164–65.

65. Translation in Miller, *Complete Gospels*, rev. and expanded ed., 200.

66. Eden, *Seneca "Apocolocyntosis,"* 3.

67. Richlin, *Garden of Priapus*, 160–61. It would seem that the Priapus cult originated in Lampsacos on the Hellespontic straits (see Parker, *Priapea*, 1). These straits connect the Achaian Sea with the Sea of Marmara and the Black Sea. The Priapus cult presumably spread from Lampsacos to Greece and from there to the remainder of the Mediterranean world. A Greek inscription found at Thera, the old city on the Achaian island (today Santorini), reads as follows: "I, Priapus, came from Lampsacos to the city Thera, and I brought along sustained prosperity. I came to help all of you and render you assistance, both citizens and foreigners" (Parker, *Priapea*, 1). The southern seaboard of the Sea of Marmara is blessed with fertile valleys where olive and fruit orchards, as well as sunflower fields, are bountiful (Brosnahan, *Turkey*, 230).

of Priapus as the protector of the garden already appeared in the earliest *Priapea*. Furthermore, he was also honored in the Greek *Priapea* as the god of fishermen in particular. This is seen in, among other works, those of Antipater of Sidon, written around the turn of the century, as well as of Antiphilus, written during the first century C.E.[68] The earliest available fragment in Latin in which a reference to Priapus appears can be found in the comical writer Aphranius (ca. 150 B.C.E.).[69] In this fragment, Priapus says: "What people say of me, namely that I was born of a long-eared parent [in other words, a donkey], is simply not true."[70] Catullus (ca. 84–ca. 54 B.C.E.) also mentioned that Priapus came from Lampsacos and that the god was honored by fishermen.

---

68. Parker, *Priapea*, 3–9.

69. We cannot, however, be sure who compiled the *Carmina Priapea*, a corpus of eighty poems included at one time among the minor works of Virgil. Similarities to the works of Catullus, Ovid, and Martial can certainly be indicated (see Richlin, *Garden of Priapus*, 143). Even though the date of Catullus's *Epigramma Dedicatorum* is uncertain (see Berkowitz and Squitier, *Thesaurus Linguae Graecae*, 78), we may date the *Priapea*, on the basis of similarities with the work of Ovid, to be from the period of the emperor Nero. The similarities with the poems of Martial situate the Latin *Priapea* in the last phase of the first century C.E. (see Richlin, *Garden of Priapus*, 143). Images of Priapus as "god of the garden" were carved from rough wood by simple peasants to serve as "scarecrows" against thieves in order to protect the garden. Horace (65–68 B.C.E.), in his *Satires* (1.8), has Priapus referring to this himself (Latin, in Page, *Seneca's Tragedies*, 97; English, in Parker, *Priapea*, 13, 82–83).

Olim truncus eram ficulnus, inutile lignum,
cum faber, incertus scamnum faceretne Priapum,
maluit esse deum, deus inde ego,
furum aviumque maxima formido;
nam fures dextra coercet obscenoque ruber porrectus ab inguine palus;
ast importunas volucres in vertice harundo terret fixa vetatque novis considere in hortis.

A fig-tree once I was, which useless wood
The carpenter in doubt was if he should
To a priapus turn, or to a chair.
He chose the god, and so my job's to scare
Away the thieves with penis painted red
From loins erect; the wreath upon my head,
From gardens new deters the birds.

Horace here mockingly refers to an extension to the gardens of Maecenas on the Esquiline hill in Rome as the "new gardens"—the place where, earlier, slaves and other poverty-stricken "expendables" had been buried (Parker, *Priapea*, 15) and "where, among the tombs, witches practiced their weird and infernal rites. Here, however, Maecenas, co-operating with Augustus in the work of city improvement, had laid out beautiful gradens, in which he later built himself a palace with a conspicuous tower" (Page, *Seneca's Tragedies*, 95). During the first century B.C.E., Columella (10.29—Parker, *Priapea*, 82–83) writes that such wooden sculptures are not exactly works of art it is merely a trunk from an old tree (*sed truncum forte dolatum*). And in the *Inscriptio Harleianus* (2578—Parker, *Priapea*, 82), Priapus is annoyed by a "stupid girl" (*insulsissima puella*), who laughs at the image of a comical piece of wood and takes him to be a joke. He is not a god who was portrayed by famed Athenian sculptors, but was carved from wood by a rustic hand (*sed lignum rude vilicus dolavit*). It is precisely "his status as a ridiculous god, a god to be mocked" (Richlin, *Garden of Priapus*, 141) that is accorded attention in the poems by Martial.

70. Parker, *Priapea*, 11.

CHILDREN CALLING GOD ABBA

We got to Priapus, who wards off the evil eye, via our earlier sidenotes on the eye of Horus, the son of Isis and Osiris. We saw that Diodorus, in the run-up to his narrative of the divine adoption of Hercules, equated Osiris with Priapus. Diodorus's material about Hercules was probably taken from the *Encomium* [Praises] *of Hercules* by Matris of Thebes.[71] In the course of retelling the story, Diodorus referred to the deification of Hercules.[72] Zeus persuaded his wife, the goddess Hera, to deify Hercules by adopting him as her son. The jealousy of Zeus's wife towards Hercules was therefore reversed and she symbolically adopted him to protect him against the shame of adultery and to legitimize his deification. The way she passed Hercules off as her own son makes use of the same ceremony that was still used in Diodorus's time by "barbarians" when they wanted to adopt a son.[73] According to the myth, Hera lay down on the bed, held Hercules close to her body and let him fall, through her clothes, onto the floor to imitate a real birth. This action by which the adoption of the child was symbolized is important because it relates to the question of who the "barbarians" might be.[74]

We have seen that Diodorus retold these myths during his residence in Alexandria in the first century B.C.E. and that he counted the Egyptians as being among the barbarians (*Bib. Tet.* 1.15.6ff.). We are also aware of the stories about divine intervention at the births of the children of Israelite women such as Sarah, Rachel, and Hannah.[75] As far as Rachel is concerned, in Gen 30:1–8 we read that she, as in the story of Sarah and Hagar (Gen 16:1–3), offered the slave Bilhah to her husband Jacob so that Bilhah could fall pregnant, give birth upon the knees of Rachel, and that Rachel, through Bilhah, could have a child.[76] The expression in the Septuagint "to make into a child" (τεκνόποιημαι) may be seen as interchangeable with "to adopt as child." (υἱοθεσία)

The expression "to give birth on one's knees" is, in a Dutch study on adoption in ancient Israel, understood as constituting a reference to the

---

71. See Oldfather, "Introduction," ix.
72. Diodorus Siculus, *Bib. Tet.* 39.2; ἀποθεωσίς (deification); υἱοποιήσασθαι (adopting).
73. Ibid., θετὸν υἱόν ποιεῖσθαι.
74. See the uncertainty in Wülfing von Martitz, υἱός, υἱοθεσία, 401, note 10.
75. See Sheres and Blau, *Truth about the Virgin*, 48–73.
76. "There was no greater sorrow for an Israelite or Oriental woman than childlessness. Even today among the Arabs the barren woman is exposed to disgrace and even grievous wrongs. These views, which derive from the human code of honor, and the customs to which they give birth also play a role in the patriarchal stories. For there was a legitimate way to avoid all these difficulties, the way that Sarah proposed to Abraham in v. 2b. To understand the conflict that now ensues, one must refer to legal customs that were apparently widespread at that time. The wife could bring to marriage her own personal maid, who was not available to her husband as a concubine in the same way his own female slaves were. If she gave her personal maid to her husband, in the event of her own childlessness, then the child born of the maid was considered the wife's child: The slave was born "on the knees" of the wife, so that the child then came symbolically from the womb of the wife herself (cf. ch. 30.3, 9)!" (Von Rad, *Genesis*, 191).

assistance rendered to Bilhah during the birth of her child.[77] In Job 3:12, the expression "knees to put me down on"[78] is used as a symbolic reference to the birth of Job. This expression is then followed in the second half of the verse with "breasts to feed me." Apart from the possibility that this is a reference to someone's birth,[79] we might also be dealing here with an adoption formula.[80] In Gen 30:3 and 50:23, the expression is clearly used as an adoption formula. The reference would in this case be to a father who took the child onto his knees as an indication that he recognized the child as his own.[81] In chapter 4, we saw that these references in Genesis pertain to Joseph's children and grandchildren born in Egypt.

When God lets Ruth fall pregnant (Ruth 4:13), she is compared to Rachel, among others (4:11). We are told that, at the birth of Obed, the ancestor of David, Naomi "laid him in her lap" (NIV) "and became his nurse" (RSV). Commentaries are virtually unanimous that the former phrase is an adoption formula.[82] Similarly, as far as the adoption of the two sons of Joseph born in Egypt (see chapter 4) is concerned,[83] the ceremony consists of Jacob picking up the boys and putting them "on his lap," while Joseph picks them up from there (Gen 48:12).[84] Joseph, just prior to his death and funeral in Egypt, still has the opportunity to adopt his grandchildren born in Egypt "as his own." In a more literal translation, "they were born on Joseph's thighs" (Gen 50:23).[85] By means of this act of adoption, he includes these children, whose grandmother (Asenath) was an impure foreigner, into God's covenant with Israel.

In his commentary on the adoption formula in Ruth 4:16, G. Gerleman relates Joseph's adoption of the children (the Makarites who were born outside the fatherland and who later became the forefathers of the Samaritans) and their subsequent inclusion among the people of the covenant to Naomi's adoption of Obed, the son of the foreigner Ruth, in the following way:

> Boas took Ruth as his wife and she gave birth to a son. It is, however, notable that the final scene of the Ruth narrative does not focus on Ruth, but on Naomi. She [Naomi] today received a redeemer [a substituting patron]; in other words, the newly born child will become a patron and provider to her. It did not suffice,

---

77. David, "Adoptie in het Oude Israel," 13–15.
78. The Septuagint reads, ἵνα τί δὲ συνεντήσαν μοι γωνάτα.
79. Rowley, Job, 46.
80. Van Selms, Genesis, 2:103.
81. E. Dhorme, cited in Rowley, Job, 46.
82. See Köhler, "Adoptionsform von Ruth 4,16," 312–14.
83. Van Selms, Genesis, 2:103.
84. The Septuagint reads, ἀπο τὸν γωνάτον αὐτοῦ.
85. The Septuagint reads, ἐτεχθέσαν ἐπὶ μερῶν Ἰωσηφ.

for the narrator, to let Ruth be included within the Israelite community. He takes care to give the newborn a true Israelite mother
by means of a distinctive act of adoption. Naomi (therefore)
presses the child to her bosom and the bystanders say: "A son has
been born to Naomi." This widespread ancient Eastern legal act
is not mentioned in the First Testament. Different narratives (in
the First Testament), however, indicate that this manner of
adopting children was not unknown to Israel. In this way the
children of Bilhah and Zilpah and Rachel and Leah were adopted
(Gen 30:3–13). Traces of the same rite of "taking on the knees"
[translated above as "laid him in her lap"] is found in the blessing of Ephraim and Manasseh (Gen 48). The sons of Makir are,
similarly, born "on the knees" of Joseph; in other words, they are
through this action adopted (legally) as children of Joseph.[86]

Apart from the apologetic context in the case of Diodorus Siculus, where
the illegitimacy of Hercules was hidden so he could enjoy the right of being
son of god, the Greek word for "adoption" (υἱοθεσία) occurs in ancient
Greece only within a juridical context. The context here is the provision of
an heir where there is none.[87] The same applies to Latin documents. Apart
from the precaution that someone could inherit legally, the adoption
appears particularly within the context of ensuring the continuation of the
imperial dynasty of the Julius-Claudius family.[88]

Even before Augustus became the first emperor of the Roman Empire,
Julius Caesar (49–44 B.C.E.) adopted Augustus (44 B.C.E.–14 C.E.), the son of
the daughter (Atia) of Caesar's son (Atius Balbus) with Iulia, as his son.
Although such a grandson (the son of the daughter of the heir's son) was
recognized by the Romans as being equal in status with the son of the heir,
Augustus's adoption by Caesar probably took place in order to ensure that
Augustus would be more than merely the equivalent of a son, but, in fact, a
son in the full sense of the word.[89] In the same manner, Augustus, in order
to continue the line of imperial succession within the Julius-Claudius family, adopted his corresponding grandsons, Gaius and Lucius, while Tiberius
adopted his daughter's son, Germanicus, and Claudius his daughter's
spouse, Nero. In the last two cases, the relation between emperor and son
was therefore bypassed.

I have now reached a point of conclusion. Paul's use of the expression
"adoption as children" in Romans 8 is not only an example of what is

86. Gerleman, Ruth—Das Hohelied, 37–38. (My translation of the original German.)
87. Schweizer, "huiothesia," 1215.
88. See Bush, Studies in Roman Social Structure, 93–96.
89. See Bush, Studies in Roman Social Structure, 93.

merely one of a number of widely recurring motifs related to the way Christians see themselves in the New Testament; indeed, it may be described as a "root metaphor." The roots of this metaphor lie deep. According to the First Testament and intertestamental evidence, Israel regarded itself as "people of the covenant" and as "children" who were adopted by God. For Israel, this metaphor possessed an enduring power, and over many years it remained one of the basic ways by means of which the "family Israel" saw itself as distinguished from other nations.

In both his epistle to the Romans and his epistle to the Galatians, Paul uses the metaphor of inheritance to refer to the reception of God's promises. It is no longer the biological children of Abraham who are to enjoy the inheritance, but those who, in Christ, have in a spiritual way become part of Abraham's family. In order to express the idea that believers in Christ are not by nature children of Abraham (in other words, children of God) but that they believe as Abraham believed and therefore have become part of God's household in a nonbiological way, Paul uses, among others, the metaphors "children of the promise" and "adoption as children."

It is clear that Paul's use of the latter expression contains connotations that can be understood against the background of the Greco-Roman and Hellenistic-Semitic world. However, biblical scholarship does not at present have much new to add regarding the usage of the term in the New Testament. However, research progresses not only through the dissemination of new information about a particular topic, but is served too through the development of different interpretations of well-known data. One way to do this is to indicate the extent to which Paul found the term "adoption as children" useful as a means of emphasizing his conviction that all people have equal access to the presence of God.

I have already indicated the considerable extent to which these values stand in opposition to the conventional views that were and are prevalent in the world of the inhabitants of the area surrounding the Mediterranean. These are values that can be traced back to Jesus himself and have been handed down by Christians who have communicated the cause of Jesus. When Paul explains who really constitutes the true "Israel of God," he uses the metaphors of family and adoption as child of God. By doing this he continues to transmit the heart of Jesus' message about children entering God's kingdom.

One can expect rhetoric related to this alternative wisdom to occur particularly in those New Testament documents where the tension between the conventional wisdom of the temple cult of Jerusalem and the "new" wisdom is in the foreground. In this regard, I am thinking in particular of the authentic letters of Paul. We have seen that the New Testament reflects the tradition of the Jesus faction in Jerusalem as being in opposition to the Pauline (e.g., Gal 2:2–14), even though authentic writings by repre-sentatives of the Jerusalem faction, such as James and Peter, do not occur in the New Testament. Robert Funk sketches this ironic situation:

> Broadly speaking, in the rivalry with Paul, Peter represents the connection with the historical Jesus. After all, Peter had been a close companion and confidant of Jesus until his arrest. Paul, on the other hand, claimed only to know the risen Jesus, the Christ of vision and spirit possession. It is perhaps ironic that it was Paul, and not Peter, who understood the heart of Jesus' parables and aphorisms.[90]

The heart of Jesus' message consisted of his vision of how God is present to people. Jesus used the metaphor of the kingdom of God as an image to communicate this message. We have seen that this is in itself shocking, as the concept of kingdom presupposes domination and hierarchy. Those in Israelite society who were the victims of the abuse of power by monarchs avidly looked forward to a future ideal "kingdom." In this apocalyptic and messianic kingdom, God will govern in the "heavenly Jerusalem" and "a temple will not be seen in the city, for its temple is the Lord God, the Almighty, and the Lamb" (Rev 21:22). Jesus' alternative definition of the kingdom of God was not portrayed in apocalyptic symbols. God's domain was for Jesus already present.[91]

Paul's pronouncement that circumcision was superfluous echoed Jesus' message that God's kingdom represents an unbrokered relation-ship to God. His use of the notion "adoption as children" forms part of the above-mentioned rhetoric. It is therefore also not surprising that this concept, or the matter to which it relates, occurs especially in Paul's letters to the Galatians and Romans. The expression "blameless children of God" also occurs in Phil 2:15 as an allusion to the concept of "Israelite sonship of God" that appears in the Greek translation (Septuagint) of Deut 32:5. The same polemical tendency occurs in 2 Cor 6:18, where Paul quotes from a different part of the Septuagint. His argument here is that Christians constitute the "temple of God" (2 Cor 6:16). In this case, Paul refers to them as "sons and daughters" of God the "Father." I am focusing, however, on Paul's use of the metaphor of adoption in Romans 8.

In order to express the idea that believers in Christ are not by nature chil-dren of Abraham but that they believe as Abraham believed and therefore have become part of "God's household" in a nonphysical way, Paul proceeds

---

90. Funk, *Honest to Jesus*, 136.
91. Ibid., 41.

with, among others, the metaphors "children of the promise" and "adoption as children." For Paul there are two Israels: the "Israel of God" and the "Israel according to the flesh." Physically speaking, the latter refers to Paul's fellow Israelites. Paul admits that they are the people whom God previously allowed to share in God's glory, with whom God made covenants, to whom God gave the law of Moses, the temple service and the gift of Jesus being born in their midst. Yet, because Paul surrendered to God (Rom 9:5b), he, on the basis of the work of the Holy Spirit (Rom 9:1), has become conscious that God in a new way places people into a proper relationship with God (Rom 10:3–4). Because Paul knows that God welcomes anyone who believes, Paul proclaims that Jesus redefined the meaningfulness of the things mentioned above. Paul summarizes this concisely in Rom 10:4 by saying that Christ is the end of the law.[92] The matter that was given a new meaning in Jesus, and that, for now, interests me, is Paul's agreement with the notion that Israel was adopted by God.

The conviction that something radical changed led Paul to distinguish between a life that is of "nature" and a life in which transience is transcended. Participation in the latter by the believer is not possible through physical means but through spiritual means. This can only be expressed with the aid of metaphors. Participants may therefore be described as the "fictive house of Abraham." In Rom 11:17, the metaphor of the wild olive that has been grafted onto the tame olive is used in this regard. In Gal 6:16, Paul refers to this household as the "Israel of God." This Israel represents a life beyond that which is "of nature." And where there is life—be it the life that is "of nature" or the life that is beyond the physical—the spirit is active: the human spirit or the Spirit of God. Paul wrote that the first way of life is a life of bondage. Bondage is dependence. Slaves are not free people, but dependent. The physical person is like a slave, someone bound to nature, transience, death. In Rom 8:15, for example, Paul says that the Spirit of God liberates. The Spirit of God does not lead to slavery. The Spirit leads to adoption.[93] Children of God are free from slavery, from bondage, from that which is physical. On the basis of these events that lead to one's adoption as child, one may call God "Father" (*Abba*), as a child would in her or his relationship toward a father.

According to Rom 8:15, Paul refers to these spiritual events concerning the adoption of the believer as child of God as something that occurred in the past. Indeed, Paul uses the past tense.[94] In Romans 8:23, however, Paul says that the Spirit received by the children of God is merely a "deposit gift," or a "first gift" (ἀπαρχή). Paul continues by saying that the children of God

---

92. Rom 10:4: τέλος γὰρ νόμου χριστὸς εἰς δικαιοσύνην παντὶ τῷ πιστεύοντι.

93. Rom 8:15: πνεῦμα δουλεία (the Spirit of God does not lead to slavery); πνεῦμα υἱοθεσίας (to adoption as child).

94. In Greek, the aoristus: ἐλάβετε.

are therefore "freed in hope" (8:24).[95] Hope is the situation in which believers live.[96] A reality built on hope is a reality that cannot be seen (8:24–25). The reality of adoption as God's children, that is, as children of Abraham, is a real event that occurred in the past. This reality must, however, be distinguished from the reality that is "of nature." The latter reality can be seen. Being a child of God while not being a child of Abraham by nature is something that cannot be seen, unlike circumcision, as a visible sign. Being a child of God is something one hopes will eventually become visible beyond this transient life, the life that is "of nature."

Paul looked forward to the liberation from a stressful, physical existence.[97] He describes this (future?) liberation in Rom 8:23 as "a redemption from our body"[98]; that is, God will free us from transience. This is definitely a reference to the "resurrection of the body."[99] Paul did not employ the idea of "immortality" or that of the "raising of the flesh."[100] He was thinking of the transition of the earthly body into a new kind of corporeality. In 1 Cor 15:44, the body of resurrection is called the "spiritual body" as opposed to the "physical body."

The resurrection faith of the earliest Christians was embedded in apocalypticism. This belief must be understood against the background of the postexilic notion of a general resurrection from death. The resurrection of the body was an unacceptable idea to Gnosticism, which despised corporeality. The assertions in Rom 8:11 about the resurrection of Jesus therefore make it impossible to interpret the expression "redemption of our body" in Rom 8:23 as Gnostic.[101] In Rom 7:14–8:30, we are dealing with a transition from a Gnostic mind-set to an apocalyptic one. The apocalyptic mind-set is closely related to the idea of switching from the transient world of daily

---

95. Rom 8:24: τῇ γὰρ ἐλπίδι ἐσώθημεν. See the translation of this verse in Barrett, *Epistle to the Romans*, 161.

96. Käsemann, *An die Römer*, 230: "Hoffnung ist die Situation, in der wir . . . als Geretteten leben." The dative translated with "in hope" (ἐλπίδι) must be understood as a dative of modality.

97. Käsemann, *An die Römer*, 229.

98. Rom 8:23: ἀπολύτρωσις τοῦ σώματος ἡμῶν.

99. Cf. Byrne, "Sons of God"—"Seed of Abraham," 109.

100. Cf. Käsemann, *An die Römer*, 229.

101. Interpreting the expression "of our body" (in the phrase "a redemption from our body") as a *genetivus separationis* might create the impression that we are dealing here with a Gnostic redemption idea (cf. Lietzmann, *An die Römer*, 85). If it is taken as an objective genitive, as in Rom 8:11, then the idea of apocalyptic liberation from afflictions at the end of time would figure more strongly (cf. Käsemann, *An die Römer*, 229; Byrne, "*Sons of God*"—"*Seed of Abraham*," 109, note 120). However, it is not necessary to see Gnosticism and apocalypticism as mutually exclusive mind-sets. On the one hand, it seems as if all of Rom 7:14–8:30, which may be seen as an independent unit dealing with the total degeneration of humanity as well as with the redemption of humanity from that state of sin, is cast in Gnostic presuppositions and mind-sets. Against the Gnostic notion that redemption primarily has the quality of presence, redemption is understood in apocalypticism as belonging to the end of time. Schmithals, *Theologiegeschichte des Urchristentums*, 82, explains this distinction by means of the respective images of Christ in apocalypticism and Gnosticism: in apocalypticism, Christ is primarily "der Kommende" (salvation is a future occurrence), while in Gnosticism he is "der Gekommene" (salvation is a present occurrence).

experience to the imaginary transcendental world. The conviction that there will be a general resurrection from death is embedded in this (mythological) idea of the switching of worlds. For the earliest Christians, the resurrection of Jesus was taken to be the start of the general resurrection from death. The Gnostic-dualistic elements, such as the dichotomy between "flesh" (σάρχ) and "spirit" (πνεῦμα) that occurs in Rom 8:2–11 and Gal 4:21–31, are not found in strongly marked apocalyptic passages of Paul's epistles.[102] On the other hand, apocalyptic concepts are connected by Paul with the Gnostic-dualistic aspect of his thought. Both Rom 7:14–8:30 and Gal 4:4–7 are examples of this.[103]

The motif "fullness of time" (which is related to the apocalyptic switching of the experiential world and the imaginary world) is in Gal 4:4–7 associated with the Gnostic preexistence Christology that God sent God's Son in order that believers may receive adoption as children of God (verse 5). Similarly, in Rom 8:12–16, Paul commences with the Gnostic "presentist eschatology," and proceeds from verse 17 to the idea of a "futuristic eschatology."[104] In this regard, he calls Christ the "first of many brothers" (Rom 8:23).

We have seen that Paul relates the announcement that God has adopted believers as God's children and, therefore, has predestined them to the resurrection from death (Rom 8:23). But we must not assume that to Paul this is only a question of hope with reference to the end of time. We must remember that the reality of faith is not dependent on physical sight, and to be a son of God is perfectly real through faith. There is therefore no tension between the past tense of Rom 8:15 and the future orientation in Rom 8:23, which describes the same reality.[105] Within the framework of Paul's apocalyptic worldview, the reality of being "adopted" as God's child is not something physical and does not create any tension.

To interpret Rom 8:24 as meaning that being a child of God can only be fully realized at the end of the time is incorrect.[106] According to Paul, being a child of God is made possible by Jesus in the world of everyday experience. The problem here lies with the use of the adverb "fully," and not with the conviction that "childhood" has already been realized. This problem is related to the well-known tension in Paul's letters between what is already

---

102. Schmithals, *Theologiegeschichte des Urchristentums*, 70.

103. Ibid., 76, 82. Cf. the combination of the second and third type Christologies discussed earlier.

104. Ibid., 83.

105. Some scholars (see Byrne, "*Sons of God*" — "*Seed of Abraham*," 2, note 1) are of the opinion that the omission of the expression "adoption as child" (υἱοθεσία) in Rom 8:23 in, for instance, the second-century papyrus manuscript Chester Beatti P⁴⁶ᵛⁱᵈ (which is damaged and legible only with difficulty at this point) may be attributed to such a tension (see Metzger, *Textual Commentary*, 517). However, the reading without the omission is without doubt the more difficult one (*lectio difficilior*) and also preferable (cf. Käsemann, *An die Römer*, 229).

106. See De Villiers, *Betekenis van HUIOTHESIA*, 69, 160.

and what is not yet.[107] The question is, however, whether it is correct to describe Paul's use of the expression "adoption as children" as only a future and transcendent reality. Such an eschatological view may perhaps correspond to John the Baptist's beliefs, as we saw earlier, but it certainly does not continue those of Jesus![108]

Paul's linking of Christians' adoption as children to a future liberation from the body, that is, the resurrection from death, must not be read separately from the apostle's conviction that Christians have already "died with Christ" (Rom 6:8) and now already believe that they live with Christ for God (Rom 6:10). According to Paul, Christ Jesus was, after all, on the basis of his resurrection from death, declared to be the Son of God (Rom 1:4)—a sonship that Jesus, according to Paul, possessed already before his resurrection (Phil 2:6). Paul argues that the Spirit already lives in the life of believers too and "will also quicken our [the believers'] mortal bodies" (Rom 8:11), but now already "makes us children of God and lets us call to God: 'Abba!' that means Father" (Rom 8:15).

In chapter 5, I indicated that the arrangements around the temple cult of Jerusalem were in essence related to the idea of who the children of God were. At the most basic level, the postexilic marriage regulations of this cult created the parameters of their view of social identity and their relationship with God. These regulations not only robbed outsiders of honor and status and of familial security, but attempted to alienate them from God. Against this background, the fatherless Jesus, victim of this systemic evil, went to John the Baptist. While he acknowledged his position as "sinner," he went with the expectation to receive forgiveness in an unconventional way. The Baptist was busy planting, as it were, "ticking time bombs":

> When people came to him [John], he kept sending them back
> from the wilderness, through the Jordan, purified and forgiven
> into the Promised Land, there to await the imminent coming of

---

107. See Ridderbos, *Paulus*, 214, 217–18.

108. Similarly, the attempt to solve this supposed tension by imposing on the text the idea of an "eschatological order of salvation" cannot be endorsed. Such a perspective yields to a "salvation-historical" explanation of Gal 3:25–26 (as well as Eph 1:5) (see Ridderbos, *Paulus*, 216–17). According to this view, Paul would argue that God acted within a linear temporal order by first electing Israel (Eph 1:5) and then, when the "fullness of time" came (Gal 4:4ff.), God sent Jesus as God's son so that believers could receive "adoption as children," which will be revealed fully at the end of time. However, the salvation-historical explanation—the "yet-not-yet" time scheme—lacks persuasiveness in view of what we today know about the concept of time in the world of the Bible. Bruce Malina ("Christ and Time," 210, 185) concludes his contribution by saying that "in the New Testament period there was no tension between the 'now' and the 'not yet.' When those writings were written and collected, there was only emphasis on a rather broad 'now.' On the other hand, the 'not yet' is a continual concern of persons from future-oriented societies." Malina argues that "the only scholarly evidence for the existence of anxiety and concern about a perceived delay of a parousia, for interest in eschatology, or some future-oriented apocalyptic was in the eyes of liberal, Enlightenment-oriented, nineteenth-century northern European biblical interpreters and their twentieth-century heirs" (125).

the avenging, saving God. In essence, John was forming a giant system of purified individuals, a network of ticking time bombs all over the Jewish homeland. Because of John, when Jesus began his ministry, he found already a vast network of people expectant, eager, waiting for God's power to be revealed.[109]

One of these time bombs already exploded before the time intended by John, that is, before the general resurrection from death could happen! Since Jesus of Nazareth, the notion of being child of God has changed for Israel. In other words, John still belonged to the old dispensation, like all of those who, up to today, still wait for God to intervene. Nonetheless, John began to invert roles. After his baptism, Jesus became convinced that the kingdom of God was a reality, and that it had already come. Radically opposed to what the conventions of the temple cult of Jerusalem prescribed, he, as an unmarried outsider, addressed God as "Father" and, like a child who, as it were, did not know what sin was, put his trust in God. Jesus went even further and called the other outsiders children and invited them to live now already as children of their heavenly Father. To enter God's kingdom as children is certainly no military coup d'état, but the image has a dynamic affect. The *Gospel of Thomas* 46 (cf. Luke 7:28 Q) gives some witness to this: "Jesus said, 'From Adam to John the Baptist, among those born of women, no one is so much greater than John the Baptist that his eyes should not be averted. But I have said that whoever among you becomes a child will recognize the [Father's] imperial rule and will become greater than John.'"[110]

The traditions about Jesus' life and work, as they have been handed down in the Gospel tradition, including within the circle of the Johannine school, have carried further the heart of this message of inclusivity and egalitarianism, of new life. Among the witnesses in the documents of early Christianity, the unmarried Paul, in my view, did this most clearly. Even though he was influenced strongly by a Greco-Roman mind-set and by Hellenistic-Semitic wisdom traditions when he referred to Jesus as preexistent "Son of God," Paul's use of the metaphor of adoption as children of God was a striking way to verbalize Jesus' invitation to enter the new world of God.

We have seen that the myths of virginal conceptions, ascensions to heaven, and being adopted by the gods are almost recycled ideas. In this regard, Seneca's tragedies of Hercules' adoption and Ovid's story of Perseus's conception are most striking. These stories were not only very familiar in the first-century Greco-Roman world, but also came to mind when (Gentile) philosophers of that period reflected on what Christians said about Jesus, child of God.

---

109. Crossan and Watts, *Who Is Jesus?* 45–47.
110. *Gospel of Thomas*, 46. Translation by Miller, *Complete Gospels*, 312.

CHAPTER 8

～

The Cradle of the Church

Jesus never conceived the church or intended to establish the church. The church is not a product of Jesus' will, intention, or action. The earliest Jesus movement in Jerusalem emanated from a faith based on the resurrection belief. However, it is an open question whether this "church" reflects a continuity or discontinuity with the cause of Jesus. The peculiar quality of Jesus' cause is its inclusiveness and antihierarchical tendency. The Jerusalem faction was known for its embeddedness in Israel's mores. It was not known for openness toward Gentiles or for egalitarianism. Yet this does not mean that there is an absolute discontinuity between Jesus and the earliest Jesus movement in Jerusalem. The historical Jesus brought his message within the scope of Israel. The Jerusalem faction searched the scriptures and found evidence that Jesus was adopted by God to be Israel's messiah.

From this messianic outlook and with an apocalyptic mind-set, the Jerusalem faction apparently started a process of institutionalizing Jesus' last meal with close followers as a table fellowship symbolizing their participation in God's spiritual kingdom. These followers of Jesus distinguished themselves from the circle of the disciples of John the Baptist. Like Jesus himself, some of them could initially have belonged to this circle. Their separation was symbolized by their distinctive understanding of the baptismal rite. The baptism by John the Baptist was a water ritual that initiated a lifestyle to be lived when and where God reigns. The fellows of the Jesus movement in Jerusalem institutionalized a "spiritual baptism" in the name of the Father, and the Son, and the Spirit of God as sign of initiation into a discipleship of the "heavenly kingdom." According to their scrutinizing exegesis of the Hebrew Scriptures, this imperial rule was inaugurated by Jesus as Israel's spirit-filled messiah, who triumphed by his victory over death as it was expected within an apocalyptic mind-set that the Child of Humanity would do. Apocalypticism can therefore be seen as the mother of the Jerusalem faction's theology[1] and unthinkable without the belief in the resurrection from the death.

The first sentence of this chapter is my paraphrase of the well-known words of Wolfgang Trilling: *Jesus never conceived the church or intended to establish the church.*[2] These words have since been repeated with approval by many historians.[3] The establishment of the church is, therefore, not to be traced back to a foundational event in the life of the historical Jesus. After Jesus' brutally maltreated body had not been laid in a family tomb, Jesus arose in the kerygma. In other words, Jesus lived on through the retelling of his cause. This process resulted in a development of Jesus movements[4] that reached back to his followers' experience of resurrection appearances of Jesus, in particular by Mary Magdalene, Peter, James, and Paul.[5]

For some in early Christianity, it was as if they experienced the appearance of the resurrected Jesus in the form of the Child of Humanity in an altered state of consciousness (for evidence in Matthew, see 24:30; 27:52–53; 28:16–20). The Child of Humanity is that triumphant apocalyptic figure who had been expected to come at that point in history when the experiences in this world were almost unendurable and God's people were fantasizing about the inauguration of the kingdom of God transcending the worrisome times that they experienced (see, e.g., Dan 7:13–14).

Others could only hold on to the kerygma of those who said that they had been sent by the exalted Jesus to convey his cause (cf. John 20:29). Paul said explicitly that he was sent by God to become an "apostle for the Gentiles" (Gal 2:8). It is reported that this commission was given to Paul when he was transformed by means of a divine light in which the risen Jesus appeared. This is, however, not described as a visual experience. It is reported that Paul heard Jesus' voice (see Acts 9:3–4; 22:6–7; 26:13–14; cf. Gal 1:25–27).

Mary Magdaline claimed to have been the first to have experienced an appearance of the risen Jesus. This is probably authentic (see Mark 16:1,

---

1. These words intentionally resemble those of Käsemann, "Anfänge christlicher Theologie," 180: "Die Apokalyptik ist—da man die Predigt Jesu nicht eigentlich als Theologie bezeichnen kann—die Mutter aller christlichen Theologie gewesen." However, Käsemann's expression "all Christian theology" should be reduced to only the theology of the Jesus faction in Jerusalem. Other "Christian" factions, contemporaneous to that in Jerusalem (e g , the communities respectively responsible for the formative stratum of the Sayings Gospel Q and the first layer of the *Gospel of Thomas*), did not interpret the Jesus event from an apocalyptic perspective but from a sapiental one.

2. Trilling, "Implizite Ekklesiologie," 68.

3. See, e.g., Vermes, *Religion of Jesus*, 214–15.

4. See Schillebeeckx, *Jezus*, 38; Schille, "Jesusbewegung und die Entstehung," 104.

5. Cf. Lüdemann, *Resurrection of Jesus*, 68, 100, 170, 176–77, with regard to Peter and Paul, and the Jesus Seminar, *The Acts of Jesus*, 478–79, with regard to Mary Magdalene, contra Lüdemann, 160.

9; Matt 28:1; Luke 24:10; John 20:1; *Gospel of Peter* 12:50; *Epistula Apostolorum* 9 [in both the Ethiopic and Coptic versions]). Only the *Epistula Apostolorum* does not place the previously demon-possessed Mary Magdalene first on the list of the women who said they had a vision of the resurrected Jesus. This story of the women *confused* (Greek: ἐξίστημι) the men (Luke 24:22–24)—the Greek word refers to amazement, astonishment—what man could believe the witness of a woman! Fortunately, for the sake of the men, another pillar of faith confirmed that the master appeared to him (cf. Luke 24:34). Paul apparently believed Peter, for the latter was actually the first to have seen Jesus (Elisabeth Schüssler Fiorenza calls 1 Cor 15:3–8 a "list intended to legitimate male authority"[6]), although Peter himself and the other "pillars of faith" fled during the turmoil surrounding Jesus' crucifixion (Mark 14:50). The rumor follows that when Peter's shame prompted him to return his heart failed him again (see Mark 14:34, 66–72). Nevertheless, it is believed that God made him an "apostle for the Israelites" (Gal 2:8).

According to Paul, Jesus also appeared to the core group of Jesus' followers, believed to be twelve, as if they could claim to represent all the sons of Israel (cf. 1 Cor 15:5; Luke 24:36–49; John 20:19–23; 26–29). Another early tradition was transmitted that the cause of Jesus began to find its way through the Roman Empire after the Spirit of God came upon a larger group of people from many different ethnic backgrounds who had come to Jerusalem as the prophets said the nations would do. This spiritual experience of an altered state of consciousness happened when Peter started "evangelizing," telling the people about the crucified Jesus whom God made to be Lord and Messiah of *all* of Israel, Israelites and Gentiles included (Acts 2:1–42). Through his death, a transformation of the temple cult took place. Instead of sacrificial rites for receiving forgiveness of sin, everyone could now be baptized in the name of Jesus Messiah as a sign of their spiritual renewal (cf. Acts 2:38ff.).

This message is referred to as *good tidings* (εὐαγγέλιον). The word *gospel* was used over the alleged "good news" of the divine birth of the emperor Augustus, who claimed to be the saving patron of the whole world. This altered state of consciousness happened when the Spirit of God came upon not only an individual but upon many sons and daughters of Israel (see Acts 2:17–21). According to an earlier transmission of probably the same story, it might have been that their numbers were more than five hundred (see 1 Cor 15:6). Paul, the source of this early testimony, said he was informed that Jesus' brother James claimed to have seen him after his crucifixion (also witnessed to in the *Gospel of the Hebrews*, fragment 7, preserved by Hieronymus, *De Viris Illustribus* 2). This reportedly happened

---

6. Schlüssler Fiorenza, *Jesus—Miriam's Child,* 122.

before the appearance to "the Twelve" as a group. The authority of James' upcoming leadership of the Jesus movement in Jerusalem probably depended on his being a primary witness (see 1 Cor 15:7). The historian Josephus (*Ant.* 20.197–203) mentioned that James became an important official in the priestly circles of Jerusalem after the Romans had killed his brother. The experience of seeing his crucified brother resurrected apparently ignited in James the desire to become a follower of Jesus. However, while Jesus was among them, James, his mother, and other kin from Nazareth did not believe in Jesus' cause. Nevertheless, he became one of the pillars of faith in Jerusalem. Having never been a follower of Jesus during his lifetime, it comes as no surprise that James did not believe that the gospel should go further, from Jerusalem through Samaria into the rest of the Roman Empire, even to the world of the barbarians who could not speak Greek. The legitimacy of his apostleship can therefore be questioned.

Another man, Paul, who apparently did not even know Jesus personally, was truly an apostle because he advocated this cause. This he did in the midst of afflictions that made him feel like a woman being crucified (according to a "reading between the lines" of 2 Cor 4:12). Likewise he considered his right to be an apostle to be based on the authority of a revelation of the resurrected Jesus (Gal 1:12). Here it seems that both parties used the resurrection belief in a way that indicates that they did not internalize Jesus' disdain for selfish superiority (cf. Mark 10:42–44). Yet Paul dissociated himself from the Jerusalem faction with his critique of the idea that obedience to cultural conventions makes right the relationship with God (see Phil 3:7–11). He also disagreed with the notion of an apostle bringing the light of the gospel to the nations outside of Jerusalem.

A MOVEMENT OF AND FOR OTHERS

Apart from those pre-Easter followers of Jesus centered in Jerusalem after his crucifixion, the cause of Jesus soon also became a movement for others— Israelites in the Diaspora and devout Hellenists who associated themselves with the religion of the children of Abraham. Pioneers like Paul played a major role in this Jesus movement. We have seen that the origins of the Jesus movement in Jerusalem apparently lie in the claims of Peter and James, and probably also the sons of Zebedee, John and James, that they saw the resurrected Jesus. We have seen that Mary Magdalene also had such a vision and that it was not brought up in the tradition of the Jerusalem faction. Paul and Mark, and Christian writers dependent on them, knew of this tradition about "the Twelve" and conveyed it further—albeit not very enthusiastically. However, Paul seems unaware of the bias that caused the astonishment among the Jerusalemites about Mary's experience of the resurrected Jesus.

Paul developed a theological construct of participation in the risen Christ Jesus. This unity with the cause of Jesus was a faith experience that can be described as an altered state of consciousness because of its spiritual nature. Spirituality was expressed by Paul with the formulae "to be in Christ," "to be in the *Kyrios*," "to be in the Spirit," and "to call upon God as *Abba*." Living in the Spirit formed an alternative to a life according to everyday cultural arrangements. In this regard, Paul differed from the Jerusalem group in his opinion that the continuing experience of the meaning of Jesus' life through the resurrection belief meant that the "old" Israel died as well. The Jesus movement in Jerusalem believed that Jesus "restored" Israel as an ethnic entity. For Paul, "the Israel of God" was totally transformed into a spiritual entity. He grounded his conviction in his understanding of Jesus' death and resurrection. The church as an altered Israel meant that it was seen as a movement of people who believed in *Christ* and in the *Kyrios*, the Jesus of faith for both Israelites and non-Israelites.[7]

The historical Jesus did not foresee that an entity like the church would be built upon such an interpretation of his death. However, Paul's altered vision of egalitarianism and cultural subversiveness was in continuity with Jesus' altered relationship with God as the Father of "nobodies." According to the core of the Pauline and Gospel traditions in the New Testament, Jesus' interpretation of the kingdom of God, his wisdom, and his redefinition of the concept "children of Abraham" constituted the essence of human self-understanding. For Paul, the essence of religion is doing what fits in with God (Rom 12:1–2). If rejection and death were seen as failure, folly or offense, then Jesus' vision would have failed. But this paradoxical and repugnant perception was what the life of Jesus pertained to be. The Pauline tradition conveyed this vision. It is a counter-cultural perspective without escaping reality. It comprises the vision that strength is possible in weakness, wisdom in folly, honor in shame, and life in death. Because God turns shame into honor, the resurrection faith is, according to Paul, the sign of a new birth, a new start, a new creation (2 Cor 5:17; Gal 6:15), the birth of the "true Israel," the "Israel of God" (Gal 6:16). According to Jesus' gospel, an altered vision, not arrogant egotism, constitutes the self-understanding of human beings.

To deny the foundation of the church in the Jesus cause (which is folly to the world but wisdom in the eyes of faith) is to deny the historic cradle of the church and to allow the essence of the church to evaporate into an ecclesiological ideology. This is in line with Paul's thinking. The core of the Pauline gospel with regard to the crucified Jesus (1 Cor 1:17–31) should be understood as "condensed history" of the historical Jesus. C. H. Dodd puts it as follows:

---

7. Cf. Bousset, *Kyrios Christos*, 76–77.

Thus Paul's preaching represents a special stream of Christian tradition that was derived from the mainstream at a point very near to its source. No doubt his own idiosyncrasy counted for much in his presentation of the Gospel, but anyone who should maintain that the primitive Christian Gospel was fundamentally different from that which we have found in Paul must bear the burden of the proof.[8]

The source behind Paul's kerygma is found in the Jerusalem faction's emphasis on Jesus' death. The kind of life Jesus lived led to his death. It is in this sense that his crucifixion should be seen as condensed history.

FROM JESUS TO THE CHURCH

We have seen that the Jesus of history did not see his death as a kerygma, as a gospel, as "good tidings." Seen as "condensed history," however, the earliest Jesus movement in Jerusalem understood the crucifixion as intended by Jesus himself. They found proof for this in the Hebrew Scriptures. Yet there were also other early factions among the followers of Jesus. An example is the audiences to whom the Sayings Gospel Q and the *Gospel of Thomas* were directed. Seemingly, they did not need the apocalyptic kerygma (i.e., an Israelite-Hellenistic notion) of Jesus dying and rising. This kerygma originated in the Jerusalem movement and was transmitted to Paul and Mark, and from them on to other New Testament writings.

The inclusive and egalitarian perspectives presented in the sayings and deeds of the historical Jesus are the ones that were mainly expressed fully within the faction that became known as the *church* (ἐκκλησία). This expression should be understood as a technical reference to the faction distinguished from the *synagogue* (συναγωγή). For this reason, the forming of the church cannot be viewed as being totally discontinuous with Jesus. The discontinuity pertains to the Paschal kerygma. The continuity pertains to the church's inclusiveness and egalitarianism.

The transition from the Jesus movement to the church represents phases of a sociological process. Historically, diversity can be indicated early. Some groups (for instance, the nonkerygmatic followers of Jesus in Northern Palestine and Trans-Jordan who, in certain later sources, were referred to as the sect of the Nazarenes and who were closely related to the Ebionites) linked themselves closely to the historical Jesus, but, in fact, theirs was an exclusive and very particularly focused nationalist ideology discontinuous with the Jesus of history. It does not really matter whether these followers

---

8. Dodd, "Primitive Preaching," 16.

of Jesus are to be mentioned in the same breath as, or alongside, the Jerusalem group.

However, they must be distinguished from that Jesus movement in Antioch designated by outsiders (Romans? Judeans in Jerusalem?) as "Christians" (χριστιανοί—see Acts 11:26; 26:28; 1 Pet 4:16). Luke's acquaintance with the Antioch tradition probably came by way of the Pauline tradition. In this regard, one can say that between Paul and the Jesus movement in Jerusalem stood the Hellenistic churches in Antioch, Damascus, and Tarsus.[9] Paul was converted to this community of believers in Damascus and Antioch—a Jesus movement with a universal and egalitarian aim. It was a conversion described by Paul himself as the experience that the Crucified One still lived, that God had made known his "Son" (Jesus) to Paul (Gal 2:12, 16), and that Paul was crucified with the Crucified One, so that he was now living with the Crucified One (Gal 2:20; Phil 3:10–11). The origins of the movement that is called Christianity are grounded in the kerygma of this "new life."

The pre-Easter Jesus movement and the establishment of the post-Easter church cannot therefore be absolutely separated from each other.[10] This continuity is, as far as the process of group forming is concerned, like links in a chain. The first link represents the phase during which an isolated group within the boundaries of a parent body comes into being.[11] The parent body in this case was "Israel" (consisting of diverse groups such as the Sadducees, Pharisees, Essenes, and Samaritans), which defined itself genealogically by means of the metaphor "family"[12] and, indeed, in the physical sense as the "children of Abraham." The start of the first phase may be situated historically in the time when Jesus was still identifying closely with John the Baptist and started attracting followers.

FROM FACTION TO SECT TO CHURCH

Christianity came into being as a set of factions within Israel. Differences and tensions about particular matters (especially as far as the resurrection faith, the nonphysical understanding of the concept "children of Abraham," and the belief in the miraculous conception of Jesus were concerned) lead to the development of Christianity into a sect that eventually became the church, independent from and opposed to the synagogue.

The nonphysical understanding of the concept "children of Abraham" is particularly well expressed in Rom 9:8.[13] Here the "children of God" form a

---

9. See Bousset, *Kyrios Christos*, 75. Cf. Schmithals, *Theologiegeschichte des Urchristentums*, 88, 90.
10. Cf. Schille, "Jesusbewegung und die Entstehung," 104.
11. Cf. White, "Shifting Sectarian Boundaries," 7–9; Stanton, *Gospel for a New People*, 89–91.
12. See Neusner, "Israel."
13. See Schmithals, *Theologiegeschichte des Urchristentums*, 156.

fictive family. As we have already seen, this concept can be traced back to Jesus. Jesus, whose relationship to his own family was tense, cherished the notion of an imaginary familial structure. In this fictive family, God fulfills the role of Father. The mutual relations between the members of the family as brothers and sisters are not necessarily determined by biological, and therefore ethnic, kinship.

This understanding of God formed the basis of the social constitution of Christianity. It is the basis of the fundamental difference between Israel and the church. Israel also used the metaphor of family to indicate the bonds that invisibly linked Israelites to one another. Herein lay the justification for the excommunication of groups such as the Samaritans and the Christians. According to the Pauline and Johannine traditions, Christians formed the "spiritual" Israel, while those belonging to the Judean temple formed the cult of "Israel in the flesh." Genealogy indicated the bonding of the latter.[14]

In this regard, the genealogical register of Jesus and the nativity and childhood narratives in the Gospel of Matthew reflect in a remarkable way the break between the church and the synagogue. Jesus' "sonship of Abraham" does not exist on the basis of physical kinship. The infancy narrative in the Gospel of Matthew emphasizes God's recognition of Jesus as a legimate child of God. The metaphor of the church as the household of God has its origins in these Jesus events. It also explains the fundamental distinction between the synagogue and the church.

Favorable conditions for change were the manipulation of the Roman Empire (and the Herodians as its client kings) and the exploitative and exclusive temple ideology of the Judeans centered in Jerusalem. During the time of the historical Jesus, the Jerusalem cult was an outrage and led to the formation of the different factions among the Jesus movement. The historical Jesus offered an alternative order for life and redefined the concept of power as compassion. He did this by his ironical use of "kingdom" as the apogee of power in the sense of imperial rule. Through his (often metaphoric) words and deeds, he himself became the living symbol of a vision that focused on both his conception of God and on society in terms of a father-child relationship. Jesus unleashed a fervor that this vision might offer special opportunities to authentic life for outcasts, in spite of their being considered alienated from God.

Historically, this conversion to a new life was a phenomenon in both pre-Easter and post-Easter Jesus movements. In the Jerusalem and Pauline movements, one finds such an alternative consciousness expressed in the resurrection faith. During the period before 70 C.E., the relative accommodating spirit prevalent within a variety of Judaisms—Sadducees, Pharisees, and

---

14. See Neusner, "Israel."

Essenes (the severe antagonism toward the "impure" Joseph tribe, the Samaritans, was an exception to the rule)—made possible the forming of Jesus factions. The increasing intolerance after 70 C.E. resulting from the Pharisaic reformation at the Jamnia academy and at centers of scribal activity in Galilee and Syria caused the Jesus factions to develop into sects and ultimately into "churches" independent of and opposed to Judaism.[15] The following phases may, sociologically speaking, be distinguished in the formation of groups: forming, storming, norming, performing, and adjourning.[16]

In the period of *forming*, Jesus shared his alternative vision with similarly disillusioned people who suffered as a result of oppressive circumstances and alienation from God. This is the phase of the pre-Easter Jesus movement. The period of *storming* pertains to the actions of the Herodian dynasty, village leaders in Galilee, and Judean "royalties" against the cause of Jesus. Against the background of the brutality of Roman imperial might, Jesus' life culminated in the traumatic events of the crucifixion. The confusion of his bewildered disciples led to a highly diverse post-Easter Jesus movement. The recovery of a section, led first by Peter and then by James the brother of Jesus, within the Jerusalem movement was accomplished through their resurrection faith.[17] The diversity was probably a result of the following set of factors:

1. The search for an identity in view of the development away from, first, the Judean ideology in Jerusalem and, later, the Pharisaic movement at Jamnia and in Galilee/Syria.
2. The issue of whether the vision of Jesus has to be seen as the "narrow gate," in contradistinction to the temple cult and the Pharisaic movement as the "wide gate."[18]
3. The issue of how to interpret Jesus' death. Foremost, one finds among the "pillars of faith" in Jerusalem the apocalyptic inference that Jesus' martyr-like vicarious death should be seen as a "ransom for many." This tradition was also taken over by Paul and Mark and authors dependent on them. It is an assessment that could be influenced by questions about how the offense caused by the scandal of the crucifixion could be overcome (Jesus' brother James), how one could make peace with intense sorrow because of denial (Peter) or because of persecution of those who proclaimed Jesus' cause (Paul), and how one could deal with intense personal reminiscences (Mary Magdalene).

---

15. See Neusner, *From Politics to Piety*.

16. See Tuckman, "Developmental Sequence in Small Groups"; cf. Malina, "Early Christian Groups."

17. Cf. Lüdemann, *Resurrection of Jesus*, 176.

18. With regard to the Sayings Gospel Q as evidence, see Horsley, *Sociology and the Jesus Movement*; Kloppenborg, "Sayings Gospel Q," 20–21.

4. The issue of the crossing of the boundaries between Israel and the Gentiles (including the Samaritans). Was this a logical consequence of Jesus' compassionate vision toward degraded people and of his pushing against the conventions of the Judean purity regulations through which the particularistic temple ideology, the calendar, and the idea of the ethnically circumcised children of Abraham were maintained?

5. The issue of whether faith in Jesus required obedience to the Torah (e.g., the Jerusalem faction and Matthew) or not (e.g., Paul).

During the *norming* phase, a degree of cohesion developed as a result of certain compromises. This was the period of the institutionalizing of the church and could also be referred to as "the institutionalization of authority." During this time, the antihierarchical and symbolic nature of Jesus' message resulted in fictive household structures. The inclusive vision of Jesus and followers like Paul was organized into structures that were not characterized by ethnic limitation, even though the biological and hierarchical family remained the metaphor for this spiritual and egalitarian movement.

The period of *performing* pertains to the transition from the initial missionary work across boundaries (the epistles of Paul and the Pauline traditions in Luke-Acts) to missionary work toward the marginalized, such as widows (also among the Hellenists), Samaritans, orphans, street children, and those possessed by demons (see, e.g., evidence in Luke-Acts and the Gospel of Matthew, the writings of Clement of Alexandria, *Diognetus,* and 1 Timothy).

The *adjourning* phase has to do with the potential destruction of the church. This was a strong possibility already in the initial phase of the pre-Easter Jesus movement. Yet, although this social-scientific theory of group formation mainly concerns the forming and dissolution of small groups, the aspect relating to the adjourning of groups may also be applied to the post-Easter church as an institution. Adjourning was, during the post-Easter period, a possibility that should not be ignored. Five facets of it may be:

First, early on, the pre-Easter Jesus movement was confronted with the scandals of Jesus' birth from a humble woman (Gal 4:4) and his crucifixion as if he were a criminal. In the post-Easter phase, the Jesus movement made a thoroughfare of what seemed to be a cul-de-sac. The words and acts of Jesus live on in the honorific names his followers granted him. The offense of the cross was overcome by means of the resurrection faith.

Second, the ascetic (later Gnostic) Christians were first confronted with the separation between the synagogue and the church, and later with the ecclesiastical councils. The former refers to the abandonment by Christians of the synagogue and the latter to the formation of the New Testament canon and the ontological-metaphysical dogma of the "two natures" of Jesus as human and divine. Gnostics did not like the First Testament. They did not like the Creator God of Israel at all. On the other hand, the synagogue did not distinguish between the Jesus factions. Some Christian communities, to a greater or lesser extent, conformed to many aspects of synogogical ideas and developed an increasing hostility against the Gnostics in their midst. Because of the anti-Arian movement[19] and the ecclesiastical councils in the fourth century, Gnostic Christianity in the end did not survive. The discovery in 1947 of the Nag Hammadi library may cause their writings to breathe new life into similar contemporary thinking.

Third, the nonkerygmatic Jesus followers did not proclaim Jesus in an apocalyptic sense in terms of the formula "buried, resurrected, and ascended." They regarded him as an ethical exemplar. This group expanded not only into an ascetic movement but also formed the group in Trans-Jordan known as the Ebionite Nazarenes. These people were ethnically oriented. As Judean Christians, they particularistically limited the meaning of the Jesus event to (Judean) Israelites. However, they were outnumbered by Christians who believed in the resurrected Jesus, by early catholicism, and by later supporters of ecumenism. In a particular sense of the word they have survived in those Christian groups where the church is seen as a "cultural" entity. Today these people would regard themselves as Christians, seemingly unaware of the universal connotation of the word *Christian* when this label was used initially to refer to the faction in Antioch (see Acts 11:26).

Fourth, at the beginning, the Constantinian Catholic church was confronted by the supporters of Arius. Later, Roman Catholicism was challenged by the influence of the Renaissance, humanism, Socinianism,[20] and the Reformation. The church of the Reformation, too, has always had to struggle against the hierarchical system hidden in its bosom.

Fifth, modern Christianity is being confronted with institutionalization and secularization. But this "offense," too, can be overcome if we can share the consciousness that the cause of Jesus has the dynamics to provide meaning to disillusioned people living in depressing circumstances in a plural and multicultural, postmodern world. But there are certain conditions: the inhibitory effect of institutionalization that dooms the church must be opposed and secularization must be seen as an opportunity for the church to be "church for the world." Seen in this way, we can still say today, in the words of Willi Marxsen, "The cause of Jesus is still on its way"![21]

---

19. Arian Christology denied that Christ was of the same "substance" as God, and thereby denied that Jesus was simultaneously "true" divine and "true" human.

20. Socinianism was a school of theological thought in the sixteenth and seventeenth centuries that denied Anselm's view of Christ's death as satisfaction. "While accepting the finality of God's revelation in Christ, it nevertheless argued as follows: If God forgives sin, satisfaction is unnecessary; if there was satisfaction, then forgiveness is an illusion. In this context Christ was seen as a supreme example to all Christians and as an ordinary man chosen by God to be head of the church" (Deist, *Concise Dictionary of Theological Terms*, 159).

21. Marxsen, "Jesus—Bringer oder Inhalt?"

CHAPTER 9

The Continued Importance of Jesus

This book is partly about the historical Jesus and partly about the early Jesus movements. Both parts are studied against the background of the intermingled contexts of the Judean, Herodian Galilean, Hellenistic-Semitic, and Greco-Roman worlds. We have seen how, in Ovid's story of the virginal conception of Perseus and in Matthew's and Luke's nativity stories, Zeus and God appear whenever what was legitimate is called into question. The implication is that the divine and the human cannot be separated wherever legitimacy is concerned. For Ovid, the legitimacy of Perseus lay in Perseus's heroic deeds that resulted in his kingly enthronement. For the early Jesus movements, the legitimacy of the fatherless and crucified Jesus lay in Jesus' claim to be God's child.

DECONSTRUCTING DOGMA

In this chapter, the focus is on the dogma of the two natures of Jesus. I will deconstruct this dogma in order to affirm the significance of the metaphor of being child of God. This is done by showing that the dogma of the two natures of Jesus as both human and divine developed out of the dialectic of the historical, fatherless Jesus who called God Father, and believers who confessed him as child of God.

My quest for Jesus does not begin at the point where Jesus meets John the Baptist. The starting point, in other words, is not when the voice from heaven declares that Jesus is the child of God. This declaration is, of course, Mark's confession. To confess means to verbalize a basic religious experience. Mark's experience is grounded in Jesus' *Abba* experience. Mark begins and ends the life of Jesus with *Abba*. In the Gethsemane episode, the words Mark chooses for Jesus to pray are the typical words spoken at meals where the eldest son asked his father if the cup could be handed to someone more worthy than himself at the table. The story of the sleeping disciples in Gethsemane is Mark's answer to this question. Jesus, and none other, was the child of God in whom God delighted. This *Abba* experience originated before Mark. It began with Jesus himself.

Jesus called God "Father." To call someone "father" presupposes conception by means of the father. Mark, like the Jesus movement in Jerusalem, however, does not contain any reference to the birth of Jesus. My book, therefore, starts before the beginning of Mark and the Jerusalem faction. Matthew and Luke also go further back than Mark. They took up the Jerusalem faction's conviction that God adopted Jesus as Israel's messiah and Mark's conviction that Jesus was adopted at his baptism as God's child. For Matthew and Luke, God adopted Jesus at his birth as God's child and declared his status again at his baptism, as though people met Jesus there for the first time.

The tradition of Jesus' dual nature is spoken in the language of confession. By means of myths and metaphors, the creeds express the experience of a special intimacy between God and humankind. Here too the articulation of this experience connects to a more foundational experience in the life of Jesus himself.

Paul, and in a certain sense, Matthew and John, extends this experience to include other believers who participated in the similar experience of being "children of God." Paul especially makes use of the metaphor of adoption. His metaphor originated in a Greco-Roman world where blood relationships between a father and his children were not of the utmost importance. Children from outside the family could be adopted as children. "Children of Abraham" should therefore be understood spiritually rather than physically. Gentiles could also become part of God's household.

Much later, John articulated this matter in a similar way when he distinguished between a natural birth and a spiritual birth. According to him (as with Paul), Jesus was born in a natural way, but, as child of God, in a spiritual way too. A further similarity between Paul and John is that both describe Jesus' sonship not as beginning at his birth but as a matter of pre-existence. John opposed the Gnostic idea that God does not engage transient humanity. God's only begotten son became human in all respects, including his birth.

John's (and Paul's) idea cannot be reconciled with the miraculous birth stories found in Matthew and Luke. They are radically opposing ideas. In his controversy with the Gnostics, Ignatius harmonized Paul and John on the one hand, and Matthew and Luke on the other hand. For the first time in the history of biblical interpretation, the virginal conception of God's eternal son was emphasized. The rest of the New Testament, besides Luke, does not attest to this idea. Ignatius was responsible for the combination of mutually exclusive myths. The point he wanted to stress is that Jesus was truly human. Seemingly, every time the early church mentioned Jesus' virginal conception in a confessional way, it was strongly communicating the message that Jesus was undoubtedly human.

My encounter with Jesus through engaging the historical and literary evidence has brought me to articulate his foundational experience of God in terms of inclusiveness and egalitarianism. In the time of Jesus, the Judeans had a very specific foundational experience in God. Outside the boundaries of the Promised Land, no meaningful existence was possible. God was only present to "full-blooded" Israelites in an exclusive way. God could only be encountered at a particular place of cultic worship, namely Jerusalem. God's saving acts were performed in the temple. The exile and the siege of Jerusalem when the temple was destroyed caused a crisis in the Judeans' religious experience. This resulted in the apocalyptic expectation of a heavenly utopia.

The fatherless Jesus grew up in Galilee of the Gentiles. His God-talk consisted of imagery that expressed an alternative experience in God. His stories about the kingdom of God and his healing acts became metaphors by which God's limitless, unmediated presence was expressed. Jesus made use of a symbol, that, in his culture, signaled a most intimate bond—that of the father-son relationship. A father without a son had no honor or credibility. A son without a father had no honor or identity. However, even in his use of this symbol Jesus subverted the cultural arrangements of his time. According to these hierarchical arrangements in the culture, the patriarch represented his family before God. No one in the family could experience God's presence without being embedded in the realm of the father.

Jesus, however, did not use the metaphor of father as the way to God, but that of child. Those not childlike could not experience the presence of God. Even more radical than this is that Jesus did not use the child who had been legitimized by the father as symbol. He pointed to an illegitimate child as a symbol of those who belonged to the realm of God.

Jesus expressed his own fundamental religious experience through this symbol. As a fatherless figure, Jesus saw himself as the protector of fatherless children in Galilee, as well as of women who did not "belong" to a man. These women and children were regarded as outcasts since they did not fit into the patriarchal system. In many ways, Jesus acted like a woman. For example, it was said that he took the last place at the table, served others, forgave wrongs, showed compassion, and healed wounds. But it was also said that he protected patriarchless women and fatherless children, not as a patriarch or father himself, not from above, but from a position of being one of them. Jesus not only called God "Father," but also lived among the outcasts as if they were all children of God. In other words, Jesus lived as their fictive brother.

As the cause of Jesus expanded, the metaphor "child of God" became part of the Christian vocabulary. The people who experienced God's presence in their lives because of their embeddedness in the cause of Jesus now became "children of God" and therefore brothers and sisters of Jesus, the "firstborn." Paul's Jesus was a Hercules figure who was publicly and mightily declared to be God's child on account of his victory over death at his resurrection. This idea influenced Luke. Luke, however, already attested to Jesus' sonship at the conception, which Luke regarded as divine. Hercules was also the product of a divine conception. Even stronger parallels are found in the myth of the birth of the healer-god Asclepios and in Ovid's story of Perseus, where divine conception canceled illegitimacy. In Luke's view, the Divine Spirit conceived Jesus and he was adopted as the child of Joseph. According to Luke, Joseph's genealogy can be traced to Adam, child of God. Other parallels can be found in Diodorus's story of Hercules' empty pyre and Seneca's story of Hercules' ascension. For Luke, Diodorus, and Seneca, the act of adoption as son is "proven" by the empty tomb/pyre and the resurrection and ascension. The Greco-Roman ideas of the emperor cult and divine-human legends are mirrored in Luke.

Luke also provides insight into the tension between the synagogue and the church. Because of the schism between the synagogue and the church, the rumors of Jesus' illegitimacy began playing a more decisive role. The legend that Joseph adopted Jesus as his child seems to have originated within this context. The First Testament Joseph was regarded as the forefather of the Samaritans. Luke emphasizes the tradition that Jesus traveled through Samaria. Jesus is even identified as a Samaritan in the parable of the Good Samaritan, in which the Samaritan plays the role of Jesus. Against the background of a schism between synagogue and church, John, in his apology, notes the label of Samaritan given to Jesus.

John refers to two origins of all of God's children. This includes Jesus and his followers. They had a physical and a spiritual birth. In the same vein, this Gospel speaks of physical bread and spiritual bread, physical water and spiritual water. This means that although people are born in a natural way, they are also spiritual people born in a spiritual way. This pertains to Jesus as well and very specifically to Jesus as the beloved child ("firstborn") of God. With this rhetoric, John wants to persuade people not to place their ultimate trust in the tradition that Jesus was the physical son of Joseph, but rather in the faith that he was God's spiritual child. The consequence of such a faith is that whoever sees Jesus sees the Father. The thrust of this rhetoric is that the humanness of Jesus should not become an obstacle to experiencing God's presence when the Jesus kerygma is proclaimed.

In Paul, Mark, Matthew, Luke, and John the metaphor "child of God" is used in a functional way. Their focus is on the events: what Jesus did and what believers did and do. In the New Testament, the proclaimer became the proclaimed. After the New Testament, the event of Jesus' sonship of God became dogma. Functional metaphors became philosophical metaphors. Functional Christology became ontological Christology. The concrete became abstract.

In the New Testament, the dual nature concept functioned to stress the human and spiritual origins of believers. After the New Testament, this metaphor became an expression of the way in which Jesus was in relationship to the heavenly Father (a static, abstract, ontological category).

The dual nature concept originated in metaphorical language usage. This language usage expressed the foundational experience that nothing physical or cultural could hinder a spiritual, unmediated presence of God. A child of humanity is born anew to be a child of God. This dual nature metaphor became a confessional formula and later the unquestionable, fixed dogma of Jesus' two natures. Against the convictions of the Arians (fourth century) and the Socinians and Anabaptists (sixteenth century), this dogma emphasized Jesus' humanness.

Fundamentalism has since reversed the emphasis, and the divine nature has become almost the only concern. Ironically, those who have participated in the Jesus cause by loving the cosmos unselfishly have become the opponents of the fundamentalists. Engaging in the cause of Jesus means taking the encounter between divinity and humanity seriously. However, in the hands of the fundamentalists, the dogma of Jesus' two natures has become a stick with which to strike and a rod with which to destroy. According to the fundamentalist view, the dogma generates justifying and saving faith. Those whose views differ from theirs are regarded as opponents of the dogma. They are therefore considered to be godless and must be excommunicated. In the process of marginalizing and eliminating opponents, the "retainers" of the dogma often lose sight of Jesus' humanness and humaneness, and of the history of the origins of the dogma.

Constructing an image of Jesus and then considering it to be the exclusive legitimate basis for God-talk operates exactly according to the principles of foundationalism and of orthodoxy. It is also in discord with the cause of Jesus. Favoritism was not part of Jesus' vision. Foundationalism favors a false fixed basement and the certainties built upon such a foundation. Thus, deconstructing dogma does not aim to recover the historical Jesus as the "foundation" of our faith assertions. Quests that have tried to do this are like waves that come and go. However, my program of deconstructing dogma is not a choice for relativism.

Engaged hermeneutics does not presuppose absolute freedom from ecclesiastical confessions. On the contrary, it takes faith seriously and respects confessional formulae in terms of their intentions. It is a search for what is foundational to faith and seeks to find it distributed through the fabric of our quest for Jesus, knowing of the dialectic between the pre-Easter Jesus *telling* of God as Father and the post-Easter church *showing* Jesus as God's child. Engaged hermeneutics presupposes a lifelong journey. Every quest will be determined by the circumstances of the time and culture in which the traveler exists. To engage is to distance oneself from one's culture to such an extent that one can see the pain that cultural measures cause. Engaging in the cause of Jesus necessitates culture critique. It asks for a critical reading of and conscious reflection on the scriptures and dogmas. It is a journey that never ceases.

It is clear that in a strategy of engaged hermeneutics, intolerant foundationalism will be unacceptable. The metaphors by which faith assertions are expressed are bound by culture and time and can lose their relevance. However, a choice for antifoundationalism is not a choice for relativism. Relativism occurs when creeds have no guiding function anymore. However, engaged hermeneutics, though antifoundationalistic in nature, does not intend that anything goes. The rhetorics of a dogma remain important. To uncover the rhetorics of the dogma, one must deconstruct it.

Deconstruction involves moving back to the building blocks. This strategy distinguishes the four phases in the development of dogma. The foundational religious experience is expressed by metaphors that in turn are transformed into confessional formulae that can lead to fixed dogmas. Power interests come into play when dogmas are formed. Those who are powerful use dogmas to manipulate or excommunicate opponents. Deconstructing dogma does not mean getting rid of the confessional formulae as such. Deconstruction in this regard has a positive and a negative motivation. On the negative side, power interests are to be exposed; on the positive side, the relevance of confessional formulae is to be ascertained. The positive strategy asks two questions: firstly, whether the metaphors used are still functional, and secondly, whether the confessional formulae are adequate vehicles for the expression of the foundational religious experience.

It is an illusion to think that worldly interests do not play a role in the formation of dogmas. The nature of these interests varies in different times and cultures. Sometimes economic and political interests will prevail, while at other times familial and political interests triumph. In the course of the development of the dogma of Jesus' two natures, familial and political interests dominated in the beginning. During the last phase, the familial was no longer a factor.

The last phase occurred in the sixteenth to the seventeenth centuries. A papal edict expanded this dogma to include the immaculate conception and the perpetual virginity of Mary. The Socinians, who did not accept the full humanity of Jesus, were thereby declared heretics. In the Netherlands, the Calvinists conformed to this edict, with the exception of the Mariology. They had a political motive for doing so. By means of the Belgic Confession, they implored the Roman Catholic Spanish king of the Netherlands to stop the persecutions of the Calvinists.

The intention of both the Belgic Confession and the papal edict was to emphasize the humanity of Jesus. With this confession, the Calvinists refuted the Anabaptists, who undervalued the humanness of Jesus. Ironically enough, the wording used to emphasize Jesus' humanness in relation to his divine origin later (since the seventeenth century) became the instrument of orthodoxy to emphasize Jesus' divinity and to downplay his humanness. The phrase "Joseph had no sexual intercourse with Mary" (used by Pope Paul IV and the Belgic Confession) was the trigger for orthodoxy to underplay the humanness of Jesus and to place the main emphasis on his divinity. The proof text that the Calvinists used to substantiate this came from the Johannine metaphoric expression of the dual nature of a child of God who was born physically and spiritually (John 1:13). The proof the papal edict used was taken from apocryphal evidence (*Proto-James, Joseph the Carpenter,* and *Pseudo-Matthew*). Both the Roman Catholics and the Calvinists were seemingly unaware of the different types of Christology that formed the context within which these metaphors were used in the first century. They simply expanded the evidence found in the Nicene Creed (from the fourth century).

The faith assertions about Jesus' dual nature expressed in the New Testament made use of metaphors from mythology and the emperor cult. Jesus, child of the heavenly emperor, described in his metaphoric stories God's kingdom in categories other than worldly hierarchies. These metaphors were utilized to express the faith, based on the words of Jesus, that Christians were children of God even though they did not physically belong to the family of Abraham. Thereby, they emphasized the unmediated access to God. The foundational experience in the life of Jesus underlying this faith is that he, as fatherless person, experienced God as his Father.

The issue is whether the rhetoric in the last phase of dogma formation is congruent with this foundational experience. It is clear that fundamentalists' understanding of the dogma of the two natures is incongruent with this foundational experience. They use the dogma to generate faith, whereas Jesus understood faith as living in the immediate presence of God. Fundamentalists use the dogma to bar people from God's presence. For Jesus, outcasts symbolized those who live in the presence of God.

Another concern is whether the metaphor "child of God" is still relevant for a postmodern era. The postmodern era has brought sensitivity for the disadvantaged, such as the street urchins who live in societies all over the world. We have seen that such children were the symbol Jesus used to express God's healing presence for disillusioned people. When the church formulates its faith assertions today, the power of this symbol should not be violated.

JESUS FOR TODAY

Is the investigation of the historical Jesus significant today? This question can be approached from a number of angles. The church, for instance, constitutes one such angle. As far as the church is concerned, the preaching and the dogmas of the church cannot claim to be free from testing. Depending on the current scientific paradigm, criteria for testing may take different forms. Here one should bear in mind that the discourse of the church should under all circumstances be bound to the gospel with regard to Jesus. The word gospel implies soteriology. Like many other technical terms used by theologians, *soteriology* points to something intrinsic and foundational to human experience. To meet God as savior is to experience serenity amidst adversity. For the Christian, God-talk is bound to the essence of Jesus' foundational religious experience. At least, God-talk for the Christian implies the quest for what this experience could have been. In its articulation of this experience, the early church referred to it soteriologically as *good tidings* (e.g., 1 Thess 1:5; Mark 1:1).

The church is supposed to be the bearer of the gospel. Therefore, it may be that people today want to test the validity of what the church says on the basis of the concrete effect of the gospel on the church and society. The church inherently faces the possibility of (mostly unknowingly) falsifying and obfuscating the gospel, and even of manipulating and exploiting others in the name of that gospel. By doing this, the church alienates itself from the One to whom it bears witness.

That possibility was already present in the earliest Jesus movement, as well as among those who handed down the Jesus tradition orally, those who put it to paper and adapted it editorially, and those who canonized the twenty-seven documents as the New Testament. Generally, we believe that this process of the handing down of tradition and the writing of the Bible took place under the guidance of the Holy Spirit. However, I do not picture or experience the work of the Holy Spirit in a mechanical way. The Holy Spirit did not detract from the humanity of the writers of the Bible, or of those who, before them, had handed down the gospel, or of those who, afterwards, interpreted it. What was included in the canon has not lost its worldly or human character.

Apart from the scientific merit of the historical Jesus investigation (because it helps us to clarify in a responsible fashion the process by which the New Testament was historically handed down) the church may with the assistance of this investigation reach greater clarity with regard to the self-understanding of Christendom. This benefit of Jesus research can be referred to as an inwardly directed desirability.

Yet there is also an outwardly directed desirability. The church also needs the investigation of the historical Jesus for the sake of interreligious debate. Christians are confronted with the question, Who is this Jesus you confess and proclaim and whom you invite us to accept as our redeemer? How is it that he, who was a particular Israelite from Galilee, is presented as universally significant? If we do not ask the questions about the historical Jesus, then the kerygma and the values of Christians could become an ideology, and be manipulated as people wish. When we remind ourselves of the images of Christ presented to people of different religious persuasions during crusades, colonization in the name of missionary work, and in gas chambers, then the historical Jesus question assists us in rediscovering the inclusive and antihierarchical meaning of the gospel.

Furthermore, Jesus of Nazareth ceased to be the sole property of the church a long time ago! Whether we like it or not, the importance of the Jesus question stretches further than Sunday services in church buildings, further than the normative documents of the official church, further than churches' programs of evangelism, further than the God-talk of Christians in the street. One need only think of library works and films, of art and music, that use Jesus as a theme.

Historical Jesus research matters. At least, it makes a significant contribution toward the historical understanding and theological application of the New Testament. The Jesus of history is either the implicit or explicit point of departure for inquiry into the sources behind, the social locations of, and the theological tendencies represented by the New Testament writings.

The fact is, in the New Testament a material relationship does exist between the proclaimer and the proclaimed. Theologians should not avoid the exegetical task of tracking this relationship to show the existence of a core continuum between the Jesus of history and the Jesus of faith. They must not, however, deny a discontinuity regarding various aspects or claim that faith, in order to be true faith, must be based on historical facts.

Historical Jesus research is fundamental to the credibility of Christianity in that Christianity is not a "book religion" but represents belief patterns witnessed in the New Testament and is modeled on the words and deeds of Jesus of Nazareth, experienced and confessed by Christians as child of God. The quest for the historical Jesus is also important with regard to interreligious dialogue. In this realm, Christianity is often, either unjustly or justly, accused of being exclusive since it was built upon the Jewishness of Jesus. But the fact is, Jesus of Nazareth, ethnically an Israelite, crossed boundaries all the way without being "un-Jewish." The kerygma about living through faith alone finds its main support historically in a gender-equitable, ethnically unbound, and culturally subversive Jesus.

Therefore, with regard to engaged hermeneutics, the quest for the historical Jesus illuminates what emancipatory living, in memory of the Jesus of history, entails existentially. As the living symbol of God's unmediated presence in terms of God's unbrokered household, the historical Jesus set people free and, as the risen Christ and Lord, still sets people (irrespective of sexual orientation, gender, age, ethnicity, or social and religious affiliation) free from distorted relationships with themselves, with others, and with God. Christian ethics is not an abstract ideology but is based on the humanness and the humaneness of the Jesus of history. Thus, the quest for the historical Jesus will play an important role in postmodern theological thinking. This opinion should be seen against the background of the conviction that postmodernity features a mondial and pluralistic perspective as a result of a broadened rationality that goes beyond foundationalism and relativism.

I still find myself within the realm of the church and therefore would like to uphold the relationship between the *historical* Jesus and the *kerygmatic* Christ. The Jesus kerygma (the faith assertions of the church modeled on the New Testament), however, seems to have increasingly lost its explanatory and heuristic power in the secular and postmodern religious age. The twenty-first century could be the time when the relevance of the church as institution and the Christian Bible as its canon become outdated for people on the street. If and when the process of secularization reaches its consummation, another Christian generation will be called to reconsider the continued importance of the historical Jesus and to reinterpret that figure as the manifestation of God.

The question about the relationship between the historical Jesus and the faith assertions that follow will have to be asked and answered over and over again. Never in history has this question been adequately and finally answered. The challenge is to find a meaningful answer to this question for the immediate present. We cannot do more. To acknowledge our limitations is no weakness. When times change, the answers will change. This does not mean that we were wrong before. To think that the journey ended in the fourth century or in the sixteenth century or in the twentieth century is a betrayal of the cause of Jesus. Or to think that the journey ended with the Old Quest or the New Quest or the Third Quest or even the Renewed Quest is to miss the reason for the search for Jesus. The direction to follow is to engage in the dialectic between Jesus and God in such a way that we today can still acknowledge him as child of God and also find ourselves as children of God living in the presence of God.

~

Conclusion

The birth of Jesus of Nazareth two millennia ago was celebrated in the year 2000. If Jesus was seen as merely a historical figure, the significance of his life would be no different from that of Socrates' or Alexander the Great's life. In Greco-Roman culture Alexander the Great, among other heroic figures and emperors, was regarded as child of God. However, since the first century C.E., followers of Jesus have worshiped Jesus as God's child. This study asks questions about the importance of Jesus within Hellenistic-Semitic and Greco-Roman contexts and his continued importance today. As in the case of Socrates, Jesus did not himself write down either the message of his words and deeds or the interpretation of his birth and death. Jesus' vision therefore needs to be deciphered from what others said about him.

Despite all their mythological elements, the starting point of the quest for the historical Jesus could be the nativity stories. Here the writers of Matthew and Luke introduce elements into Jesus's story that allow us to ask new questions about his identity. Because Joseph, the father of Jesus, should be seen as a legendary figure, the historical Jesus emerges as a fatherless figure in ancient Galilee. What would it be like for someone in first-century Herodian Palestine to bear the stigma of being fatherless, but who trusted God as Father? The myth of the absent father was very well known in antiquity. In addition, there are ancient stories that feature heroes who are divinely conceived, who are adopted by Zeus, and who ascend to heaven. Jesus' followers would have been familiar with these stories and would have understood the dishonor of his fatherlessness. Because of his own fatherlessness, Jesus focused his ministry on "fatherless" children and "patriarchless" women.

One of the most urgent social problems of our time is that millions of children are growing up fatherless. We can look to the historical Jesus as a model for addressing this contemporary issue, for the historical Jesus filled the emptiness caused by his fatherlessness with his trust in God as his father.

~

Bibliography

Adams, P. L., J. R. Milner, and N. A. Schrepf. *Fatherless Children*. Wiley Series in Child Mental Health. New York: John Wiley & Sons, 1984.

Aland, B., K. Aland, J. Karavidopolos, C. M. Martini, and B. Metzger, eds. *The Greek New Testament*. 4th rev. ed., in cooperation with the Institute for New Testament Textual Research, Münster, Westphalia. Stuttgart: Deutsche Bibelgesellschaft, 1994.

Aland, K. *Die Säuglingstaufe im Neuen Testament und in der alten Kirche: Eine Argument an Joachim Jeremias*. Munich: Kaiser Mainz, 1961.

Allison, D. C. *The New Moses: A Matthean Typology*. Minneapolis: Fortress Press, 1993.

Angel, R. J., and J. L. Angel. *Painful Inheritance: Health and the New Generation of Fatherless Children*. Madison, Wis.: University of Wisconsin Press, 1993.

Aptovitzer, V. "Aseneth, the Wife of Joseph." *Hebrew Union College Annual* 1 (1924) 239-306.

Argyle, A. W. "The Influence of the Testaments of the Twelve Patriarchs upon the New Testament." *Expository Times* 63 (1951–52) 256–58.

———. "Joseph the Patriarch in Patristic Teaching." *Expository Times* 67 (1956) 199–202.

Arndt, W. F. and F. W. Ginrich. *A Greek-English Lexicon of the New Testament and Other Early Christian Literature*. Chicago: University of Chicago Press, 1957.

Art and History of Pompeii: With the Reconstructions of the City. Florence: Centro Stampa Editoriale Bonechi (Casa Editrice), 1995.

Atkins, R. A. *Egalitarian Community: Ethnography and Exegesis*. Foreword by Mary Douglas. Tuscaloosa, Ala.: University of Alabama Press, 1991.

Baarda, T. "Concerning the Date of the Gospel of Thomas." Unpublished paper presented at the Annual Meeting of the Society of Biblical Literature, San Francisco, November 1997.

Bach, G. R. "Father-Fantasies and Father-Typing in Father-Separated Children." *Child Development* 17 (1946) 63–79.

Bakon, S. "Jacob, Man of Destiny: His Youth." *Dor le Dor. Our Biblical Heritage* 10, no.1 (1981) 10–19.

Ball, A. P. *The Satire of Seneca on the Apotheosis of Claudius.* New York: Columbia University Press, 1902.

Barr, J. "Abba Isn't 'Daddy.'" *Journal of Theological Studies* 39 (1988) 28–47.

Barrett, C. K. *The Epistle to the Romans.* London: SCM Press, 1967.

Barthes, R. *Mythologies.* Translated by A. Lavers. New York: Hill & Wang, 1957.

Beare, F. W. *The Gospel according to Matthew: A Commentary.* Oxford: Basil Blackwell, 1981.

Berger, P. L., and T. Luckmann. *The Social Construction of Reality: A Treatise in the Sociology of Knowledge.* Harmondsworth, England: Penguin Books, 1967.

Berguer, G. *Some Aspects of the Life of Jesus from the Psychological and Psycho-Analytical Point of View.* New York: Harcourt, Brace & Co, 1923.

Berkowitz, L., and K. A. Squitier. *Thesaurus Linguae Graecae: Canon of Greek Authors and Works.* 2d ed. New York: Oxford University Press, 1986.

Bertrand, F.-G., and G. Ponton. "Textes patristique sur saint Joseph." *Cahiers de Josephologie* 3 (1955) 141–74; 4 (1956) 325–57; 5 (1957) 125–67, 289–320; 6 (1958) 139–79, 265–321; 7 (1959) 151–72, 275–333; 8 (1960) 171–86, 347–74; 9 (1961) 333–57; 10 (1962) 149–82.

Best, E. *Mark: The Gospel as Story.* Studies of the New Testament and its World. Edinburgh: T. & T. Clark, 1985.

Betz, H. D. "Jesus as Divine Man." In *Jesus and the Historian*, edited by F. T. Trotter, 114–33. Philadelphia: Westminster Press, 1968.

Blankenhorn, D. *Fatherless America: Confronting Our Most Urgent Social Problem.* New York: Basic Books, 1995.

Borg, M. J. *Conflict, Holiness, and Politics in the Teaching of Jesus.* New York: Edwin Mellen Press, 1984.

———. "The First Christmas." *Bible Review,* December 1992, 4, 10.

———. "From Galilean Jew to the Face of God: The Pre-Easter and Post-Easter Jesus." In *Jesus at 2000*, edited by M. J. Borg, 7–20. Boulder, Colo.: Westview Press, 1997.

———. *Jesus: A New Vision—Spirit, Culture, and the Life of Discipleship.* San Francisco: HarperSanFrancisco, 1991.

———. *Jesus in Contemporary Scholarship.* Valley Forge, Pa.: Trinity Press International, 1994.

———. "The Meaning of the Birth Stories." In *The Meaning of Jesus: Two Visions*, by M. J. Borg and N. T. Wright, 179–88. San Francisco: HarperSanFrancisco, 1999.

————. *Meeting Jesus Again for the First Time.* San Francisco: HarperSanFrancisco, 1994.

————. "Portraits of Jesus in Contemporary North American Scholarship." *Harvard Theological Review* 84 (1991) 1–22.

————. "A Renaissance in Jesus Studies." *Theology Today* 45 (1988) 280–92.

————. "Seeing Jesus: Sources, Lenses, and Method." In *The Meaning of Jesus: Two Visions,* by M. J. Borg and N. T. Wright, 3–14. San Francisco: HaperSanFrancisco, 1999.

Borg, M. J. and R. Riegert, eds. *Jesus and Buddha: The Parallel Sayings.* Berkeley, Calif.: Ulysses Press, 1997.

Bornkamm, G. *Jesus of Nazareth.* Translated by I. and F. McLuskey with J. M. Robinson. San Francisco: Harper & Row, 1975.

Boshoff, P. B. "The Proclaimer Became the Proclaimed: Walter Schmithals's Point of View." *Journal of Higher Criticism* 4, no. 1 (1997) 89–119.

Bossman, D. "Ezra's Marriage Reform: Israel Redefined." *Biblical Theology Bulletin* 9 (1979) 32–38.

Boswell, J. E. "*Exposito* and *Oblatio*: The Abandonment of Children and the Ancient and Medieval Family." *American Historical Review* 89 (1984) 10–33.

Botha, P. J. J. "Herodes die Grote." *Hervormde Teologiese Studies* 51, no. 4 (1995) 996–1028.

Bourguignon, E. *Psychological Anthropology: An Introduction to Human Nature and Cultural Differences.* New York: Holt, Rinehart & Winston, 1979.

Bousset, W. *Kyrios Christos: Geschichte des Christusglaubens von den Anfängen des Christentums bis Irenaeus.* Göttingen: Vandenhoeck & Ruprecht, 1926.

Bowen, G. L., and D. K. Orthner. "Effects of Organizational Culture on Fatherhood." In *Fatherhood and Families in Cultural Context,* edited by F. W. Bozett and S. M. H. Hanson, 187–217. New York: Springer Publishing Co., 1991.

Bozett, F. W., and S. M. H. Hanson, eds. *Fatherhood and Families in Cultural Context.* New York: Springer Publishing Co., 1991.

Brandon, S. G. F. *Jesus and the Zealots: A Study of the Political Factor in Primitive Christianity.* Manchester: Manchester University Press, 1967.

Breech, J. *Jesus and Postmodernism.* Minneapolis: Fortress Press, 1989.

————. *The Silence of Jesus: The Authentic Voice of the Historical Man.* Philadelphia: Fortress Press, 1983.

Breytenbach, A. P. B. "Die Herfsfees en die Koningsrite by Bet-El as Interteks van Amos 7:10–8:14 en Hosea 9:1–9." *Hervormde Teologiese Studies* 53, no. 3 (1997) 513–28.

————. "Meesternarratiewe, Kontranarratiewe en Kanonisering: 'n Perspektief op Sommige Profetiese Geskrifte." *Hervormde Teologiese Studies* 53, no. 4 (1997) 1157–82.

————. "'Seun van Josef' uit 'n Noord-Israelitiese Perspektief." *Old Testament Essays* 11, no. 3 (1998) 415–26.

Breytenbach, C. "Jesusforschung: 1990–1995. Neuere Gesamtdarstellungen in deutscher Sprache." *Berliner Theologische Zeitschrift* 12, no. 2 (1995) 226–49.

Broshanan, T. *Turkey.* 3d ed. Hawthorn, Australia: Lonely Planet Publications, 1990.

Brown, R. E. *The Birth of the Messiah: A Commentary on the Infancy Narratives of Matthew and Luke.* First Image Edition. New York: Doubleday, 1979.

————. *The Death of the Messiah: From Gethsemane to the Grave.* 2 vols. The Anchor Bible Reference Library. New York: Doubleday, 1994.

————. *The Virginal Conception and Bodily Resurrection of Jesus.* New York: Paulist Press, 1973.

Brown, R. M. *Theology in a New Key: Responding to Liberation Themes.* Philadelphia: Westminster Press, 1978.

Bultmann, R. "Antwort an Ernst Käsemann." In *Glauben und Verstehen: Gesammelte Aufsätze,* by R. Bultmann, vol. 4, 190–98. Tübingen: J. C. B. Mohr (Paul Siebeck), 1965.

————. "Das christologische Bekenntnis des Ökumenischen Rates." In *Glauben und Verstehen: Gesammelte Aufsätze,* by R. Bultmann, vol. 2, 246–61. Tübingen: J. C. B. Mohr (Paul Siebeck), 1952.

————. "Die Erforschung der synoptischen Evangelien." In *Glauben und Verstehen: Gesammelte Aufsätze,* by R. Bultmann, vol. 4, 1–41. Tübingen: J. C. B. Mohr (Paul Siebeck), 1952.

————. *Das Evangelium des Johannes.* Göttingen: Vandenhoeck & Ruprecht, 1968.

————. *Die Geschichte der synoptischen Tradition.* 7th ed. Göttingen: Vandenhoeck & Ruprecht, 1967.

————. *The Gospel of John: A Commentary.* Edited by R. W. N. Hoare and J. K. Riches. Translated by G. R. Beasley-Murray. Philadelphia: Westminster Press, 1971.

————. *The History of the Synoptic Tradition.* Rev. ed. Translated by J. Marsh. Oxford: Basil Blackwell, 1972.

————. *Jesus.* New ed. Tübingen: J. C. B. Mohr (Paul Siebeck), 1988.

————. *The Second Letter to the Corinthians.* Translated by R. A. Harrisville. Minneapolis: Augsburg, 1985.

————. "The Significance of the Historical Jesus for the Theology of Paul." In *Faith and Understanding,* by R. Bultmann, vol. 1, 220–46.

Edited by R. W. Funk.Translated by L. P. Smith. London: SCM Press, 1969.

―――. *Theologie des Neuen Testaments*. 6th ed. Neue Theologische Grundrisse. Tübingen: J. C. B. Mohr (Paul Siebeck), 1968.

―――. *Theology of the New Testament*. Vol. 1. Translated by K. Grobel. London: SCM Press, 1974.

―――. *Das Verhältnis der urchristlichen Christusbotschaft zum historischen Jesus*. 4th ed. Heidelberg: Carl Winter/Universitätsverlag, 1965.

―――. *Der zweite Brief an die Korinther*. Edited by E. Dinkler. Göttingen: Vandenhoeck & Ruprecht, 1976.

Burchard, C. *Untersuchungen zu Joseph und Aseneth: Überlieferung-Ortbestimmung*. Tübingen: J. C. B. Mohr (Paul Siebeck), 1965.

Burn, L. *Greek Myths*. London: British Museum Press, 1996.

Burton, R. V., and J. W. M. Whiting. "The Absent Father and Cross-Sex Identity." *Merrill-Palmer Quarterly* 7 (1961) 85–95.

Bush, A. C. *Studies in Roman Social Structure*. Washington, D.C.: University Press of America, 1982.

Butterfield, H. *The Origins of Modern Science: 1300–1800*. London: Bell & Hyman, 1975.

Byrne, B. *"Sons of God"—"Seed of Abraham."* Analecta Biblica 83. Rome: Biblical Institute Press, 1979.

Cain, M. *Jesus the Man: An Introduction for People at Home in the Modern World*. Sonoma, Calif.: Polebridge Press, 1999.

Callagher, E. V. *Divine Man or Magician? Celsus and Origen on Jesus*. SBL Dissertation Series 64. Chico, Calif.: Scholars Press, 1982.

Calvert, D. G. A. "An Examination of the Criteria for Distinguishing the Authentic Words of Jesus." *New Testament Studies* 18 (1971) 209–18.

Capps, D. "The Desire to Be Another Man's Son: The Child Jesus as an Endangered Self." In *The Endangered Self* by R. K. Fenn and D. Capps. 21–35. Princeton, N.J.: Center for Religion, Self and Society, Princeton Theological Seminary, 1992.

Casey, M. *From Jewish Prophet to Gentile God: The Origins and Development of New Testament Christology*. Cambridge: James Clarke & Co., 1991.

Chesnutt, R. D. "From Text to Context: The Social Matrix of Joseph and Aseneth." In *SBL 1996: Seminar Papers*, 285–302. Atlanta: Scholars Press, 1996.

Cimok, F. *Pergamum*. Istanbul: Publishers A Turizm Yayinlari, 1998.

Coggins, R. J. *Samaritans and Jews: The Origins of Samaritanism Reconsidered*. Atlanta: John Knox Press, 1975.

Collins, J. J. *The Apocalyptic Imagination: An Introduction to the Jewish Matrix of Christianity*. New York: Crossroad, 1984.

Collins, R. F. *Introduction to the New Testament.* Garden City, N. Y.: Doubleday, 1983.

Connick, C. M. *Jesus, the Man, the Mission, and the Message.* 2d ed. Englewood Cliffs, N.J.: Prentice-Hall, 1974.

Conzelmann, H. "History of Early Christianity." In *Interpreting the New Testament: An Introduction to the Principles and Methods of N.T. Exegesis,* by H. Conzelmann and A. Lindemann, 336–53. Translated by S. S. Schatzmann from the 8th rev. German ed. Peabody, Mass.: Hendrickson, 1988.

————. *Jesus.* Translated by I. and F. McLuskey with J. M. Robinson. San Francisco: Harper & Row, 1973.

Corbett, J. H. "The Foster Child: A Neglected Theme in Early Christian Life and Thought." In *Traditions in Contact and Change: Selected Proceedings of the XIVth Congress of the International Association for the History of Religions,* edited by P. Slater and D. Wiebe, 307–21, 710–13. Waterloo, Ont.: Canadian Corporation for Studies in Religion/Wilfrid Laurier University Press, 1983.

Corley, K. "Gender and Class in the Teaching of Jesus: A Profile." Unpublished paper presented at a meeting of the Jesus Seminar, Santa Rosa, Calif., October 1997.

Coser, L. A. *The Functions of Social Conflict.* New York: Free Press of Glencoe, 1964.

Countryman, L. W. *Dirt, Greed, and Sex: Sexual Ethics in the New Testament and Their Implications for Today.* Philadelphia: Fortress Press, 1989.

Crossan, J. D. *The Cross That Spoke: The Origins of the Passion Narrative.* San Francisco: Harper & Row, 1988.

————. "Divine Immediacy and Human Immediacy: Towards a New First Principle in Historical Jesus Research." *Semeia* 44 (1988) 121–40.

————. *The Essential Jesus: Original Sayings and Earliest Images.* San Francisco: HarperSanFrancisco, 1994.

————. *The Historical Jesus: A Revolutionary Biography.* San Francisco: HarperSanFrancisco, 1994.

————. "The Historical Jesus in Earliest Christianity." In *Jesus and Faith: A Conversation on the Work of John Dominic Crossan,* edited by J. Carlson and R. A. Ludwig, 1–21. Maryknoll, N.Y.: Orbis Books, 1994.

————. *The Historical Jesus: The Life of a Mediterranean Jewish Peasant.* San Francisco: HarperSanFrancisco, 1991.

————. "The Infancy and Youth of the Messiah." In *The Search for Jesus: Modern Scholarship Looks at the Gospels,* edited by H. Shanks, 59–81. Washington, D.C.: Biblical Archaeology Society, 1994.

————. "Jesus and the Kingdom: Itinerants and Householders in Earliest Christianity." In *Jesus at 2000,* edited by M. J. Borg, 21–53. Boulder, Colo.: Westview Press, 1997.

————. "The Life of a Mediterranean Jewish Peasant." *Christian Century,*
18–25 December 1991, 1194–204.

————. *Who Killed Jesus? Exposing the Roots of Anti-Semitism in the Gospel
Story of the Death of Jesus.* San Francisco: HarperSanFrancisco, 1995.

————. "Why Christians Must Search for the Historical Jesus." *Bible
Review,* April 1996, 35–45.

Crossan, J. D., with R. G. Watts. *Who Is Jesus? Answers to Your Questions
about the Historical Jesus.* San Francisco: HarperSanFrancisco, 1996.

Cullmann, O. *The Early Church.* Edited by A. J. B. Higgins. Philadelphia:
Westminster Press, 1956.

————. "Spuren einer alten Taufformel im Neuen Testament." In *Die
Tauflehre des Neuen Testament,* 65–73. Zürich: Theologischer Verlag, 1948.

Dahrendorf, R. *Class and Class Conflict in Industrial Society.* Stanford, Calif.:
Stanford University Press, 1959.

————. *Essays in the Theory of Society.* Stanford, Calif.: Stanford University
Press, 1968.

Daly, M., and Wilson, M. "A Sociobiological Analysis of Human
Infanticide." In *Infanticide: Comparative and Evolutionary Perspectives,*
edited by G. F. Haustafer and S. Hardy, 487–502. New York: Aldine
Publishing Co., 1984.

Darroch, J. 1947. "An Interpretation of the Personality of Jesus." *British
Journal of Medical Psychology* 21, 75–79.

David, M. "Adoptie in het Oude Israel." Mededelingen Kon. Ned. Akademie,
afd. Letterkunde, Nieuwe Reeks 18, no. 4 (1955).

Davies, S. L. *Jesus the Healer: Possession, Trance, and the Origins of
Christianity.* New York: Continuum, 1995.

Deissmann, A. *Light from the Ancient East.* Grand Rapids, Mich.: Baker
Book House, 1965.

Deist, F. *A Concise Dictionary of Theological Terms.* Pretoria: Van Schaik,
1984.

De Jonge, M. J. *The Testaments of the Twelve Patriarchs: A Study of Their
Text, Composition, and Origin.* Assen, Netherlands: Gorcum, 1975.

Denaux, A. "Did Jesus Found the Church?" *Louvain Studies* 21 (1966)
25–45.

Den Heyer, C. J. *Opnieuw: Wie is Jezus? Balans van 150 Jaar Onderzoek naar
Jezus.* 2d ed. Meinema: Zoetermeer, 1996.

Deroux, M. P. "Les origines de l'oblature benedictine." *Revue Mabillion* 17
(1927) 1–16, 81–113, 193–216.

Derrett, J. D. M. *Jesus's Audience: The Social and Psychological Environment
in which He Worked.* New York: Seabury Press, 1973.

————. "Why Jesus Blessed the Children (Mk 10:13–16 par)." *Novum
Testamentum* 25 (1983) 1–18.

Devenish, P. E. "Introduction: The Jesus-Kerygma and the Christian Theology." In *Jesus and the Church: The Beginnings of Christianity*, by W. Marxson, xi–xxxv. Philadelphia: Trinity Press International, 1992.

De Villiers, J. L. *Die Betekenis van HUIOTHESIA in die Briewe van Paulus.* Amsterdam: Academisch Proefschrift, Vrije Universiteit Amsterdam, 1950.

Dibelius, M. *Jungfrauensohn und Krippenkind: Untersuchungen zur Geburts geschichte Jesu im Lukas-Evangelium*. Heidelberg: Carl Winters Universitäts buchhandlung, 1932.

———. "Seneca, Lucius Annaeus." In *Religion in Geschichte und Gegenwart* 5. Tübingen: J. C. B. Mohr (Paul Siebeck), 1961.

Dickemann, M. "Concepts and Classification in the Study of Human Infanticide: Sectional Introduction and Some Cautionary Notes." In *Infanticide: Comparative and Evolutionary Perspectives*, edited by G. F. Haustafer and S. Hardy, 427–38. New York: Aldine Publishing Co., 1984.

———. "Demographic Consequences of Infanticide in Man." *Annual Review of Ecology and Systematics* 6 (1975) 107–37.

Dittenberger, W. *Sylloge Inscriptionum Graecarum*. Vol. 2. 4th ed. Hildesheim, Germany: Olms, 1960.

Dodd, C. H. "The Primitive Preaching." In *The Apostolic Preaching and Its Developments: Three Lectures with an Appendix on Eschatology and History*, 7–35. London: Hodder & Stoughton, 1956.

Doherty, E. *The Jesus Puzzle: Did Christianity Begin with a Mythical Christ?* Ottawa: Canadian Humanist Publications, 1999.

Duling, D. C. "Matthew's Infancy in Social Scientific Perspective: Conflict and Legitimation." Unpublished paper presented at the Context Group Meeting, Portland, Ore., March 1991.

———. "Matthew's Son of David in Social Science Perspective: Kinship, Kingship, and Magic." Unpublished paper presented at the First International Conference on the New Testament and Social Sciences at Medina del Campo, Spain, 1991.

Du Toit, A. B. "Die Historiese Jesus en die Verkondigde Christus van die Evangelies." In *Handleiding by die Nuwe Testament*, edited by A. B. Du Toit, vol. 4, 267–93. 2d rev. ed. Pretoria: NG Kerkboekhandel, 1985.

———. "Kanoniek van die Nuwe Testament." In *Handleiding by die Nuwe Testament*, edited by J. H. Roberts and A. B. Du Toit, vol. 1, 81–294. 2d rev. ed. Pretoria: NG Kerkboekhandel, 1984.

Eden, P. T., ed. *Seneca "Apocolocyntosis."* Cambridge: Cambridge University Press, 1984.

Egger, R. *Josephus Flavius und die Samaritaner: Eine terminologische Untersuchung zur Identitätsklärung der Samaritaner.* Novum Testamentum et Orbis Antiquus. Freiburg, Switzerland: Universitätsverlag; Göttingen: Vandenhoeck & Ruprecht, 1986.

Eliade, M. *Myth and Reality*. Translated by W. R. Trask. New York: Harper & Row, 1963.

Elliott, J. H. "The Evil Eye and the Sermon on the Mount: Contours of a Pervasive Belief in Social Scientific Perspective." *Biblical Interpretation* 2, no. 1 (1994) 51–84.

———. "Household and Meals versus the Temple Purity System: Patterns of Replication in Luke-Acts." *Biblical Theology Bulletin* 21, no. 3 (1991) 102–8.

———. "Paul, Galatians, and the Evil Eye." *Currents in Theology and Mission* 17 (1990) 262–73.

———. "Temple versus Household in Luke-Acts: A Contrast in Social Institutions." In *The World of Luke-Acts: Models for Interpretation*, edited by J. H. Neyrey, 211–40. Peabody, Mass.: Hendrickson, 1991.

Epstein, L. M. *Marriage Laws in the Bible and Talmud*. Cambridge: Harvard University Press, 1942.

Erikson, E. "The Galilee Sayings and the Sense of 'I.'" *Yale Review* 70 (1982) 321–62.

———. *Young Man Luther: A Study in Psychoanalysis and History*. New York: W. W. Norton, 1958.

Ernst, J. *Johannes der Täufer: Interpretation—Geschichte—Wirkungsgeschichte*. Berlin: Walter de Gruyter, 1989.

Evans, C. A. *Life of Jesus Research: An Annotated Bibliography*. Rev. ed. Leiden: E. J. Brill, 1996.

Evans, D. "Academic Scepticism, Spiritual Reality, and Transfiguration." In *The Glory of Christ in the New Testament*, edited by L. D. Hurst and N. T. Wright, 175–86. Oxford: Clarendon Press, 1987.

Eybers, I. H. "Relations between Jews and Samaritans in the Persian Period." In *Biblical Essays*, edited by the Ou-Testamentiese Werkgemeenskap in Suid-Afrika. Pretoria: Unisa Publishing House, 1966.

Farid, S., and D. Busath. *The Temple of Philae*. Simpkins Splendour of Egypt. Salt Lake City: Simpkins Souvenirs, 1990.

Ferguson, E. *Backgrounds of Early Christianity*. Grand Rapids, Mich.: Wm. B. Eerdmans, 1987.

Fiensy, D. A. *The Social History of Palestine in the Herodian Period: The Land Is Mine*. Studies in the Bible and Early Christianity 20. Lewiston, N.Y.: Edwin Mellen Press, 1991.

Ford, M. J. "The Crucifixion of Women in Antiquity." *Journal of Higher Criticism* 3, no. 2 (1996) 291–309.

Fortna, R. T. *The Fourth Gospel and Its Predecessor: From Narrative Source to Present Gospel*. Philadelphia: Fortress Press, 1988.

Foucault, M. *The Archaeology of Knowledge*. New York: Harper & Row, 1972.

————. *Power Strategies, in Power/Knowledge: Selected Interviews and Other Writings 1972–1977*. Edited by C. Gordon and translated by C. Gordon and others. New York: Pantheon Books, 1980.

Francis, L. J., and J. Astley. "The Quest for the Psychological Jesus: Influences of Personality on Images of Jesus." *Journal of Psychology and Christianity* 16, no. 3 (1997) 247–59.

Franzmann, M. *Jesus in the Nag Hammadi Writings*. Edinburgh: T. & T. Clark, 1996.

Freyne, S. *Galilee, Jesus, and the Gospels: Literary Approaches and Historical Investigations*. Philadelphia: Fortress Press, 1988.

Freyne, S. "Galilean Questions to Crossan's Mediterranean Jesus." In *Whose Historical Jesus?* Edited by W. E. Arnal and M. Desjardins, 63–91. Studies in Christianity & Judaism 7. Waterloo, Ont.: Wilfrid Laurier University Press, 1997.

Fuchs, E. *Zur Frage nach dem historischen Jesus: Gesammelte Aufsätze*. Vol. 2. Tübingen: J. C. B. Mohr (Paul Siebeck), 1960.

Funk, R. W. "Criteria for Determining the Authentic Sayings of Jesus." *The Fourth R* 3, no. 6 (1990) 8–10.

————. "Demons, Identity, and Worldview." *The Fourth R* 5, no. 3 (1992) 15.

————. *Honest to Jesus: Jesus for a New Millennium*. San Francisco: HarperSanFrancisco, 1996.

————. "The Jesus That Was." *The Fourth R* 5, no. 6 (1992) 1–6.

Funk, R. W., and R. W. Hoover, and the Jesus Seminar. *The Five Gospels: The Search for the Authentic Words of Jesus*. New York: Macmillan Publishing Co., 1997.

Funk, R. W., and the Jesus Seminar. *The Acts of Jesus: What Did Jesus Really Do?* San Francisco: HarperSanFrancisco, 1998.

Funk, R. W., with M. H. Smith. *The Gospel of Mark: Red Letter Edition*. Sonoma, Calif.: Polebridge Press, 1991.

Gabra, G. *Cairo: The Coptic Museum and Old Churches*. With contributions by A. Alcock. Cairo: Egyptian International Publishing Co., 1993.

Gärtner, B. *The Temple and the Community in Qumran and the New Testament: A Comparative Study in the Temple Symbolism of the Qumran Texts and the New Testament*. Cambridge: Cambridge University Press, 1965.

Gaston, L. "Paul and Jerusalem." In *From Jesus to Paul: Studies in Honour of Francis Wright Beare*, edited by P. Richardson and J. C. Hurd, 61–72. Waterloo, Ont.: Wilfrid Laurier University Press, 1984.

Gerleman, G. *Ruth—Das Hohelied*. Biblischer Kommentar Altes Testament. Neukirchen-Vluyn: Neukirchener Verlag, 1963.

Gloege, G. "Zur Geschichte des Schriftverständnisses." In *Das Neue Testament als Kanon: Dokumentation und kritische Analyse zur gegenwärtigen Diskussion*, edited by E. Kasemann, 13–40. Göttingen: Vandenhoeck & Ruprecht, 1970.

Gnilka, J. *Das Evangelium nach Markus.* Vol. 2, *Mk 8,27–16,20.* Zürich: Theologischer Verlag, 1979.

Goodnick, B. "The Saga of the First Born." *Dor le Dor. Our Biblical Heritage* 16, no. 3 (1988) 170–78.

Grant, F. C. "The Economic Background of the New Testament." In *The Background of the New Testament and Its Eschatology: In Honour of Charles Harold Dodd*, edited by W. D. Davies and D. Daube, 96–114. Cambridge: Cambridge University Press, 1956.

Grenfell, B. P., A. S. Hunt, and E. Bell, eds. *The Oxyrhynchus Papyri.* 17 vols. London: Egypt Exploration Fund, 1898–1927.

Grønseth, E. "The Impact of Father Absence in Sailor Families upon the Personality Structure and Social Adjustment of Adult Sailor Sons, Part 1." In *Studies of the Family,* vol. 2, edited by N. Anderson, 97–114. Göttingen: Vandenhoeck & Ruprecht, 1957.

Hahn, F. *Christologische Hoheitstiteln: Ihre Geschichte im Frühen Christentum.* 4th ed. Göttingen: Vandenhoeck & Ruprecht, 1974.

———. "Methodologische Überlegungen zur Rückfrage nach Jesus." In *Rückfrage nach Jesus: Zur Methodik und Bedeutung der Frage nach dem historischen Jesus*, edited by K. Kertelge, 11–77. 2d ed. Freiburg: Herder, 1974.

Hamerton-Kelly, R. *God the Father: Theology and Patriarchy in the Teaching of Jesus.* Overtures to Biblical Theology. Philadelphia: Fortress Press, 1979.

Hamilton, W. *A Quest for the Post-Historical Jesus.* New York: Continuum, 1994.

Hanfmann, G. M. A. "The Crucified Donkey Man: Achaios and Jesus." In *Studies in Classical Art and Archaeology: A Tribute to P. H. van Blanckenhagen*, edited by G. Kopke and M. B. Moore, 206–8. Augsburg: Locust Valley, 1979.

Harper, M. "Village Administration in the Roman Province of Syria." *Yale Classical Studies* 1 (1928) 105–68.

Harris, M. J. *Jesus as God: The New Testament Use of "Theos" in Reference to Jesus.* Grand Rapids, Mich.: Baker Book House, 1992.

Harris, W. V. *Ancient Literacy.* Cambridge: Harvard University Press, 1989.

Hengel, M. *The Son of God: The Origin of Christology and the History of Jewish-Hellenistic Religion.* Translated by J. Bowden. Philadelphia: Fortress Press, 1976.

Hennecke, E. *New Testament Apocrypha.* Vol. 1, *Gospels and Related Writings.* Edited by W. Schneemelcher and translated by R. McL. Wilson. Louisville, Ky.: Westminster Press, 1973.

Herzog, J. M. "On Father Hunger: The Father's Role in the Modulation of Aggressive Drive and Fantasy." In *Father and Child: Developmental and Clinical Perspectives,* edited by S. H. Cath, A. R. Gurwitt, and J. M. Ross, 163–74. Boston: Little, Brown and Co., 1982.

Hill, B. *Jesus the Christ: Contemporary Perspectives.* Mystic, Conn.: Twenty-Third Publications, 1991.

Hollander, H. W. *Joseph as an Ethical Model in the Testaments of the Twelve Patriarchs.* Studia in Veteris Testamenti Pseudepigrapha. Leiden: E. J. Brill, 1981.

Hollenbach, P. "The Conversion of Jesus: From the Baptizer to Jesus the Healer." In *Aufstieg und Niedergang der Römischen Welt,* edited by W. Haase, vol. 25, 196–219. Berlin: Walter de Gruyter, 1982.

Hollenbach, P. "Defining Rich and Poor: Using Social Sciences." In *SBL Seminar Papers,* edited by K. H. Richard, 50–63. Atlanta: Scholars Press, 1987.

———. "Social Aspects of John the Baptizer's Preaching Mission in the Context of Palestinian Judaism." In *Aufstieg und Niedergang der römischen Welt,* edited by W. Haase, vol. 19, 850–57. Berlin: Walter de Gruyter, 1979.

Hooker, M. "On Using the Wrong Tool." *Theology* 75 (1972) 570–81.

Horsley, R. A. *Jesus and the Spiral of Violence: Popular Jewish Resistance in Roman Palestine.* San Francisco: Harper & Row, 1987.

———. "Josephus and the Bandits." *Journal of Jewish Studies* 10 (1979) 37–63.

———. *The Liberation of Christmas: The Infancy Narratives in Social Context.* New York: Crossroad, 1989.

———. *Sociology and the Jesus Movement.* New York: Crossroad, 1989.

Horsley, R. A., and J. S. Hanson. *Bandits, Prophets, and Messiahs: Popular Movements in the Time of Jesus.* Minneapolis: Fortress Press, 1985.

Horsley, R. A., and N. A. Silberman. *The Message and the Kingdom: How Jesus and Paul Ignited a Revolution and Transformed the Ancient World.* New York: Penguin Putnam, 1997.

Horst, F. "Segen und Fluch." In *Religion in Geschichte und Gegenwart,* vol. 5. Tübingen: J. C. B. Mohr (Paul Siebeck), 1961.

Innes, M. M. *The Metamorphoses of Ovid.* London: Penguin Books, 1955.

Ishak, Amram. *The History and Religion of the Samaritans.* Jerusalem: Greek Convent Press, n. d.

Jacobs-Malina, D. *Beyond Patriarchy: The Images of Family in Jesus.* New York: Paulist Press, 1993.

Jacobson, A. D. *The First Gospel: An Introduction to Q.* Sonoma, Calif.: Polebridge Press, 1992.

Jeppesen, K. "Then Began Men to Call upon the Name of Yahweh: An Idea." In *In the Last Days: On Jewish and Christian Apocalyptic and Its Period,* by K. Jeppesen, K. Nielsen, and B. Rosendal, 158–63. Aarhus: Aarhus University Press, 1994.

Jeremias, J. "Der gegenwärtige Stand der Debatte um das Problem des historischen Jesus." In *Der historische Jesus und der kerygmatische Christus,* edited by H. Ristow and K. Matthiae, 12–25. Berlin: Evangelische Verlagsanstalt, 1960.

———. *Heiligengräber in Jesu Umwelt.* Göttingen: Vandenhoeck & Ruprecht, 1985.

———. *Jerusalem in the Time of Jesus: An Investigation into Economic and Social Conditions during the New Testament Period.* Translated by F. H. and C. H. Cave from the 3d German ed. London: SCM Press, 1969.

———. *Die Kindertaufe in den ersten vier Jahrhunderten.* Göttingen: Vandenhoeck & Ruprecht, 1958.

———. *New Testament Theology.* Vol. 1, *The Proclamation of Jesus.* Translated by J. Bowden. New York: Charles Scribner's Sons, 1971.

———. *The Problem of the Historical Jesus.* Translated by N. Perrin. Philadelphia: Fortress Press, 1964.

Johnson, L. T. *The Real Jesus: The Misguided Quest for the Historical Jesus and the Truth of the Traditional Gospels.* San Francisco: HarperSanFrancisco, 1996.

———. "The Search for (the Wrong) Jesus." *Bible Review,* December 1995, 20–44.

Joy, C. R. "Introduction: Schweitzer's Conception of Jesus." In *The Psychiatric Study of Jesus: Exposition and Criticism,* by A. Schweitzer. Boston: Beacon Press, 1948.

Jung, C. G. "Symbols of Transformation." In *The Collected Works of C. G. Jung,* edited by H. Read, M. Fordham, and G. Adler, vol. 5. New York: Pantheon Books, 1956.

Jüngel, E. "The Dogmatic Significance of the Question of the Historical Jesus." In *Theological Essays,* by E. Jüngel, vol. 2, 82–119. Edited by J. B. Webster and translated by A. Neufeldt-Fast and J. B. Webster. Edinburgh: T. & T. Clark, 1995.

Jurich, A. P., M. B. White, C. P. White, and R. A. Moody. "Internal Culture of the Family and Its Effects on Fatherhood." In *Fatherhood and Families in Cultural Context,* edited by F. W. Bozett and S. M. H. Hanson, 263–74. New York: Spring Publishing Co., 1991.

Kahen, H. W. *Samaritan History, Identity, Religion and Subdivisions, Literature and Social Status.* Jerusalem: Greek Convent Press, 1996.

Kähler, M. *Der sogenannte historische Jesus und der geschichtliche, biblische Christus*. 4th ed. Munich: Kaiser Verlag, 1969.

Käsemann, E. *An die Römer*. 3d ed. Tübingen: J. C. B. Mohr (Paul Siebeck), 1974.

———. "Die Anfänge christlicher Theologie." *Zeitschrift für Theologie und Kirche* 57 (1960) 162–85.

———. "Blind Alleys in the 'Jesus of History' Controversy." In *New Testament Questions of Today*, 23–65. Translated by W. J. Montague. New Testament Library. London: SCM Press, 1969.

———. "Das Problem des historischen Jesus." In *Exegetische Versuche und Besinnungen*, vol. 1, 187–214. Göttingen: Vandenhoeck & Ruprecht, 1960.

Katz, S. T. "Issues in the Separation of Judaism and Christianity after 70 C.E.: A Reconsideration." *Journal of Biblical Literature* 103 (1984) 43–76.

Keck, L. E. *A Future for the Historical Jesus: The Place of Jesus in Preaching and Theology*. Philadelphia: Fortress Press, 1981.

Kee, H. C. *What Can We Know about Jesus?* Cambridge: Cambridge University Press, 1990.

Kertelge, K. "Die Funktion der 'Zwölf' im Markusevangelium." *Trierer Theologische Zeitschrift* 78 (1969) 193–206.

Kirkwood, G. M. *A Short Guide to Classical Mythology*. New York: Holt, Rinehart & Winston, 1966.

Klein, G. "Jesus und die Kinder: Bibelarbeit über Markus 10, 13–16." In *Ärgernisse: Konfrontationen mit dem Neuen Testament*, 58–81. Munich: Kaiser Verlag, 1970.

———. *Die zwölf Apostel: Ursprung und Gehalt einer Idee*. Göttingen: Vandenhoeck & Ruprecht, 1961.

Kloppenborg, J. S. *The Formation of Q: Trajectories in Ancient Wisdom Collections*. Studies in Antiquity and Christianity. Philadelphia: Fortress Press, 1987.

———. *Q Parallels: Synopsis, Critical Notes, and Concordance*. Sonoma, Calif.: Polebridge Press, 1988.

———. "The Sayings Gospel Q: Recent Opinion on the People behind the Document." *Currents in Research: Biblical Studies* 1 (1993) 9–34.

Koester, H. *Ancient Christian Gospels: Their History and Development*. Harrisburg, Pa.: Trinity Press International, 1990.

———. *Introduction to the New Testament*. Vol. 2, *History and Literature of Early Christianity*. New York/Berlin: Walter de Gruyter, 1987.

———. "One Jesus and Four Primitive Gospels." In *Trajectories through Early Christianity*, by J. M. Robinson and H. Koester, 158–204. Philadelphia: Fortress Press, 1971.

Köhler, L. "Die Adoptionsform von Ruth 4,16." *Zeitschrift für Alten Testamentliche Wissenschaft* 29 (1909) 312–14.

Kopfensteiner, T. R. "Historical Epistemology and Moral Progress." *Heythrop Journal* 33, no. 1 (1992) 45–60.

Kristeva, J. *The Kristeva Reader.* Edited by T. Moi. New York: Columbia University Press, 1986.

Kümmel, W. G. "Notwendigkeit und Grenze des neutestamentlichen Kanons." In *Das Neue Testament als Kanon: Dokumentation und kritische Analyse zur gegenwärtigen Diskussion,* edited by E. Kasemann, 62–97. Göttingen: Vandenhoeck & Ruprecht, 1970.

Lake, K., trans. "The Epistle to Diognetus." In The Apostolic Fathers, vol. 2, 348–79. London: William Heinemann, 1965.

LeMarquand, G. "The Historical Jesus and African New Testament Scholarship." In *Whose Historical Jesus?* edited by W. E. Arnal and M. Desjardins. Studies in Christianity & Judaism 7. Waterloo, Ont.: Wilfrid Laurier University Press, 1997.

Lenski, G. *Power and Privilege: A Theory of Social Stratification.* New York: McGraw-Hill, 1966.

Lenski, G., J. Lenski, and P. Nolan. *Human Societies: An Introduction to Macrosociology.* 6th ed. New York: McGraw-Hill, 1991.

———. *Human Societies: An Introduction to Macrosociology.* 7th ed. New York: McGraw-Hill, 1995.

Levinson, D. *The Seasons of a Man's Life.* New York: Alfred A. Knopf, 1978.

Liddell, H. G., and R. Scott. *A Greek-English Lexicon.* A new edition revised and augmented by H. S. Jones. Oxford: Clarendon Press, 1961.

Lietzmann, H. *An die Römer.* Tübingen: J. C. B. Mohr (Paul Siebeck), 1993.

Lindemann, A. *Die Kinder und die Gottesherrschaft.* Darmstadt: Wissenschaftliche Buchgesellschaft, 1983.

Louw, J. P., and E. A. Nida. *Greek-English Lexicon of the New Testament Based on Semantic Domains.* Vol. 1, *Introduction and Domains.* New York: United Bible Societies, 1988.

Lüdemann, G. *The Resurrection of Jesus: History, Experience, Theology.* Translated by J. Bowden. Minneapolis: Fortress Press, 1994.

———. *Virgin Birth? The Real Story of Mary and Her Son Jesus.* Translated by J. Bowden. Harrisburg, Pa.: Trinity Press International, 1998.

Ludolphy, I. "Zur Geschichte der Auslegung des Evangelium Infantium." In *Die Kinder im Evangelium,* edited by G. Krause, 31–51. Göttingen: Vandenhoeck & Ruprecht, 1973.

Lührmann, D. "The Gospel of Mark and the Sayings Collection Q." *Journal of Biblical Literature* 108 (1989) 51–71.

Luther, M.. *Vorrede auf die Episteln S. Jacobi und Judae.* In *Die Werke Luthers in Auswahl.* Vol. 5, *Die Schriftauslegung.* 4th ed. Edited by Kurt Aland. Göttingen: Vandenhoeck & Ruprecht, 1990.

Lynn, D. B., and W. L. Sawrey. "The Effects of Father-Absence on Norwegian Boys and Girls." *Journal of Abnormal Social Psychology* 59 (1959) 258–62.

Mack, B. L. *The Lost Gospel: The Book of Q and Christian Origins*. San Francisco: HarperSanFrancisco, 1993.

———. *A Myth of Innocence: Mark and Christian Origins*. Philadelphia: Fortress Press, 1988.

——. *Who Wrote the New Testament? The Making of the Christian Myth*. San Francisco: HarperSanFrancisco, 1995.

Mahl, G. F. "Father-Son Themes in Freud's Self-Analysis." In *Father and Child: Developmental and Clinical Perspectives*, edited by S. H. Cath, A. R. Gurwitt, and J. M. Ross, 33–64. Boston: Little, Brown and Co., 1982.

Malina, B. J. "Christ and Time: Swiss or Mediterranean?" In *The Social World of Jesus and the Gospels*, 179–214. London: Routledge & Kegan Paul, 1996.

———. *Christian Origins and Cultural Anthropology: Practical Models for Biblical Interpretation*. Atlanta: John Knox Press, 1986.

———. "Dealing with Biblical (Mediterranean) Characters: A Guide for US Consumers." *Biblical Theology Bulletin* 19, no. 4 (1989) 127–41.

———. "Early Christian Groups: Using Small Group Formation Theory to Explain Christian Organizations." Unpublished paper presented at the International Context Group Meeting, St. Andrews University, Scotland, 1994.

———. "Interpreting the Bible with Anthropology: The Case of the Poor and the Rich." *Listening* 21 (1986) 148–59.

———. "Is There a Circum-Mediterranean Person? Looking for Stereotypes." *Biblical Theology Bulletin* 22, no. 2 (1991) 66–87.

———. *The New Testament World: Insights from Cultural Anthropology*. Rev. ed. Louisville, Ky.: Westminster/John Knox Press, 1993.

———. "The Question of First-Century Mediterranean Persons." In *The Social World of Jesus and the Gospels*, 35–66. London: Routledge & Kegan Paul, 1996.

Malina, B. J., and J. H. Neyrey. *Calling Jesus Names: The Social Value of Labels in Matthew*. Sonoma, Calif.: Polebridge Press, 1988.

Maluleke, T. S. "What Africans Are Doing to Jesus: Will He Ever Be the Same Again?" In *Images of Jesus*, edited by C. Du Toit, 185–205. Pretoria: University of South Africa Press, 1997.

Manns, F. *Essais sur le Judéo-Christianisme*. Studium Biblicum Franciscanum Analecta 12. Jerusalem: Franciscan Printing Press, 1977.

Marciano, T. D. "Religion and Its Impact on Fatherhood." In *Fatherhood and Families in Cultural Context*, edited by F. W. Bozett and S. M. H. Hanson, 138–61. New York: Springer Publishing Co., 1991.

Marsh, C. "Quests of the Historical Jesus in New Historicist Perspective." *Biblical Interpretation* 5, no. 4 (1997) 403–37.

Marxsen, W. *Christologie—Praktisch.* Gütersloh: Gütersloher Verlagshaus Gerd Mohn, 1978.

———. *Der Exeget als Theologe: Vorträge zum Neuen Testament.* 2d ed. Gütersloh: Gütersloher Verlagshaus Gerd Mohn, 1969.

———. *Introduction to the New Testament: An Approach to Its Problems.* Translated by G. Buswell. Philadelphia: Fortress Press, 1968.

———. *Jesus and the Church: The Beginnings of Christianity.* Translated by P. E. Devenish. Philadelphia: Trinity Press International, 1992.

———. "Jesus—Bringer oder Inhalt des Evangeliums?" In *Die Sache Jesu geht weiter,* 45–62. Gütersloh: Gütersloher Verlagshaus Gerd Mohn, 1976.

———. *Das Neue Testament als Buch der Kirche.* Gütersloh: Gütersloher Verlagshaus Gerd Mohn, 1968.

———. "Das Problem des neutestamentlichen Kanons." In *Das Neue Testament als Kanon: Dokumentation und kritische Analyse zur gegenwärtigen Diskussion,* edited by E. Käsemann, 233–46. Göttingen: Vandenhoeck & Ruprecht, 1970.

Matthews, V. C., and D. C. Benjamin. *Social World of Ancient Israel, 1250–587 B.C.E.* Peabody, Mass.: Hendrickson, 1993.

Maulucci, F. P. *The National Archaeological Museum of Naples.* Naples: Publisher Carcavallo, 1996.

Maurer, W. "Luthers Verständnis des neutestamentlichen Kanons." In *Die Verbindlichkeit des Kanons,* 47–77. Hamburg: Luthers Verlaghaus, 1969.

McDonald, L. M. *The Formation of the Christian Biblical Canon.* Rev. and expanded ed. Peabody, Mass.: Hendrickson, 1995.

McVann, M. "Baptism, Miracles, and Boundary Jumping in Mark." *Biblical Theology Bulletin* 21 (1991) 151–57.

Meadow, M. J. "Archetypes and Patriarchy: Eliade and Jung." *Journal of Religion and Health* 31, no. 3 (1992) 187–95.

Meier, J. P. "The Brothers and Sisters of Jesus in Ecumenical Perspective." *Catholic Biblical Quarterly* 54 (1992) 1–28.

———. "The Circle of the Twelve: Did It Exist during Jesus' Public Ministry?" *Journal of Biblical Literature* 116, no. 4 (1997) 635–72.

———. *A Marginal Jew: Rethinking the Historical Jesus.* Vol. 1, *The Roots of the Problem and the Person.* New York: Doubleday, 1991.

———. *A Marginal Jew: Rethinking the Historical Jesus.* Vol. 2, *Mentor, Message, and Miracles.* New York: Doubleday, 1994.

Meijer, A., and A. Meijer. "Matriarchal Influence in the Bible: A Medical-Psychological Study." *Dor le Dor. Our Biblical Heritage* 13, no. 1 (1984) 81–87.

Metzger, B. *A Textual Commentary on the Greek New Testament.* Stuttgart: United Bible Societies, 1971.

Meye, R. P. *Jesus and the Twelve*. Grand Rapids, Mich.: Wm. B. Eerdmans, 1968.

Meyer, B. *The Aims of Jesus*. London: SCM Press, 1979.

————. *Critical Realism and the New Testament*. Princeton Theological Monograph Series. Allison Park, Pa.: Pickwick Publications, 1989.

————. s.v. "Jesus Christ." *Anchor Bible Dictionary*, 773–96. New York: Doubleday, 1992.

Meynell, H. "On Knowledge, Power, and Michel Foucault." *Heythrop Journal* 30 (1989) 419–32.

Michaud, R. *L'Histoire de Joseph, le Makirite (Genese 37–50)*. Paris: Les éditions du Cerf, 1976.

Miller, J. W. *Jesus at Thirty: A Psychological and Historical Portrait*. Minneapolis: Fortress Press, 1997.

Miller, R. J. *The Complete Gospels: Annotated Scholars Version*. Sonoma, Calif.: Polebridge Press, 1992.

————. *The Complete Gospels: Annotated Scholars Version*. Rev. and expanded ed. Sonoma, Calif.: Polebridge Press, 1994.

————. *The Jesus Seminar and Its Critics*. Sonoma, Calif.: Polebridge Press, 1999.

Mitscherlich, A. *Society without the Father: A Contribution to Social Psychology*. Translated by E. Mosbacher. London: Tavistock Publications, 1969.

Montgomery, J. A. *The Samaritans: The Earliest Jewish Sect. Their History, Theology, and Literature*. New York: KTAV Publishing House, 1968.

Mott, F. L. "When Is a Father Really Gone? Paternal-Child Contact in Father-Absent Homes." *Demography* 27, no. 4 (1990) 1–27.

Mouton, J., and J. C. Pauw. "Foundationalism and Fundamentalism: A Critique." In *Paradigms and Progress in Theology*, edited by J. Mouton, A. G. Van Aarde, and W. S. Vorster, 176–86. HSRC Studies in Research Methodology 5. Pretoria: HSRC, 1988.

Murphy-O'Connor, J. *The Holy Land: An Oxford Archaeological Guide from Earliest Times to 1700*. 4th ed., rev. and expanded. Oxford: Oxford University Press, 1998.

————. "Tradition and Redaction in 1 Cor. 15:3–7." *Catholic Biblical Quarterly* 43 (1981) 582–89.

Mussner, F. "Methodologie der Frage nach dem historischen Jesus." In *Rückfrage nach Jesus: Zur Methodik und Bedeutung der Frage nach dem historischen Jesus*, edited by K. Kertelge, 118–47. Freiburg: Herder, 1974.

Neirynck, F. "Duality in Mark: Contributions to the Study of the Markan Redaction on the 'Two-step Progression' as a Markan Device." In *Ephemerides Theologicae Lovanienses* 47, 394–463.

Neusner, J. *Formative Judaism: Religious, Historical, and Literary Studies*. Brown Judaic Studies 37. Chico, Calif.: Scholars Press, 1982.

————. *From Politics to Piety*. Englewood Cliffs, N.J.: Prentice-Hall, 1973.

————. "Israel: Judaism and Its Social Metaphors." *Journal of the American Academy of Religion* 55 (1987) 331–61.

————. *The Way of Torah: An Introduction to Judaism*. North Scituate, Mass.: Duxbury Press, 1979.

Neyrey, J. H. "The Symbolic Universe of Luke-Acts: 'They Turn the World Upside Down.'" In *The World of Luke-Acts: Models for Interpretation*, edited by J. H. Neyrey, 271–304. Peabody, Mass.: Hendrickson, 1991.

Niehoff, M. *The Figure of Joseph in Post-Biblical Jewish Literature*. Arbeiten zur Geschichte des Antiken Judentums und des Urchristentums 16. Leiden: E. J. Brill, 1992.

Nyamiti, C. "African Christologies Today." In *Jesus in African Christianity*, edited by J. N. K. Mugambi and L. Magesa, 17–39. Nairobi: Initiatives Publishers, 1989.

————. "The Incarnation Viewed from the African Understanding of Person." *C.H.I.E.A. African Christian Studies* 6, no. 2 (1990) 23–76.

Oakman, D. E. *Jesus and the Economic Questions of His Day*. Studies in the Bible and Early Christianity 8. Lewiston, N.Y.: Edwin Mellen Press, 1986.

Oberlinner, L. *Historische Überlieferung und christologische Aussage*. Stuttgart: KBW, 1975.

Oepke, A. *Der Brief des Paulus an die Galater*. Revised by J. Rohde. Theologischer Handkommentar zum Neuen Testament. Berlin: Evangelische Verlagsanstalt, 1973.

Ogden, S. M. *Doing Theology Today*. Valley Forge, Pa.: Trinity Press International, 1996.

Oldfather, C. H. "Introduction." In *Diodorus of Sicily*. Loeb Classical Library. Cambridge: Harvard University Press, 1935.

Osborn, R. T. "The Christian Blasphemy: A Non-Jewish Jesus." In *Jews and Christians: Exploring the Past, Present, and Future*, edited by J. H. Charlesworth, 211–38. New York: Crossroad, 1990.

Osiek, C. "Jesus and Cultural Values: Family Life as an Example." *Hervormde Teologiese Studies* 53, no. 3 (1997) 800–14.

————. "The Women at the Tomb: What Are They Doing There?" *Ex Auditu* 9 (1993) 97–107.

Overman, J. A. *Matthew's Gospel and Formative Judaism: The Social World of the Matthean Community*. Minneapolis: Fortress Press, 1990.

Pace Tour Guide of the West Bank and Gaza Strip ("Palestine"): Historical and Archaeological Guide. Ramallah and Gaza: PACE (The Palestine Association for Cultural Exchange) and PACL (The Palestinian Abraham Center for Languages) 1999.

Page, T. E., ed. *Seneca's Tragedies*. Translated by F. J. Miller. 2 vols. London: William Heinemann, 1960.

Painter, J. *Theology as Hermeneutics: Rudolf Bultmann's Interpretation of the History of Jesus.* Historical Texts and Interpreters in Biblical Scholarship. Sheffield: Almond Press, 1987.

Pannenberg, W. *Jesus—God and Man.* Translated by L. L. Wilkins and D. A. Priebe. London: SCM Press, 1968.

Parker, W. H. *Priapea: Poems for a Phallic God.* Croom Helm Classical Studies. London: Croom Helm Routledge, 1988.

Patte, D. *The Gospel according to Matthew: A Structural Commentary on Matthew's Faith.* Philadelphia: Fortress Press, 1987.

Patterson, S. J. *The Gospel of Thomas and Jesus.* Foundations and Facets Reference Series. Sonoma, Calif.: Polebridge Press, 1993.

P'Bitek, O. *Two Songs: Song of Prisoner. Song of Malaya.* Nairobi: Heinemann, 1971.

Perkins, P. "Canon, Paradigms, and Progress?" *Biblical Interpretation* 1, no. 1 (1993) 88–95.

———. "The Historical Jesus and Christology." In *Who Is This Christ? Gospel Christology and Contemporary Reflection,* edited by P. Perkins and R. H. Fuller. Garden City: Doubleday, 1983.

Perrin, N. R. *Jesus and the Language of the Kingdom: Symbol and Metaphor in New Testament Interpretation.* Philadelphia: Fortress Press, 1976.

———. *Rediscovering the Teaching of Jesus.* London: SCM Press, 1967.

Pesch, R. *Das Markusevangelium.* Vol. 1, *Einleitung und Kommentar zu Kap. 1,1–8,26.* Freiburg: Herder, 1977.

Philonenko, M. *Joseph et Aseneth: Introduction, Texte Critique et Notes.* Leiden: E. J. Brill, 1968.

Pilch, J. J. "Altered States of Consciousness: A 'Kitbashed' Model." *Biblical Theology Bulletin* 26, no. 3 (1996) 133–38.

———. "'Beat His Ribs While He Is Young' (Sir 30:12): Cultural Insights on the Suffering of Jesus." Unpublished Paper presented at the Context Group Meeting, Portland, Ore., March 1992.

———. "Insights and Models from Medical Anthropology for Understanding the Healing Activity of the Historical Jesus." *Hervormde Teologiese Studies* 51, no. 2 (1995) 314–37.

———. "Psychological and Psychoanalytical Approaches to Interpreting the Bible in Social-Scientific Context." *Biblical Theology Bulletin* 27, no. 3 (1997) 112–16.

———. Review of *Jesus the Healer: Possession, Trance, and the Origins of Christianity,* by S. L. Davies. *Biblical Theology Bulletin* 27, no. 2 (1997) 71–72.

———. "Sickness and Healing in Luke-Acts." In *The Social World of Luke-Acts: Models for Interpretation,* edited by J. H. Neyrey, 181–210. Peabody, Mass.: Hendrickson, 1991.

————. "Understanding Biblical Healing: Selecting the Appropriate Model." *Biblical Theology Bulletin* 18 (1988) 60–66.

————. "Visions in Revelation and Altered Consciousness: A Perspective from Cultural Anthropology." *Listening: Journal of Religion and Culture* 28, no. 3 (1993) 231–44.

Pirani, A. *The Absent Father: Crisis and Creativity.* London: Arkana, 1989.

Porkorny, P. *Der Gottessohn: Literarische Übersicht und Fragestellung.* Zürich: Theologische Verlag, 1971.

Pratt, N. T. *Dramatic Suspense in Seneca and in His Greek Precursors.* Princeton, N. J.: Princeton University Press, 1939.

Price, R. M. "Implied Reader Response and the Evolution of Genres: Transitional Stages between the Ancient Novels and Apocryphal Acts." *Hervormde Teologiese Studies* 53, no. 4 (1997) 909–38.

Pummer, R. *The Samaritans.* Iconography of Religions 23, 5. Leiden: E. J. Brill, 1987.

Rahlfs, A., ed. *Septuaginta.* Editio Nona. Stuttgart: Würtembergische Bibelanstalt, 1971.

Rawson, B. "Children in the Roman 'familia.'" In *The Family in Ancient Rome: New Perspectives,* edited by B. Rawson, 170–200. London: Croom Helm, 1986.

Reumann, J. "The Quest for the Historical Baptist." In *Understanding the Sacred Text: Essays in Honor of Morton S. Enslin,* edited by J. Reumann, 175–91. Valley Forge, Pa.: Judson Press, 1972.

Rhoads, D., and D. Michie. *Mark as Story: An Introduction to the Narrative of a Gospel.* Philadelphia: Fortress Press, 1982.

Richard, L. *What Are They Saying about Christ and World Religions?* New York: Paulist Press, 1981.

Richardson, N. *Was Jesus Divine?* London: Epworth Press, 1979.

Richardson, P. "'Why Turn the Tables?' Jesus' Protest in the Temple Precincts." In *SBL Seminar Papers,* edited by E. H. Lovering. Atlanta: Scholars Press, 1992.

Riches, J. *Jesus and the Transformation of Judaism.* London: Darton, Longman & Todd, 1980.

Richlin, A. *The Garden of Priapus: Sexuality and Aggression in Roman Humor.* New Haven, Conn.: Yale University Press, 1983.

Ricoeur, P. "Philosophische und theologische Hermeneutik." In *Metapher: Zur Hermeneutik religiöser Sprache,* edited by P. Ricoeur and E. Jüngel, 24–44. Evangelische Theologie Sonderheft. Munich: Chr. Kaiser Verlag, 1974.

Ridderbos, H. *Paulus: Ontwerp van zijn Theologie.* Kampen, Netherlands: Kok, 1973.

Riley, G. J. "The Gospel of Thomas in Recent Scholarship." *Currents in Research: Biblical Studies* 2 (1994) 227–52.

Ringshausen, G. "Die Kinder der Weisheit: Zur Auslegung von Mk 10, 13–16 par." *Zeitschrift für die neu-testamentliche Wissenschaft* 77 (1986) 43–63.

Robbins, V. K. "Pronouncement Stories and Jesus' Blessing of the Children: A Rhetorical Approach." *Semeia* 26–29 (1983) 43–74.

Robinson, F. "Coptic Apocryphal Gospels: Translations Together with the Texts of Some of Them." In *Texts and Studies: Contributions to Biblical and Patristic Literature*, by F. Robinson and J. Armitage. Cambridge: Cambridge University Press, 1896.

Robinson, J. M. "Introduction: The Dismantling and Reassembling of the Categories of New Testament Scholarship." In *Trajectories through Early Christianity*, by J. M. Robinson and H. Koester, 1–19. Philadelphia: Fortress Press, 1971.

———. *A New Quest of the Historical Jesus and Other Essays*. Philadelphia: Fortress Press, 1983.

———. "Sethians and Johannine Thought." In *The Rediscovery of Gnosticism*, edited by B. Layton, vol. 2, 643–63. Leiden: E. J. Brill, 1981.

Roloff, J. *Apostolat—Verkündigung—Kirche*. Gütersloh: Gütersloher Verlagshaus Gerd Mohn, 1965.

Rowley, H. H. *Job*. Century Bible. New Series. Aylesbury, England: Hazell Watson & Viney Ltd., 1970.

Saldarini, A. J. *Matthew's Christian-Jewish Community*. Chicago Studies in the History of Judaism. Chicago: University of Chicago Press, 1994.

———. *Pharisees, Scribes, and Sadducees in Palestinian Society: A Sociological Approach*. Wilmington, Del.: Michael Glazier, 1988.

Saler, B. "Supernatural as a Western Category." *Ethos* 5 (1977) 31–53.

Salyer, G. "Myth, Magic, and Dread: Reading Culture Religiously." *Literature and Theology* 9, no. 3 (1995) 261–77.

Sand, A. *Das Gezetz und die Propheten: Untersuchungen zur Theologie des Evangeliums nach Matthäus*. Regensburg, Germany: Pustet, 1974.

Sanders, E. P. *The Historical Figure of Jesus*. New York: Allen Lane Penguin, 1993.

———. *Jesus and Judaism*. Philadelphia: Fortress Press, 1985.

Sandmel, S. "Parallelomania." *Journal of Biblical Literature* 81 (1962) 1–13.

Sauer, J. "Der ursprüngliche 'Sitz im Leben' von Mk 10, 13–16." *Zeitschrift für die neu-testamentliche Wissenschaft* 72 (1981) 27–50.

Schaberg, J. "The Canceled Father: Historicity and the NT Infancy Narratives." Unpublished paper presented at a meeting of the Jesus Seminar, Santa Rosa, Calif., October 1994.

———. *The Illegitimacy of Jesus: A Feminist Theological Interpretation of the Infancy Narratives*. San Francisco: Harper & Row, 1987.

———. "The Infancy of Mary of Nazareth (Proto-James and Pseudo-Matthew)." In *For Searching the Scriptures*. Vol. 2, *A Feminist Commentary*, edited by E. Schüssler Fiorenza, 708–27. New York: Crossroad, 1994.

Schille, G. "Die Jesusbewegung und die Entstehung der Kirche." *Theologische Literatur Zeitschrift* 119 (1994) 100–112.

Schillebeeckx, E. *Jezus: Het Verhaal van Een Levende.* 2d ed. Bloemendaal: H. Nielsen, 1974.

———. *Jesus in Our Western Culture: Mysticism, Ethics, and Politics.* London: SCM Press. 1987.

Schimmel, S. "Joseph and His Brothers: A Paradigm for Repentance." *Judaica* 5 (1981) 60–65.

Schlier, H. *Der Brief an die Galater.* Rev. ed. Kritisch-Exegetischer Kommentar. Göttingen: Vandenhoeck & Ruprecht, 1971.

Schmahl, G. "Die Berufung der Zwölf im Markusevangelium." *Trierer Theologische Zeitschrift* 81 (1972) 203–13.

Schmidt, D. D. "Albert Schweitzer's Profile of Jesus." Unpublished paper presented at a meeting of the Jesus Seminar, Santa Rosa, Calif., October 1997.

Schmithals, W. *Die Apostelgeschichte des Lukas.* Zürcher Bibelkommentare. Zürich: Theologischer Verlag, 1982.

———. *Einleitung in die drei ersten Evangelien.* Berlin: Walyer de Gruyter, 1985.

———. *Das Evangelium nach Lukas.* Zürcher Bibelkommentare. Zürich: Theologischer Verlag, 1980.

———. *Das Evangelium nach Markus: Kapitel 1,1–9,1.* 2d ed. Ökumenischer Taschenbuch-Kommentar zum Neuen Testament 2/1. Gütersloh: Gütersloher Verlagshaus Gerd Mohn, 1986.

———. *Jesus von Nazareth in der Verkündigung der Kirche: Aktuelle Beiträge zum notwendige Streit um Jesus.* Neukirchen-Vluyn: Neukirchener Verlag, 1972.

———. "Der Markusschluss: Die Verklärungsgeschichte und die Aussendung der Zwölf." *Zeitschrift für Theologie und Kirche* 69 (1972) 379–411.

———. "Nachwort." In *Jesus,* by R. Bultmann, 149–58. New ed. Tübingen: J. C. B. Mohr (Paul Siebeck), 1988.

———. *The Office of Apostle in the Early Church.* Nashville: Abingdon Press, 1969.

———. *Theologiegeschichte des Urchristentums: Eine problemgeschichtliche Darstellung.* Stuttgart: Kohlhammer, 1994.

Schnackenburg, R. *The Gospel according to St John.* Vol. 1, *Introduction and Commentary on Chapters 1–4.* Translated by K. Smyth. Chippenham, England: Burns & Oates, 1968.

Schneider, G. *Die Apostelgeschichte.* Vol. 1. Freiburg: Herder, 1980.

Schönberger, O. *Lucius Annaeus Seneca—Apocolocyntosis Divi Clavdii: Einführung, Text und Kommentar.* Würzburg: Königshausen & Neumann, 1990.

Schrage, W. "'Ekklesia' und 'Synagoge': Zum Ursprung des urchristlichen Kirchenbegriffs." *Zeitschrift für Theologie und Kirche* 60 (1963) 178–202.

Schürmann, H. *Das Lukasevangelium.* Vol. 1, *Kommentar zu Kap. 1,1–9,50.* Freiburg: Herder, 1969.

Schüssler Fiorenza, E. *Jesus—Miriam's Child, Sophia's Prophet: Critical Issues in Feminist Christology.* New York: Continuum, 1994.

Schweizer, E. *Das Evangelium nach Markus.* Göttingen: Vandenhoeck & Ruprecht, 1975.

——. s.v. "huiothesia." In *Theological Dictionary of the New Testament*, edited by G. Kittel and G. Friedrich and translated by G. W. Bromiley. Abridged in one volume. Grand Rapids, Mich.: Wm. B. Eerdmans, 1985.

Schweitzer, A. *Geschichte der Leben-Jesu-Forschung.* 2d rev. and expanded ed. of *Von Reimarus zu Wrede.* Tübingen: J. C. B. Mohr (Paul Siebeck), 1913.

——. *The Psychiatric Study of Jesus: Exposition and Criticism.* Translated by C. R. Joy. Boston: Beacon Press, 1948.

——. *The Quest of the Historical Jesus: A Critical Study of Its Progress from Reimarus to Wrede.* New York: Macmillan, 1968.

Scobie, C. H. H. "The Origins and Development of Samaritan Christianity." *New Testament Studies* 19 (1973) 390–414.

Scott, B. B. "From Reimarus to Crossan: Stages in a Quest." *Currents in Research: Biblical Studies* 2 (1994) 253–80.

——. *Hear Then the Parable: A Commentary on the Parables of Jesus.* Minneapolis: Fortress Press, 1990.

Scrimshaw, S. C. M. "Infanticide in Human Populations: Societal and Individual Concerns." In *Infanticide: Comparative and Evolutionary Perspectives*, edited by G. F. Haustafer, 439–62. New York: Aldine Publishing Co., 1984

Seim, T. K. *Patterns in Gender in Luke-Acts.* Edinburgh: T. & T. Clark, 1994.

Sellew, P. "Death, Body, and the World in the Gospel of Thomas." In *Studia Patristica*, edited by E. A. Livingstone, 31, 530–34. Louvain: Peeters, 1990.

——. "Heroic Biography and the Literary Intent of the Protevangelium Jacobi." Unpublished paper presented at the Christian Apocrypha Section, Annual Meeting of the Society of Biblical Literature, San Francisco, November 1997.

Sheres, I., and A. K. Blau. *The Truth about the Virgin: Sex and Ritual in the Dead Sea Scrolls.* New York: Continuum, 1995.

Sim, D. C. "Are the Least Included in the Kingdom of Heaven? The Meaning of Matthew 5:19." *Hervormde Teologiese Studies* 54, nos. 3–4 (1998) 573–87.

Sissa, G. *Greek Virginity*. Translated by A. Goldhammer. Cambridge: Harvard University Press, 1990.

Sklar, H. W. "The Fighter of Horizons: The Story of Joseph as a Model for Social and Spiritual Reconciliation." Master's thesis, Graduate Theological Union, Berkeley, Calif., 1996.

Snyman, J. J., and P. G. W. Du Plessis, eds. *Wetenskapsbeelde in die Geesteswetenskappe*. RGN-studies in Navorsingsmetodologie 3. Pretoria: RGN, 1987.

Stager, L. E., and S. R. Wolff. "Child Sacrifice at Carthage: Religious Rite or Population Control? Archaeological Evidence Provides Basis for a New Analysis." *Biblical Archaeological Review* 10, no. 1 (1984) 31–51.

Standartinger, A. *Das Frauenbild im Judentum der hellenistischen Zeit: Ein Beitrag anhand von 'Joseph & Aseneth.'* Arbeiten zur Geschichte des Antiken Judentums und des Urchristentums. Leiden: E. J. Brill, 1995.

———. "From Fictional Text to Socio-Historical Context: Some Considerations from a Textcritical Perspective on Joseph and Aseneth." In *SBL 1996 Seminar Papers*, translated by Dieter Georgi, 303–18. Atlanta: Scholars Press, 1996.

Stanton, G. N. *A Gospel for a New People: Studies in Matthew*. Edinburgh: T. & T. Clark, 1992.

———. *The Gospels and Jesus*. Oxford: Oxford University Press, 1989.

———. "Jesus of Nazareth: A Magician and a False Prophet Who Deceived God's People?" In *Jesus of Nazareth: Lord and Christ—Essays on the Historical Jesus and New Testament Christology*, edited by J. B. Green and M. Turner, 164–80. Grand Rapids, Mich.: Wm. B. Eerdmans, 1994.

Stearns, P. N. "Fatherhood in Historical Perspective: The Role of Social Change." In *Fatherhood and Families in Cultural Context*, edited by F. W. Bozett and S. M. H. Hanson, 28–520. New York: Springer Publishing Co., 1991.

Stegemann, E. W., and W. Stegemann. *Urchristliche Sozialgeschichte: Die Anfänge im Judentum und die Christusgemeinden in der mediterranen Welt*. Stuttgart: Kohlhammer, 1995.

Stein, R. H. *Jesus the Messiah: A Survey of the Life of Christ*. Downers Grove, Ill.: InterVarsity Press, 1966.

Stockton, I. "Children, Church, and Kingdom." *Scottish Journal of Theology* 36 (1983) 87–97.

Strathmann, H. "Die Krisis des Kanons der Kirche." In *Das Neue Testament als Kanon: Dokumentation und kritische Analyse zur gegenwärtigen Diskussion*, edited by E. Käsemann, 42–61. Göttingen: Vandenhoeck & Ruprecht, 1970.

Stuhlmacher, P. *Schriftauslegung auf dem Wege zur biblischen Theologie*. Göttingen: Vandenhoeck & Ruprecht, 1975.

Tabor, J. "Firstborn of Many Brothers: A Pauline Notion of Apotheosis." In *SBL 1984 Seminar Papers*, edited by K. H. Richards, 295–303. Chico, Calif.: Scholars Press, 1984.

Tatum, W. B. *In Quest of Jesus*. Rev. and enlarged ed. Nashville: Abingdon Press, 1999.

———. *John the Baptist and Jesus: A Report of the Jesus Seminar*. Sonoma, Calif.: Polebridge Press, 1994.

Taylor, L. R. *The Divinity of the Roman Emperor*. Chico, Calif.: Scholars Press, 1981.

Telford, W. R. "Major Trends and Interpretive Issues in the Study of Jesus." In *Studying the Historical Jesus: Evaluations of the State of Current Research*, edited by B. Chilton and C. A. Evans, 33–74. Leiden: E. J. Brill, 1994.

Tellenbach, H., ed. *Das Vaterbild im Mythos und Geschichte: Ägypten, Griechenland, Altes Testament, Neues Testament*. Stuttgart: Kohlhammer, 1976.

Theissen, G. *The Miracle Stories of the Early Christian Tradition*. Translated by F. McDonagh and edited by J. Riches. Edinburgh: T. & T. Clark, 1983.

———. *Urchristliche Wundergeschichte: Ein Beitrag zur formgeschichtliche Erforschung der synoptischen Evangelien*. Studien zum Neuen Testament. Gütersloh: Gütersloher Verlagshaus Gerd Mohn, 1974.

Thompson, T. L. *The Bible in History: How Writers Create a Past*. London: Jonathan Cape, 1999.

Thompson, W. M. *The Jesus Debate: A Survey and Synthesis*. New York: Paulist Press, 1985.

Thompson, Y. "A Missing Hexateuchal Narrative Concerning Child Sacrifice." *Dor le Dor. Our Biblical Heritage* 15 (1986) 38–42.

Tiller, P. O. "Father Absence and Personality Development of Children in Sailor Families: A Preliminary Research Report, Part II." In *Studies of the Family*, edited by N. Anderson, vol. 2, 115–37. Göttingen: Vandenhoeck & Ruprecht, 1957.

Tracy, D. *The Analogical Imagination: Christian Theology and the Culture of Pluralism*. New York: Crossroad, 1981.

Trilling, W. "Zur Entstehung der Zwölferkreises: Eine geschichtkritische Überlegung." In *Die Kirche des Anfangs: Heinz Schürmann Festschrift*, edited by R. Schnackenburg, J. Ernst, and J. Wanke, 201–22. Leipzig: St. Benno, 1977.

———. "Implizite Ekklesiologie: Ein Vorschlag zum Thema 'Jesus und die Kirche.'" In *Die Botschaft Jesu: Exegetische Orientierung*, 57–72. Freiburg: Herder, 1978.

Tripp-Reimer, T., and S. E. Wilson. "Cross-Cultural Perspectives on Fatherhood." In *Fatherhood and Families in Cultural Context*, edited by

F. W. Bozett and S. M. H. Hanson, 1–27. New York: Springer Publishing Co., 1991.

Tromp, J. *The Assumption of Moses: A Critical Edition with Commentary.* Leiden: E. J. Brill, 1993.

Tuckman, B. W. "Developmental Sequence in Small Groups." *Psychological Bulletin* 63 (1965) 384–99.

Ulanov, A. B. "The Search for Paternal Roots: Jungian Perspectives on Fathering." In *Fathering: Fact or Fable?* edited by E. V. Stein, 47–67. Nashville: Abingdon Press, 1977.

Vaage, L. E. "Recent Concerns: The Scholar as *Engagé.*" In *Whose Historical Jesus?* edited by W. E. Arnal and M. Desjardins. Studies in Christianity and Judaism 7. Waterloo, Ont.: Wilfrid Laurier University Press, 1997.

Van Aarde, A. G. "The Continued Importance of Jesus." *Hervormde Teologiese Studies* 53, no. 3 (1997) 773–99.

———. *God-with-us: The Dominant Perspective in Matthew's Story, and Other Essays.* Pretoria: University of Pretoria Press, 1994.

———. "'He Has Risen from the Dead' (Mt 28:7): A Textual Evidence on the Separation of Judaism and Christianity." *Neotestamentica* 23 (1989) 219–33.

———. *Kultuurhistoriese Agtergrond van die Nuwe Testament: Die Eerste-Eeuse Mediterreense Sosiale Konteks.* Pretoria: Kital, 1994.

———. "Matthew 27:45–53 and the Turning of the Tide in Israel's History." *Biblical Theology Bulletin* 28, no. 1 (1998) 16–26.

———. "Tracking the Pathways Opened by Willem Vorster in Historical Jesus Research." *Neotestamentica* 28 (1994) 235–51.

Van der Watt, J. G., and S. J. Joubert. "Hoe is Jesus Gekruisig?" *Hervormde Teologiese Studies* 52, no. 4 (1996) 633–52.

Van Eck, E. *Galilee and Jerusalem in Mark's Story of Jesus: A Narratological and Social Scientific Reading.* Pretoria: University of Pretoria Press, 1995.

Van Selms, A. *Genesis.* Vol. 2. De Prediking van het Oude Testament. Nijkerk: Uitgeverij G. F. Callenbach, 1967.

———. *Marriage and Family Life in Ugarit Literature.* London: Luzac & Co., 1954.

Van Tilborg, S. *The Jewish Leaders in Matthew.* Leiden: E. J. Brill, 1972.

Veitch, J. *The Birth of Jesus: History or Myth?* Presbyterian Church of Aotearoa New Zealand, 1997.

Vellanickal, M. *The Divine Sonship of Christians in the Johannine Writings.* Rome: Biblical Institute Press, 1977.

Vergote, A., and A. Tamayo. *The Parental Figure and the Representation of God.* The Hague: Mouton, 1981.

Vergote, A., and others. "Concept of God and Parental Images." *Journal for the Scientific Study of Religion* 8 (1969) 79–87.

Vermes, G. *The Religion of Jesus the Jew*. Minneapolis: Fortress Press, 1993.

Von Rad, G. *Genesis: A Commentary*. Translated by J. H. Marks. Rev. ed., based on the 9th German ed. Old Testament Library. London: SCM Press, 1972.

Von Wahlde, U. C. *The Earliest Version of John's Gospel: Recovering the Gospel of Signs*. Wilmington, Del.: Michael Glazier, 1989.

Vorster, W. S. "Jesus: Eschatological Prophet and/or Wisdom Teacher." *Hervormde Teologiese Studies* 47, no. 2 (1991) 526–42.

———. "Jesus the Galilean." *Hervormde Teologiese Studies* 47, no. 1 (1991) 121–35.

Vorster, W. S., with P. J. J. Botha. "The Jewishness of Jesus: Presuppositions and the Historical Study of the New Testament. A Research Report on a Project That Forms Part of the HSRC's 'Investigation into Research Methodology.'" Pretoria: Human Science Research Council, 1992.

Weaver, P. R. C. "The Status of Children in Mixed Marriages." In *The Family in Ancient Rome: New Perspectives*, edited by B. Rawson, 145–69. London: Croom Helm, 1986.

Webb, R. L. "John the Baptist and His Relationship to Jesus." In *Studying the Historical Jesus: Evaluations of the State of Current Research*, edited by B. Chilton and C. A. Evans, 179–230. New Testament Tools and Studies. Leiden: E. J. Brill, 1994.

———. *John the Baptizer: A Socio-Historical Study*. JSNT Supplement Series 62. Sheffield: Sheffield Academic Press, 1991.

Weber, M. *Max Weber on the Methodology of the Social Sciences*. Translated and edited by E. A. Shils and H. A. Finch. Glencoe, Ill.: Free Press, 1949.

Wenham, D. "A Note on Mark 9:33–42/Matt.18:1–6/Luke 9:46–50." *Journal for the Study of the New Testament* 14 (1982) 113–18.

Whiston, W., trans. *Josephus Complete Works*. Grand Rapids, Mich.: Kregel Publications, 1978.

White, L. M. "Shifting Sectarian Boundaries in Early Christianity." *Bulletin of the John Rylands Library Manchester* 70 (1988) 7–24.

White Fathers—Saint Anne. "Bethesda: St. Anne" pamphlet. Jerusalem, Israel, n.d.

Whitelam, K. W. *The Invention of Ancient Israel: The Silencing of Palestinian History*. London: Routledge & Kegan paul, 1996.

Whiting, J. W. M., R. Kluckhorn, and A. Anthony. "The Function of Male Initiation Ceremonies at Puberty." In *Readings in Social Psychology*, edited by E. E. Maccoby, T. M. Newcomb, and E. L. Hartley, 359–70. New York: Henry Holt, 1958.

Wilson, S. "Infanticide, Child Abandonment, and Female Honour in Nineteenth-century Corsica." *Comparative Studies in Society and History* 30, no. 1 (1988) 762–83.

Witherington, B. *Jesus the Sage: The Pilgrimage of Wisdom*. Minneapolis: Fortress Press, 1994.

Wolf, E. R. *Peasants*. Englewood Cliffs, N.J.: Prentice-Hall, 1966.

Wright, G. E. "The Samaritans at Shechem." In *Die Samaritaner*, edited by F. Dexinger and R. Pummer, 263–73. Wege der Forschung 604. Darmstadt: Wissenschaftliche Buchgesellschaft, 1992.

Wright, N. T. *Christian Origins and the Question of God*. Vol. 1, *The New Testament and the People of God*. Minneapolis: Fortress Press, 1992.

————. *Christian Origins and the Question of God*. Vol. 2, *Jesus and the Victory of God*. London: SPCK, 1996.

————. "Knowing Jesus: Faith and History." In *The Meaning of Jesus: Two Visions*, by M. J. Borg and N. T. Wright, 15–27. San Francisco: HarperSanFrancisco, 1999.

————. "The Mission and Message of Jesus." In *The Meaning of Jesus: Two Visions*, by M. J. Borg and N. T. Wright, 31–54. San Francisco: HarperSan Francisco, 1999.

————. *Who Was Jesus?* Grand Rapids, Mich.: Wm. B. Eerdmans, 1992.

Wright N. T., and S. Neill. *The Interpretation of the New Testament 1861–1986*. New York: Oxford University Press, 1988.

Wülfing von Martitz, P. s.v. "υἱός, υἱοθεσία." *Theologisches Wörterbuch zum Neuen Testament*. Vol. 8. Stuttgart: Kohlhammer, 1969.

Yaghijan, L. "How Shall We Read? A Preface to Matthew's Protocols of Reading." Unpublished paper presented at The Context Group Meeting, Portland, Ore., March 1992.

Zerbe, G. M. *Non-Retaliation in Early Jewish and New Testament Texts*. Sheffield: JSOT Press, 1993.

Index